IN THE LONG RUN
WE ARE ALL DEAD

# IN THE LONG RUN
# WE ARE ALL DEAD

*Keynesianism, Political Economy, and Revolution*

## Geoff Mann

**VERSO**

London • New York

First published by Verso 2017
© Geoff Mann 2017

1 3 5 7 9 10 8 6 4 2

**Verso**
UK: 6 Meard Street, London W1F 0EG
US: 20 Jay Street, Suite 1010, Brooklyn, NY 11201
versobooks.com

Verso is the imprint of New Left Books

ISBN-13: 978-1-78478-599-4
eISBN-13: 978-1-78478-602-1 (US)
eISBN-13: 978-1-78478-601-4 (UK)

**British Library Cataloguing in Publication Data**
A catalogue record for this book is available from the British Library

**Library of Congress Cataloging-in-Publication Data**
Names: Mann, Geoff, author.
Title: In the long run we are all dead / Geoff Mann.
Description: Brooklyn : Verso, 2017. | Includes bibliographical references
  and index.
Identifiers: LCCN 2016030966 (print) | LCCN 2016045446 (ebook) | ISBN
  9781784785994 (hardback) | ISBN 9781784786021 ()
Subjects: LCSH: Economic history—1945- | Keynesian economics. | Financial
  crises. | Economic policy—21st century. | BISAC: POLITICAL SCIENCE /
  Economic Conditions. | POLITICAL SCIENCE / Political Ideologies /
  Democracy.
Classification: LCC HC59 .M2486 2017 (print) | LCC HC59 (ebook) | DDC
  330.15/6—dc23
LC record available at https://lccn.loc.gov/2016030966

Typeset in Adobe Garamond by Hewer Text UK, Ltd, Edinburgh
Printed in the UK by CPI Group (UK) Ltd, Croydon CR0 4YY

The plague ends too; it rights itself. But hundreds of thousands have perished of it; they're all dead. Everything has thereby been straightened out again.

—G. W. F. Hegel

But this long run is a misleading guide to current affairs. In the long run we are all dead. Economists set themselves too easy, too useless a task if in tempestuous seasons they can only tell us that when the storm is long past the ocean is flat again.

—J. M. Keynes

# Contents

*Preface*                                                              ix

### PART 1. KEYNESIANISM

1. Keynes Resurrected?                                                  4
2. What Is Keynesianism?                                               32
3. The Tragedy of Poverty                                             58

### PART 2. BEFORE KEYNES

4. Poverty, Honor, and Revolution                                     83
5. Freedom After Revolution                                          119
6. Necessity and the Rabble                                          144
7. The State and the Masses                                          163
8. A Theory of Political Economy                                     182

### PART 3. KEYNES

9. How to Read *The General Theory* I                                217
10. How to Read *The General Theory* II                              240
11. How to Read *The General Theory* III                             257

## PART 4. AFTER KEYNES

12. Keynesian Political Economy and the Problem of
    Full Employment                                          281
13. The (New) Keynesian Economics of
    Equilibrium Unemployment                                 304
14. From Unemployment to Inequality in the
    Twenty-First Century                                     335
15. Revolution After Revolution?                             366

    *Index*                                                  397

# Preface

John Maynard Keynes is commonly called the most influential economist of the twentieth century. That may well be true, but the reasons, I think, are not to be found in his originality or his argumentation. As creative and fascinating a thinker as he was, his ideas became extraordinarily powerful for the same reason anything else becomes extraordinarily powerful: his audience empowered them. He did not discover Truth, fleeting or permanent. In a time of war, economic collapse, and fascism, he answered questions many people desperately wanted answered. The Truth of his answers was entirely secondary to the fact that they explained the catastrophe and legitimized the panicked anxiety that suffused the politics of his time and place. Keynes told people they were correct to be terrified, but he also told them that it didn't have to be terrible. When the world seems at risk of falling apart, who would not want to hear that?

I suppose this figure of the "economist as saviour" (the subtitle of the second installment in Robert Skidelsky's excellent three-volume biography of Keynes) is imaginable in all kinds of political economic systems, but Keynes's particular diagnosis and consequent prescription were a product of their historical moment in the development of liberal capitalism.[1] When he published *The General Theory of*

---

1 Robert Skidelsky, *John Maynard Keynes, volume 2: The Economist as Saviour, 1920–1937*, London: Macmillan.

*Employment, Interest, and Money* in 1936, liberal capitalism had already been around, in at least a broadly recognizable form, for more than a century. Today, eighty years after *The General Theory*, it is still around, if of course in a slightly different variety. The persistence of liberal capitalism matters in multiple ways, but the one I want to emphasize here is that as long as it persists, so too will Keynesianism. The anxiety and hope beating at the heart of Keynes's ideas is endemic to capitalist modernity in this sense, and it becomes especially visible in moments of crisis.

A generous and detailed engagement with *The General Theory* is of course essential to this account. Because the anxiety and hope that suffuses it, however, is expressed in more or less technical language (some of it of Keynes' own coinage), and is presented as a critique of an older set of ideas that may be unfamiliar, its analysis might require a little decoding for some readers. At the political-economic and conceptual level, this is the purpose of Part 3 of this book, three chapters entitled "How to Read *The General Theory*" I, II and III. Yet in the course of writing *In the Long Run We Are All Dead*, I have learned—and it is no surprise—that most people (even economists) are largely unfamiliar with the contents and argument of *The General Theory*, and hardly anyone has read it. Many of us have learned what we think we know about the specifics of the book's arguments from vague references to "effective demand," "liquidity preference," or the "enthanasia of the rentier." But, as I try to show in the chapters that follow, there is much more to *The General Theory* than is often thought, and the ways in which the distinctively Keynesian critique animates it can tell us a great deal not only about Keynes and Keynesianism, but about political economy as a way of grasping the world.

Consequently, I think it is quite possible—indeed, I hope it is likely—that readers may want to have access to the somewhat more "technical" details of *The General Theory*'s argumentation and structure. With this in mind, I have put together an e-book supplement to *In the Long Run*, entitled *A Companion to* The General Theory of Employment, Interest, and Money. It contains a brief introduction to *The General Theory* and identifies some of the important contributions to subsequent debates concerning the varieties of Keynesian economics. Most of the text, however, is a series of reasonably detailed chapter-by-chapter summaries. The summaries attempt to take Keynes's ideas on their own terms—they *describe* as opposed to *critique*, the latter being the task of the book you hold in your hands. The *Companion* is intended to lay out the way that Keynes builds up the argument of *The General Theory*, and to explain his terms and claims in a way that is accessible to those new to them, but avoids oversimplification. It is available for download at Verso's website (versobooks.com), and I hope those interested will take advantage of it. It is worth noting that I have written it in the hope that it might also serve as a helpful reader's aid for anyone reading or teaching *The General Theory* or Keynesian economics, whether or not they read *In the Long Run*.

Understanding *The General Theory* and Keynes's ideas in this dual sense, both in some detail and in their broader political-economic implications, allows us to see the ways in which—as I argue in what follows—Keynes was in no way the first Keynesian, he was not the last, and there will be more yet. What we call Keynesianism is as old as liberal capitalism, and as long as it is the hegemonic mode of social and political economic organization, as it remains in much of the world, Keynesian politics and political economy will find themselves empowered when they are deemed most desperately necessary. In this sense, Keynes and Keynesianism were not "resurrected" following the financial meltdown of 2007–2008, because neither was ever "dead," however hard some mainstream economists might have tried to convince us otherwise. Capitalist modernity, in fact, is and always has been Keynesian on the inside, as it were—the call for the state when disorder looms or revolution threatens has always been an option, one that, like a panic button, is essential even when we never use it. Indeed, political economy is—or at least I try to show that it is—Keynesian by definition: when the social order is fraying, it is the art and science of revolution without revolutionaries. Revolution is its *raison d'être*; born in the wake of the French Revolution, the ghost of Robespierre forever stalks it.

If Keynesianism returned with the most recent crisis, it is not because of Keynes's theory of effective demand or his employment function, but because climate change, war and accelerating inequality seem to have put what many think of a "civilization" on the ropes. Robespierre—or Hitler (Keynes understood them as two sides of the same populist coin)—might be right around the corner. The panic that gripped Europe and North America following the bankruptcy of Lehman Brothers in fall 2008 was partly motivated by rich people's frantic effort to stay rich, but it was also motivated by lots of not-that-rich people's fears that we were at some tipping point in the social order. Those people, were not, primarily, trying to save capitalism, they were trying to stave off a calamity caused by capitalism, in the hope that something better will come along. That is what Keynesianism is, and always has been, all about. This book is a (mostly) sympathetic critique of that sensibility, which I cannot help but see everywhere I look, perhaps because I have yet been unable, despite my best efforts, to escape it completely myself.

Which is to say that this is a book written, as I understand it, in the shadow of calamity we can attribute entirely to liberal capitalism, and in this assessment, at least, I am a Keynesian. There is much to be hopeful about in emergent creative radicalisms and emancipatory politics all over the world, and there is lots of long-term struggle that has brought millions of people great gains, but I admit to having to work very hard to be optimistic. To speak honestly, the future looks mighty bleak. I realize that this will stand as reason to accuse me of "defeatism" or a lack of imagination. Both are perhaps fair. Be that as it may. What you hold in your hands is an effort, however limited by my own privilege and ignorance, to elaborate a sympathetic but skeptical critique of the politics and knowledge at the core of that structure of feeling.

That has proven to be a great struggle, and it has taken a very long time—and I don't mean to suggest I have finished the job, or that it is something someone could ever finish. But it has been a long road. I began this project a couple of months after my younger son entered grade one, and he just started high school. The intervening years have been quite a time, full of all the things lives are full of. And yet the whole time I have been, and continue to be, surrounded by so much love and support it would make your head spin. It's a cliché to say writing a book is a long and lonely process, but in this case, I didn't have much of the lonely. This book, or what is worthwhile in it, is entirely a product of that good fortune, and for that I have colleagues, friends, and family to thank.

Much of the research was supported by an Insight Grant from the Social Sciences and Humanities Research Council of Canada; research funding like that is no small thing these days, I assure you, and I appreciate it. Bits and pieces of the text have appeared in three previously published articles: parts of "Keynes Resurrected?" in *Dialogues in Human Geography* (volume 6, number 2) and "Poverty in the Midst of Plenty: Unemployment, Liquidity, and Keynes' Scarcity Theory of Capital" in *Critical Historical Studies* (volume 2, number 1) are scattered throughout, and much of Chapter 14 was printed as "A General Theory for Our Times: On Piketty" in *Historical Materialism* (volume 23, number 1). Sage, the University of Chicago Press, and Brill have helpfully agreed to have that material reappear here. In addition, the editors and reviewers for each of those articles have provided (for the most part anonymously) enormously valuable help with my thinking and writing. Earlier versions of some of the ideas here also benefited more than a little from discussions following presentations at the University of Wisconsin—Madison, University of Wisconsin—Milwaukee, University of British Columbia, University of Minnesota, the University of Northern British Columbia, University of California—Berkeley, University of Georgia, University of Toronto, and the Historical Materialism conference in London a few years ago.

At Verso, Sebastian Budgen has guided the whole process, moved it along when it slowed, and gave me the kind of scholarly feedback one only gets from someone of his extraordinarily broad insight and energy. In addition to Sebastian, Marjam Idriss, and Cian McCourt have shepherded me through the administrative side of the process, and the editorial work of Duncan Ranslem, Ida Audeh, and Elena-Maria Georgiou made the manuscript much better, and the last steps straightforward.

In Vancouver, my work on the book has benefited from both the unflagging support of excellent coworkers at Simon Fraser (Chris

Au-Yeung, Anke Baker, Joyce Chen, Liliana Hill, B-Jae Kelly, Tiina Klassen, John Ng (who made the figure in Chapter 13), Kellie Smith, Justin Song, and Marion Walter), and a few other great minds to which I have regular access on Burnaby Mountain—Eugene McCann, Janet Sturgeon, Paul Kingsbury and Nick Blomley in particular. Tracy Brennand has provided fantastic leadership in an increasingly austere, marketized institutional setting. Also in Vancouver, there are quite a number of people who have helped me in ways of which they are probably unaware: I write a lot in coffee shops, two in particular, and I have chatted about these ideas, and about lots of other stuff, with many of the people who work there and who have sometimes inspired me to rethink things I thought were settled. So to all of them, and especially to Grady Buhler, Spencer James, and the Murdocco family (Frank, Nick, Vince and Frank Sr.), I offer my sincere thanks for the great friendship and coffee, and a place to set up shop a couple of times a week. A couple of these coffee people were also, fortunately, my students. Eilish Rodden and Sarah-Ellen Whitford are two of a crew of inspiring young people it is the professional luck of a university teacher to get to know. The others, each of whom has significantly shaped my thinking about this book, include Heather Hamilton, Mike Fabris, Chanel Ly, Peggy Lam and Gabe Boothroyd. These are "students" with whom you spend enough time to discover who is really the "teacher." This is especially true of Chloe Brown, Dawn Hoogeveen, Emilia Kennedy, Emily LeBaron, Howard Tenenbaum, Becky Till, Maria Wallstam, and Mark Kear, who each contributed enormously to this project. Their work and their ideas have fundamentally changed how I conceive the world, and whether they can see themselves in it or not, they have shaped this book in crucial ways.

Speaking of crucial, let me tell you about my "colleagues" (as I have often said before, the term is sorely inadequate). Academic life can be strange, and one of the ways that strangeness plays out is that some of your closest collaborators and co-thinkers are thousands of miles away. Matt Hern might be here in Vancouver, but Brad Bryan is in Victoria, Joel Wainwright is in Ohio, Nik Heynen and Dani Aiello are in Georgia, Sanjay Narayan, Jake Kosek and Gill Hart are in Berkeley, Scott Prudham, Deb Cowen and Shiri Pasternak are in Toronto, Alberto Toscano is in London, and Brett Christophers is at this very moment causing all sorts of trouble in Sweden. Kris Olds, Andy Leyshon, Jamie Peck, Am Johal, Trevor Barnes, Gerry Pratt, Vinay Gidwani, Jesse Goldstein, Neil Brenner, Manu Goswami, Jim Glassman, Carla Bergman, Rosemary Collard, Glen Coulthard, Emilie Cameron, Stuart Poyntz and Michel Feher are near and far. And yet every one of them has read or discussed these ideas and given me generous but incisive advice on how to make it better. Some of those folks are now central to my life beyond the professional realm, too. Despite the distance, Joel, Jake, Nik, Brad and Brett, along with Sanjay Narayan, have become a big part of the way I understand not just my work, but also my world.

Jessica Dempsey is, thankfully, here with me in Vancouver—just up the street, in fact. There are others, family and friends, I wish were as close, and whose support matters so much to me: Mom & Ian, Dad & Lo, Gie & Andy, Pete & Sarah, Andrew & Lori, Chris & Anna, Sanj & Shalini. Their absence is made easier by Sally & Steve, Robin & Neib, Pete & Shirley, Panos & Anabel, Ziff & Barb, Nora & John, Jess & Ry, Ger & Steve, Brad & Deb, Mark & Goo and Matt & Selena. But it really would be awesome to have everyone close by, if only for a while. If I could ever pull that off, then I could enjoy with them (even though they already know) my unbelievably good luck: my wise and beautiful lady and our courageous, crazy boys. Here's to a world as fearless and hopeful as you.

# PART I

# Keynesianism

# CHAPTER I

# Keynes Resurrected?

When the world's financial markets fell off a cliff in 2007 and 2008, it seemed to some as if the upheaval might drag the whole global economic order over the precipice. After a brief and wide-eyed confrontation with Karl Marx, economic and public policy insiders quickly turned to the ideas of John Maynard Keynes.[1] Although his most famous work, *The General Theory of Employment, Interest, and Money* (1936), appeared to remain almost as unread as it was in the heady anti-Keynesian heyday preceding the meltdown, there followed a veritable explosion in books, articles, and digital media concerning his ideas, and "Keynesianism" in general.[2]

As with everything to do with Keynes, it seems, almost all of these additions to the bloated shelves of crisis books take a strong position

---

1 The *Guardian* (October 15, 2008) declared, "Karl Marx is back," and the *Wall Street Journal* (November 6, 2008) reported that "as capital struggles, *Das Kapital* moves units." A more ironic redemption is hard to imagine.

2 There are some good reasons for the mismatch between Keynes's readership and the influence of his ideas. Accessibility is one. Although *The General Theory of Employment, Interest, and Money* (volume VII of Keynes's *Collected Writings*, originally published in 1936) is a technical stroll-in-the-park compared to today's academic economics, it was explicitly aimed at experts and was not an easy read for many of them. Keynes was a finer stylist than is often thought—as his *Economic Consequences of the Peace* (volume II of Keynes's *Collected Writings*, originally published in 1919) attests—but it is not always evident in *The General Theory*.

either for or against, in celebration or condemnation. The most notable effect of the financial crisis is that the revitalized Keynes industry
is largely driven by those proud to call themselves Keynesians. The
most prominent to affirm their faith are, unsurprisingly, self-identified Keynesians like Paul Krugman (*New York Times* columnist and
winner of the 2008 Nobel Prize in Economic Sciences) and Joseph
Stiglitz (former chief economist of the World Bank, US policy advisor, and 2001 Nobel laureate).[3] But others, across a wide swath of the
political spectrum—from the archconservative Richard Posner, to
the measured Martin Wolf of the *Financial Times*, to the inimitable
Thomas Geoghegan of *The Nation*—have also found themselves
propounding Keynes's wisdom.[4]

Even more emphatic was the onslaught of popular and scholarly
media announcing Keynes's crisis-driven return. *Time* announced
"The Comeback Keynes," and the *Wall Street Journal* anointed
Keynes "The New Old Big Thing in Economics."[5] (The citations are
so numerous that a footnote can list only a sample.[6]) There can be no

---

3    For exemplary and well-argued contributions to post-Lehman Brothers Keynes reviv-
alism from prominent Keynesian scholars, see Axel Leijonhufvud, "Out of the Corridor:
Keynes and the Crisis," *Cambridge Journal of Economics* 33, 2009, 741–57; Robert Skidelsky,
"The Relevance of Keynes," *Cambridge Journal of Economics* 35, 2011, 1–13.

4    Richard Posner, "Liberals Forgetting Keynes," *The Atlantic,* July 27, 2009; Martin
Wolf, "Keynes Offers Us the Best Way to Think about the Financial Crisis," *Financial
Times,* December 23, 2008; Thomas Geoghegan, "What Would Keynes Do?" *The Nation,*
October 17, 2011.

5    *Time,* October 23, 2008; *Wall Street Journal,* January 8, 2009.

6    The Keynesian boom spanned such diverse outlets as US National Public Radio's
*This American Life*, the British Broadcasting Corporation's Radio 4, the *International
Socialist Review*, to the Argentine daily *La Nación*. Since 2009 alone the list of books
published in English alone includes Robert Skidelsky, *Keynes: The Return of the Master*,
London: Penguin, 2010; Lance Taylor, *Maynard's Revenge: The Collapse of Free Market
Economics*, Cambridge, MA: Harvard University Press, 2011; Paul Davidson, *The Keynes
Solution: The Path to Global Economic Prosperity*, London: Palgrave Macmillan, 2009; John
Eatwell and Murray Milgate, *The Fall and Rise of Keynesian Economics*, Oxford: Oxford
University Press, 2011; Peter Clarke, *Keynes: The Rise, Fall, and Return of the 20th Century's
Most Influential Economist*, London: Bloomsbury Press, 2009; Roger Backhouse and Bradley
Bateman, *Capitalist Revolutionary: John Maynard Keynes*, Cambridge: Cambridge University
Press, 2011; and Jonathan Schlefer, *The Assumptions Economists Make*, Cambridge: Harvard
University Press, 2012. For a sampling in languages other than English, see Axel Kicillof,
*Volver a Keynes: Fundamentos de la Teoría General de la Ocupación, el Interés y el Dinero,*

doubt that, whatever it might mean exactly, Keynes returned with the subprime collapse—or, as the libertarian screed *The Freeman* had it, "HE'S BAAAAACK!" like some horror-film zombie.[7]

This book is an inquiry into the content and meaning of the Keynesian return. This is not the first reported return: Despite the common wisdom that Keynes disappeared from theoretical and policy circles sometime in the late 1960s or early 1970s (the various autopsies disagree), the news of his death was, and is, "greatly exaggerated" (to steal a phrase from Mark Twain). In fact, Keynesian ideas have been an essential component of political life in capitalist liberal democracy since long before Keynes himself walked the earth. The chapters that follow examine these ideas—which I call "Keynesianism" or the "Keynesian critique"—from their origins in the liberal reaction to the French Revolution to their most recent "return"—in an attempt to understand their fundamental assumptions and claims, and why they continue to appeal, especially but not only to those on the Left (in the broadest sense of the term).

For it seems to me undeniable that Harvard legal scholar and Brazilian politician Roberto Unger's complaint is true: "Keynesianism is the default economic creed of progressives around the world today."[8] Every time capitalism is beset by crisis, many of its most engaged critics clamor for Keynes. What I would add, however, and what Unger unwittingly obscures, is that this is not a new problem. Keynesianism has been the "default economic creed" of "progressives" at least since

Madrid: Clave Intelectual, 2012; Giovanni Mazzetti, *Ancora Keynes?! Miseria o Nuovo Sviluppo?*, Trieste: Asterios, 2012; Luis Ángel Rojo, *Keynes, Su Tiempo, y el Nuestro*, Madrid: El Hombre del Tres, 2012. Then there are the many bestselling how-it-happened books on the crisis that lean more or less heavily on a Keynesian account of what went wrong, from Joseph Stiglitz, *Freefall: America, Free Markets, and the Sinking of the World Economy* (New York: W. W. Norton, 2010) to Nouriel Roubini and Stephen Mihm, *Crisis Economics: A Crash Course in the Future of Finance* (New York: Penguin, 2011). Even the billionaire rentier George Soros, trying desperately to avoid Keynes in his *The New Paradigm for Financial Markets: The Credit Crisis of 2008 and What It Means*, (New York: PublicAffairs, 2008) cannot help resuscitating simple versions of his most basic conclusions, clothed ill-fittingly in the antipathetic dogma of Karl Popper.

7  *The Freeman* 59: 3, April 2009.
8  Roberto Mangabeira Unger, "Misusing Keynes," YouTube video, part 1 of 3-part lecture, posted by Roberto Mangabeira Unger, July 19, 2011.

18 Brumaire, year VIII (more familiar to us as November 9, 1799), when Napoleon dissolved the Directory, effectively putting an end to a tumultuous decade of revolution and reaction.[9]

To put it thus, of course, is to invite all sorts of questions, since it would seem to attribute a rather idiosyncratic meaning to "Keynesianism"—a term subjected to more than its fair share of definitional dispute. Indeed, it sometimes seems as if there is very little ground shared by what we might call the "varieties of Keynesianism." Yet I will argue that although its political, technical, and institutional apparatuses have changed significantly since the end of the eighteenth century, the "stuff" of Keynesianism, the logic and concepts and politics that make it what it is, has been pretty consistent. Keynes's own variety of Keynesianism, and the many ways in which it has been interpreted since, makes this difficult to perceive, so pointing out these connections is part of the task ahead.

## The Left in a Foxhole?

In *The Tailor of Ulm*, his farewell before assisted suicide in 2011, the Italian communist Lucio Magri remarks that the post–World War II Left's constant "gesture to Keynes" has no "clear-cut content": Keynes is "never read, never reflected upon."[10] The book you hold in your hands is, among other things, an attempt to understand that gesture to Keynes and its unreflective persistence, by reading and reflecting upon Keynes and other Keynesians. It reexamines the force of the Keynesian critique of capitalism and its relation to political economy as both knowledge and a way of knowing. It argues that the Keynesian critique—always constructed in light of a historical, pragmatic, and intuitive Reason—is a distinctively postrevolutionary political economy, assembled and reassembled again and again to address an

---

9   The late Charles Kindleberger—an eminent Keynesian economic historian—goes back a bit further in his discussion of eighteenth-century French "Keynesians" like John Law; Charles Kindleberger, *Keynesianism vs. Monetarism and Other Essays in Financial History*, London: George Allen & Unwin, 1985, 41–60.

10   Lucio Magri, *The Tailor of Ulm*, London: Verso, 2011, 54.

existential anxiety at the heart of liberal modernity. Like all things social, it has taken a variety of forms, each of which reflect the world in which it seemed necessary. Yet it is always, at its core, a reluctantly radical but immanent critique of liberalism, a science and sensibility that allows us to name "the crisis"—poverty, unemployment, inequality—when everything hangs in the balance and "something must be done." For Keynesians, from Hegel to Piketty, it is always ultimately civilization itself that is at stake.

This stance, and the critical theory of liberal capitalism upon which it rests, are not confined to the "centrist" or "progressive" political realm we might immediately associate with nominally Keynesian ideas or policies. In other words, to say that Keynesianism is distinctively postrevolutionary is not to say that "we" (whoever that might be) are past the time of revolution. Rather it is to say that whatever the fate of future revolutions, Keynesianism is a critique of liberal modernity that could only be formulated *after* revolution. It would never have emerged without a revolutionary past to endlessly haunt it. As a result, the same forces that have animated two centuries of the *immanent* "reform" of liberalism have also animated much—although certainly not all—of the nominally *radical* critique of liberalism in what we now call the global North. As Robert Lucas, among the most influential economists of the "counterrevolution" against Keynesianism in the 1970s and 1980s, put it in 2008, "everyone is a Keynesian in a foxhole", and there is wisdom in this.[11]

I say this not to undermine or dismiss the radical politics or political economy that has developed in the Euro-American tradition, as if it is not "really" what it claims to be. Rather, to lean on Magri once more, I say so because "we need to confront the true evolution of the situation, without despondency but also without pretence."[12] There are threads the Left must trace, leading twisted and knotted but basically unbroken from Hegel's response to the French Revolution to our twenty-first century triple crisis and, more important, to the

---

11    Justin Fox, "Bob Lucas on the Comeback of Keynesianism", *Time*, October 28, 2008.

12    Magri, *Tailor of Ulm*, 7.

politics of our attempt to conceptualize and confront that crisis. Moreover, these threads are not necessarily red: the ghost of Robespierre haunts the contemporary Left, but not always in the manner in which some might hope. On the contrary, some of the threads to which we unwittingly cling touched Robespierre's finger-tips only briefly. Together, they lead us back and tie us irrevocably to both a revolutionary tradition and a collection of modern anxieties that he and his colleagues also felt and inspired and which have never gone away.

At the risk of making claims regarding a broader political condition sure to misrepresent many, I would contend that Keynes's most recent return thus presents a propitious opportunity to undertake a critical accounting of his particular political economy so as to understand what Keynesianism means for "progressives." Why does Keynesian reason have such a hold on progressive thought, and why, at moments of crisis like the present, does a "progressive" knee-jerk Keynesianism seem to reappear? Why does Keynesianism make so much sense to much of the Left, especially in times of crisis, and does that signify some sort of longer term imaginative or ideological crisis? What facets of the modern varieties of "Keynesian" policy and political economy reproduce the wisdom that seems so consistently appealing, and on what historical premises could they possibly deliver on their promises?

*The General Theory's* great contribution—also its express purpose—was to develop a pragmatic, general theory of liberal capitalism, one that confronted the fact that there was no single, timeless answer to its shortcomings. Keynes presented it, immodestly but honestly, as the most coherent and useful theory yet developed of civil society and its relation to the state: coherent because it pertained, he believed, to all capitalist societies, and useful because it identified the mecha-nisms that made what he called "modern communities" tick.

Taken at face value, this contribution justifies the truism that Keynes was no radical. As Eric Hobsbawm famously remarked, he came to save capitalism from itself.[13] But to leave it at that is to miss the most important point. The crucial question is not merely what

---

13   Eric Hobsbawm, "Goodbye to All That," *Marxism Today*, October 1990, 20.

Keynes was trying to save—and the term "capitalism" does not adequately capture the object of his rescue efforts—but why he came to save it and what he came to save it from. Keynes himself was unequivocal on the matter: *"Civilization,"* he said in 1938, "is a thin and precarious crust, erected by the personality and will of a very few, and only maintained by rules and conventions skillfully put across and guilefully preserved."[14] This is the single most important premise of all things Keynesian. If it were possible to define the fundamental Keynesianism proposition in a phrase, this is about as close as we could get.[15]

---

14 John Maynard Keynes, *Collected Writings*, vol. X, Cambridge: Cambridge University Press, 1971–1989, 446–47 (emphasis added). (Hereinafter, all citations from the *Collected Writings* take the following form: *CW*, volume number, page.) *CW*, X is *Essays in Biography*, first published in 1930.

15 Unfortunately, nowhere does Keynes tell us what defines "civilization" as such. We can, however, assume he had in mind Sigmund Freud's *Civilization and Its Discontents*, which appeared in 1930. Keynes read all of Freud's work and was close with one of his translators, James Strachey. Although he refers to Freud only once in his major "economic" work—the "Freudian theory of the love of money" is mentioned in *A Treatise on Money*, *CW*, VI, 258–59—traces of his influence can be found elsewhere. The "fetish of liquidity" analyzed in *The General Theory* surely has partially Freudian conceptual origins, as does the famous account of entrepreneurial "animal spirits."

I want to be clear that I am not proposing that Keynesianism is ultimately an "economic" Freudianism or psychoanalysis. There is a great deal that separates Freud from Keynes and Keynesianism, but it is nonetheless true that on the question of civilization, Keynes thought along lines almost exactly the same as those laid out by Freud. In *Civilization and Its Discontents*, Freud posits civilization [*Kultur*] as a specifically evolutionary phenomenon, "the whole sum of the achievements and the regulations which distinguish our lives from those of our animal ancestors and which serves two purposes—namely to protect men against nature and to adjust their mutual relations." Keynes shared Freud's contentions that the "replacement of the power of the individual by the power of a community constitutes the decisive step in civilization," that human life "in common is only made possible when a majority comes together which is stronger than any separate individual and which remains united against all separate individuals." The question as to whether Keynes was a "Freudian" in the all-or-nothing sense the term has come to have, then, is misplaced. But on some key conceptual issues, Freud clearly helped him think and see things in a new light. See Sigmund Freud, *Civilization and Its Discontents*, trans. James Strachey, New York: Norton, 1961, 40, 46–47, 56–57, 100–101. See especially Bernard Maris, *Keynes ou l'Économiste Citoyen*, Paris: Presses de Sciences Po, 2007 29–41; Gilles Dostaler, *Keynes and his Battles*, Cheltenham: Edward Elgar, 2007, 39–42; and E. G. Winslow, "Keynes and Freud: Psychoanalysis and Keynes's Account of the 'Animal Spirits' of Capitalism," *Social Research* 53: 4, 1986, 549–78.

(Obviously, "civilization" is a debatable translation of *Kultur*. I myself have wondered whether it makes the connection seem closer than it really is. Nevertheless, it is the term

This argument, and the pragmatic, elitist approach to governance it suggests, retains extraordinary appeal, and not only among self-identified Keynesians. Understanding its logic and ideological basis is the key to understanding not only what made Keynes a Keynesian and what it means to be Keynesian today; it is crucial to the construction of any politically viable post-2008 liberal-capitalist political economy, for which Piketty's *Capital in the Twenty-First Century* might one day stand as the crowning achievement.[16] As I argue in Chapter 14, a Keynesian critique saturates Piketty's analysis—indeed, it is the very reason it met such an extraordinarily enthusiastic audience.

Many Left critics of Piketty will disagree, insisting that he is just another in a long line of "third-way" liberal apologists. It is true that *Capital in the Twenty-First Century* shares with all of modern liberalism—classical, neoclassical, and everything in between—a quasi obsession with the containment of problems to their "proper" sphere.[17] Keynesians also share this obsession, most evident in the emphasis on techno-bureaucratic solutions, which demand that regulatory authorities enjoy as much jurisdictional definition and independence as possible. All varieties of Keynesianism propose what Hegel called a "universal class" that can surgically remove social questions like poverty from the everyday messiness of politics and address them properly in the expert realm of reason and reasonableness.

But the problem of separating the economic from the political is perhaps even more visible, and considerably more elaborate, in Keynesianism than in more dogmatic commitments to liberalism. In the Keynesian critique, there is more than just an effort to keep political and economic or social questions separated; the content of the political, as a category of social life, not only shifts over time and

---

Freud suggested to his translators and the one Keynes read. Moreover, Freud goes on to say that we "recognize as cultural all activities and resources which are useful to men for making the earth serviceable to them, for protecting them against the violence of the forces of nature, and so on." See James Strachey's "Editor's Introduction" to the 1961 English edition of *Civilization and Its Discontents*, 6.)

16    Belknap Press, 2014.

17    Ellen Meiksins Wood, "The Separation of the Economic and the Political in Capitalism," *New Left Review* I: 127, 1981, 66–95.

space but is also constantly redefined so as to determine as clearly as possible what it does *not* contain.

This categorical malleability, however, should not be taken to represent a Keynesian faith in the liberal gospel of the "natural" separation of the political and economic realms. On the contrary, one of the most fundamental elements of Keynesianism's immanent critique of liberalism is its apostasy concerning the doctrine of separation. On the contrary, Keynesianism endorses a very Machiavellian position on this front. Keynesians certainly understand the separation between politics and economy as essential to social order, but they are under no impression it is "natural" or a given. They know it is nothing other than a necessary political-historical artifact, and a terribly unstable one at that. A separation of the political and economic realms, and the liberal capitalist civilization that depends upon it, tend inescapably toward disintegration because the liberal "freedom" they cultivate and celebrate—yield-seeking, entrepreneurial atomicity—inevitably and endogenously produces scarcity and poverty, both of which make the separation difficult to maintain. This is the looming "Ricardian apocalypse" that motivates Piketty's entire project.[18] Capitalist modernity's internal dynamics erode the very social fabric upon which it relies. The grandiose Utopia that Keynes sometimes proposes, like the virtuous full-employment "communism of capital" he envisions at the close of *The General Theory*, might occasionally give his futurology a rosy glow. But none of his professed hopes or predictions have prevented his sharpest readers from arguing that his analysis of modern political economy is "pessimistic."[19] I would go further: it is tragic.[20]

---

18 Thomas Piketty, *Le Capital au XXI<sup>e</sup> Siècle*, Paris: Seuil, 2013, 23: "if the tendencies observed in the period 1970–2010 were to continue until 2050 or 2100, we will approach social, political and economic disequilibria of such magnitude, both within and between countries, that it is hard not to think of the Ricardian apocalypse."

19 Antonio Negri, "Keynes and the Capitalist Theory of the State post-1929" [1968], in *Revolution Retrieved: Writings on Marx, Keynes, Capitalist Crisis and New Social Subjects*, London: Red Notes, 1988, 33–34, 41–42, n.69; Maris, *Keynes ou l'Économiste Citoyen*, 59.

20 Norman Schofield, "The Heart of the Atlantic Constitution: International Economic Stability, 1919–1998," *Politics and Society* 27: 2, 1999, 189–94; David Scott, *Conscripts of Modernity: The Tragedy of Colonial Enlightenment*, Durham: Duke University Press, 2004, 156–60.

The tragic core of *The General Theory* lies in its analysis of modern poverty and unemployment, in its demonstration that while there is no universal or natural necessity to either, they nonetheless persist. Capitalist scarcity is produced by capitalism. For Keynesians, this has crucial, permanent, and tragic political-economic consequences. It means liberal-capitalist civil society's internal contradictions render it impossible to forever contain poverty to its own "proper" compartment of the social. Consequently, the ultimate tragedy, and the ultimate paradox, is that despite modernity's perpetual production of the poor, *poverty has no proper place.* Although poverty and the poor are as much a product of modern life as technical automation and the capitalist firm, there is nowhere in modern life proper to them, nowhere they belong or are supposed to be. As a result, the economic problem and the social question can never be finally solved. Poverty is always a condition imposed upon the poor and in this true sense it is not the opposite of abundance or wealth, but the opposite of freedom.

This is the radical truth Keynes was unable to see in what he offered: that poverty serves no purpose, has no place, and cannot be justified. He knew the traditional bourgeois rationalizations—that poverty is "natural" or "good" for the poor because it motivates them; that government requires a core of elites with a disproportionate stake in the maintenance of social order; or that inequality ensures that the wealthy can play their part as savers (what Schumpeter called "the last pillar of the bourgeois argument")—were nothing but lies.[21] To force people to be poor is not only morally indefensible—a moral failure classical and neoclassical theories dismiss by blaming the poor for their poverty—but also foolish. This, combined with his realization (but unwillingness to admit) that capitalist abundance is a self-destructive proposition, is the radical kernel at the heart of Keynes, a kernel he planted but could not or did not want to nurture. If he has "returned" to us, then, as we embark on the twenty-first century, what exactly he resurrects is an appropriate object of struggle.

---

21    Mancur Olson, *The Logic of Collective Action*, Cambridge: Harvard University Press, 1965; Joseph Schumpeter, "John Maynard Keynes, 1883–1946," *American Economic Review* 36: 4, 1946, 516.

## Why Keynesianism? Why Now?

In 1930, as things seemed to be falling apart, Keynes published an essay entitled "Economic Possibilities for Our Grandchildren." "We are suffering just now," he declared, "from a bad attack of economic pessimism," based on "a wildly mistaken interpretation of what is happening to us." The slump, he promised, was merely a bump in the road on the way to abundance,

> only a temporary phase of maladjustment. All this means in the long run *that mankind is solving the economic problem.* I would predict that the standard of life in progressive countries one hundred years hence will be between four and eight times as high as it is to-day . . . This means that the economic problem is not— if we look to the future—*the permanent problem of the human race.*[22]

Seven years later, the world was a much bleaker place. Stuck in economic depression, with fascism on the rise and bread lines across the "progressive countries," the slump no longer seemed a merely "temporary phase of maladjustment." Had the "economic problem" proven itself permanent? It no longer seemed so clear to Keynes:

> It is our duty to prolong peace, hour by hour, day by day, for as long as we can. We do not know what the future will bring, except that it will be quite different from anything we could predict. I have said in another context that it is a disadvantage of "the long run" that in the long run we are all dead. But I could have said equally well that it is a great advantage of "the short run" that in the short run we are still alive. Life and history are made up of short runs. If we are at peace in the short run, that is something. The best we can do is put off disaster, if only in the hope, which is

---

22   Keynes, *CW,* IX, 326 (emphasis in the original). [*CW,* IX is *Essays in Persuasion,* originally published in 1931.]

not necessarily a remote one, that something will turn up. While there is peace, there is peace.[23]

Juxtaposing these two assessments, it is tempting to read a narrative of the fall. Even those most optimistic in 1930 could no longer deny the terrible reality that had become the capitalist world's new normal. Certainly this is part of what was on his mind in 1937. But it would be a mistake to understand this shift as an indicator of an "early" and "later" Keynesian political economy.[24] Instead, the two propositions—that "economic bliss" is on the horizon, but "the best we can do is put off disaster"—describe the dialectic of hope and fear at the heart of Keynesianism. They coexist, commingle; in fact, they are essentially simultaneous "glass-half-full" and "glass-half-empty" views of the very same Keynesian glass.

Keynesianism always combines an extraordinary optimism concerning the quasi-Utopian potential of human communities and human ingenuity with an existential terror at the prospect that it might not be realized. There is a sense in which, for Keynesians, liberal capitalism is always at a historical tipping point or precipice on which we balance in an inherently unstable "normality." Keynes would have vehemently rejected the claim that his words in 1937 suggested he had abandoned the hope of 1930. For him, and for all Keynesians, they are one and the same, for they proceed from the same foundational argument he made in 1924: in the long run we are all dead. If we forget that—that "life and history is made up of short runs"—then we will neglect the possibilities, both disastrous and blissful, that comprise a radically uncertain future. The long run absolves us of the untenable arrogance of certainty and occludes the extraordinary dynamic complexity of the world "in which we actually live" (a crucial Keynesian idea and phrase, which comes up again and again in what follows).[25]

---

23   Keynes, *CW,* XXVIII, 61.
24   One might make an "early" and "later" distinction in his approach to economic theory, however, for he did not always reject the "classical economics" he destroys in *The General Theory*. That shift mostly took place in the late 1920s and early 1930s.
25   Keynes, *CW,* VII, 3, 13, 247.

The key, therefore, is to understand the relation between bliss and disaster. Both are more or less immediately at hand:

The *pace* at which we can reach our destination of economic bliss will be governed by four things—our power to control population, our determination to avoid wars and civil dissension, our willingness to entrust to science the direction of those matters which are properly the concern of science, and the rate of accumulation as fixed by the margin between our production and our consumption; of which the last will easily look after itself, given the first three.[26]

Keynes himself thought the first and third nothing to worry about. Population, he believed, had become a nonissue.[27] And his faith in the capacities of scientific management by an enlightened intelligentsia was unshakeable.[28]

The real threat to prosperity, the political purpose of the Keynesian project, lay in the second "thing": avoiding "wars and civil dissension." In the conditions in which it was formulated, Keynes's political economy—and all varieties of Keynesianism—are about the production of credible stability in the face of crisis. The problem is not so much the "radical uncertainty" that features prominently in Keynes's thought, but the constant threat that radical uncertainty will precipitate a collapse of the social order. In other words, the fear is not that capitalism's contradictions produce the conditions for its own supersession in the radical sense. On this, at least, Antonio Negri's remarkable analysis of Keynes is wrong: Keynesianism is *not* a reaction "to the working class, to a mass movement which has found a political identity, to a possibility of insurrection and

---

26   Keynes, *CW,* IX, 331 (emphasis in the original). Keynes's "bliss" is a reference to a much-admired article written by his student and friend, Frank Ramsey: "A Mathematical Theory of Saving," *Economic Journal* 38, 1928, 543–59.

27   Keynes, *CW,* XIV, 124–33.

28   His remark in a radio address of the early 1930s is indicative: "The economic problem is not too difficult to solve. If you leave it to me, I will look after it" (Keynes, *CW,* XXVIII, 34).

subversion of the system."[29] Keynes might, I suppose, have been "a clear-sighted, intelligent conservative preparing to fight what he knows is coming," but it was not for the revolutionary realization of proletarian justice that he was preparing himself. He knew those dreams were out there among fractions of the masses, and he even granted their legitimacy in a way. But he was absolutely convinced they would remain unfulfilled. Like most liberals, Keynes did not believe the masses could achieve anything constructive on their own, let alone something so sophisticated as a new social order. They were, despite their aspirations perhaps, only capable of destruction.[30]

If, as Negri says, "the necessity of Keynesian ideology" arises in a "tension born of desperation," it is not provoked by communism but by the onset of *bellum omnium contra omnes* that looms on the Keynesian horizon.[31] This is the tension that motivates Keynes's most famous contribution, *The General Theory*. That work, and virtually all those concepts and policies we call Keynesian, are essentially moments in a political economy of anxiety and hope—efforts to subdue the sources of social disorder and animate the untapped social and economic wealth immanent to what Keynes called "modern communities."

Finding a way to tap that supposedly immanent wealth when prospects seem so bleak is referred to as the "economic problem," and it is the true reason we often hear that Keynes is "back." Admittedly, the surge of popular and scholarly work that cheered Keynes's return from the wilds of economic crankdom did subside after the first two or three years of the post-Lehman Brothers "current situation," and the "Keynesian" label eventually faded away, at least

---

29    Negri, "Keynes and the Capitalist Theory of the State post-1929," 24. I engage Negri more fully in the Chapter 15.

30    Jürgen Habermas, in many ways a consummate Keynesian, captures this liberal sentiment: "The people from whom all governmental authority is supposed to derive does not comprise a subject with a will and consciousness. It only appears in the plural, and *as* a people it is capable of neither decision nor action as a whole"; Jürgen Habermas, "Appendix I: Popular Sovereignty as Procedure," in *Between Facts and Norms: Contributions to a Discourse Theory of Law and Democracy*, trans. William Rehg, Cambridge: MIT Press, 1998, 469.

31    Negri, "Keynes and the Capitalist Theory of the State post-1929," 24.

relative to the initial furor. To some extent this is a function of the normalization of elements of nominally "Keynesian" macropolicy (low long-term interest rate policies perhaps most prominently). But even if we are willing to believe he was dead prior to 2008, the anxiety that resurrected Keynes at that point has not subsided one bit. Indeed, while unevenly distributed, it has produced capitalism's most significant legitimation crisis since the interwar years and has sowed the seeds for a political volatility the state and elites are addressing with what can only be described as regulatory and technocratic panic. By late spring 2015, both negative interest rates on banks' reserves and negative yields on the most secure sovereign debt had become almost standard financial fare, even though most economists and policy-makers have in no uncertain terms long considered the very idea to be bonkers. Negative rates! Silvio Gesell (one of the heroic heretics Keynes celebrates in Chapter 23 of *The General Theory*) must be laughing in his grave.[32]

This is the world—at least that disproportionately powerful part of it we call the capitalist global North—that welcomed Thomas Piketty's *Capital au XXe siècle* in 2013–2014. It is, or at least one could be forgiven for thinking it is, a somewhat paradoxical world, one in which, as Piketty puts it, "capital is back," just as capitalism itself seems to have stalled. By every measure, it is increasingly unequal, increasingly undemocratic, and, it seems, increasingly precarious. It is plagued with political and economic fragmentation and volatility, decades of geopolitical order seem to be coming

---

32   If his name was familiar to *The General Theory*'s readers at all, Gesell was usually thought of as little more than a crank. Keynes praised his proposal to date-stamp money, which would motivate investment because if money holders hoarded cash, it would fall in value over time. The idea has enjoyed some renewed interest; see, for example, the March 30, 2015 edition of Martin Sandbu's engaging "Free Lunch" column in the *Financial Times*. Axel Leijonhufvud, a prominent postwar Keynesian, has investigated these dynamics with a thought experiment he calls the "blueback scheme." Reflecting on the possible effects of "Gesell money," he proposes the "blueback" as a sort of inversion of Gesell's progressive depreciation. A blueback would be indexed to expected inflation, so that unlike regular old "greenbacks," its real value would always be (expected to) equal its nominal value. Leijonhufvud uses the thought experiment to demonstrate the inadequacy of monetarist theories of inflation. See Axel Leijonhufvud, "Theories of Stagflation," in *Macroeconomic Stability and Coordination*, Cheltenham: Edward Elgar, 2000, 134–50.

unstuck, rising ethno-nationalist populisms trouble formerly dependable liberalisms in the core, and all this is unraveling against a background of accelerating global climate change and ecological degradation.

Far more than the renewed interest in Keynesian economics, or Keynes the economist or statesman, it is the precariousness of "civilization" that makes the question of Keynesianism urgent. We are witness to the desperate refusal to abandon the belief that a non-revolutionary bliss is out there to be realized, that "something will turn up." This anxious hope and trepidation are not confined to elites, governors, or the ruling class, and they exceed the realm of liberal politics. They are, rather, widespread across otherwise quite rigid lines of difference—millions of us have become, as Keynes was once described, "Geiger counters of future headlines."[33]

These overlapping ecological and political economic crises in which we are stuck challenge us all (albeit extraordinarily unequally), but they produce a particular kind of existential anxiety in fractions of the Left in the capitalist global North. Despite enormously important movements like Occupy and the radical hope they have instilled in some, for many the general trend at present is at best intimidatingly ambiguous. While a burgeoning radicalism appears to have more to offer than at any time since the 1960s, so too, it seems, does a hateful nationalist-racist populism. Fundamentalist religious authoritarianism and xenophobic and reactionary far-right movements—protofascisms and worse—seem to be exploding, and the vindictive austerity-capitalism that one would think was the root of the problem seems to have survived the financial crisis many thought would kill it. It seems to me fair to say—although perhaps I put too much emphasis on their electoral-legislative form—that twenty-first century mass politics presents at least as daunting a problem as it does a hopeful radical alternative.[34]

---

33  George Stigler, *Five Lectures on Economic Problems*, Freeport, NY: Books for Libraries, 1949, 7. Stigler, a key contributor to Chicago School economics and no fan of Keynes, did not mean this as a compliment.

34  Paul Mason, *Why It's Kicking Off Everywhere: The New Global Revolutions*, London: Verso, 2012.

I have a hard time imagining a nonviolent, "democratic" response to the long-term implications of both liberal capitalism's current trajectory and ecological disintegration driven by climate change and other processes—the two forces being of course bound up in one another. I am willing to accept the logical proposition that a nondemocratic response (at least in the liberal sense of a bureaucratic-technical "fix") need not necessarily be violent, but it seems very likely to be. The likely liberal response to these new planetary challenges has the potential to further concentrate power and resources in the hands of elites, a condition more than likely to render progressives even more beholden to a political status quo that might seem the only thing between us and political chaos. In the realm of climate change, for example, it is this sentiment that justifies the widely shared "progressive" assumption that what Joel Wainwright and I have called "climate Leviathan"—a sovereign invested with the authority to force us to save ourselves from catastrophic climate change—is the only possible answer.[35] This is what drove much (but not all) of the mass mobilization around the Copenhagen and Paris climate meetings of 2010 and 2015.

This cul-de-sac is precisely where Keynesian reason leads us. Many of those political features that make Keynesianism make sense to "progressives" are significant obstacles to a vital, mass-based progressive or Left movement—that is at least part of Keynesianism's *raison d'être*. I am of course far from the first to point this out; some variation on it is a "radical" axiom. The problem that is almost never mentioned, however, is that recognizing Keynesianism's limits, or even excoriating it for its "reformist" or "collaborationist" bases (as some "radicals" are often wont to do), does not thereby cut the ties that bind the Left to Keynesianism. Keynesianism is not something that the Left in the liberal capitalist North can just disavow at will. It has always been a crucial element of that social formation, and there is no politics that can escape its time. Keynesianism has been at the core of both liberalism and the critique of liberalism for more than

---

35   J. Wainwright and G. Mann, "Climate Leviathan," *Antipode* 45, 2013, 1–22; see also J. Wainwright and G. Mann, *Climate Leviathan*, London: Verso, forthcoming.

two hundred years.[36] It is, unintentionally but inescapably, no small part of what "progressive" or "Left" has come to mean, however much some might wish it were otherwise.

I raise these questions at this early stage partly in the interests of honesty and partly because much of what follows concerns the fact that these quasi-paralyzing conclusions—that is, a justifiable skepticism regarding the capacity of representative democracy, however radical, to lead us out of the woods, a fear of the seemingly inevitable violence that will follow, and a turn to the centralizing state as the only answer—have always partly defined the condition and critique I call Keynesianism. In other words, this situation is not merely the result of the recent and broad-based recognition of looming environmental catastrophe or accelerating inequality and mass displacement. It is much older than that. It follows not from our novel historical or geographical context, but instead from a logic fundamental to the very notion of politics in liberal capitalism—for most of its critics and its proponents—for at least two centuries: a distrust of the masses.

Take, as a contemporary example, the common critique of Donald Trump's 2016 presidential candidacy or the Tea Party in the United States. Any perusal of the analyses in the US "progressive" media— from the decidedly nonradical *New York Review of Books*, to the muckraking *Nation*, to the traditional Marxism of the *Monthly Review*—will confirm a generalized distrust of the people or at least of their present judgment. Only ignorance, abandonment, or false consciousness could possibly explain the appeal of such vindictive, antipoor, racist nationalism. Moreover, the wariness of mass politics' seemingly inevitable populist manipulability is not diminished by the celebrations of "community" and the "grassroots" one encounters in "progressive" discourse. Even these more "participatory" commitments are embedded in elite managerialism. The "progressive" organizations and activists who claim to speak for "everyday people" often have little intention of giving the grassroots a voice per se, but in

---

36    Alan Ryan, *The Making of Modern Liberalism*, Princeton: Princeton University Press, 2012, 69.

giving "citizens" an opportunity to speak with a particular and prede-termined voice. If community meetings, planning charettes, and marches across town produced a consensus that the problem is non-white immigrants, unionized labor markets, environmental regula-tion, and the "nanny state," these conclusions will not find a way into progressive or Left op-eds and policy analysis. The point of participa-tory progressivism is usually to elicit a response consonant with what progressives want the grassroots to say.

This is not to say that such an orientation distinguishes progressive politics, as if other organizations or movements are "true" to their constituents even if it means undermining their own causes. Certainly not. But it is to say that there are some good reasons for Tea Party attacks on the "liberal elite."

The disdain for the Tea Party cannot be easily separated from the Left or progressive engagement with popular democracy. Attempts by left intellectuals like Thomas Frank to frame the problem as merely the product of manufactured reactionary populism rather than as a fundamental part of liberal democracy—which, in its "true" form is instead posited as an incorruptible goodness machine—are just obfuscations. The fact is that a substantial proportion of "the people" appear to be either easily swayed or terrifyingly mean-spir-ited. Populism as it animates a movement like the Tea Party may not be equivalent to democracy, but it is undoubtedly democratic, at least according to the liberal definition. Moreover, if antipopulism comes from the nominally "democratic" Left (however nominal the modifier), it is marked by deep historical irony, since some of the most important moments of radical social change in history were in no small part premised on ideological appeals of a similarly populist tenor. (The French and Haitian revolutions come to mind.)

Ultimately, however, this irony is a big part of what is at stake: much (if not all) of the Left wants democracy without populism; it wants transformational politics without the risks of transformation; it wants revolution without revolutionaries. This is the legacy of the Terror and Stalinism, and it is the logic at the heart of Keynesianism. Much of the self-described Left is not as far as we would like to think from the Keynes who declared that if it came down to it, he would side with the bourgeoisie.[37] The grip of this antipopulism is so strong and complex that the solution is not to be discovered merely by committing to the "other side"—and even if it were, it is not easy to know which side that is and where we can go to find it.

This means it is a grave mistake for "progressives" or "radicals" (and I include myself in these groupings) to take liberal or capitalist elites' fear of the masses as somehow, deep down, a fear of "us" or "our ideas." Contemporary liberals are neither nineteenth-century relics nor Cold War nostalgists. They do not fear the specter of communism or radical redistribution according to socialist principles. That is a *conservative* bogeyman, one that conservative elites like the Koch brothers probably hardly believe in themselves. The contemporary liberal variation of the antidemocratic premise is no more founded on a fear of left-wing revolution than contemporary Left politics is founded on the imminence of that revolution. On the contrary, contemporary liberalism in the capitalist global North is constituted, more than anything else, by an effort to ensure that capital does not alienate a large enough proportion of the people to destabilize the social order, thus putting its historical achievements at risk and precipitating what Keynes's avatar Piketty calls the "Marxian apocalypse."[38]

I do not mean that modern liberalism is an unwitting or accidental Marxist analysis stripped of its politics. Among liberals, the effect of the twin ecological and economic crises has been to exacerbate an anxiety that has always been there but has recently resurfaced more energetically than at any time since the "Keynesian" heights of the Cold War. The contemporary liberal recognizes that if capital does not understand the precariousness of its position, it risks losing it. Against anything deserving the name Marxism, liberals believe that a scientific assessment of their power will give them the tools to hold on to it forever. The corollary of this proposition is not that, should they fail, the proletariat or the 99 percent or the multitude will rise

---

37   Keynes, *CW*, IX, 258.
38   And he does not mean communist revolution, he means unrelenting immiseration and reactionary revolt: Piketty, *Capital*, 16, 368.

("heads we win, tails we get socialism")—but rather that if bourgeois civil society falls, so will everyone and everything else. The entire social order will go with it.

This is the logical conclusion of what we might call the liberal syllogism, with the following propositional structure: (a) liberalism produced modern civilization; (b) liberalism is capitalist; therefore (c) all modern civilization is capitalist. We can trace inchoate forms of the syllogism in Hobbes and some of his contemporaries, including Locke, but it is really with Kant that it comes together as a mode of "practical logic."[39] All forms of Keynesian reason are a sympathetic critique of this syllogism.

As Keynes's theory of civilization makes clear, because the bourgeoisie cannot imagine a nonbourgeois society, it cannot conceive of its own end as anything other than the end of the world. The specter behind its fear, therefore, is neither the multitude, nor the 99 percent as the-truth-of-the-working-class, nor the-people-as-historically-"autonomous" force striving to overthrow the existing order to free itself or take power. Rather, the multitude or the 99 percent represents the potential destruction of the social stability that keeps disorder at bay. Liberalism has little fear of the masses' historical mission. On the contrary, the core premise of liberalism is that the masses, by definition, have no mission—only conservatives think the multitude are actually trying to achieve something "positive." For liberals, the multitude is either a contented populace or the rabble, the people or the antipeople that always lurks within it.[40]

One of the conclusions of this examination of Keynesianism is that this fear of power in the hands of the ignorant is far from specifically liberal. As a friend of mine, active on the radical Left, said to me recently, "give a moron a gun, and anything can happen." There are many ways in which I agree; in a world that includes the Tea Party (and worse), I am all for gun control. That is why Keynes makes

---

39    Immanuel Kant, *Critique of Pure Reason*, Cambridge: Cambridge University Press, 1998, 627.

40    José Ortega y Gasset, *La Rebelión de las Masas*, Madrid: Austral, 2010, 79; Ryan, *Making of Modern Liberalism*, 73–76.

intuitive sense to me—and, I would venture, to so many others—despite my own struggles for political clarity and despite my recognition that he helped save capitalism *and* liberalism, both of which I oppose. Keynesianism appeals even though we know its dangers. For the figure and thought of Keynes stands as the most compelling modern response to the dark spirit we perceive beneath the reassuring hustle and bustle of civil society. His eternal return to the center of "progressive" political thought is proof of the depth and persistence of this distrust, a vast sea of anxiety in which a significant proportion of all liberal capitalist societies seem to swim.

Witness, for example, the response of prominent socialists and social democrats to the financial crisis. Rather than welcoming the meltdown (as, say, Marx did the financial turmoil of 1857), radical political economists like Robin Blackburn, Robert Wade, and others have been mostly interested in stabilizing a system so that unrest does not destroy the whole kit and caboodle, thus ruining the lives not only of the rich who nevertheless deserve it, but of as many or more of the innocent poor. Their proposals are more or less unqualified attempts to save the institutions of capitalism while dethroning capital.[41] There is much worth considering in that idea, but whether it is possible—especially in the face of environmental catastrophe—is a key question, and the answer is not at all clear.

I hasten to emphasize that none of this is to point fingers; I aim this critique at myself as much as anyone. That Blackburn and Wade make a lot of sense is a result of a shared and, in my opinion, justifiable condition; to call it paralysis is not to suggest it could be otherwise. It is the reason that Marx, among others, remains a crucial resource in our current condition. For Marx makes one acutely aware of the need for social transformation radical enough to seem quite

---

41   See, for example, Robin Blackburn, "The Subprime Crisis," *New Left Review* II: 50, 2008, 63–105; Robert Wade, "Financial Regime Change," *New Left Review* II: 53, 2008, 5–21; Robert Wade, "From Global Imbalances to Global Reorganisations," *Cambridge Journal of Economics* 33, 2009, 539–62; Graham Turner, *The Credit Crunch: Housing Bubbles, Globalization and the Worldwide Economic Crisis*, London: Pluto Press, 2008; Larry Elliott and Dan Atkinson, *Going South: Why Britain Will Have a Third World Economy by 2014*, London: Palgrave, 2012.

risky, and therefore quite frightening. While I would not want to suggest that Marx provides us with all the intellectual resources we need, it remains true that taking his work seriously enables Leftists to see that one's world—especially if one is among the more fortunate—does not match one's political or moral claims. And the only way to make it do so would be to embrace the kind of change that quite possibly means throwing it all away. That is a very unsettling experience, one not a few of us prefer to avoid, or at least defer. We are not unreasonably tempted to turn instead to something—Keynesianism—that allows us to contemplate the chasm between "is" and "ought" without demanding the same fear and trembling. The persistent power of this temptation is hard to overestimate.

At the same time, however, while our current condition reaffirms the ethics and politics of the Marxian wager, it also demands an honest confrontation with its limits. The historical logic upon which Marx made his wager offered a guarantee. That guarantee is not a function of his supposed belief that "historical necessity" was equivalent to inevitability. Contrary to a century and a half of misreading, he did not believe that at all. He knew history does not just happen, it has to be made. Instead, the Marxian wager—the *salto mortale*—was based on the guarantee that however long it might take, unrelenting struggle will eventually be rewarded. In other words, when Marx urged the proletariat to make history, he did so by positing—through analysis, not prophecy—a light at the end of the tunnel. For reasons both material and ideological, this guarantee is not possible at present and may never be again. Whatever radical wagers we choose to make in the face of capitalism, liberalism, and their occasional fascist and totalitarian guises, there is a very real possibility that we make them in vain. There is no certain victory, even in the longest run or the latest instance—or if there is, it is presently unimaginable. No matter how long and hard the path, it may still end in disaster. This only seems to make Keynesianism more sensible than ever.

Indeed, one might even say of liberal capitalism that if in the long run it's dead, in the short run it is Keynesian. The Keynesian return in the moment of liberal-capitalist crisis is thus axiomatic, since it is a Keynesian sensibility that recognizes and names the crisis per se, that is, a conjuncture or condition that by definition cannot go unaddressed. Keynesianism might be that variety of liberalism the Left cannot shake precisely because, among the varieties of liberalism currently circulating, it is the one that allows us to hope, and thus to undertake crisis mitigation, at least at the fundamental level of the social.

As Georges Sorel put it in 1919, excoriating Keynesianism before Keynes: "Our middle class desire to die in peace—after them the deluge."[42] Are many of us not, in the end, really afraid we will *all* go down with the ship—that it will not merely bring down those who deserve it? Should a "real" radical not embrace the inevitably radical revolution financial crisis and environmental crisis and political crisis will bring? I do not think that is the correct path; but that is, of course, not a necessarily "radical" conclusion. It is, rather, a part of a broader politics whose valence is much more ambiguous and whose nature we must struggle to understand.

As much as any other recent figure, it is in Keynes, the varieties of Keynesianism, and the much longer tradition of Keynesian critique upon which they are predicated, that we can discover the political origins and limits of these problems, and the potential, if any, to overcome them. Indeed, I believe that we cannot grasp a way out of our current, and eminently rational, road to ruin without understanding Keynesianism, what it offers, and what it forecloses. Contemporary capitalism and liberalism are literally unimaginable without it, and, as a result, so too are any feasible plans to escape the binds in which they tie us.

## An Outline of This Book

To make this case, the book uses a wide-angle lens, conceptually and historically. Part I gives an overview of the key elements of the argument. Chapter 2 details my proposed conception of Keynesianism

---

42    Georges Sorel, *Reflections on Violence*, Glencoe, IL: Free Press, 1950 [1919], 120.

(or the Keynesian critique; I use the terms interchangeably) and through which the rest of the book works. It may at first seem somewhat removed from its namesake, but part of the task of the chapters that follow is to demonstrate the ways in which this critique is not only the foundation of Keynes's Keynesianism, but of a wide range of critiques of modern liberalism, sometimes explicitly, sometimes implicitly. Chapter 3 calls upon Keynes himself to substantiate the way this Keynesianism works at the broadest level, that is, in an essentially tragic reading of the seeming ineradicability of poverty from a modern liberal capitalism that cannot, either conceptually or politically, come to grips with it.

In part II, Before Keynes, I return to the French Revolution and Hegel, where the Keynesian critique is clearly articulated for the first time in the aftermath of the Terror and the roiling instability that rippled across Europe. Chapter 4 exposes the fundamental problems to which Keynesianism is a response in the Revolution, and in particular in the figure of the Jacobin leader Maximilien Robespierre. Robespierre, whose political career culminated in his leadership of the Committee of Public Safety—the principal coordinators of the Terror of 1793–1794—represented, and continues to represent, much of what revolution has come to mean for liberal modernity. In the heart of revolutionary Paris, Robespierre formulated two of the ideas around which the rest of the book revolves: the revolution without revolution and the question of the possibility of "honorable poverty" in the modern age. These ideas, which he forced upon his bourgeois compatriots, go some way to explaining why, since the late eighteenth century, he has for Euro-American elites stood as the purest, and therefore most terrifying, figure of the explosive instability and violence they take to be latent in "the people." At precisely the moment when liberalism and capitalism are coming into being in Europe, Keynesianism—as a distinctively Eurocentric political stance—coalesces as a critique of both with Robespierre on its mind.

Chapters 5, 6, and 7 undertake an engagement with Hegel, for whom the Revolution not only marked the historical beginning of the modern age but also radically transformed the experience of the world, materially and ideologically, and Robespierre was its most complex protagonist. I am far from the first to say the Revolution is the event around which Hegel's entire life's work was oriented. He is the appropriate place to begin because his political philosophy was purposefully constructed to offer a way out of revolutionary turmoil, to shore us up against it, without forsaking the changes the Revolution (and Robespierre) had wrought. His struggle not only to avoid "taking sides" but also (as he saw it) to see beyond or above the politics of his day is characteristic of Keynesianism and the stance it takes toward the world.

Hegel is important here not only because he had such a significant influence on the thought of a Europe in transition—like Keynes, he was very well-known and controversial—but because of the often remarkable if surprising resonances between his political thought and that of Keynes. As I hope to show, a reading of Hegel with Keynes in our minds allows us to turn to Keynes and Keynesianism with a sharper, more critical, but also more sympathetic eye. Chapter 5 examines Hegel's response to the Revolution and revolution more broadly. Chapter 6 considers the problems of necessity, scarcity, and poverty—captured in the figure of the "rabble"—that he took to characterize the post-Revolutionary age, and the theory of civil society he developed to understand it. Chapter 7 focuses on his thoughts on the role of political economy as the science of government appropriate to that age.

Chapter 8, which closes part II, is something of a transitional moment in the book's account of Keynesianism, both historically and logically. Following up on Hegel's illumination of the key role of political economy to modern government (meaning both the state and Foucault's broader sense, that is, the conduct of social conduct), the chapter lays out what is effectively—I ask readers to pardon the grandiosity of the claim—a theory of political economy. It describes political economy as a postrevolutionary pharmaceutical science of government, crucial to the process of legitimation that is the focus of the Keynesian critique. In other words, Keynesianism is not equivalent to political economy, but rather political economy is crucial to the project of Keynesianism in distinctive ways. Tracing an admittedly fragmented and selective (but not unwarranted) history, the chapter examines some of the problems around which classical political economy coalesced into what Marx called its fully developed "final shape" and links Keynes's critique of the economic orthodoxy of his age to the arguments of Hegel's time. (These links are not too difficult to make, since they are the ones Keynes himself emphasized in his theoretical-intellectual lineage.)

All of these questions and themes return in part III, Keynes, which comprises an extended reading of *The General Theory of Employment, Interest and Money*. In these chapters, and throughout the book, I do draw frequently from Keynes's other writings, but since it is the most comprehensive and influential of his works—surely there is no better known twentieth-century political economy—in these three chapters I focus specifically on *The General Theory*. The point is neither to summarize the book nor to explain the "economic" dynamics Keynes intended to describe. I do, of course, work out some of his key ideas—his critique of Say's Law (the idea that "free" markets always lead to full employment), effective demand, and liquidity preference, for example—but others, like the multiplier or propensities to consume, go largely undiscussed. (Readers interested in the details of these ideas and how they matter to Keynes's argument should consult *A Companion to* The General Theory—available online on the Verso website, versobooks.com—which provides a straightforward chapter-by-chapter summary of *The General Theory*.)

Part III proceeds from the proposition that Keynes is our Hegel—a reference to the younger Marx's attempt to critique the politics of his age through an engagement with the thinker he took to capture his time so effectively. This does not mean reading *The General Theory* as a Marxist, although it might, and it does not mean engaging it in the hyperdetailed "commentary" mode with which Marx read *Philosophy of Right*. Rather, I attempt to read *The General Theory* along lines similar to those Antonio Negri did half a century ago—as a "political manifesto." My reading both resonates with and contradicts Negri's on important matters, but I hope that, like his, it uncovers the political struggles that defined Keynes's particular variety of Keynesianism, a Keynesianism that, like Hegel's, was formulated in response to a world-historical upheaval that exposed elites to the terror that lay just beneath the surface of modernity. That upheaval was not the

Bolshevik Revolution of 1917, but World War I—and in this distinction lies the source of most of my differences with Negri. Chapter 9
introduces *The General Theory* and the world of economics in which
Keynes felt the book necessary. Chapter 10 works through Keynes's
theory of effective demand and unemployment in light of the over-
arching Keynesian critique, and Chapter 11 follows this up through
Keynes's theories of liquidity and capital.

The first three chapters of part IV, After Keynes, bring the concept of
Keynesianism developed in the preceding chapters to the terrain of
post–World War II economics, with a focus first on the economics of
unemployment and then on inequality. Each chapter engages in detail
with an influential intervention in the political and sometimes policy
realms concerning causes and consequences, examining the ways in
which the Keynesian critique continued (and continues) to animate a
wide range of "Keynesian economics," despite its up-and-down fortunes
since *The General Theory* appeared in 1936. Chapter 12 briefly surveys
the here-enthusiastic, there-reluctant "Keynesianization" of economics
in the years immediately following the war, with special attention paid
to developments in the United States and the United Kingdom, where
most of the work took place. It then turns to an examination of an
(eventually) widely read paper by Keynes's sometime colleague Michał
Kalecki, "The Political Aspects of Full Employment." I argue that
Kalecki's analysis of unemployment, influenced heavily by both Marx
and Keynes, marks one end of the postwar Keynesian spectrum.

Chapter 13 takes up the daunting task of situating contemporary
"New Keynesian" economics in the context of the Keynesian critique.
New Keynesian economics took a recognizable shape in the 1980s,
after the widely announced death of Keynesian policy and economics, and is particularly dominant in the United States. It is not entirely
"new" however; it developed directly out of the bread-and-butter
analysis of the Fordist–Keynesian Golden Age following World War
II, the "neoclassical synthesis" of neoclassical approaches with non-
Walrasian markets (markets not assumed to be in full employment
equilibrium). New Keynesian economics is thought by some to
represent the "betrayal" of Keynes's vision and contribution, and in
many ways this is undeniable. Here, though, through a reading of

important contributions from New Keynesian economists Carl Shapiro and Joseph Stiglitz, I try to show that there are crucial ways in which New Keynesians retain central aspects of Hegel's and Keynes's Keynesianism.

The penultimate chapter (14) is an extended critique of Thomas Piketty's best-selling *Capital in the Twenty-First Century*. Piketty's massive and justifiably widely discussed tome, like *The General Theory*, appeared in a moment of crisis-ridden trepidation in the liberal capitalist global North, and it was received with a similar mix of celebration and condemnation. I argue that the similarities go far deeper than reception, however: it is a thoroughly Keynesian work. In its motivation, in its structure, and (to a surprising degree) its argument, it is a *General Theory* for our time.

Chapter 15 offers as much of a "conclusion" as I know how to give to the broad and ultimately uncloseable questions with which the book wrestles. The threads that run through a project either arrogant or foolish enough to attempt to trace a critical liberal anxiety across the political economy of two centuries are not easily tied off, and that is entirely appropriate. In place of a final riposte, I return to the questions of revolution, political economy, and legitimacy that run through the book, with special attention to the figure of the bourgeois who lies at the heart of many powerful radical critiques of Keynesianism. In these last pages I also return to the crisis of faith or hope (I am not sure which) the current conjuncture seems to solicit: a caricature of Robert Louis Stevenson's bipolar Doctor Jekyll and Mister Hyde in the form of an internal struggle between Doctor Marx and Mister Keynes.

# CHAPTER 2

# What Is Keynesianism?

What is Keynesianism? Posterity bestows few honors more uncertain than the slip from proper name to adjective. Although some syntactical transformations seem to capture their inspiration intuitively enough—Stalinist, say, or Dickensian—others are so inadequate to their eponym's thought or practice as to be the etymological equivalent of a lie. Neither Hobbes nor Machiavelli, I am sure, could in a thousand years have imagined the collection of politics now qualified by their names, and Marx was eagerly distancing himself from Marxism long before the advent of the authoritarian state socialisms that so twisted his legacy. If he had been around in the mid-twentieth century, he might very well have chosen to change his family name.

Such imprecision is probably unavoidable. No single adjective can be expected to capture an inevitably contradictory lifetime of thought and action, and any misrepresentation will only be more glaring in familiar eyes, since the deeper the knowledge of the figure, the less the modifier will seem sufficient to its descriptive task. Nevertheless, these terms circulate, evolve, and come to express—in an attitude to the world, a way of thinking, a historical condition—not only the times and places in which the adjectives are uttered, but also the times and places of the individual with whom "it all began": the force of the category is always retroactive. Despite themselves, Marx is canonized as a Marxist, Machiavelli as Machiavellian. The adjective becomes a household word, the name its ghostly emanation, as if the predicate produced the subject. This process has the paradoxical effect of foregrounding the individual, while simultaneously rendering invisible the conditions and content of his or her real contribution. It is easy to forget that Christ was not a Christian.

In our own times, the term "Keynesian" epitomizes these problems. Its status in political and economic discourse was a point of conflict from the very beginning. The difference between "Keynesian economics and the economics of Keynes" (as the title of Axel Leijonhufvud's influential 1968 book frames it) has been a subject of heated debate since the days of Keynes himself.[1] Economists and policy makers were denouncing or applauding one another for "Keynesianism" within five years of Keynes's death in 1946; and in the 2010s, influential New Keynesians in the Obama administration constructed policies on the basis of ideas that "post-Keynesian" economists claim not only are not Keynesian, but would have horrified old Maynard.

The meanings of "Keynesianism" are thus always controversial, usually unclear, and often, it must be said, based in little more than econo-babble of one variety or another. It is a rare reader of the financial pages or lay observer of capitalism who would feel unable to define "Keynesianism" loosely, although it would very often be an inaccurate representation of Keynes's own ideas. Admittedly, the disconnect from its origins may not quite match that of "Marxist" or "Christian," but the adjective has for most people similarly overwritten the life and thought of its namesake retroactively. Keynesianism has limited our capacity to understand Keynes and has thus substantially obscured its own origins and some of its most fundamental dynamics. Other than the claim to being more "realistic" (because it takes into account nominal rigidities and other "frictions"), I wager most economists are unable to say why "Keynesian economics" is Keynesian. This is confirmed by thumbing through the index of the vast majority of economics texts, both for academic and general

---

1   Axel Leijonhufvud, *On Keynesian Economics and the Economics of Keynes*, Oxford: Oxford University Press, 1968.

readers: almost all entries under "Keynes" refer the reader not to discussion of John Maynard Keynes but rather to "Keynesianism," as if they were the same.

Keynes and Keynesianism have thus merged, and for many it would seem their shared meaning is captured in the idea that the first two words in the phrase "Keynesian welfare state" are synonyms. In fact, they are not synonymous at all—neither on the terms of twenty-first century "Keynesian economics" nor on those of the political economy and policy analysis of Keynes. If the welfare state was Keynesian—and that is not a given—it does not follow that its Keynesian-ness is what made it a welfare state.

Confronted with this messiness, two responses predominate in contemporary discussions of Keynes and Keynesianism. The first, common among both post-Keynesians (who would celebrate Keynes) and those who would condemn him is to analyze the ways in which what gets passed off as Keynesianism is more or less compatible with Keynes's thought, especially as presented in *The General Theory*. The second, a strategy shared somewhat surprisingly by most orthodox economists and popular economic literature, is to ignore the problem entirely and to assume—not unreasonably—that if there is a meaningful historical distinction between "Keynesian economics and the economics of Keynes," it is of no "practical" significance. As Paul Krugman puts it: "my basic reaction to discussions about . . . What Keynes Really Meant—is, I Don't Care."[2] Keynesianism is as "Keynesianism" does.

**What Keynes "Really Meant"**

As someone interested in the details of the problem, I believe the post-Keynesian strategy is always important. It is (as I hope to show) essential to an understanding not just of Keynes and Keynesianism, but also of contemporary politics and political economy. Nevertheless, we cannot wholly dismiss the latter. Where readability or the norms

---

2   Paul Krugman, "Minsky and Methodology," from his *New York Times* blog "Conscience of a Liberal," posted March 27, 2012.

of scholarly communication make the historical mismatch seem irrelevant, it is surely understandable. If a whole community of economists calls itself "New Keynesian," what is there to be achieved by "outing" its members as not "truly" Keynesian? If the problem ultimately lies in this or that position's relative fidelity to the Word, is that grounds for a meaningful critique? I hope not.

What the two responses share is a definitional approach to the problem. The task becomes one of categorization: what content should the word "Keynesian" have? The first strategy involves determining what Keynes truly meant to say and including or excluding later ideas based on their relative compatibility with the original. The second accepts the colloquial "welfare-state" definition, or the "sticky" variables of modern New Keynesian models, and moves on, whether Keynes himself is on board or not. Since this is a book about both Keynesianism and Keynes's thought, both of these approaches matter, but neither of them suffices. I am of course often focused on what Keynes "really meant." However, the importance of his "real" meaning is not that it represents the thought of the "origin" or "father" of something called Keynesianism; what is important is that his thinking is *not* an origin, but, instead, an extraordinarily powerful instance of what I am calling the Keynesian critique. This is what we must tackle if we want to understand what the concept Keynesianism "really means." We must identify the fundamental grounds of Keynesianism—to ask not of the differences between Keynes and Keynesianism, but rather to consider the ways in which their premises, if not their arguments, are shared, driven by politics neither can contain.

In other words, the point is to *understand Keynes as a Keynesian thinker*—to situate Keynesian reason in its longer historical trajectory, to examine Keynes's ideas as a product of the conditions that constitute capitalist modernity as such. I hope readers forgive this self-aggrandizing comparison, but my objective is to read Keynes as Marx read Hegel: recognizing that ideas can never be anything but (as Hegel himself said) their "own times apprehended in thought."[3]

---

3   G. W. F. Hegel, *Philosophy of Right*, Cambridge: Cambridge University Press, 1991, Preface. (Hereinafter cited as *PhR*.)

On these terms, Keynes poses a particularly important challenge, because he is the most influential theorist of capitalism of the twentieth century—to which, for all intents and purposes, we still belong. And, despite all claims to the contrary, he is very far from dead. In the wake of the financial crisis that began in 2007-2008, the relentless waves of nominally "Keynesian" reappraisals—especially those that declare the crisis solicited the "return of the master"—amply demonstrate that his thought apprehends something of import to more than just his time and place. Keynes's political economy is the outcome of a set of historical and geographical conditions endemic to capitalism in the global North—and in some cases beyond it—and Keynesian reason is neither the property nor the product of Keynes alone.

Keynesianism so understood has had several lives since Keynes. But just as important, it also had a life before him. Keynes the thinker is in effect one star in a constellation whose Keynesian shape is visible because of a specific set of relations in historical and theoretical space. Keynes is a key to understanding the politics of modern capitalism and liberal democracy, just as Marx found in Hegel a key to understanding their early consolidation. Keynes is our Hegel.

As the economist Paul Baran put it in 1957, with the economic collapse of the interwar period:

> Keynesian economics found itself face to face with the entire irrationality, the glaring discrepancy between the productive potentialities and the productive performance characteristic of the capitalist order.
>
> At the risk of grossly exaggerating the intellectual performance of Keynes, it might be said that what Hegel accomplished with respect to German classical philosophy, Keynes achieved with regard to neoclassical economics. Operating with the customary tools of conventional theory, remaining well within the confines of "pure" economics, faithfully refraining from considering socioeconomic processes as a whole, the Keynesian analysis advanced to the very limits of bourgeois economic theorizing, and exploded its entire structure. Indeed, it amounted to an "official" admission on

the part of the "Holy See" of conventional economics that instability, a strong tendency toward stagnation, chronic underutilization of human and material resources, are inherent in the capitalist system. It implicitly repudiated the zealously guarded "purity" of academic economics by revealing the importance for the comprehension of the economic process of the structure of society, the relations of classes, the distribution of income, the role of the state, and other "exogenous" factors.[4]

Baran was a Marxist, a key member of the orthodox *Monthly Review* school of political economy, and like his comrades, he hardly was willing to grant Keynesianism much legitimacy—a reluctance, presumably, that results in the contradiction (in the same paragraph) of accusing Keynes of remaining within "pure" economics while admitting that *The General Theory* repudiated that "purity." But even Baran could not deny the significance of what Keynes was confronting in his time and what he was trying to achieve.

His proposed parallel with Hegel is also apt: like Hegel, Keynes's work is a wholesale attempt to re-interpret a radically uncertain moment for a tattered social fabric. It is no surprise, I suppose, that Baran uncritically adopts the standard Marxist stance on Hegel, that is, he took German idealism to its absolute limits but could go no further and thus remained "on his head." This critique is certainly powerful and offers an insight into Keynes no less than Hegel, but not for the reasons Baran provides. Lucio Colletti—in my view the most brilliant proponent of this critique—concentrates our attention on Marx's insistence, time and again, that Hegel inverts the subject and predicate of history, so that the predicate (thought) becomes the subject (being), and the subject becomes the predicate. In other words, what Marx found in Hegel's *Philosophy of Right* was a true account of a world viewed upside down.[5] If Keynes is our

---

4  Paul Baran, *The Political Economy of Growth*, New York: Monthly Review Press, 1957, 7–8.

5  Lucio Colletti, "Introduction," in Karl Marx, *Early Writings*, London: Penguin, 1975, 33; Lucio Colletti, *Marxism and Hegel*, London: New Left Books, 1973, 278; Karl Marx, "Contribution to the Critique of Hegel's Philosophy of Law" [1843], in *Marx-Engels*

Hegel—he who accurately captures the world in the thought of his time, but errs in hypostatizing it as the essence of all times—then we can say that Keynes elaborated the most sophisticated subject-predicate inversion of our age in his analysis of the Hegelian concept of *bürgerliche Gesellschaft*: civil society or "modern community." With Keynes, the concept's predicate, *bürgerliche* or bourgeois-civil, becomes the subject, and society/*Gesellschaft* is in turn rendered predicate. Which is to say that society is a "realization" of the bourgeois, an emanation of an idealized "educated bourgeoisie"—indeed, it is only possible as bourgeois. This is merely a variation on what earlier I called the liberal syllogism.

What Baran misses is that the parallel resides not only in Keynes's and Hegel's intellectual challenges or in their necessary historical limitations, but also in their common origin in a tremulous postrevolutionary moment. Neither of them began their massive undertakings because it just seemed like an interesting thing to do or because they wanted to satisfy mere scholarly curiosity. They were both driven by the constant specter of a calamitous past and a volatile present that seemed about to explode. The respective worlds of Reason they inhabited clearly were entirely inadequate to the world in which they "actually lived": as Hannah Arendt said, "reason had foundered on the rock of reality."[6] They both thus felt themselves compelled to reconstruct the intellectual scaffolding of their time—using, to be sure, the tools at hand, for they had no other. And, as immanent critics of liberalism—the ideological constellation within which they

---

*Collected Works*, vol. III, New York: International Publishers, 1973, 75: "It shows Hegel's profundity that he feels the separation of civil from political society as a *contradiction*. He is wrong, however, to be content with the appearance of this resolution and to pretend it is the substance, whereas the "*so-called theories*" he despises demand the "*separation*" of the civil from the political estates—and rightly so, for they voice a *consequence* of modern society, since there the *political-estates* element is precisely nothing but the factual expression of the actual relationship of state and civil society, namely, their *separation*. Hegel does not call the matter here in question by its well-known name. It is the undisputed question of a *representative* versus *estates* constitution. The representative constitution is a great advance, since it is the *frank, undistorted, consistent* expression of the *modern condition of the state*. It is an *unconcealed contradiction*." (Emphasis in the original.)

6   Hannah Arendt, *The Human Condition*, Chicago: University of Chicago Press, 1958, 301.

both felt simultaneously at home and unsettled—they were perhaps unsurprisingly driven to do so in a strikingly similar manner.

Indeed, it is to Hegel we must turn, for Hegel was, if not the first Keynesian, then his closest previous incarnation.[7] This is of course not exactly why he was so central to Marx's thinking, but it is not so far from it, either. There is a reason both Hegel and Keynes have inspired "left-" and "right-" traditions. Hegel, struggling to make sense of the French Revolution, was the first to fully elaborate a Keynesian reason, the reluctantly radical but immanent critique of liberalism that ultimately found its fullest and (at least at present) most powerful historical realization in *The General Theory of Employment, Interest, and Money*.[8]

**From Hegel to Keynes?**

Keynes would almost certainly have rejected out of hand the suggestion that his work resonated with Hegel's. Despite some notable exceptions like the philosopher T. H. Green and Keynes's teacher

---

7   See especially Chapters 4–6. I have been able to find only two other writers who have made the Hegel–Keynes connection (and only suggestively at that): David MacGregor, *Hegel and Marx After the Fall of Communism*, Cardiff: University of Wales Press, 1998, 105, 208; and Raymond Plant, *Hegel: An Introduction*, 2nd ed., Oxford: Basil Blackwell, 1983, 227. See also Raymond Plant, "Hegel and Political Economy—I," *New Left Review* I: 103, 1977, 79–92 and Raymond Plant, "Hegel and Political Economy—II," *New Left Review* I: 104, 1977, 103–13. Plant does not name Keynes in these articles, but they are clearly part of a path that led him to Hegel's Keynesianism. Many others have outlined the general economic policies a reading of Hegel suggests, the vast majority of which resemble post-World War II Keynesianism without using the terminology. See, for example, Timothy Luther, *Hegel's Critique of Modernity: Reconciling Individual Freedom and Community*, Lanham, MD: Lexington Books, 2009, 347–63; Andrew Buchwalter, *Dialectics, Politics, and the Contemporary Value of Hegel's Practical Philosophy*, London: Routledge, 2012, 214–18; Bruce Gilbert, *The Vitality of Contradiction: Hegel, Politics, and the Dialectic of Liberal-Capitalism*, Montréal: McGill-Queen's University Press, 2013, 186–209.

8   Serge Audier says Walter Lippmann—a friend of Keynes and an extraordinarily influential Keynesian—developed "a critique of liberalism in the name of liberalism." Something similar could be said of all Keynesians, including Keynes himself. Serge Audier, *Néo-liberalisme(s): Une archéologie intellectuelle*, Paris: Éditions Grasset, 2012, 83. See Walter Lippmann, *The Good Society*, Guildford: Billing & Sons, 1944.

Alfred Marshall, by the time Keynes appeared on the scene, many took it for granted that Hegel's work was at best irrelevant and possibly malevolent obfuscation.

Keynes's own rejection was grounded in the thinking of his teacher G. E. Moore. Moore's "anti-idealist" *Principia Ethica* was all the rage with the Apostles, the exclusive club of privileged Victorians with whom Keynes ran as a student at Cambridge. Moore advocated what has been called "ethical non-naturalism." He argued that qualities like "good" or "just" are neither material nor metaphysical; they are only attributed properties of those things we call "good" and "just." As Moore put it, "there is no criterion of goodness."[9] Unlike heat, say, it has no independent "natural" existence in the world. Ethics, consequently, is a matter of "realistic" "common sense." We have no reason to suspect there is anything more to the world than what we can know empirically, and ethical judgments are made on those terms alone.

Moore took these positions to be radically opposed to Hegel on two grounds. First, he said that Hegel was part of a tradition (which included Spinoza and Kant, among others) that founded ethics in metaphysics, that is, in principles or properties that exist beyond human sensation, almost like Platonic forms.[10] Second, and more important, he posited Hegel as the basis of an antiscientific, antirealist "organicism" that took the whole as proof that the "part" was incomprehensible outside of it.[11] In contrast, Moore defended a

---

9    G. E. Moore, *Principia Ethica*, Cambridge: Cambridge University Press, 1993, §83.

10    Ibid., §66.

11    Ibid., §20: "I have said that the peculiar relation between part and whole which I have just been trying to define is one which has received no separate name. It would, however, be useful that it should have one; and there is a name, which might well be appropriated to it, if only it could be divorced from its present unfortunate usage. Philosophers, especially those who profess to have derived great benefit from the writings of Hegel, have latterly made much use of the terms organic whole, organic unity, organic relation. The reason why these terms might well be appropriated to the use suggested is that the peculiar relation of parts to whole, just defined, is one of the properties which distinguishes the wholes to which they are actually applied with the greatest frequency. And the reason why it is desirable that they should be divorced from their present usage is that, as at present used, they have no distinct sense and, on the contrary, both imply and propagate errors of confusion."

strong empiricism. He insisted that even when the part was de facto inseparable from the whole, it must always be analytically distinct. The result of Hegel's influence was in his eyes an unfortunate antirigorous "idealism" which created confusion and justified weak-mindedness:

> Hegel's main service to philosophy has consisted in giving a name to and erecting into a principle, a type of fallacy [the idea of an "organic unity"] to which experience had shown philosophers along with the rest of mankind to be addicted. No wonder that he has followers and admirers.[12]

Although it is not susceptible to definitive proof, I am certain that Moore and his acolytes never read Hegel any more seriously than Keynes read Marx (or at least they never got past the *Phenomenology of Spirit*, which does seem quite metaphysically inflationary at times). For it is as hard to reconcile Moore's account with what Hegel actually wrote as it is to find anything in Marx that might make sense of what Keynes says of him. This is not the place for a full engagement with Hegel's philosophy, but it is a sorry caricature to describe him as an "organicist," and it is willful misrepresentation to suggest that he is uninterested in the differences within a unity. If there is a

---

To say that a thing is an organic whole is generally understood to imply that its parts are related to one another and to itself as means to end; it is also understood to imply that they have a property described in some such phrase as that they have no meaning or significance apart from the whole; and finally such a whole is also treated as if it had the property to which I am proposing that the name should be confined. But those who use the term give us, in general, no hint as to how they suppose these three properties to be related to one another. It seems generally to be assumed that they are identical; and always, at least, that they are necessarily connected with one another. That they are not identical I have already tried to shew; to suppose them so is to neglect the very distinctions pointed out in the last paragraph; and the usage might well be discontinued merely because it encourages such neglect. But a still more cogent reason for its discontinuance is that, so far from being necessarily connected, the second is a property which can attach to nothing, being a self-contradictory conception; whereas the first, if we insist on its most important sense, applies to many cases, to which we have no reason to think that the third applies also, and the third certainly applies to many to which the first does not apply."

12    G. E. Moore, "A Refutation of Idealism," in Thomas Baldwin (ed.), *G. E. Moore: Selected Writings*, London: Routledge, 1993, 34.

fundamental organicism to his thought, then "organic" must mean
something quite different than what Moore means by the term—
something much less like "mystical" and "complete," and more like
"historical" and "dynamic." Hegel's aim was to understand ever-
changing unities and the differences within and between them *at the
same time*. There are no static monoliths in Hegel, because nothing is
fixed and homogenous in content. Even the great unfolder of history,
*Geist*, is internally dynamic.

I would suggest it is no exaggeration to say that the stupidity of
the rejection of Hegel's political thought—the most common wrong-
headed reasons cite quasi-theological mysticism, the "philosophy of
the Prussian Restoration," or the philosophical origin of fascism—
has impoverished liberalism for more than 150 years.[13] Liberalism's
legacy from that century and a half is very different from the story it
tells about itself. The liberal world, the world Europeans (especially
British) and Euro-Americans posit as proof of liberalism's normative
superiority, was founded upon racial slavery, the subordination of
women, and colonial exploitation and genocide. Rather than recognizing Hegel's thought as the subtle and sophisticated (if ultimately
limited) critique that it is, liberals have struggled in vain to bridge
the yawning chasm between liberalism as a normative ideal and
liberalism as political practice. The history of nineteenth-century
liberalism is a series of more or less ridiculous anti-Hegelian contor-
tions, an ultimately futile attempt to justify its moral claims to a
world that proved their mendacity.

Of those who recognized these shortcomings and tried to create a
"new" liberalism to address them—John Stuart Mill, John Hobson,
Leonard Hobhouse, John Dewey, for example—many built on
Hegelian foundations, some explicitly so.[14] And yet, by the time the

---

13   Domenico Losurdo, *Hegel et les Liberaux: Liberté, Egalité, État*, Paris: Presses
Universitaires de France, 1992, 121–53; Domenico Losurdo, *Hegel et le Catastrophe
Allemande*, Paris: Albin Michel, 1994.

14   Alan Grimes, "Introduction," in Leonard Hobhouse, *Liberalism*, Oxford: Oxford
University Press, 1964, 5–6; Nicholas Capaldi, *John Stuart Mill: A Biography*, Cambridge:
Cambridge University Press, 2004, 93, 144, 254; Michael Freeden, "J. A. Hobson as a New
Liberal Theorist: Some Aspects of his Social Thought Until 1914," *Journal of the History of*

Great Depression of the interwar period finally forced even orthodox liberals to reconsider the relationship between the state and civil society, between the universal and the particular, Hegel had been definitively abandoned by all but a few Marxists and social democrats. To be sure, this is partly due to Hegel's posthumous ties to Marxism. But that can hardly be the only factor. The philosophers of liberal apology, then as now, had no familiarity with Hegel, no idea that more than a century earlier he had identified liberalism's self-destructive tendencies and suggested powerful ways to conceive what freedom could mean beyond classical *laissez-faire* dogma. Instead, Hegel's political thought ironically nourished a radicalism he would certainly have understood but never have endorsed. Marxists should be thankful, because Marx and Marxism are impossible without Hegel.

Keynes, perhaps, is not "impossible" without Hegel. The very fact that he refused to engage Hegel's thought, misunderstood what little he may have read, and endorsed its "rigorous" opposite, makes the case. But the point is not that Keynes was a secret Hegelian. Instead (and as I discuss in Chapters 5–7), Hegel, like Keynes, was a Keynesian. Keynesian political economy is the product of an anxious analysis of liberalism's crisis tendencies that manifests the same logical structure as that of Hegel's attempt to understand the meaning and legacy of the French Revolution. To discover in Hegel the critic of liberalism, a critique developed with a particular understanding of the trajectory of history and politics, is to open a window on the structure and function of Keynesian political economy, the most influential form of this thinking in our own time.

Theodor Adorno said of Hegel that he "simply cannot be understood rigorously."[15] The same is true of Keynes, who once wrote to a friend struggling with an economic model that he

---

*Ideas* 34: 3, 1973, 421–43; James Good, "John Dewey's 'Permanent Hegelian Deposit' and the Exigencies of War," *Journal of the History of Philosophy* 44: 2, 2006, 293–313; Dina Emundts, "Hegel as Pragmatist," *British Journal for the History of Philosophy* 23: 4, 2015, 611–31. Many of the Anglophone "new liberals" came to their Hegelianism through the work of T. H. Green.

15   Theodor Adorno, *Hegel: Three Studies*, trans. Sherry Weber Nicholsen, Cambridge: MIT Press, 1993, 95.

ought not to feel inhibited by a difficulty in making the solution precise. It may be that part of the error of the classical analysis is due to that attempt. As soon as one is dealing with the influence of expectations and of transitory experience, one is, in the nature of things, outside the realm of the formally exact.[16]

The key is that the Keynesian critique is not only Keynes's critique, but a thematic, and a set of concerns, that runs throughout the history of liberal capitalism since its first moments. In fact, Hegel thought the crisis of the French Revolution was the most important influence on liberalism's birth, an irrevocable if necessarily bloody leap forward in history. Like Keynes, Hegel celebrated the progress, the decisive end of the old order, and yet at the same time put all his effort into making future revolutions unnecessary. To understand our present palliative moment, we will do well to turn to the revolution and then to Hegel. This is the best way to uncover the threads through which Keynesianism weaves an immanent critique of both revolution and liberalism.

None of which is to suggest that Keynes marks the end of the lineage—on the contrary, Keynesian reason is alive and well, if difficult to see in the way of all things that become common sense. Despite a thousand obituaries, from his own passing in 1946 to his notorious theoretical and policy deaths in the 1970s, Keynes has been with us since the day he died, and Keynesian reason has been with us at least since the early nineteenth century. The ongoing financial crisis has merely cast off the shadows in which they stood, and in so doing has illuminated, if not explained, the relentless anxiety of modern progressive politics. We are left to confront the paradoxical certainty that the unknown rushes toward us.

I hasten to add that to claim Hegel was a Keynesian is not to say that there is no sense to the unfolding of thought and action over time, as if we can simply jumble up the past and reorder it willy-nilly for the purposes of conveniently ad hoc categories. While it is true that in an age of looming political economic and ecological

16    Keynes, Letter to G. Shove (April 21, 1936), *CW* XIV, 2.

calamities it seems increasingly useless to try to keep history in its proper order—indeed, in which for many (the Syrian people, for example) calamity arrived long ago—the wholesale rejection of a once unquestionable historical logic has its perils. If we should not regret the disintegration of the myth of universal progress, which for so long legitimized narratives as fantastical as they were false, it is not necessary to abandon the linear experience of the past. The problem, rather, is that the effort to put Keynes (or Hegel) in his proper historical "place"—which would obviously rule out the idea that Hegel was a Keynesian—is a holdover from an age commanded by progress, part of the problem the rejection of history identifies but cannot resolve. The task is to trace both a knowledge's history and the "structures of feeling" that produce it and the way in which it changes.

## Defining the Keynesian Critique

The fulcrum of the Keynesian critique is what Hegel called civil society—*bürgerliche Gesellschaft*—not a "community" (*Gemeinschaft*), but an increasingly urban, commercial "society" (*Gesellschaft*) of modern individuals and firms, bourgeois (*bürgerliche*) by definition. Indeed, Keynes's theory of liberal civil society is essentially Hegelian: what he called "modern communities" are animated by a sphere of self-interested particularity, riven with contradictions eventually bound, without adequate administrative or ideological attention, to render it inoperable. In its very movement it produces the potential seeds of its own destruction—thus Albert O. Hirschman, in his engaging "Rival Views of Market Society," labels the emergent social theory of Hegel's time the "self-destruction thesis."[17]

At the most general level, this critique appears to share much with Marx's own analysis of the capitalist mode of production, destined to tear itself apart. But the Hegelian-Keynesian critique differs in crucial ways. Rather than the technological and political contradictions

---

17    Albert O. Hirschman, *Rival View of Market Society and Other Essays*, Cambridge: Harvard University Press, 1986, 109–17.

between the relations and forces of production, it emphasizes the ways in which contradictions arise largely because of civil society's structural incapacity to overcome the logical, material, and ideological conflicts produced by social relations in which individual interest is unmoored from collective welfare. The result, in both Keynes's and Hegel's accounts (and in all Keynesian analyses) is effectively anti-Mandevillean, a Nightmare of the Bees: the "corruption of civil society," that notorious "poverty in the midst of plenty" that gives birth to the ruinous "rabble."[18]

This contradiction between the liberty of the one and the interests of the whole is a signature problem of modernity.[19] There is nothing distinctively Keynesian about it (or, for that matter, Hegelian or Hobbesian or Rousseauian), and it has troubled Euro-American politics and governance at least since the seventeenth century. It is basically the same problem modern liberals call the "trade-off" between "freedom and equality" or "freedom and security," and it frames (for example) struggles over both redistributive taxation and state surveillance.

There are, however, three features that distinguish the Keynesian–Hegelian response from other means of thinking about these dynamics. The first is not solely a property of Keynesianism, but it bears emphasis regardless. This is the unstated but fundamental character of the Keynesian critique captured by the adjective "Euro-American." In the effort to untangle Keynesianism, an ideological and intellectual development immanent to the liberal capitalist "core," it is easier than it should be to forget that Europe and North America are not just its historical–geographical "origin," but also delimit its unspoken object. It is true that both Hegel ("modern societies") and Keynes ("modern communities") do make explicit reference to the "modern" as their subject, and given the worlds in and of which they wrote, it is safe to assume that for them, that did not include the world outside the

---

18 Hegel, *PhR*, §244, note to §243, 453–54; Keynes, *CW*, VII, 30–3-1. The term "rabble" is the standard translation of the Jacobins' *canaille* and Hegel's *Pöbel*.

19 "The idea that the social order—intermediate between the fortuitous and the unchangeable—may be an important cause of human unhappiness became widespread only in the modern age"; Hirschman, *Rival Views of Market Society*, 105.

"West." But it is also the case that for both of them, the implied spatial equivalence of "modernity" and the "West" entailed a bracketing of the rest of the world and of any relations between it and the modern.

In other words, Keynesianism has almost always been not just a critique elaborated from within liberal capitalist "industrial" nation-states in western Europe and North America—it has also been a critique that almost entirely ignores everywhere else. This is not an accidental or trivial feature, although it is analytically convenient for both Hegel and Keynes since, among other things, it allows them to claim to identify universals on the basis of what are actually very provincial histories. That much is obvious. Just as important, though, is the fact that the critique mirrors perfectly the white, masculine, colonialist, and bourgeois worlds in and to which they spoke. There is no outside to either of their accounts. Even taking into account compelling arguments like those made recently regarding the Haitian Revolution's importance to Hegel's *Phenomenology of Spirit* (see Chapter 8), the reader of either the *Philosophy of Right* or *The General Theory* would never know that a world outside the liberal capitalist "modern" even existed.

This remains true for virtually all of Keynesianism. Despite its enormous role in shaping the trajectory of modern capitalism, it has hardly reached beyond western Europe and North America. "Keynesian" policy became part of a limited conversation in Latin America in the 1950s and 1960s, and Japan has experimented with it on and off, but the Keynesian critique of liberal capitalism has been confined almost entirely to its "home range." Since World War II, when the Bretton Woods Agreements "internationalized" some aspects of Keynes's thought in the structure of world trade and, later, self-described Keynesian economists began slowly to "relax" the assumption of a "closed economy," there has been more and more interest in "open economy" dynamics. Keynesian politics and political science, epitomized by "embedded liberalism" and the massive literature it has spawned, also identify themselves as more-than-Euro-American.[20] But

---

20 John Ruggie, "International Regimes, Transactions, and Change: Embedded Liberalism in the Postwar Economic Order," *International Organization* 36: 2, 1982, 379–415.

they are not, and really never have been, even in their Bretton Woods glory days.

Embedded liberalism certainly does stand, as its most influential academic advocate puts it, in "stark contrast" with the "disembedded liberalism" of the nineteenth century, that is, the classical political economy and free trade imperialism Keynes and Hegel attacked. But it is premised, like even the most enlightened Keynesianisms, on an understanding of the non-West as effectively one undifferentiated realm from which liberal-capitalist nation-states extract resources, the rule of which they negotiate among themselves on the basis of "norms," as opposed to the play of pure power. With post-World War II embedded liberalism, "multilateralism and the quest for domestic stability were coupled and even conditioned by one another," reflecting the "shared legitimacy of a set of social objectives to which the industrial world had moved, unevenly but 'as a single entity.'"[21] "Multilateralism" is nothing more than a term for the relations between members of the liberal capitalist core concerning the social order in spaces and territories that exceed their jurisdiction.[22]

The second distinguishing feature of Keynesianism's approach to the relation between individual liberty and the social collective is that it neither refuses nor embraces the knee-jerk liberal response: an a priori prioritization of the individual (assumed to be the only subject of "freedom"), modified by a series of ad hoc qualifications. Instead, it accepts liberal premises as necessary but not sufficient. Keynesianism involves a combination of a modern commitment to individual liberty—and against, say, an account based in a Rousseauian "general will"—with a radical distrust of the formalisms or abstract universalisms that subtend the priority of either the

---

21  Ibid., 397.

22  Ibid., 399: "The essence of embedded liberalism . . . is to devise a form of multilateralism that is compatible with the requirements of domestic stability. Presumably, then, governments so committed would seek to encourage an international division of labour which, while multilateral in form and reflecting *some* notion of comparative advantage (and therefore gains from trade), *also* promised to minimize socially disruptive domestic adjustment costs as well as any national economic and political vulnerabilities that might accrue from international functional differentiation." (emphasis in the original)

general or the particular. In other words, it acknowledges liberalism as *one* legitimate means through which to negotiate the relation between individual liberty and the social collective, but not the *only* legitimate means, or even necessarily the ideal to which we should aspire. This is a critique of liberalism that rejects both dogmatic individualism à la Locke and essentialist collectivism à la Bodin.

It tends, thus, toward what might be called a "third way," a phrase that has unfortunately become saturated with the politics of Anthony Giddens and Tony Blair, whose "third way" is really a soft neoliberalism, closer to a compromise aligned quite far to one side. Despite occasional attempts to liken the Blairite "third way" to Keynesianism on the part of both its detractors and supporters, Keynes's and Hegel's is a third way in a radically different sense, the "third" in a dialectical triad: a simultaneous cancellation and preservation of the two previous moments in a new if not-necessarily-stable unity. In other words, the explicit goal of Keynesian reason is to expose the apparently "natural" or "inevitable" antinomy between individual liberty and collective solidarity as in fact merely a historical stage. The point is definitively *not* to create some "hybrid" or "mixed economy" with a little bit of individualism and a little bit of collectivism.[23] It is, rather, to propose something novel; to describe a means by which freedom, solidarity, and security can be fully realized at once in a rational social order. The point is to overcome the modern condition, in which (as Arendt put it) it seems "reality and human reason have parted company,"[24] so as to escape (in Hegel's words) the "confusion" or (in Keynes's term) the "colossal muddle" to which history has unfortunately led.[25]

The third distinguishing feature of the Keynesian–Hegelian response to the self-destructive forces produced by civil society is its concern to demonstrate that such tragic tendencies need not

---

23 The term "mixed economy" was popularized by some Keynesians in the late 1940s; see especially Paul Samuelson, *Foundations of Economic Analysis*, Cambridge: Harvard University Press, 1947, Chapter 3.

24 Arendt, *Human Condition*, 300.

25 G. W. F. Hegel, *Political Writings*, Cambridge: Cambridge University Press, 1999, 150; Keynes, *CW*, IX, 139.

necessarily lead to a tragic ending, or even to temporary disruption or penance. On the contrary, with patient and pragmatic oversight, existing institutions, ideas, and social relations have the potential to produce, without rupture, a radically transformed social order. If conservatives argue that we can attain the "best of all possible worlds" by zealously protecting the status quo, liberals that we can get there through principled commitment to a set of abstract ideals, and radicals that we can only get there through a root-and-branch reconstruction of social life, Keynesians tell us that a radically different world is peacefully contained *in potentia* in the existing (liberal-capitalist, Euro-American) order.

In other words, when an outraged Robespierre asked the bourgeois Convention of 1792, "Citizens! Would you have a revolution without revolution?" Keynesians were those who thought to themselves, "Yes, actually. That sounds just right."[26] Unlike the younger Hegel in the postrevolutionary moment, modern Keynesians do not trust that this new world will come about of its own accord, but they are convinced that revolution is now unnecessary—a symptom of muddled confusion, not progress.[27] All that is needed is a problem-solver's intuition, wise expert administration, and the social stability to which these lead. If we do things right, we can use what we have to gradually, pragmatically, build a world that is radically different but still contains all that is good in the one we have.

*The Fundamental Keynesian Propositions*
Both Hegel and Keynes (at least by the time of *The General Theory*) know there is no magic formula to realize the transformation they anticipate.[28] The point is not to develop precise and transferable political-economic or ideological cure-alls like "Lower interest rates!" "Fund public works!" or "Build community!" There is no single

---

26    Maximilien Robespierre, *Oeuvres Complètes*, vol. IX, Paris: Presses Universitaires de France, 1910, 89: "*Citoyens, vouliez-vous une révolution sans révolution?*"

27    Take, for example, the promise of redemption in *Geist*'s unfolding in *Phenomenology of Spirit*, Oxford: Oxford University Press, 1979.

28    Roger Backhouse and Bradley Bateman, *Capitalist Revolutionary: John Maynard Keynes*, Cambridge: Cambridge University Press, 2011, 111–12.

means to this end, policy or otherwise. Instead (in stark contrast to how both Hegel and Keynes are usually characterized), their critique does not advocate a retreat to the realm of abstraction, where problems become "clearer" or more "manageable," but constructs a propositional framework with which to approach "actually existing" historically and geographically particular "modern communities." Linked together in a coherent whole, these propositions (some but not all of which can be found in non-Keynesian approaches) define the terms of analysis not by laying out the principles by which modern communities are to be evaluated or analyzed, but by always subordinating questions of principle to those of practice. This pragmatism is essential to all things Keynesian.

The propositional framework runs as follows. The identification of civil society's inescapable limits—particularly its inability to self-regulate—triggers Keynesian reason's most fundamental driver: a fear of disorder, or the breakdown of what we might now call the social contract, and the emergence of a "state of nature" for either the whole "community" or some part thereof. Keynesians are as terrified as Hegel of the rule of "absolute necessity." They are certain that neither civilization nor capitalism is natural; if left to self-regulate, things will *not* take care of themselves. Keynes's most famous remark—"in the long run we are all dead. Economists set themselves too easy, too useless a task if in tempestuous seasons they can only tell us that when the storm is long past the ocean is flat again"—is a remarkably faithful echo of Hegel, who in the 1820s told his students that "no one should trust a principle according to which 'things will adjust, they will take care of themselves.'"[29]

This anxiety is Hobbesian in the colloquial sense, and, although Keynes reflected on it far less, and far less critically, than Hegel, it is derived about as "directly" from the conventional reading of Hobbes as political theory can be.[30] Basically, Keynesian reason holds that it

29    Keynes, *CW,* IV, 65; Hegel, quoted in Domenico Losurdo, *Hegel and the Freedom of Moderns*, Durham, NC: Duke University Press, 2004, 81. It is worth noting how much this admonition upsets the standard story of the "mystical" and "teleological" Hegel.

30    As Keynes—Lord Keynes by then—sat out the terrible summer of 1940 awaiting German invasion in London (the Blitz began three months later), he wrote to an American

is only possible to be a liberal after the Hobbesian problem of securing social order has been solved, and not only is that problem unlikely
to be solved once and for all, but it is certain that the solution cannot
be "purely" liberal: it depends absolutely on the state that prioritizes
collective security over individual liberty. Only in a polity in which
these foundations are laid and carefully maintained can someone like
Locke or Jefferson (or Milton Friedman, for that matter) make any
sense at all.

This analysis of civil society, and the anxiety it produces, underwrites a categorical distrust of democracy, because faith in democracy
is premised on the proposition that civil society, if given concrete
political form beyond its subordination to the state, can conceive the
answers to its own problems. "Democracy is content and form," said
Marx in his critique of Hegel's theory of civil society.[31] According to
the Keynesian critique, however, the "facts of experience" demonstrate the futility of the young Marx's faith.[32] The failures of civil
society are part of its very logic; visions of "true" democracy are quix-
otic illusions. Indeed, Keynesian reason demands a fundamental
skepticism regarding all popular (and populist) modes of politics,
since the claims on which these are grounded are by definition a
product of civil society's internal dynamics and thus always unwittingly contain in themselves the very obstacles they attempt to
overcome.

The most important conclusion to which this theory of civil society leads, however, is that any attempt to contain democratic sentiment, or to limit the populist urge, is also itself historically

---

colleague: "The events of the modern world are surely a dreadful confirmation of Hobbes'
diagnosis of human nature and of what is required to preserve civilization. From one point
of view, we can regard what is now happening as the final destruction of the optimistic
liberalism which Locke inaugurated. Our age forces us to return to that pessimistic view
which the horrors of the seventeenth century impressed on Hobbes." Letter to Sterling
Lamprecht, June 19, 1940, quoted in Lamprecht, "Review of J. Bowle, *Hobbes and His
Critics: A Study in Seventeenth Century Constitutionalism*," *Political Science Quarterly* 67: 4,
1952, 612.

    31  Marx, "Contribution to the Critique of Hegel's Philosophy of Law," 29.

    32  Keynes, *CW*, VII, 3, 96, 250; Gilles Dostaler, *Keynes and his Battles*, Cheltenham:
Edward Elgar, 2007, 89.

constrained. Merely to quell civil society's dynamic responses to its own internal limits is not to address those limits, but only to stall, to play at distraction. Ultimately, without changes both inside and outside the sphere of civil society, these limits will be met, whether we like it or not. What is variable, however, is the outcome of such transformation. Deferral is therefore a possibility, sometimes necessary, sometimes simply the best one can hope for—but it is always, in the end, deferral. Modern civil society is a historical force, in all cases shaped by the contingencies and structural limits of time and place, which in the long run generates dynamics rendering social transformation absolutely unavoidable. But the direction, form, and content of that change is radically uncertain.

### A State-Led Revolution without Revolutionaries

Taking this as a basic, fundamental fact of modern life, to the Keynesian the task ahead is obvious: the inevitable transformation must be accomplished without disorder—without revolution, or at the very least without revolutionaries. Since a modern liberal commitment to individual liberty is necessarily incompatible with more direct means to this end—fascism, for example—the revolution without revolution poses a remarkably complex problem. In contrast to the rather dramatic means of social overhaul on the antiliberal menu, Keynesian reason demands—in the interest of ongoing social stability—a more gradual collection of institutional, political economic, and ultimately sociocultural tweaks, or "fine-tuning."

Designing and administering this process presents itself as a technical problem: if change is coming, and one cannot entrust its management to democratic means, then the changes must involve the complex coordination of many institutions and types of knowledge, and expertise and discretion are the answer. Depending upon the context in which problems arise, the timeline is judged to demand something between careful consideration and panicked emergency management—but in all cases, Keynesian reason points to the *centrality of centrality*: to the political function of the state as the sole, if flawed, legitimate universal institution, and to the rational, scientific bureaucracy at the core of modern state function.

Indeed, from the Keynesian perspective, an appropriate division of the labor of government would immediately expose many of the seemingly most intractable problems as really quite straightforward. Keynes himself, in the depths of the Great Depression, told the British public: "The economic problem is not too difficult to solve. If you leave it to me, I will look after it."[33] Krugman, channeling this Keynesian spirit, recently put it this way:

The depression we're in is essentially gratuitous: we don't need to be suffering so much pain and destroying so many lives. We could end it both more easily and more quickly than anyone imagines— anyone, that is, except those who have actually studied the economics of depressed economies and the historical evidence on how policies work in such economies.[34]

Ultimately, the role of the state enlightened by Keynesian reason is that of the great reconciler—the "sublator"—of individual and collective interests. Again, however, it bears emphasis that this is not a question of "mixed economy" compromise. While the fear of disorder that founds Keynesianism takes Hobbesian form, the role of the state it anticipates is radically different than that Hobbes proposes, because Keynesian reason posits a means through which to pass through Leviathan, to attain the "real freedom" to be realized at the end of history. The means to this end take particular form: neither by forever managing private difference—the impossible task assigned to liberalism by Hobbes, Locke, and Kant—nor by subordinating the individual to the general à la Rousseau or Lenin. Instead, the Keynesian state is posited as that social institution, both part of and apart from society, that can harmonize the particular and the universal, materially and ideologically, without sacrificing either. The citizen bathed in the light of Keynesian reason understands his or her

---

33   Keynes, *CW,* XXVIII, 34. Recall Keynes in 1930: "We are suffering just now from a bad attack of economic pessimism," based on "a wildly mistaken interpretation of what is happening to us"; *CW,* IX, 364.

34   Paul Krugman, "How to End This Depression," *New York Review of Books,* May 24, 2012, 12.

own interests as commensurate with, but in no way necessarily the same as or subordinate to what Keynes called the "social interest."

The appeal of this analysis, seemingly founded simultaneously in science, pragmatic "realism," and quasi-utopian faith in human governance, reaches far beyond the community of self-described Keynesians. Figuring out the nature of this appeal and its implications is crucial, because it can help us understand both the social conditions in which it operates and the limits to political (economic) imagination it imposes. As noted in Chapter 1, the complicated stance Keynesianism takes toward politics and the political as a category of social life is crucially important here. Like its parent liberalism, Keynesianism is obsessed with containing problems to their "proper" sphere.[35] But unlike liberals, for whom the separation is a matter of principle, for Keynesians it is a matter of practice, the logic behind its unshakeable faith in techno-bureaucratic expertise, clear jurisdictional definition, and policy independence from interested "meddling." The separation of the political and the economic is not "given," but it is necessary. This helps explains the largely ad hoc redefinition of the content of the political as a category of social life which various Keynesianisms adapt across time and space. At certain moments in time, in the interests of social order some dynamics must *not* be political or politicizable.

The point is not, contrary to what is commonly said of bureaucratization or so-called managerial capitalism, that Keynesianism is an attempt to neutralize politics, in the interests of an apolitical society stripped of debate and public life. On the contrary, and although civil society is the very source of the difficulties, Keynesianism understands it as in many ways an idealized arena for the exercise of modern liberal citizenship, the "bourgeois public sphere" of Arendt and Habermas. The problems Keynesian reason identifies at the heart of civil society are not attributed to principled debate over questions appropriate to the classical *agora* (justice, for example, or the

---

35 This position is epitomized by a book only a liberal could write, Michael Walzer's influential *Spheres of Justice: A Defense of Pluralism and Equality*, New York: Basic Books, 1984.

meaning of the good or the right). Such "properly" political discussion is to be celebrated. Instead, the problems Keynesians worry about are attributed to the fact that in the modern public sphere, the political cannot be isolated from concerns that are not "properly" political: the "economic problem," the "social question," or, more prosaically, "the pressure of the street."[36] In a "modern community," politics is continuously distorted by the inescapable fact of *poverty*, a problem that should be economic, not political.

The problem according to Keynesians, therefore, is not that public life has been emptied of politics, but rather that the political realm is inadequately isolated from "economic" problems, or displaced by "the economy" as the sphere of citizenship, and liberal civil society is structurally incapable of handling it. Reining in the "economic problem"—taking poverty out of politics—and doing the unending work required to keep it out is the most important task of the nonrevolutionary revolution. This is exactly what Keynes meant when he said, "If you leave it to me, I will look after it." He believed this was readily achievable. He knew it was true, as Hegel said, that the "important question of how poverty can be remedied is one which agitates and torments modern societies especially," but that did not mean we could do nothing about it: the "problem of want and poverty and the economic struggle between classes and nations, is nothing but a frightful muddle, a transitory and *unnecessary* muddle."[37] We should be filled with hope, but instead we find ourselves shaking with fear.

The urgency of overcoming this "confusion" is the foundation of all Keynes's work, from the critique of Versailles in 1919 to his death twenty-seven years later. The following, from 1924's *Tract on Monetary Reform*, is representative:

No man of spirit will consent to remain poor if he believes his betters to have gained their goods by lucky gambling. To convert

---

36  Keynes, *CW*, IX, 364–65; Hannah Arendt, *On Revolution*, London: Penguin, 2006, 49–52; Jürgen Habermas, *The Structural Transformation of the Public Sphere: An Inquiry into a Category of Bourgeois Society*, Cambridge: MIT Press, 1989, 132.

37  Hegel, *PhR*, §244A; Keynes, *CW*, IX, vii.

the business man into the profiteer is to strike a blow at capitalism, because it destroys the psychological equilibrium which permits the perpetuance of unequal rewards. The economic doctrine of normal profits, vaguely apprehended by every one, is a necessary condition for the justification of capitalism. The business man is only tolerable so long as his gains can be held to bear some relation to what, roughly and in some sense, his activities have contributed to society.[38]

The same fear drives *The General Theory*: "It is certain that the world will not much longer tolerate the unemployment which, apart from brief intervals of excitement, is associated—and, in my opinion, inevitably associated—with present-day capitalistic individualism."[39] If we can put off disaster, the possibility of bliss can again light the (not-too-distant) horizon.

---

38  Keynes, *CW*, IV, 29.
39  Keynes, *CW*, VII, 381.

CHAPTER 3

# The Tragedy of Poverty

K eynes was convinced that our inability to contain modern
civil society's self-destructive tendencies was the result of our
theories of how it worked. The dominant economic knowledge of his time, which he called "classical economics," was wrong,
and it had led us to believe things about the inner workings of liberal
capitalism that were just not true. What the situation required, therefore, was not mere policy proposals, but a new foundation of basic
knowledge that would give us the theoretical tools for economic
bliss. Without this foundation, any new ideas regarding what is to be
done would always seem mere exceptions to an orthodox rule, and
the fundamental theoretical errors would go unaddressed.

In a now-famous letter of New Year's Day 1935, a year before the
publication of *The General Theory*, Keynes boasted to George Bernard
Shaw that the book he was writing would "revolutionise" the way
"the world thinks about economic problems."[1] Its publication
certainly did attract attention: Keynes's arguments, in combination
with his timing and public persona, quickly cemented the book's
status as controversial classic. And yet the "revolution" was far from
universally acknowledged, let alone endorsed. Addressed to his
"fellow economists," much of the book's audience was unconvinced
by his attack on their "classical" thinking. As he predicted, many

1  Keynes, *CW*, XXVIII, 42.

argued that where *The General Theory* was not wrong, it was merely old wine in new bottles. If his critics are to be taken at their word, it was not at all clear to them what the book was good for, other than sowing confusion or creating a stir (for which Keynes had something of a reputation).[2]

There were, however, apostles and early adopters. By the middle of the war, one could find those we would now call "Keynesians" on both sides of the Atlantic. They varied substantially in the extent to which they understood themselves as participants in a "revolution" in economics, but they did not doubt the importance of *The General Theory*: in the midst of the Great Depression, it offered a much-needed correction to the now-terrifyingly obvious errors of *laissez-faire* liberalism.[3] For them, it was never, as is sometimes thought, a how-to manual for the welfare state. This is hardly surprising. *The General Theory* contains little if any direction, "policy recommendations" are virtually absent, and empirical examples are rare and barely elaborated. It is best described as a theoretical manifesto.

Like another famous manifesto, argument over *The General Theory* has been virtually incessant since its publication. Even during the 1980s and 1990s, decades when Keynes was supposedly forgotten or dead or dismissed, debate continued. Then came Keynes's animated return in 2007–2008, when near-global crisis put state-coordinated

---

2   Keynes, *CW*, VII, v. (*CW*, VII is *The General Theory of Employment, Interest, and Money*.) Roger Backhouse and Bradley Bateman, "Inside Out: Keynes's Use of the Public Sphere," *History of Political Economy* 45(annual suppl.), 2013, 68–91. For exemplary reactions from the discipline, see the four reviews in the *Quarterly Journal of Economics* 51: 1, 1936, 147–203: Dennis Robertson, "Some Notes on Mr Keynes' General Theory of Employment," Jacob Viner, "Mr Keynes on the Causes of Unemployment," Wassily Leontief, "The Fundamental Assumption of Mr. Keynes' Monetary Theory of Unemployment," and Frank Taussig, "Employment and the National Dividend." See also Bertil Ohlin, Dennis Robertson, and Frank Hawtrey, "Alternative Theories of the Rate of Interest: Three Rejoinders," *Economic Journal* 47: 187, 1937, 423–43; Joseph Schumpeter, "A Review of J. M. Keynes's *General Theory of Employment, Interest and Money*," *Journal of the American Statistical Association* 31, 1937, 791–95; Frank Knight, "Unemployment: and Mr. Keynes's Revolution in Economic Theory," *Canadian Journal of Economics* 3: 1, 1937, 100–123.

3   See the essays in Peter Hall (ed.), *The Political Power of Economic Ideas: Keynesianism Across Nations*, Princeton: Princeton University Press, 1989.

fiscal and monetary management back on all but the most libertarian policy menus.[4] This "fall and rise" of Keynesian economics has reanimated a long-running controversy, especially among self-described Keynesians. Should we revive the ideas of Keynes himself today, or do we require a radically renovated Keynesianism, either to correct for Keynes's own errors or to render it more appropriate to twenty-first century capitalism?[5] Oversimplifying somewhat, in the world of academic economics these positions are occupied by two schools of self-consciously "Keynesian" thought. On one hand, so-called "post-Keynesians" are dedicated to the wisdom of Keynes and the faithful among his students and colleagues, like Joan Robinson or Roy Harrod. Generally of a social-democratic tendency (sometimes called "left-Keynesian"), post-Keynesians hew to a close, if not exegetical, reading of Keynes's later work, *The General Theory* in particular—so close, in fact, that they feel justified in denouncing Keynes's "betrayal" by various forms of "bastard Keynesianism."[6] On the other hand, the thinking of some "New Keynesians" is not always so close to the "economics of Keynes." New Keynesians take Keynes as inspiration for skepticism in the face of classical and neoclassical claims to completeness or perfection, rather than as a sage to be turned to again and again.[7]

Paul Krugman, perhaps the most prominent of the New Keynesians, weighed in on this distinction at a 2011 celebration of *The General*

---

4   Post-subprime crisis discussions of Keynes are so numerous as to defy summary. See Chapter 1, n.8.

5   John Eatwell and Murray Milgate, *The Fall and Rise of Keynesian Economics*, Oxford: Oxford University Press, 2011.

6   Geoff Tily, *Keynes' Betrayed*, New York: Palgrave, 2010; Joan Robinson and John Eatwell, *An Introduction to Modern Economics*, New York: McGraw-Hill, 1973, 47.

7   The labels "New Keynesian" and "post-Keynesian" came into common usage only in the 1980s. I have taken the liberty of projecting the labels back in time, since a similar division has existed among self-described "Keynesian" economists throughout the post-World War II era, between those working in the "neoclassical synthesis" vein and those Allan Coddington called "fundamentalist Keynesians"; Coddington, "Keynesian Economics: The Search for First Principles," *Journal of Economic Literature* 14: 4, 1976, 1259–63. Coddington identifies two other groups—"hydraulic" and "reconstituted reductionist" Keynesians—that I lump together in the retrospective "New Keynesian" category, since both work on a neoclassical synthesis foundation.

*Theory's* seventy-fifth anniversary. Krugman suggested that its readers could be divided into two groups, which he labeled "Chapter 12ers" and "Book 1ers." Chapter 12ers (also known as post-Keynesians) focus on Keynes's account of uncertainty and long-term expectations, which Krugman says shows that "investment decisions must be made in the face of radical uncertainty to which there is no rational answer."[8] Book 1ers (also known as New Keynesians) take Keynes's principal contribution to be the "refutation" of Say's Law, the recognition of "the possibility of a general shortfall in demand." Krugman says the former are skeptical of the effort to shoehorn *The General Theory* into neoclassical-style quasi-equilibrium models. The latter, in contrast, read the principle of effective demand as a quasi-equilibrium concept and see no problem combining Keynes's ideas with an orthodox framework in what has come to be called the "neoclassical synthesis."[9] For them, the adjective "Keynesian" is basically equivalent to "disequilibrium" or "non-Walrasian."[10]

---

8   See, for example, Angel Asensio and Dany Lang, "The Financial Crisis, Its Economic Consequences, and How to Get Out of It," *International Journal of Political Economy* 39: 2, 2010, 58–69.

9   Paul Krugman, "Mr. Keynes and the Moderns," paper presented to the Cambridge conference commemorating the seventy-fifth anniversary of the publication of *The General Theory of Employment, Interest, and Money*, June 18, 2011, 2–3. (For more on the neoclassical synthesis, see Chapter 13.) While the expectation that a market left to its own devices always clears is as essential to the work of David Ricardo as it is to that of Milton Friedman, the framework that has probably most influenced the way in which Say's Law is operationalized is the so-called "Walrasian" general equilibrium system developed by the political economist Léon Walras and others in the 1870s. Walras—a socialist, it turns out—argued that prices are determined as if there were an economy-wide grand auctioneer, who gradually "discovered" equilibrium prices through *tatônnement*, or "groping" (the word's connotations in English have led even English texts to use the French). Walras was the first to posit—but could not prove—that this process of discovery could determine a set or "vector" of prices that simultaneously clear all markets. The logical possibility such a vector exists is the formal condition of "general equilibrium." When Gérard Debreu and Kenneth Arrow finally proved this in the early 1950s, and in the process further emboldened the burgeoning "mathematization" of economic thought, they provided an *ex post facto* formal foundation for Say's Law. Indeed, Arrow-Debreu (or AD) is the "scientific" basis for contemporary capital's opposition to state "meddling." See Kenneth Arrow and Gérard Debreu, "Existence of an Equilibrium for a Competitive Economy," *Econometrica* 20, 1954, 265. For more on Keynes's critique of Say's Law, see Chapters 9, 10, and 11.

10   Anthony Atkinson and Joseph Stiglitz, *Lectures on Public Economics*, Princeton: Princeton University Press, 2015, 185.

Although Keynes himself (if forced to choose sides) would almost certainly have joined the Chapter 12ers, in Cambridge Krugman went on to argue that Book 1ers are on to something more important.[11] But his larger argument regarding the relevance of Keynes's work is more aggressive and sweeping, and he has made it before and since. Krugman holds that "moderns" (you and I) interested in the present-day value of *The General Theory* need not bother to historicize it. What Keynes thought, what motivated him, what he was reacting to—in short, what made Keynes a Keynesian? "I Don't Care," says Krugman.[12]

This is a grave error. Certainly, the word of Keynes must not be treated as the Word of Keynes, as if the fact He said it makes it True. This is apparently an error to which post-Keynesians would seem prone if they feel it necessary to denounce "betrayal." Marxists will be more than familiar with this problem. But what is at issue here is not merely "academic" interpretation (trivial terrain Krugman abandons to "biographers and intellectual historians").[13] Rather, what is at issue is in fact so foundational to Krugman's work he cannot see it: the question of how and why we read *The General Theory* today.

It is true there is no single puzzle the book is clearly attempting to solve. Instead, it is an uneven and wide-ranging affair, jumping from critique of specific pricing models, to "fundamental psychology," to questions of the "general interest." It is also true that in the years between the appearance of *The General Theory* and his death in 1946, Keynes ambiguously, and sometimes uncritically, linked his own work to a broad and arguably inconsistent collection of ideas.[14] But

---

11    John Maynard Keynes, "The General Theory of Employment," *Quarterly Journal of Economics* 51: 2, 1937, 209–23; Krugman, "Mr. Keynes and the Moderns," 21.

12    Paul Krugman, "Minsky and Methodology," from his *New York Times* blog *Conscience of a Liberal*, posted March 27, 2012.

13    Krugman, "Mr. Keynes and the Moderns," 2.

14    Roger Backhouse and Bradley Bateman, *Capitalist Revolutionary: John Maynard Keynes*, Cambridge: Cambridge University Press, 2011, 124–26; Robert Skidelsky, *Keynes: The Return of the Master*, New York: Penguin, 2009, 102. Among Keynes's more free-market leaning critics and acolytes, there are some who claim that near the end of his life, Keynes returned to a defense of *laissez-faire* that had lain hidden all those years. They even trade in third-hand rumors, whispering to each other that someone talked to someone who once

that does not mean What Keynes Really Meant is irrelevant. Because if we do not try to understand What Keynes Really Meant, then we will never understand why he felt it needed to be said, that is, what features of the world had to be confronted anew in the mid-1930s. And if we do not understand the relationship between his thought and the world in which he formulated it, we cannot confront the extraordinarily important question of whether his answers are appropriate to our own historical and geographical contexts. As Giovanni Mazzetti put it succinctly in 2012, "Keynes Again?!"[15] Why? What made Keynes a Keynesian, and are his reasons good reasons for us to be Keynesians, too?

This chapter is an attempt to get at these questions. It examines both the argument of *The General Theory* and its political subtext, and links it to a historically specific theory of capitalist civil society, a theory which did not begin with Keynes, but which he developed in crucial ways. To take up an argument initiated in Chapter 1, these developments are based on the fact that Keynes's political economy is rooted in a theory of "civilization" and not a theory of capitalism. This analysis can help us understand both the tragic paradox of poverty in the richest societies in history and the irrepressible anxiety that tragedy generates in the continued force of "Keynesian" ideas.

## A General Theory of Civilization

In Keynes's own time, it was his radical critics who took most seriously his assertion that his theory "revolutionized" economics, if not in the manner he intended. To them, *The General Theory* was indeed a manifesto, but of the counterrevolutionary variety. Capitalism,

---

heard Keynes say (echoing Marx!) "I am not a Keynesian"; see, for example, T. W. Hutchison, *Keynes vs. the "Keynesians"* . . .? London, Institute for Economic Affairs, 1977, 23.

15   Giovanni Mazzetti, *Ancora Keynes?!* Trieste, Italy: Asterios Editore, 2012. Mazzetti's short book is a powerful argument that the Keynesian policies of the post-World War II era are woefully inadequate for the twenty-first century. Deficit-financed investment and incomes policies were designed for a world long gone; only a massive redistribution of work will do.

with its post-1929 political economic integrity in tatters and shad-owed by a viable Bolshevik alternative, had emboldened its own false messiah. Book in hand, Keynes had come to bring salvation.

Radicals generally have never abandoned this critique of Keynes, and over time it has become axiomatic for some—so obvious it requires no explanation.[16] It has also been widely endorsed beyond the Left. As Albert O. Hirschman once put it, "after Keynes, any theory purporting to show that, short of revolution, there was no way out . . . was bound to have a hard time."[17] Outside the world of Tea Party bloggers, the *Daily Telegraph,* and the Hoover Institute— where the idea that Keynes was a "socialist" is idiotic common sense—this historical interpretation is noncontroversial. Today, in venues as different as the *Economist* and the *International Socialist Review,* it is assumed that Keynes developed his ideas in an effort to "save capitalism."[18] In stark contrast to his suspicious Treasury School detractors in the late 1920s and 1930s, post-subprime main-stream consensus has it that Keynes's plan was not to abandon *lais-sez-faire* in the interests of collectivist meddling or utopian wishful thinking, but to bring the state to capital's rescue.

This much is taken for granted, even by some of the most ortho-dox of contemporary anti-Keynesians. Heated debate continues, certainly, but not over what he was trying to do. The questions today concern how he meant to do it, whether his arguments were politi-cally acceptable, theoretically sound, and realizable. "New Keynesians" like Krugman take him to have been proposing an

16    Paul Baran, *The Political Economy of Growth,* New York: Monthly Review Press, 1957, 8; Paul Mattick, *Marx and Keynes: The Limits of the Mixed Economy,* Boston: Porter Sargent, 1969; Antonio Negri, "Keynes and the Capitalist Theory of the State post-1929" [1968], in *Revolution Retrieved: Writings on Marx, Keynes, Capitalist Crisis and New Social Subjects,* London: Red Notes, 1988; Eric Hobsbawm, "Goodbye to All That," *Marxism Today,* October 1990, 18–23.

17    Albert O. Hirschman, "Hegel, Imperialism, and Structural Stagnation," *Journal of Development Economics* 3, 1976, 6.

18    "A Keynes for All Seasons," *The Economist,* November 26, 2013; Petrino DiLeo, "The Return of Keynes?" *International Socialist Review* no. 63, 2009. See also Martin Wolf, "Keynes Offers Us the Best Way to Think about the Financial Crisis," *Financial Times,* December 23, 2008; J. B. Foster and R. W. McChesney, "Listen Keynesians, It's the System," *Monthly Review* 61: 11, 2010, 44–56.

essentially universal technical solution to chronically sub-optimal capitalist markets. Many progressives see Keynesianism as simply the "social-liberal" acknowledgment that capitalism requires kinder, gentler, and more intelligent management.[19] Others read *The General Theory* as the epitome of pragmatic "realism."[20]

In fact, the story is considerably more complicated. There was, and is, much more at stake in *The General Theory* and the "varieties of Keynesianism" than the mere fate of a historical mode of production. It is not true that Keynes aimed to "save capitalism" or not true enough. Keynes became a Keynesian not to save capitalism or liberalism per se, but to save the "thin and precarious crust" of civilization itself.[21] He was, to be sure, a capitalist, and he believed that something like capitalism—although in a more or less radically different form—would be a central pillar in the construction of more robust, peaceful, and secure social formation. But to read his commitment to capitalism as his priority is to misunderstand his politics and that of many elites of his time. He understood capitalism to be intimately interwoven with but not identical to civilization. His work, especially but not only *The General Theory*, is an attempt to do via "economics" what, since the French Revolution, others had tried to do through other modes of analysis—philosophical, political, even literary: to understand the ways in which modernity puts civilization at risk and to uncover the means by which we might rescue civilization from modernity's self-destructive tendencies.

That Keynes could imagine no better mode of production than capitalism by which to advance civilization should in no way suggest that he thought classical liberal capitalism anything less than fatal or even of special merit in its own right. He was committed to rewriting capitalism because he could not conceive a better method for salvaging what he took for granted as the best of modernity: the social

---

19  Gilles Dostaler, *Keynes and His Battles*, Cheltenham: Edward Elgar, 2007, 99; Skidelsky, *Keynes: The Return of the Master*; Thomas Geoghegan, "What Would Keynes Do?" *The Nation*, October 17, 2011.

20  Dani Rodrik, *The Globalization Paradox: Democracy and the Future of the World Economy*, New York: W. W. Norton, 2012, 121.

21  Keynes, *CW*, X, 446.

order of "the bourgeois and the intelligentsia who, with whatever faults, are the quality in life and surely carry the seeds of all human advancement."[22]

The Keynesian question, therefore, is not what Keynes "really" said on this or that technicality or which concepts or policies should count as "truly" Keynesian, but rather why, and from what perils, civilization might need saving. This is a question of the underexamined political bases of Keynesian thought, of which we should think of Keynes as neither the only practitioner nor even the first. He is, rather, one prominent contributor to a well-established historical tradition. I want to propose an interpretation of Keynes's politics and Keynesian political economy that situates them in the fascinating and much longer line of thought to which they have contributed so significantly. This can help us understand not only what Keynes was trying to save, why he came to save it, and what he came to save it from, but also the origins of his efforts and why and how they continue to matter enormously. In effect, it can help us understand what made Keynes a Keynesian, while also, I think, helping us understand why so many rediscover the Keynesian in themselves each time capitalism threatens to fall apart.

This is why those who say Keynes came to "save capitalism" only understand part of why he is so important and why he retains such intuitive appeal to so many. It is not an accident that he did not write "*capitalism* is a thin and precarious crust." He would never have written that, because he knew it was not true. Capitalism's problem was not its fragility, but its mindless irrationalism. In its *laissez-faire* liberal variation—the one many of his "fellow" economists and policy-makers favored—it was so unthinking, so unreasonable and inflexible, that it would not even slow down as it steamed toward the precipice, taking the rest of civilization with it. This is why, unlike many of his "fellows" then and now, he did not participate in the chorus of simplistic denunciations of socialism and communism. He disagreed strongly with the radical Left and

---

22   Keynes, *CW,* IX, 258; see Peter Clarke, *The Keynesian Revolution in the Making, 1924–1936,* Oxford: Clarendon Press, 1988, 10–17.

was particularly wary of the Soviet experiment (for aesthetic as much as political economic reasons). But in contrast to much of the rhetoric one hears from the curates of contemporary neoliberal liturgy, he knew there was nothing innately eternal or natural about capitalism. He sympathized with what he thought capitalism's critics were after, the "emptiness," selfishness, and arbitrary inequalities against which they struggled.[23] Like them, he too took these as endemic to modern capitalism.

Consequently, and contrary to what many critics wrongly assume, his diagnosis of liberal capitalism's ills and prognosis for its future cannot be reduced to a bold rescue of the status quo. Keynes was definitively *not* committed to capitalism at all costs. His most passionate political commitment was his antifascism, but he never fooled himself into thinking fascism was or could ever be noncapitalist. On the contrary, it was for him the "capitalist branch of the totalitarian faith." His critique of communism was almost kindly in comparison: it was the "confused stirrings of a great religion"; fascists, on the other hand, were "enemies of the human race."[24]

What Keynes constructed to address these concerns is a reluctantly radical, immanent critique of liberalism, a critique with a long history. The main obstacle to grasping what is at stake in this critique, consequently, is the ideological hegemony of liberalism itself. The Keynesian critique cannot adequately be grasped on the terrain of orthodox liberalism's fundamental axioms. Together, these axioms—that there is an inescapable contradiction between liberty and equality; that the individual is the privileged political subject (and thus equality is subordinate to liberty); and, finally, that history is the result of ahistorical and aspatial linear developmentalism—suggest a priori the necessary interdependent unfolding of freedom and modern capitalism.[25] Indeed,

23   Keynes, "Reply to Shaw," *New Statesman & Nation,* November 10, 1934, in *CW,* XXVIII, 31–35.

24   Keynes, "Mr Chamberlain's Foreign Policy," *New Statesman & Nation,* October 8. 1938, in *CW,* XXVIII, 126; "A Short View of Russia," in *CW,* IX, 269; "British Foreign Policy," *New Statesman & Nation,* July 10, 1937, in *CW,* XXVIII, 63.

25   By "ahistorical and aspatial linear developmentalism" I mean a refusal to grant any political status to history or geography—the result of which is to make a *tabula rasa* the

they are often taken to prove that freedom and capitalism are the same thing.

Keynes rejected these articles of faith. For him, if liberals naïvely endorsed this stance it was only evidence of how deep they had stuck their heads in the sand. "Economic" liberalism, especially in its classical variety, was for him a quasi-mythical Utopia, one he expected would never be realized. His explicitly "political" variety of liberalism could only be reached through "economically" illiberal means, that is, granting substantial control to the state and "technicians" like himself: "the achievement of economic reform would make the defense of political liberty much easier."[26] If "central controls" on the economy were effective and everything worked out—an eventuality upon which we could never plan, things being as radically uncertain as they always are—then someday it might just be possible to enable classical liberalism to finally "come into its own." But only after a lot of careful illiberal political economy and economic policy had laid the foundations.[27]

What attractions Keynes found in liberalism are primarily due to its historical links to bourgeois order, with which he enthusiastically announced his sympathies: "the *Class* war will find me on the side of the educated *bourgeoisie*."[28] It is not the capitalist but the bourgeois in him that made him dismiss a Left political alternative. The bourgeois in him was convinced that the working class was structurally incapable of anything so positive or constructive as self-organization, social reconstruction, or governance on any basis

---

default ethical–political condition. There can be neither "past" victims—or at least none whose claims can fundamentally challenge the distributional concerns of the present (that is, past wrongs are forgotten or erased, even if "recognized")—nor any places or spaces deemed worthy of particular consideration. At any given moment, every one in every place is assumed formally "equal," at the starting line in a "fair" race that only looks and moves forward from this moment in logical development time. To state the obvious, colonialism, slavery, and gendered oppression are thus erased by definition, because no other places and times have any ethical claim on a status quo that always begins now.

26    Keynes, The Listener, April 2, 1942, in *CW*, XXVII, 266–67; Letter to the Editor, *New Statesman & Nation*, August 11, 1934, in *CW*, XXVIII, 28–29.

27    Keynes, *CW*, VII, 378.

28    Keynes, *CW* IX, 258, 297 (emphasis in the original).

whatsoever—communist, anarchist, or otherwise. He did not fear working class radicals for their egalitarian passion for social justice. In fact, he had a kind of paternalistic soft spot for them. What he feared was the social disorder and demagoguery he believed such politics solicit, the unwitting reactionaries he believed radicals always eventually become.[29] Without proper elite direction—in the full sense of Gramsci's *direzione* (direction *qua* organization and leadership)—he was certain that all the working class could accomplish on its own was destruction, with the results not only unlikely to represent proletarian "class interest," but, more important, disastrous for everyone.[30]

Consequently, if "left-Keynesians" from John Galbraith in the 1960s to James Galbraith today have commonly recruited Keynes to the cause of social democracy, it is not because he was a "left" thinker. Contrary to his own occasional claims in the 1910s and 1920s, he was not.[31] Rather, he can be mobilized in the service of social democracy only because at its roots it is and always has been as much an elite civilizing project as a "Left" political program. Given the option, Keynes would never have endorsed social democracy, and it is

---

29    Indeed, he labeled the Left of the Labour Party the "Party of Catastrophe"; Keynes, "Am I a Liberal?" in *CW*, IX, 297, 299–300, 308.

30    "A Short View of Russia" (*CW*, IX, 253–71) recounts Keynes's 1925 visit to the newly founded Soviet Union. He understood his experience there to be proof that this judgment regarding working class politics was fully warranted. This is the tacit claim behind his shockingly empty critique of Marx. Keynes may indeed have "never in the least been influenced by Marx," as his best biographer claims—even if one might argue that no one writing about political economy in Keynes's time, least of all someone with Keynes's broad professional circle, can reasonably be said to be entirely uninfluenced by Marx; Robert Skidelsky, *John Maynard Keynes, 1883–1946: Economist, Philosophy, Statesman*, London: Pan Macmillan, 2003, 402. The more important point is that if he was "never in the least" influenced by Marx, it is because he barely, and maybe never, actually read Marx or made any effort to understand him, as the remarks in his private and public writing make clear (see *CW*, VII, 355; *CW*, IX, 258; *CW*, XXVIII, 28–29, 32–34, 42; *CW*, XXIX, 76–87). For a person of such insight, ignorance is the only plausible explanation for his blatant mischaracterizations.

31    In a letter to his mother soon after October 1917, Keynes described himself as "buoyantly Bolshevik" (*CW*, XVI, 265). More notoriously, in his famous "Liberalism and Labour" lecture of 1926, Keynes told his audience that the "Republic of my imagination lies on the extreme left of celestial space" (*CW*, IX, 309). See also Letter to the Editor, *New Statesman & Nation*, November 24, 1934, in *CW*, XXVIII, 36.

baseless to imagine he was more "radical" than he let on, as if he kept his true politics a secret. He was definitively not a democrat, because anything approaching popular sovereignty was in his view antithetical to the long-term interests of civilization.

On these grounds, capitalism was a crucial, but ultimately derivative, concern, and today's liberal faith that capitalism and democracy are necessary complements—despite substantial historical evidence to the contrary—was for him a historical relic, an irrational nineteenth-century piety. In the days of high liberalism, perhaps, one might imagine good reasons that the "standard system" of economic thought only "bred two families—those who thought it true and inevitable, and those who thought it true and intolerable." But such narrowness of vision no longer made sense:

> There was no third school of thought in the 19th century. Nevertheless, there is a third possibility—that *[the standard system] is not true* . . . It is this third alterative which will allow us to escape. The standard system is based on an intellectual error . . . Our pressing task is the elaboration of a new standard system which will justify economists in taking their seat beside other scientists . . . Thus, for one reason or another, Time and the Joint Stock Company and the Civil Service have silently brought the salaried class into power. Not yet a proletariat. But a salariat, assuredly. And it makes a great difference . . . There is no massive resistance to a new direction. The risk is of a contrary kind—lest society plunge about in its perplexity and dissatisfaction into something worse. Revolution, as Wells says, is out of date.[32]

Revolution is out of date. Once upon a time, certainly, there was revolutionary work to be done. But those days are long gone, Keynes tells us, and *The General Theory* is the theoretical substitute for revolution and a "solution" to the economic problem and a looming "something worse." These are the stakes as he understood them. They

---

32   Keynes, *New Statesman & Nation,* November 10, 1934, in *CW,* XXVIII, 31–34, emphasis added.

are truly existential. Indeed, he argued the book lays the conceptual groundwork for "the only practicable means of avoiding the destruction of existing economic forms in their entirety."[33] As José Ortega y Gasset, who helped organize *The General Theory*'s Spanish translation, put it in 1930:

> Civilization is not simply here, it is not self-sustaining. It is artificial, and demands an artist or artisan. If you want to enjoy the advantages of civilization, but are not concerned with sustaining civilization—well, you are done. In the blink of an eye you find yourself without civilization. Just a slip, and when you look around everything has vanished into thin air![34]

Keynes is not the first one to trouble himself with maintaining civilization. His analysis of its dynamics and the resulting diagnosis are not new, but in fact represent a specific kind of response to liberalism, elements of which we can trace back as far as Hobbes, but which really are consolidated after the French Revolution. The origins of that analysis are to be found first and foremost in the complex politics of the Revolution itself and in the liberal "reaction" which followed. Keynesianism is in itself synonymous with neither of these revolutionary dynamics, but is rather a distinctive response to them both. It is an immanent critique of both revolutionary radicalism and the "classical" liberalism that was emerging at the end of the eighteenth century, and held sway in Europe until World War I. It is thus a specifically post-revolutionary politics, both historically and theoretically. Historically, it arose after Napoleon's *coup d'état* definitively ended the Revolution and the reaction in 1799. Theoretically, it represents a mode of political and economic analysis that was and is only possible after revolution; in other words, it only makes sense, and could only have been fully formulated, after the

---

33  Keynes, *CW*, VII, 380.
34  José Ortega y Gasset, *La Rebelión de las Masas*, Madrid: Austral, 2010, 152; see also Serge Audier, *Néo-liberalisme(s): Une Archéologie Intellectuelle*, Paris: Éditions Grasset, 2012, 111.

historical experience of revolution, because the shadow of revolution—revolutionary terror in particular—animates it, gives it
momentum, and constantly reinvigorates it.

## The Tragedy of Capitalist Poverty

A. C. Bradley once defined tragedy in the following terms: "That
men may start a course of events but can neither calculate nor
control it, is a *tragic* fact."[35] These modern anxieties, motivated by
both fear and bafflement, concern a tragedy in precisely this unin-
tended-but-inevitable sense, perhaps *the* tragedy of modernity: the
persistence of mass poverty in the midst of modern, liberal democratic, capitalist societies, societies in which the "economic problem" was supposed to have disappeared. This is what lies at the heart
of Keynes's "economic problem"—the tragedy that we are not only
unable to eradicate poverty, but we have not even been able to
contain poverty to a bounded sphere, to keep it a purely "economic"
concern. And in this failure, we have been unable to found real freedom for all. The tragedy lies in the fact that the poverty is of our
making, the inevitable corollary of individuals competitively pursu-
ing their own good.[36]

What lies at the base of all this, and determines the limits of
liberalism itself, is that ultimately it is impossible to contain
poverty to its own proper sphere because in the liberal order
poverty *has no proper sphere*. Since liberal capitalism cannot and
will not hold itself responsible for poverty—which is, on its terms,
a condition insufficiently or not yet liberal and capitalist—then
poverty is always the fault of the poor. There is nowhere, systemi-
cally or geographically, the poor are "supposed" to be.[37] The

---

35   A. C. Bradley, quoted in David Scott, *Conscripts of Modernity: The Tragedy of Colonial Enlightenment*, Durham: Duke University Press, 2004, 159 (emphasis in the original).

36   Ibid., 11–14, 156–60, 189–90.

37   For Keynes, this tragedy is not a *Homo sacer* problem—it is not the case that the poor by definition exist in a state or space of exception, as outlined by Giorgio Agamben, *Homo Sacer: Sovereign Power and Bare Life*, Stanford: Stanford University Press, 1998.

possibility of what Robespierre called an "honourable poverty" is categorically denied.

With no proper domain for the poor and their poverty, liberalism is incapable of containing the economic problem to distinct realms of the social. Poverty—in the sense of absolute and relative material deprivation—cannot remain a merely "economic" problem, sufficiently bounded to enable a political realm free to operate on the basis of pristine abstractions like formal equality or the universal rights of citizenship. The recognition that poverty is a product of modern liberal political economy is also a recognition that it is always imposed upon the poor by social relations that have no ideological capacity to come to grips with it. Poverty in this sense—again, surely the truest possible sense—is not the opposite of abundance or riches, but of freedom. This is perhaps the fundamental materialist lesson— a "radical" lesson, but a Keynesian one, too.

If we are to understand the political significance of this tragedy, however—and thus of what I am calling Keynesianism or the Keynesian critique—it is essential to understand its potential as evidence not only of the failure of liberalism to deliver on its promises, but of the failures of revolution also. This, at least, is how history looks through the Keynesian lens, one first ground by Hegel. Through it, the tragedy of poverty is proof of the historical and political limits of both liberalism and revolution.[38] Revolution's failure to realize its ideal is the reason that Keynesianism begins from the proposition that revolution's necessity can only reside in that it must have been, but can no longer be. Revolution is acknowledged as a necessary tragedy, or perhaps a tragic necessity, whose ultimate and inevitable failure now stands exposed.

This Keynesian lens is definitively not reactionary or conservative. Rather, it is closer to what remains of transformative political thought

---

Rather, it is closer to the condition Jeremy Waldron identifies in "Homelessness and the Issue of Freedom," *UCLA Law Review* 39, 1991, 295–324. The conduct of modern civil society makes it impossible to understand poverty as immanent, either historically, socially, or—as Waldron shows so clearly—spatially.

38 Christoph Menke offers a compelling account of Hegel's diagnosis of "tragedy in ethical life" in *Reflections of Equality*, trans. Howard Rouse and Andrei Denejkine, Stanford: Stanford University Press, 2006, 129–32.

when stripped of its revolutionary energy. Keynesianism represents a specifically postrevolutionary shift in the conception of historical possibility and the limits of historical agency. From this perspective, *laissez-faire* liberalism can only perpetuate poverty in the midst of plenty, while the revolution has taught us that the poor, the ignorant, the downtrodden—whose cause is in many ways just and whose outrage is legitimate—cannot undo these bonds but inevitably only tighten them in the construction of a new, and usually worse, tyranny. For Keynesians, Robespierre and Lenin make sense in the context of their time and place, but in retrospect we know that revolution cannot accomplish what they envisioned. The masses, however well-meaning, are unable to effect the changes they advocate. They cannot erect civilization, and cannot be entrusted with its preservation. The Keynesian thus arrogates historically meaningful action to the state and elites.

As I mentioned, Keynes was in no way the first to isolate this historical dynamic, and to draw Keynesian conclusions from it. The chapters that follow examine in some detail several moments in the post-Bastille history of political economic reflections on this dynamic. That history is not confined to thinkers of liberal or "reformist" ilk. At least in the global North, a critique of liberal capitalism combined with a wariness of the people, of popular sovereignty, and mass politics has also often been a key, if repressed, feature of the Left in some of its manifestations, from progressive to radical. This is no accidental historical convergence. Rather, it arises from a shared historical experience in the revolutionary era of the late eighteenth to the mid-nineteenth century, the era in which liberal capitalism achieved its hegemony in that part of the world. Even for many of those thought to be among the more revolutionary thinkers of the last two centuries, the poor are sometimes objects rather than subjects of knowledge, historical agents that must be coaxed or directed by others to fulfill their historical role, and the leaders of revolutions or rebellions of the poor or downtrodden are often not poor or downtrodden themselves. There is little question in many revolutionary intellectuals' minds that even those whose historical mission is to overturn the world cannot conceive that mission on their own.

One might presume that the historical basis for this conclusion is straightforward, even if the efforts it underwrites differ. At least in their capacity to deliver the freedom and security they all claimed as their ultimate ends, the list of revolutionary failures is long. One need only think of the big ones: the Terror of 1793–1794, Bonaparte's *coup d'état*, the revolutions of 1848 ("poor incidents—small fractures and fissures in the dry crust of European society," according to Marx), the Paris Commune in 1871, Stalinism, and Spanish republicanism.[39] All revolutionary moments that could not unreasonably be understood as cataclysmic or catastrophic in one way or another, all were crushed by the overwhelming power of terrible reaction or were victims of more endogenous disaster. One might, of course, take the optimistic view that in the long run, these moments represent halting and painful steps toward freedom. But that view is antithetic to all Keynesianisms, and is not necessarily endorsed by all radicalisms. Consequently, without the metaphysical embrace of cataclysm one occasionally finds in the work of Alain Badiou or Slavoj Žižek, many who wish for a radically different world have consequently deemed it reasonable to conclude that the revolutionary means of the last two centuries have either been futile, caught up in populist irrationalism or utopian naïveté, or simply cost too many lives. Many, across the political spectrum, have concluded that the masses cannot necessarily be trusted with the tasks of social change or social order.

This stance clearly contrasts with what is in many ways the Left's signal claim, often a defining feature in its own eyes: that it speaks for the poor, that it stands for what the poor "really" want or to which they have legitimate claim. But this is by no means *necessarily* true, and the problem is not merely due to the possibility that what the masses want has been misunderstood. Some of the self-important "bourgeois socialists" derided by Marx and Engels remain; elite Left intellectuals continue to represent themselves as undistorted channels for workers' or poor people's politics.[40] In addition, the historical

---

39    Marx, "Speech at the Anniversary of the *People's Paper,*" in *Political Writings,* vol. 2, New York: Verso, 296.

40    "Protective duties; for the benefit of the working class. Prison reform; for the

legacy of Left and radical politics in Europe and North America contains significant elements as dismissive of poor people's politics as many a conservative. Think, for example, of the distraught soul-searching that consumes the Left in the United States or the United Kingdom every time the working class votes for a Thatcher or a Bush.

I will suggest that one of the most important reasons that Keynes remains so compelling to so many, wittingly or unwittingly, whether or not they understand themselves as on the Left, is that the specter of this rabble haunts the "progressive" political imagination. Moreover, in the fundamentalist garb of the Tea Party or political Islam, it seems less and less spectral in recent years. Jacques Rancière impugns "the philosopher and his poor," but he could just as readily have trained his sights on "the economist and his poor." "The economist" can invoke both Marx *and* Keynes.

We could take this invocation of Marx cynically, even go so far as to suggest that for him the revolutionary proletariat was a capricious rabble that must be led by other historical actors. This is Rancière's position. For Marx, according to Rancière, the rabble problem arises from the fact that the "working and thinking proletarian" must become "someone *who has only one thing to do*—to make the revolution—and who *cannot not do that* because of what he is": a worker in whom the social relations of production engender the "potential capitalist." If so, Rancière tells us, then Marx understands the burden of creating the new world to fall squarely on the non-worker, that is, the bourgeois who understands the historical mission of the poor *qua* workers, "masters of a virtue" they are "not at liberty to choose." The poor worker, who owns little but strives for more, "condemned to the shameful privileges of thrift, accumulation, and wealth" is

---

benefit of the working class. This is the last word and the only seriously meant word of bourgeois socialism. It is summed up in the phrase: the bourgeois is a bourgeois—for the benefit of the working class." Marx and Engels, "Manifesto of the Communist Party" [1847], in K. Marx, *Political Writings*, vol. 1, New York: Verso, 2010, 94. While the accusation is different, this recalls Gayatri Spivak's well-known critique of Michel Foucault and Gilles Deleuze for representing themselves as able to disavow their own power to represent "the people"; see Spivak, "Can the Subaltern Speak?" in Cary Nelson and Lawrence Grossberg (eds.), *Marxism and the Interpretation of Culture*, Urbana: University of Illinois Press, 1988, 271–313.

"always a potential capitalist."[41] Thus, as Marx himself said, the point is not what the poor think they want, but to what ends history recruits them, whether they wish it or not:

> It is not a question of what this or that proletarian, or even the whole proletariat, *regards* as its aim at the moment. It is a question of *what the proletariat is* and what, in accordance with this *being*, it will historically be compelled to do.[42]

"Communism is a faith in the suicide of the bourgeoisie," Rancière writes; the proletarians of the *Manifesto* are "gravediggers, not even assassins."[43]

Rancière's larger critique concerns not just Marx, but the long history of the philosopher's invocation of the poor. The status of that inorganic intellectual deserves his close attention. But with Marx, I would argue, this is what can only be called a misreading. Marx was not the "socialistic bourgeois" who, in the words of the *Manifesto*, wants "the existing state of society minus its revolutionary and disintegrating elements."[44] And yet it is true he did not always or necessarily "trust in the masses." Contrary to a common interpretation, what Hegel calls the "rabble"—the spectral, anticipated agent of chaos, demagoguery, and violence central to the argument of this book—is not redeemed by Marx in the figure of the proletariat.[45] Marx too had his "rabble," but it was not the coalescent proletarian industrial working class. It was the "mob," the *lumpenproletariat*, "drawn from the midst of the working masses in the sense of being *precipitated out of them* (to use the chemical term) by the processes of developing bourgeois society."[46] The

41    Jacques Rancière, *The Philosopher and His Poor*, Durham: Duke University Press, 2004, 12, 20.

42    Marx, *The Holy Family*, in Karl Marx and Friedrich Engels, *Collected Works*, vol. IV, London: Lawrence and Wishart, 1975, 36–37.

43    Rancière, *The Philosopher and His Poor*, 80, 92.

44    Marx and Engels, "Manifesto," 93.

45    See, for example, Slavoj Žižek, "Two Types of Rabble," from his blog on Southbank Centre, posted July 20, 2010.

46    Hal Draper, *Karl Marx's Theory of Revolution*, vol. II: *The Politics of Social Classes*, New York: Monthly Review Press, 1978, 453–54, 462.

*lumpenproletariat*, which can be found, Marx says, "fighting against the working and thinking proletariat":

> in all towns, forms a mass quite distinct from the industrial prole-
> tariat. It is a recruiting ground for thieves and criminals of all sorts,
> living off the garbage of society, people without a definite trace,
> vagabonds, *gens sans feu et sans aveu*, varying according to the
> cultural level of their particular nation, never able to repudiate
> their *lazzarroni* character; during their youthful years—the age at
> which the Provisional Government recruited them—they are
> thoroughly tractable, capable of the greatest acts of heroism and
> the most exalted self-sacrifice as well as the lowest forms of banditry
> and the foulest corruption.[47]

This

> passively rotting mass thrown off by the lowest layers of the old
> society, may, here and there, be swept into the movement by a
> proletarian revolution; its conditions of life, however, prepare it far
> more for the part of a bribed tool of reactionary intrigue.[48]

This "tool of reaction" that falls out of bourgeois civil society is framed in almost identical terms by Hegel (see Chapter 6), and it is crucial to his politics, and no less central to Keynes's understanding of modern liberal capitalism. For Keynes, the problem of political transformation is also a problem for the bourgeoisie: the "euthanasia of the rentier" and the possibility of an "honourable poverty." The

---

47   Marx, "Review: May-October 1850," *NRZ Revue*, November 1, 1850. See also "The Victory of the Counter-Revolution in Vienna," *Neue Rheinische Zeitung*, November 7, 1848, in *Political Writings*, vol. 1, 306, 176; "The Class Struggles in France: 1848 to 1850," *Political Writings*, vol. 2, 52–53. The phrase *"gens sans feu et sans aveu"* means "people without fire or commitment" (with neither hearth nor home). In feudal times, *sans aveu* described someone without the status of vassal and thus "placeless," without the right to a lord's protection.

48   Marx and Engels, "Manifesto," 77: *"Das Lumpenproletariat, diese passive Verfaulung der untersten Schichten der alten Gesellschaft, wird durch eine proletarische Revolution stellen-weise in die Bewegung hineingeschleudert, seiner ganzen Lebenslage nach wird es bereitwilliger sein, sich zu reaktionären Umtrieben erkaufen zu lassen."*

"free" masses (democracy) can no more be expected to eliminate the tragedy than "free" markets.

This is what I mean when I say that the ghost of Robespierre haunts the contemporary Left, but not only in the "emancipatory" manner in which some might hope. Neither he, nor even Marx and Engels, were entirely free of this anxiety. To be sure, Marx wagers that history will redeem the poor—if not now, then later. That optimism retains its power. But the upshot of these revelations—that the masses have power, but that it is not something in which we can trust unconditionally—is that radical transformation is potentially devoid of a reliable agent. And yet, on both the Marxian and Keynesian accounts, liberal capitalism is unsustainable if left to self-regulate. In response to this perceived absence, Keynesianism takes up the burden of ensuring a sustainable social order. Radical transformation is inevitable, but only elite direction can ensure it realizes its "proper" ends. The tragedy can be redeemed, the moment of rupture is not inevitable. *The General Theory* is, ultimately, an answer to the problems identified by the *Manifesto*. In its response, it accepts much of the *Manifesto's* analysis (contradictions of capitalist civil society, unsustainable levels of inequality) and shares many of its premises (earthly utopianism, materialism, recognition of the power of the masses, and so on). But to the revolutionary road of the *Manifesto* it proposes a scientific detour, by way of a longer but much less tumultuous route. The destination is somewhat different, but it is, in Keynesians' eyes, an eminently reasonable option. Only confusion, or mysticism, could justify choosing revolution when we really have no need of it.

Which is to say that, if Marx was correct when he claimed to have inverted an upside-down Hegel, and put him on his feet, Keynes puts Hegel back on his head again. In doing so, he attempts to outline a scientific justification for the "German road" of transformation—the careful, reasoned, state-managed "revolution without revolutionaries" celebrated by Hegel—that avoids the "perilous road" of the French or Russians.[49] *The General Theory* unwittingly reasserts

49   Stathis Kouvelakis, *Philosophy and Revolution: From Marx to Kant*, trans. G.M. Goshgarian, New York: Verso, 2003, 12, 42–43.

the Hegelian analysis of revolution that drove Marx crazy: that it is no longer necessary, or at least will no longer work. To the extent that liberal ideology grants this assessment the status of Truth—epitomized, perhaps, in the popular idea that the twentieth century exposed Marx's critique of Hegel's civil society as a historical and theoretical failure—*The General Theory* is simultaneously one of its most important effects and, since its publication, one of its most powerful defenses.

But Keynes's proposition is not a mere liberal reversal of Marx's critique. It is, perhaps in paradoxical ways, a Marxist Hegel turned "back" on his head, a materialist Hegel. The realization of the revolution without revolutionary upheaval—which was for Hegel the task of history, via the cunning of reason—is for twentieth- and twenty-first-century Keynesians the task of worldly affairs. It is not the unfolding of the Idea, but the technical-managerial problem of governing human behavior and institutions. With *The General Theory* comes (or at least definitively emerges) the end of faith in a "natural" or rational order, either divine or Newtonian, and those problems that Hegel displaced to the realm of metaphysics are brought down to Earth. Keynes rediscovers the key to this in the analysis of civil society's limits and the production of a state-civil society equivalence that overcomes them. Part II of this book argues that we can learn much about Keynes and Keynesianism by coming to them through Hegel's struggle with the same questions. But first, we must begin where Hegel himself found he could not avoid beginning: with Robespierre.

PART 2

# Before Keynes

## CHAPTER 4

# Poverty, Honor, and Revolution

I n the broadest possible sense, this book is about "crisis": instability, disorder, and unrest, and their irrepressible effects on modern political economy and political imagination. The phenomena I have in mind include great (capital-R) Revolutions—both "political" (something akin to regime change) and "social" (the emergence of new historical paths or epochs)—but also what Keynes called "civil dissension": subrevolutionary activity like populist rebellions, strikes, and less organized or unorganized demonstrations of widespread discontent and resistance, like riots and mass protests.

Despite the obviously broad range of social dynamics this includes, I collect them in the convenient category "revolution." I embrace this broad version of the category not because the analytical or historical particularities do not matter or do not help us understand the world better. They do. But the catchall revolution concept I lean on is important because the significance of this broad collection of social phenomena registers in the mind of those who govern—the state and elites—largely because of their historical relation to revolution. In the places and times with which this book is most concerned—western Europe and North America during the last two centuries—political and economic conditions are identified as "crises" precisely because they risk precipitating revolution in this broad sense. A riot daunts the governors not as an isolated incident, but in the larger processes it threatens to precipitate. I would argue that this risk is in

fact what defines a situation as crisis; it is less about present conditions than the trajectory they indicate we are on. Crisis is the name
we give to a condition we are afraid will not return to "normal."

If political economy is the science of (the) liberal capitalist government—as Michel Foucault said, and which is surely true—then
much of it is a science of crisis, and its key concepts, formulas, and
occasional self-reconstruction are born of crisis.[1] Consequently,
despite the fact that capital-R Revolution in the capitalist global
North has been more an absent presence than a "present presence," it
remains an irrepressible determinant of the modern political imagination and also of political economy. There are certainly crucial revolutionary presents that have come and gone in this part of the
world—Spain in the 1930s, ongoing struggles in Ireland, the violent
rise of national fascisms—not to mention the very real anticolonial
revolutions that challenged European and North American imperialism "extraterritorially" throughout the twentieth century. But if we
confine ourselves to actually existing revolutions and popular resistance, we miss some of the most significant ways in which the idea of
revolution reaches beyond specific times and places to shape the
world. Revolution and social upheaval always matter, even when the
streets are quiet and all is calm. Modern liberal capitalism has always
been shaped by the anxious memory of revolution, and thus by a
consciousness of the potential, the *menace*—however isolated or
consistently unrealized—of popular rejection of the existing order.

Much of my account of Keynesianism is about liberal capitalist
anxiety and the ways in which the most powerful and affluent societies of the modern world have tried to address this menace—and
thus, most important, about their confrontation with the constant
tragic fact of poverty in the midst of their plenty. Consequently, an
extensive and historically loose idea of revolution is most useful
because in the part of the world in question, revolution has frequently
remained merely that: an idea. This is not to say that "real"

---

1   Michel Foucault, *Birth of Biopolitics: Lectures at the Collège de France, 1978-1979*,
London: Palgrave, 16-17, 320; Michel Foucault, *The Essential Foucault*, New York: New
Press, 2003, 234.

revolutions and resistance are not, in the last instance, behind the idea and the anxiety it induces for many. Of course they are. Real events (maybe even "Events," à la Badiou) engender that anxiety, even in the minds of those ignorant of the historical reasons for it. Nor is it to suggest that the evolving political economic rationalities of liberal capitalism are strictly antirevolutionary or counterrevolutionary by definition. They are not. The very idea of something like a "bourgeois revolution," a term often used to describe the English, French, and American revolutions, suggests that liberals have not always been on the "No" side of movements for massive social change. To take only the most obvious example, the status among liberals of the Big One, the French Revolution—de Tocqueville called it the "universal earthquake"—has always been complex, soliciting everything from rapturous celebration, to regret, to vilification.[2]

In fact, the revolutionary moment in France, and its broader dynamics like the contemporaneous slave revolution in Haiti, mark precisely the moment at which one should begin an examination of Keynesianism, because they herald the revolutionary birth of modern political liberalism, and Keynesianism is liberalism's most significant critical development in the face of revolutionary menace. If an immanent critique is one that accepts the basic principles of its object, Keynesianism is simultaneously an immanent critique of liberalism *and* of revolution. It is the liberalism of those who (however reluctantly) acknowledge the continued historical legitimacy of revolution but claim to render it unnecessary, to "revolutionize" without revolution. One certainly might say this is impossible, and perhaps, in the long run, that is true. But, as Keynes himself said—and his point was not metaphorical—"in the long run we are all dead." In the endless "short run" moments of deferral between now and then, the problem of maintaining civilization itself is the most pressing task of all.

---

2 Alexis de Tocqueville, *The Old Regime and the French Revolution*, Mineola, NY: Dover, 2010, vi.

## Robespierre and the Ends of Revolution

And so we turn to de Tocqueville's earthquake, and to the individual whose historical reputation is tied most closely to it, Maximilien Robespierre: lawyer, pamphleteer, orator, and influential member of the Jacobin Club. He is best known for his eventual leadership of the Committee of Public Safety, the organizing institution behind the Terror. Arrested by his opponents on July 27, 1794—a day better known by its date in the Revolutionary calendar, 9 Thermidor, Year II—he and 21 colleagues went to the guillotine the next day.

Robespierre's brilliant political rise, relentless commitment, and eventual bloody downfall are often taken as a metaphor for the French Revolution and revolutionary radicalism *tout court*. Critics of more than a few revolutionary movements of the last two and a half centuries (in the broad sense described above) have invoked Robespierre's name as either a dire warning against the perils of "ideology," "the masses," and "demagoguery" or simply as a rebuke to the demand for too much change too quickly. Hannah Arendt, who called Robespierre Marx's "teacher in revolution," said that his "emotion-laden insensitivity to reality," inspired by Rousseau, ultimately determined his enormous contribution to

> the greater perfidy which was to play such a monstrous role in the revolutionary tradition. Since the days of the French Revolution, it has been the boundlessness of their sentiments that made revolutionaries so curiously insensitive to reality in general and to the reality of persons in particular, whom they felt no compunctions in sacrificing to their "principles," or to the course of history, or to the cause of revolution as such.[3]

Walter Lippmann saw Robespierre's legacy wherever "extremism" held sway: "It is one of the ironies of history that Mussolini and

---

3    Hannah Arendt, *On Revolution*, New York: Penguin, 2006, 54, 80.

Hitler should have taken their conception of sovereignty from the extremist doctrinaires of the French Revolution."[4]

Yet precisely because the French Revolution so quickly, and uncritically, became a lens through which to assess the progress of modernity, and Robespierre made out to be the "lamentablest sea-green Chimera" stalking all radical politics, we should be wary of these sweeping assessments.[5] The stakes are too high for conservative simplicities. Like the legacies of the Revolution itself, Robespierre's thought was much more complex, and far less static, than these superficialities suggest. He has much to teach us that we would not expect to learn, I think, particularly with regard to the relation between liberalism and revolution. This relation defines Keynesianism, and Robespierre helped shape it, and in so doing, shaped both what liberalism and revolution mean.

Like the Revolution itself, Robespierre's ideas and strategies became more rigid, less subtle and supple, as the struggle wore on and the forces opposing revolution chased him across the ideological terrain of his times.[6] By 9 Thermidor, he had clearly trespassed its limits. The only legitimacy he retained, perhaps, lay in the fact that his end endorsed the justice of his means. Many have attributed the "excesses" of this idealism, and that of the Jacobins in general, to Rousseau's deification of the "general will" and the abstractions of a Kantian "kingdom of ends."[7]

But we must be careful not to underestimate Robespierre's own ideological contributions. He was an admirer of Rousseau, to be

---

4   Walter Lippmann, *The Good Society*, Guildford: Billing & Sons, 1944, 311 n.14.

5   Thomas Carlyle, *The French Revolution*, London: Continuum, 2010 [1837], 184.

6   Throughout, I follow the practice of capitalizing the noun "Revolution" when it refers to the French Revolution specifically. Lowercase "revolution" refers to the broader concept.

7   Stathis Kouvelakis, *Philosophy and Revolution: From Marx to Kant*, trans. G. M. Goshgarian, New York: Verso, 2003, 30–32; Charles Taylor, *Hegel*, Cambridge: Cambridge University Press, 1975, 370–75. It is worth noting, however, that although the notion of a "kingdom of ends" arguably does link Kant and the Revolution, and Kant defended the Revolution throughout his life, he was not an inspiration for the Jacobins in the manner of Rousseau, and his work was largely unknown to them at the time; see Ferenc Fehér, "Practical Reason in the Revolution: Kant's Dialogue with the French Revolution," in Ferenc Fehér (ed.), *The French Revolution and the Birth of Modernity*, Berkeley: University of California Press, 1990, 201–14.

sure, and was prone to dramatically conjuring Rousseau's judgmental spirit to condemn his compatriots' failure to keep the Revolution in mind.[8] But he knew nothing of Kant or Kantians and had no need of their retroactive inspiration. Robespierre was himself a theorist of revolution and popular mobilization of the highest order, an ideologue in the truest sense of the word, working tirelessly to shape a new common sense. If he shared anything with Kant, it was, as we will see, his emphasis on the clear and present power of necessity. If Kant envisioned a long-run "kingdom of ends," he also recognized the short-run irrepressible demand for the means of subsistence. Those without such means are beyond ethics, beyond law. They exist in the realm of the most fundamental necessity, and exercise the right appropriate to that realm, *Ius necessitatis*. That right, the "right of necessity," defines the limits of law, property, and government: "*Necessitas non habet legem*"—necessity has no law.[9] But Kant— sometimes called the "philosopher of the French Revolution"—wrote these words three years after Robespierre's execution.[10] In truth, he only came to grips with *necessitas* through Robespierre and the Revolution. History realized what Kant then tried to rationalize, but ultimately failed to grasp.

Robespierre was nothing if not a product of his time. In the months surrounding the fall of Louis XVI in August 1792, he was a force to be reckoned with in Paris, consolidating his position as the most influential member of the revolutionary leadership. At that moment, before the Terror, the focus was shifting from taking power to exercising it. For all his commitment to popular sovereignty and

---

8    Maximilien Robespierre, "Sur la nécessité de révoquer les décrets qui attachent l'exercice des droits du citoyen à la contribution du marc d'argent, ou d'un nombre determine de journées d'ouvriers [On the necessity of revoking the decrees that impose the contribution of a silver mark or a particular number of working days to the exercise of the rights of the citizen]" April 1791, *Oeuvres Complètes*, vol. VII, Paris: Presses Universitaires de France, 1910, 170. (All quotes from Robespierre are from the collected works, hereinafter cited as *OC*, volume number, page. My translations.)

9    Immanuel Kant, "The Metaphysics of Morals," in *Practical Philosophy*, Cambridge: Cambridge University Press, 1996 [1797], 392.

10    Hans Reiss, "Introduction," in Immanuel Kant, *Political Writings*, Cambridge: Cambridge University Press, 1970, 3.

universal citizenship, Robespierre was forced to consider the problem of "the people" not merely as one of representation, but of government, and the world to be governed looked, at least in 1791 and 1792, like a substantially *liberal* world (even if he did not have the term at his disposal). He could hardly be insensitive to the need to lay the groundwork for a new order which, whether he wished it or not, would include bourgeois merchants, small landowners, and professionals. These were the people with whom he had made the Revolution.

He approached this problem with characteristic fury. There were many moments in which he played the part for which he is famous: the outraged populist, equating the "general will" of "the people" with justice and truth à la Rousseau. In those moments the political was reduced to the kind of Manichean opposition for which revolutionaries are so often caricatured—"if you don't do everything for liberty, you have done nothing. There are no two ways of being free: one must either be completely free, or return to slavery."[11] Live free or die.

Nevertheless, the moment also required an understanding of the political as a more complex realm, in which what is worked out is not the victory of one truth and the obliteration of another, virtue over corruption, but the political problem per se: the relation between governors and governed. In contrast to what we have been taught to expect from the cartoon Robespierre, he did not think the solution was simply to erase the line between the people and the legislature or to eradicate material inequality and begin *tabula rasa*. Indeed, he did not even believe that was possible:

> Doubtless we have no need of a revolution to teach the world that the extreme inequality in fortunes is the source of so much evil and so many crimes; but we are no less convinced that equality of

---

11 Robespierre, "Sur le marc d'argent," *OC,* VII, 164. Anders Stephanson remarks that "the stark contrast between 'liberty or death'" has always been "much beloved by Western revolutionary liberals"; "The Philosopher's Island," *New Left Review* II: 61, 2010, 199.

property is a chimera. To my mind, I believe equality is less essential to private wellbeing than to public contentedness: it is more
important to render poverty honourable than it is to outlaw
opulence.[12]

The task of governance was to make it possible for the poor to be
"active citizens," to disassemble the machine that gives dignity and
power to the wealthy and propertied and denies them to the poor
solely because of their poverty.

The law, the public authority: is it not established to protect weakness against injustice and oppression? It is thus an offence to all
social principles to place it entirely in the hands of the rich . . . I
envy not at all the advantageous share you have received, since this
inequality is a necessary or incurable evil: but at least do not take
from me the imprescriptible property of which no human law can
strip me. Let me even be proud sometimes of an honourable
poverty.[13]

In this transitional moment, the possibility of an honorable
poverty was the key to Robespierre's vision of the world the Revolution
was making. If a social order could exist in which material inequality
had no moral or political relevance, in which one's wealth and income
had no impact on one's participation as *citoyen*, then bourgeois liberalism might well be commensurable with the new world inaugurated
by the Revolution. Only when he no longer believed the bourgeois
order capable of accommodating an honorable poverty did
Robespierre abandon this position and commit himself to the necessarily violent construction of a new society founded on a more radical equality, one in which poverty would not exist and hence would
have no meaning.

The centrality to Revolutionary ideology of this "formal" equality—which posits a clean division of the social between an abstract

---

12  Robespierre, *OC,* IX, 459.
13  Robespierre, "Sur le marc d'argent," *OC,* VII, 164–65.

political realm in which all are equal and a concrete and unequal domain of labor and everyday life—is sometimes missed, since today it is a fundamental principle of liberalism. Indeed, it is nowadays closely associated with Kant, whose founding father status among liberals like political philosopher John Rawls has proved more than compatible with his status as the "philosopher of the French Revolution." The fact that for some he might be both can seem strange now that two centuries have gradually made liberalism into the antithesis of revolution. But the hope for honorable poverty in a fundamentally liberal order remains with us. It is the Keynesian dream, and insofar as he shared that dream, however briefly, Robespierre too was tempted by the vision of a Keynesian society— one for which revolution was like a midwife: essential at birth, but no longer necessary.

## Honorable Poverty

We can isolate a decisive moment in this struggle for honorable poverty if we enter the drama in Paris, late autumn 1792, immediately following the founding of the National Convention and the inauguration of the First Republic. Crisis gripped the city. Essential commodities were in very short supply, and prices were rising. The urban poor knew scarcity as a quasi-permanent condition—some even say that bread shortages precipitated the events of 1789—but forces combined to make this a hard time even by the standards of the age. For a newly elected revolutionary assembly, riven with factionalism and mistrust, the situation in the streets only made an already challenging political environment worse. On December 2, just days before the imprisoned Louis XVI went to trial, Robespierre rose before the Convention to "address the people's representatives on ways of providing for its subsistence."[14] With the population up in arms, demanding higher taxes and expropriation of the property of wealthy citizens, Robespierre ("The Incorruptible") took on the

---

14  Robespierre, "Sur les subsistances," December 2, 1792, *OC*, IX, 110.

distributional problems at the heart of the discontent: scarcity and private property. What rights, and whose rights, matter? Where and when do they matter? And why?

To those who think of Jacobinism as irrational proto-communist radicalism driven by uncompromising ideological purity, Robespierre's answer might come as something of a historical surprise. Jacobin politics was neither so rigid nor so unsubtle as is often thought, nor was the Jacobin Club static or homogeneous. From the beginnings of the Revolution, Jacobins shared a commitment to property rights with the provincial elites who dominated the Convention at the time and who later came to be known as the Girondins, after the region around Bordeaux from which many of their leaders hailed. (Indeed, the idea that the two groups were always clearly distinct is a convenient simplification; the line between them was often blurrier than canned histories make it seem.) If the Revolution undoubtedly "inaugurated a liberal commercial order," the Jacobins played their role.[15] In the months that followed Robespierre's speech, the two factions united, if uneasily, in defense of private property as central to the revolutionary cause and in condemnation of calls for radical redistribution from *les Enragés*.[16]

Since Robespierre in particular is so commonly written off as the political ancestor of Josef Stalin or Pol Pot, the fact that he could respect anything other than unforgiving "divine violence"—let alone something so *liberal* as private property rights—seems hard to reconcile with his reputation.[17] This is partly due to the

---

15   Richard Biernacki, *The Fabrication of Labor: Germany and Britain, 1640–1914*, Berkeley: University of California Press, 1995, 343.

16   *Les Enragés* were a loose group of radicals at the far Left of the Revolutionary movement (beyond even Robespierre's *Montagnards*). Led by the radical cleric Jacques Roux, they were involved in the termination of the Girondins and the beginning of the Terror in Fall 1793. Long in direct conflict with Robespierre and his Jacobin allies, the leadership was eliminated soon after. Their great historian is the socialist Albert Mathiez; see in particular "La Révolution et les subsistances. Les Enragés et les Troubles du savon (juin 1793)," *Annales Révolutionnaires* 13: 5, 1921, 353–71; and "La Révolution et les subsistances. La fin des Enragés," *Annales Révolutionnaires* 15: 2, 1923, 89–112.

17   Slavoj Žižek, *In Defense of Lost Causes*, London: Verso, 2008, 161–62. The title of a recent biography in English (Ruth Scurr, *Fatal Purity*, New York: Henry Holt, 2007) succinctly expresses the common assessment of Robespierre's character.

one-dimensional caricature of Robespierre that is easily constructed by reading his biography backwards, so that his role in the Terror retrospectively defines the entire life that preceded it. (In 1789 he actually opposed the death penalty.) Such misrepresentation is the common curse of those who become a metaphor for their times, and in this case it has crucial historiographical effects. Robespierre's reputation for vicious dedication to revolutionary communism *avant la lettre* has been enthusiastically confirmed not only by liberals but by radicals too. Slavoj Žižek's defensive account of Jacobin terrorism is almost as one-sidedly revisionist as François Furet's condemnation thereof.[18] Both make it seem impossible that Robespierre might have had anything at all to do with an emergent liberalism.

But it is not just such politically and historically thin accounts of Robespierre's life and thought that produce the mismatch between his reputation and much of what he actually said and did. The mismatch is attributable at least as much, if not more so, to a misunderstanding of liberalism, which (as discussed in Chapter 2) has effectively rewritten its own illiberal history by determining the very terms through which the past is comprehended. "Radicalism," "extremism," coercion—all have been excised from liberalism's account of itself. Yet the violence and terror that Robespierre's politics ultimately visited upon the world were and are more than matched by the violence and misery perpetrated in the name of liberal "freedom" (think of Atlantic slavery, for example, or British and American imperialism). There is nothing necessarily un-liberal about immiseration and the politics of the blade.

But if your definition of "progress" is the inevitable unfolding of liberal principle over time, then its history is a just-so story in which justice and legitimacy are imputed a priori. Obstacles to freedom's actualization can never arise from within that process itself; they are, by definition, only attributable to backward or irrational interests.

---

18   See Žižek's engaging commentary in the brief selection of Robespierre's speeches, *Robespierre: Virtue and Terror*, London: Verso, 2007; and François Furet, *Interpreting the French Revolution*, Cambridge: Cambridge University Press, 1981.

After the Terror, there is no place for Robespierre and the Jacobins in liberalism's autobiography.

Liberal erasure and radical narrow-mindedness thus combine to make it difficult to understand Robespierre's point on that day in December, because it just does not fit the standard narratives. His speech to the Convention was intended neither to denounce, nor to reaffirm, the Jacobin "position" on property rights. It was actually to make a pragmatic recommendation regarding a Girondin proposal to reinstate "freedom of commerce" (by terminating price controls), which had been legislated by the Constituent Assembly in 1791 but suspended since the imprisonment of the King and the abolition of the monarchy on August 10, 1792.[19]

Robespierre opposed the reinstatement of commercial freedom—not in principle, but at that moment. Noting that the masses were up in arms—as he spoke, 10,000 peasants were marching on Tours to demand a fixed price on wheat—he reminded the delegates that meeting the people's needs was not only their "most sacred duty," but it was also in "their most precious interests."[20] In conditions of scarcity [disette] and desperation, the right of necessity held sway, and necessity has no law. "The first social law guarantees all members of society the means to live; all others are subordinate to that one." He thus spoke to "plead not only the cause of indigent citizens, but that of property-owners and merchants too":

> I would take from them no honest profit, no legitimate property; I would take from them only the right to infringe upon those of others; I would not destroy commerce at all, only the monopolist's brigandage; I would sentence them only to the punishment of allowing their fellows to live.[21]

---

19   Biernacki, *The Fabrication of Labor*, 217–18.

20   Eric Hazan, *A People's History of the French Revolution*, trans. David Fernbach, London: Verso, 2014, 211.

21   Robespierre, "Sur les subsistances," *OC*, IX, 110, 117.

One need not bother with a complex set of legislative rules or with lofty principle. In the midst of the crisis, it is all about short-run immediacy, "less about creating brilliant systems than about returning to simple, common sense solutions; it does not require a system of legislation either, but an instant and provisional law."[22]

For Robespierre, the errors of the bourgeois insistence on freedom of commerce lay in the fact that the *practical* problem of securing private property—how to ensure it survived the crisis—demanded a very different approach than many in the Convention understood. The situation in the streets meant a strict commitment to an abstraction like "pure" economic liberty—what today would be called "free markets" and the individual pursuit of self-interest—was foolish given the actually existing world upon which it was to be imposed. "Freedom of commerce" would mean the end of commerce. If the Girondins' plan entailed "unlimited freedom of trade, and bayonets to calm fears or appease hunger," then it very clearly crossed a crucial threshold: "freedom of trade is necessary up to the point where homicidal greed starts to abuse it; the use of bayonets is an atrocity; the system is essentially incomplete because it fails to touch on the real principle."[23]

The *real principle.* Robespierre understood that the answer to the crisis was not "exceptional," only an expedient but temporary respite from the otherwise implacable unfolding of freedom and reason. The situation might be conjunctural, demanding immediate action, but it was not to be grasped as simply a brief moment of exception from truth or justice, as if it had no lasting implications for the meaning of freedom and reason.[24] On the contrary, "the real principle" was the very fact that exception was necessary. The "real principle" the conjuncture revealed is the inescapable fact and priority of material necessity, *Ius necessitatis*—what Hegel would later call *Notrecht*. The people must be fed, or they will do what is necessary to feed themselves.

---

22 Robespierre, *Gazette Nationale*, December 2, 1792, *OC,* IX, 117.
23 Robespierre, "Sur les subsistances," *OC,* IX, 111.
24 Ibid., 113.

This iron law (*Ius*) means the liberal *practice* of freedom demands substantial sacrifices from the liberal *principle* of freedom. The revolution against the *ancien régime* embraced the principle of private property, but for Robespierre, it had also to embrace moral and practical "common sense" [*bon sens*]. It is self-evident that no one "has the right to amass piles of wheat beside a neighbour who is dying of hunger." "It is not necessary that I be able to purchase brilliant fabrics; but I do need to be rich enough to buy bread, for myself and my children."[25]

One might argue that Robespierre's proposal—distribute the means of subsistence so that all can afford them—is founded in a conception of bourgeois self-interest that is just as self-interested, merely less myopic. As long as the poor are our neighbors, he seems to be saying, it is worth our while to subdue our neighbors' hunger. At the very least, it is a safer bet than letting them starve and become more and more desperate.

That is certainly part of Robespierre's point—he repeatedly argues that to leave hunger unaddressed is nothing less than "dangerous": it puts the Revolution and all it has achieved at risk.[26] But his is simultaneously a much deeper critique of bourgeois "freedom." Confronted with the fact that some amassed piles of wheat beside neighbors dying of hunger—in other words, that it was (and to this day remains) entirely possible that neighbors could be subject to such radically different fortunes—Robespierre pressed the "real principle" further. If one can starve while one's neighbor can "amass piles of wheat," then regardless of what the accumulators say, the problem is clearly not a scarcity of wheat. If there are piles of it, then there is more than enough for everyone.

If so—and it was, and still is, obviously so—then the world behind skyrocketing prices and bread riots is not the outcome of "natural" scarcity and a consequently "inevitable" Malthusian poverty for some unfortunate portion of society. On the contrary, scarcity is a problem only because "men" themselves produce it:

---

25    Ibid., 112.
26    Ibid., 116–18.

In every country where nature provides for the needs of men with prodigality, scarcity [*disette*] can only be due to the vices of the administration or the laws themselves; bad laws and bad adminis- tration originate in false principles and bad morals. It is a well- known fact that the soil of France produces far more than is needed to feed her inhabitants, and that the current scarcity is artificial [*une disette factice*].[27]

And yet, for all his talk of brigandage and greed, Robespierre does not blame the crisis solely on the avarice of the Convention's "bour- geois aristocracy" (although he does attack the greed of the Revolution's enemies, "great men, ministers, the rich").[28] On the contrary, "the people," which for him always includes the Convention, which is of and for it, "is naturally right and peaceful; it is always guided by a pure intention."[29] Once the aristocracy is expropriated, scarcity can no longer be solely attributed to property owners' selfish infidelity to the revolutionary purpose. Instead, it is also, and more importantly, the result of misunderstanding what liberty truly entails, what the practice of freedom actually requires. Liberty is not an abstraction that precedes or supersedes materiality and to which the real world must be made to bend. At least at this point in his political evolution, Robespierre understood that it is far more complicated and contextual than that.

He points to two ideas in particular that led the administration of the law astray. First, he says, the theorists of freedom of commerce had no appreciation for the force of *Ius necessitatis*, for the fact that *necessitas non habet legem*. They "treated foodstuffs [*denrées*] the most necessary for life like ordinary merchandise, and made no distinction between trade in wheat, for example, and that in indigo; they concerned themselves more with grain markets than with the people's subsistence." Consequently, "because they failed to account for the

---

27   Ibid., 110. In a footnote (n.6), the editors of Robespierre's works remark that *une disette factice* involves "hoarding and rising speculation."

28   Ibid., 110, 112.

29   Ibid., 112, 116.

fact of this difference in their calculations, they made a faulty application of principles evident in general; it's this mix of truth and falsity
that put something specious into an already incorrect system."[30]

In other words, the merchants' abstract principles had little relation to the substance of the world in which we actually live. "Common
sense" tells us that commodities that

> are in no way necessities can be abandoned to the merchant's
> limitless speculations; any momentary shortage is always bearable;
> and in general it makes sense that unconstrained freedom in such
> markets should be to the greatest profit of the state and some indi-
> viduals; but the lives of men cannot be subjected to such
> uncertainty.[31]

To defend the right to amass piles of indigo beside a neighbor who
has none is something qualitatively different than when one speaks
of wheat and hunger.

The second error the new governors committed was to adhere to
ideas that originated in a society long expired, ruled by the "great
men, ministers, the rich." Consequently, they failed to describe a
"liberty" adequate to human needs, and

> they did even less to adapt it to the stormy circumstances that
> revolutions bring; and their vague theory, even it if had been good
> for ordinary times, turns out to have no application to the instan-
> taneous measures that moments of crisis can require of us. They
> counted for much the profits of merchants and landowners, and
> the lives of men for basically nothing. And why? It was great men,
> ministers, the rich who were writing, who governed. If it had been
> the people, the system would likely have received a few
> modifications![32]

---

30   Ibid., 111–12.
31   Ibid., 112.
32   Ibid., 112.

Robespierre's critique here is crucial and merits some elaboration. His point is not simply that sometimes emergency measures are necessary, true as that may be. He is also saying something more, and more fundamental. He is arguing two absolutely essential points: first, that the inescapable demands of the material world (*Ius necessitatis*) have radical implications for "universal" abstractions like freedom and reason; and second, that the so-called "universality" of principles like freedom of commerce is a lie. It is not that this or that current crisis (temporary shortages of grain or riots in the streets, for example) demands a merely momentary exception to a general principle like free trade, which otherwise holds always and everywhere. The general principle is not, in fact, general. It is, rather, always and inescapably subject to the current situation.

And the current situation, the lived material conditions of life, is all there ever is. The "stormy circumstances that revolutions bring" mean that in the unavoidable confrontations between liberal principle and necessity, it is principle that must relent. "It is not true that property never gets in the way of human subsistence. The food necessary to life is as sacred as life itself. Everything indispensable to life is the whole of society's common property."[33] Necessity is history's challenge to all the universal principles that human communities convince themselves must be true and natural. There are no laws so pure that before them even hunger and the force of history itself give way. *Necessitas non habet legem.*

## Liberty and Equality

It is sometimes said that the ideological differences between the Gironde and the Jacobins lay in opposing priorities concerning the liberal "trade-off" between liberty (Girondins) and equality (Jacobins). There is some superficial truth to this, but for either party, liberty and equality were both essential. For Robespierre, the link between them is necessity, the unrelenting constraint on the material

---

33   Ibid., 112.

and moral structure of all organized forms of social life. To let the people starve is both evil and promises the destruction of the social order. Recognizing and accepting this constraint is not an unfortunate amendment to our common liberty, but essential to it: "freedom consists in obeying the laws we make for ourselves." If necessity imposes itself upon us, freedom consists in its embrace, in recognizing it as our own principle.[34] Indeed, Robespierre turns this necessity into virtue. Acknowledging our irreducible equality before the law of necessity is an eminently *practical* morality. It establishes the one obligation that always holds, precisely because it is obliged to respect no other—*necessitas non habet legem.*

This is what Robespierre meant when he cried "the people asks only for what is necessary, it only wants justice and peace." The right of necessity is not a limit to the abstract realm of "justice and peace." Necessity is the ground of that realm, and the right of necessity is in and of itself an outright and undeniable claim thereto. "The people have a natural tendency to seek out means to reduce their misery, a natural and legitimate tendency in itself."[35] To take from those who put their property rights or freedom of commerce before their neighbors' hunger is no crime against justice or peace, and to the extent that the poor must assert the right of necessity to the detriment of the social order, that social order is exposed as neither just not peaceful.

For Robespierre, therefore, it is true that the principle of equality in this fuller sense became the foundation of revolution—as, some say, it must always be.[36] The most powerful counterrevolutionary force was neither popular unrest nor the return of a foreign-backed *ancien régime*, but the "horror of equality" shared by "bourgeois aristocrats" and "stupid merchants" who "reserve for artisans the same disdain with which the nobility treated the merchants themselves."[37] When he asked the Convention, "Citizens, would you want a

34   Robespierre, "Sur le marc d'argent," April 1791, *OC,* VII, 162.

35   Robespierre, "Sur les troubles de subsistances," February 25, 1793, *OC,* IX, 275.

36   Christoph Menke, *Reflections of Equality,* trans. Howard Rouse and Andrei Denejkine, Stanford: Stanford University Press, 2006, 153–76.

37   Robespierre, May 10, 1793, *OC,* IX, 498.

revolution without revolution?," it was equality that determined the distinction between an event and true transformation.[38]

These are the grounds on which he attacked the argument, common then and now, that an excess of democracy—a logical corollary of radical equality—made governance unworkable, impracticable. To this merchants also added the qualification—less explicit today, perhaps—that "the people" were not fit for power. They had nothing, and nothing to lose. They were prone to corruption, caprice, and violence. They had no honor, no dignity.[39] These arguments enraged Robespierre. He set upon them with a vengeance. But it was not just the bourgeoisie's "delirious arrogance" he targeted. He also claimed their position was "practically" untenable even on its own terms. First, it was unjust:

> General practicality, you say! But is there nothing practical in what is just and honest? And doesn't this eternal maxim hold above all for the organization of society? If the goal of society is the well-being of all and the protection of the rights of man, then what are we to think of those who would found it on the power of a few individuals and the debasement and irrelevance of the rest of humanity!

Second, their position was stupid:

> The people who "have nothing to lose"!? How unjust and false this language of delirious arrogance is in the eyes of truth! The people of whom you speak are apparently men who somehow live, who survive in society without the means to live and survive. Yet if they are provided with those means they have, it seems to me, something to lose or preserve.[40]

Excluding "the people" would never work, because it denied the irrepressible force of necessity on both moral and material registers.

---

38   Robespierre, November 5, 1792, *OC* IX, p. 89.
39   Robespierre, "Sur le marc d'argent," *OC*, VII, 163–66.
40   Ibid., 164.

The attempt to construct an equivalence between justice and pragmatism is key to Robespierre's arguments, but it is not easy. It cannot help but expose the inevitable tensions in a concept of equality sufficiently complex—even unstable—to do the work he required of it. In general Robespierre relied on rhetorical force to manage the trouble. But even his legendary oratorical capacities cannot suppress the truth that the abstract demands of justice and equality are not so easily imposed on a substantive world framed by "necessity" and "utility." The claim that justice is not just the most correct but also the most useful foundation for practice can readily lead to the sort of blood-soaked performativity to which Robespierre was, arguably, ultimately led. The common idea that a "fatal purity" obsessed him is based on precisely this interpretation of his approach to the world, that is, that true justice can only be realized in a world purged of the features that make it inadequate, too messy, for the pure formality of principle.[41]

As noted earlier, this interpretation is a staple narrative of otherwise quite different historiographical approaches to the French Revolution and to Robespierre in particular. On the one hand we have liberal histories filled with regret that the Revolution and Robespierre went too far, effectively committing political suicide. On the other we have the presumably much more radical work of writers like Žižek, who accept the fatal purity argument, only to celebrate the commitment to "divine violence" as a historical Truth-event that must be embraced if the revolutionary task is to be revived.

This fatal purity seems a reasonable characterization of Robespierre's stance in the last year of his life, as the Terror reached its height under the Committee for Public Safety, and the death penalty was imposed for counterrevolutionary crimes like hoarding coffee and

41   Hannah Arendt, for example, considers Robespierre's fixation with popular "virtue" among the most important (and, however unintended, evil) legacies he left all revolutionaries since his time; *On Revolution*, especially 64–101; compare with Jürgen Habermas, "Appendix I: Popular Sovereignty as Procedure," in *Between Facts and Norms: Contributions to a Discourse Theory of Law and Democracy*, trans. William Rehg, Cambridge: MIT Press, 1998, 488.

sugar.[42] It is also true that his speeches and writings before these last months are filled with denunciations of the bourgeoisie's "hypocritical moderation," his threats to one day "avenge those you call 'the people' for your sacrilegious calumnies."[43]

And yet it is more complicated than his rhetoric makes it seem. It was not a question of pure principle, and the concept of equality that Robespierre actually worked with was not exactly Kantian, however much "pure reason" might retrospectively seem to animate "fatal purity." Kant had declared that the

> uniform equality of human beings as subjects of a state is, however, perfectly consistent with the utmost inequality of the mass in the degree of its possessions, whether these take the form of physical or mental superiority over others, or of fortuitous external property and of particular rights (of which there may be many) with respect to others.[44]

He wrote these words in 1793, Robespierre's moment, and the endorsement of such "formal equality"—and thus, one must assume, honorable poverty—would appear to resonate with Robespierre. Indeed, Heinrich Heine, brilliant poet and friend of Marx, once wrote that "Kant was our Robespierre."[45]

But it is worth remembering that while he asserted the *principle* of equality, for Kant it was in *practice* a "fantasy." It was a "pleasant dream," even a useful moral guide, as long as it did not provoke rebellion. He was almost certainly thinking of Robespierre when he remarked that

> a political artist, just as well as an aesthetic one, can guide and rule the world by deluding it through images in place of reality; for

---

42   Robespierre, July 27, 1793, *OC,* X, 9.

43   Robespierre, 17 Pluviôse II, *OC* X, 361; "Sur le marc d'argent," p. *OC*, VII, 166.

44   Immanuel Kant, "On the Common Saying: This May Be True in Theory but It Does not Apply in Practice," in *Political Writings*, 75.

45   Heinrich Heine, *The Romantic School and Other Essays*, New York: Continuum, 1831/2002, 246.

example, the *freedom* of the people (as in the English Parliament), or their rank and *equality* (as in the French Assembly), which consist of mere formalities.

In the conflict between the fantasy of universal equality and the real world of authority, Kant unequivocally endorsed authority, however unjust, including that of Louis XVI. Progress can only proceed "*from the top downwards.*"[46]

If it is true that the idea of an honorable poverty is no less a "fantasy" today than it was in eighteenth-century Europe, it is due less to the violence with which Robespierre sought to realize it and more to the force of Kant's politics, which have for all intents and purposes become liberal common sense. The concept of equality to which Robespierre turned was clearly built upon the formal abstraction, but it was more than that. It was a product of his pragmatism; not a useful moral guide, but a useful abstraction. It was fluid, opportunistic, and above all "realistic," combining (not without contradiction) a commitment to the formal equality enjoyed by each individual will regardless of one's station in life with a substantive demand for a recognition of the lived constraints on the exercise of equality. This equality, simultaneously radical and liberal, formal and substantive, is the only equality that makes room for an honorable poverty.[47] It is less a "human rights" argument than an effort to adapt liberty to a real world defined by irrepressible necessity, a force of nature itself.

In the face of necessity, artificial scarcity of essential goods like grain is a crime against morality *and* nature. To justify scarcity as the regrettable result of commercial freedom was a stain on the concept

---

46    Immanuel Kant, *Anthropology from a Pragmatic Point of View* [1798], Cambridge: Cambridge University Press, 2002, 75; Immanuel Kant, "Contest of the Faculties," *Political Writings*, 188 (emphasis in the original); compare with Fehér, "Practical Reason in the Revolution"; Lewis Beck, "Kant and the Right of Revolution," *Journal of the History of Ideas* 32: 3, 1971, 411–22; Sidney Axinn, "Kant, Authority and the French Revolution," *Journal of the History of Ideas* 32: 3, 1971, 423–32; Jacques Droz, *L'Allemagne et la Révolution Française*, Paris: Presses Universitaires de France, 1949.

47    This conception is much closer to Hegel than to Kant.

"freedom," if that concept has any foundation in the world in which we actually live:

> Now, what are the means of repressing these abuses? It is said they are impracticable; I maintain they are as simple as they are infallible. It is said the problems are insoluble, even for genius; I maintain they present no difficulty, at least for common sense and good faith; I maintain they injure neither commercial interests nor property rights . . . For the scourge of the people, the source of the scarcity, is the obstacles placed in the way of circulation, under the pretext of rendering it unlimited. Is public subsistence circulating when greedy speculators are keeping it piled up in their granaries? Is it circulating when it is accumulated in the hands of a small number of millionaires who withhold it from the market, to make it more valuable and more scarce; who coldly calculate how many families must starve before they reach a price fixed by their terrible greed? Is it circulating when all it does is cross the regions that produce it, before the very eyes of destitute citizens suffering the tortures of Tantalus, to be swallowed up in the unknown pits of some entrepreneur in public scarcity? Is it circulating when beside the most abundant harvests the needy citizen languishes, unable to give a gold piece or a slip of paper precious enough to purchase a little bit? Circulation is that which puts essential foodstuffs within reach of all men, and carries abundance and life to humble cottages.[48]

This is an eminently practical policy stance, because "in general, there is nothing so just or so good as the people"—except when "irritated by excessive oppression."[49] A "contented people was never a turbulent people."[50] The alternative is that the people must and will rise up, to survive, and to "bring down the brigands."[51] Justice and nature will join forces in the form of necessity.

---

48  Robespierre, "Sur les subsistances," *OC,* IX, 114.
49  Robespierre, "Sur le marc d'argent," *OC,* VII, 166.
50  Robespierre, "Sur les subsistances," *OC,* IX, 116.
51  Robespierre, "Sur les troubles de subsistances," *OC,* VII, 275.

It bears emphasis that while the moment in Robespierre's political career from which these words are drawn (April 1791–April 1793) was certainly marked by increasingly consolidated revolutionary radicalism, it is still quite far from his bloody crescendo in the first half of 1794. In other words, while he was already being labeled a despot and tyrant, there remain in Robespierre's arguments at this point frayed threads of the very politics that eventually brought him down. Those politics and those committed to them—eventually known as Thermidorian, because of the date of Robespierre's arrest and execution—were no less products of the Revolution than the Terror and its commitments. Indeed, one might argue that the most powerful inheritance the French Revolution bequeathed modern liberal capitalism was not the fury of the Terror, but the Thermidorian reaction that ended it.

That reaction has received a little less attention than the Terror and Robespierre in the centuries since, but given the extraordinary volume of scholarship on the French Revolution, this in no way means it has been underexamined. It, too, has been controversial. Was it merely the reassertion of liberal reasonableness, stemming the tide of Jacobin excess? Was it a conjunctural response to developments that had run their course? Or was it an essentially bourgeois dictatorship whose failures inadvertently enabled the triumph of Napoleon in 1799? Was it the realization of counterrevolutionary aims or a "conservative reaction" immanent to the revolution's own dynamic?[52] I would like to set aside the historiographical concerns momentarily, to emphasize Thermidor's political resonance, and in particular its relation to Robespierre's analysis of necessity, scarcity, and "the people."

---

52   Leon Trotsky, *The Revolution Betrayed*, New York: Pathfinder, 1937/1970, 87–89, 105–6; Neil Davidson, *How Bourgeois Were the Bourgeois Revolutions?* Chicago: Haymarket, 2012, 309.

### Necessity After Thermidor

When I first read these passages—"a contented people was never a turbulent people"—from Robespierre's speeches, I thought I had identified a logic from which both Thermidor and radical or even permanent revolution were born. On one hand, they suggest Thermidor was logically consistent with Robespierre's account of the natural and moral priority of necessity to the contentedness of the people and the suppression of the "danger" posed by their deprivation. And while Robespierre's own sentiments are rarely linked to it, it is true that Thermidor is often framed in this manner, that is, that in the interests of necessity and the stability of social order, the Revolution was inevitably sacrificed. As Robespierre himself acknowledged in the Legislative Assembly in 1791, the people did not necessarily need or want Revolution. On the contrary, it "is grateful for the most trivial considerations shown it, the smallest good done for it, even for harm not done to it."[53]

On the other hand, the idea that "a contented people was never a turbulent people" can—and for Robespierre, it seems, did—posit revolution itself as a radical solution to the same problem, an attempt to finally rid the world of the rule of necessity through so perfect and harmonious a virtue that individual needs would be indistinguishable from those of the social whole. It seemed to me that in Robespierre, however briefly, the two politics were twins, or at least siblings. From this moment they parted company, but for an instant they were entangled in one another.

While I still think there is some truth to this, its characterization of the meaning of Thermidor, or what was "really going on," is too clunky. Putting it all down to the "necessity" of stability obviously misses a lot of what was going on and can even be accused of a sort of tendential functionalism, as if things "naturally" revert to equilibrium. Antonio Negri, in contrast, takes the significance of Thermidor to be of an entirely different order, almost endowing it with the status of a theoretical or political category: "Thermidor marked the moment

---

53    Robespierre, "Sur le marc d'argent," *OC*, VII, 166.

at which constituent power realized itself for the purposes of a paradoxical act of self-denial, power realized so as to erase itself immediately after."[54]

The extent to which this claim is historically accurate depends on
the historiographical questions we set aside for the moment. The
extent to which it is politically adequate, however, is not so readily
open to empirical evaluation. Negri does not say so, but it seems safe
to assume he would never suggest that a Thermidorian moment is
inevitable, as if it were the necessary recoil of the Revolutionary gun.
On this account, rather, Thermidor is a conjunctural dynamic immanent to the Revolution itself, evidence neither of a "natural" equilibrating tendency nor an exogenous counterrevolutionary force. This
makes a lot of sense. But it leaves aside a key problem, because recognizing Thermidor's immanence and contingency leaves us no better
apprised of its particular origins or causes. It just tells us where to
look for them. Negri does not indicate how he would respond to the
most immediate questions his concept of Thermidor provokes: Why
would "constituent power" realize itself only to negate itself? What
conditions or objectives could make that make sense?

We can begin by noting that any historical-theoretical category
"Thermidor" takes a limited range of forms in the conditions of
bourgeois revolution, specifically because its effect is always "to secure
the replacement of one ruling class with another."[55] Bourgeois revolution is, in that sense at least, "political" revolution. Moreover, the
fact that no small fraction of the agents of "constituent power" are
bourgeois merchants, smallholders and professionals (even bankers!)
committed to an emergent liberal social order surely distinguishes a
"bourgeois revolution" from peasant-based contexts, for example.
Taking the role of the bourgeoisie seriously—as Robespierre himself
certainly did—we can tentatively propose some responses to the
questions above. First, "constituent power" might negate itself when

---

54    "Thermidor représentait le moment où le pouvoir constituant se réalisait pour que
l'on puisse paradoxalement le nier, l'effacer immédiatement après"; Antonio Negri, "La
démocratie contre la rente," *Multitudes* 1: 32, 2008, 127.

55    Davidson, *How Bourgeois Were the Bourgeois Revolutions?* 71.

its own power poses an obstacle to the realization of its goals. In other words, Thermidor for Negri is a politics for those who understand the Revolution as having gone too far, as something of which they have lost control. In this sense, it need not mark a moment of apocalyptic violence or terror, but only a recognition that the constructive work required of the revolution has already been completed. What follows can only be destructive. Thermidor hands the Revolutionary reins to forces deemed capable of stopping the horse, even turning it around.

This is partially confirmed by events in France. Aware of both rapidly dwindling popular support for the Terror and the weakening of Robespierre's personal political foundations, the bourgeoisie of the Jacobin and non-Jacobin camps (the Gironde had been eliminated by mid-1793) took control in an attempt to roll back the Revolution to within the limits it had originally intended. These bourgeois revolutionaries had cringed to find themselves sitting in the Convention, listening to Robespierre attack them for "degrading the vast majority of the human race with the words 'rabble' and 'masses,'" reminding them that "we"—the members of the Convention—"are the sans-culottes and the rabble."[56] The point for them had never been mass democracy, universal citizenship, and the end of wealth and privilege. It had always been to found what Domenico Losurdo calls the "community of the free," in which class, race, regional and imperial distinctions would most certainly remain.[57] Robespierre was absolutely correct to denounce them for "designating by the word 'people' a separate class of men, which they associate with a certain idea of inferiority and contempt"; he reminded them that their system, "the system we are attacking, proscribes nine-tenths of the nation."[58]

The Revolution had thus become not only no longer useful, it had actually abetted a power that could no longer be wielded

---

56  Robespierre, "Sur le marc d'argent," *OC*, VII, 166; "Sur l'influence de la calomnie sur la Révolution," October 28, 1792, *OC*, IX, 59.

57  Domenico Losurdo, *Liberalism: A Counter-History*, New York: Verso, 2011.

58  Robespierre, "Sur le marc d'argent," *OC*, VII, 167.

productively. Given the opportunity to re-assert the limits of the "community of the free" that had always been the bourgeoisie's objective, it did so. Thermidor was "above all the moment [in the Revolution] when those who had inspired it and participated in it declared they did not wish to begin its history anew or relive their experience."[59]

But the result was not the self-erasure or negation Negri suggests, because the "constituent power" at the heart of the Revolution was never as unified nor as "humble" as Robespierre hoped. It was neither of "one will," nor was it only "the people," but included elites who were not mere witnesses to a popular uprising but were themselves revolutionary. Robespierre himself knew this well and was constantly wary of its reactionary potential. As he said to the Jacobin Club in early 1792:

> Alongside yourselves, it is the parliaments, the nobility, the clergy, the rich that set the revolution in motion; only afterwards did the people arrive. Then, when they saw that the people could recover their sovereignty, they changed their minds, or at least wanted to stop the revolution. But it was they who had started it; without their resistance and their mistaken calculations, the nation would still be under the yoke of despotism.[60]

For much of the bourgeoisie, then, Thermidor was far from a moment of self-denial or erasure. It was closer to something like the victorious consolidation of a short-term hegemony, if such a thing is possible. It was hegemonic insofar as the Thermidorians were granted significant (short-term) legitimacy by the fact that the much broader revolutionary constituency, in the cities and the countryside, could no longer tolerate the violence and fear the Terror precipitated. Their interests were the general interests.

But it was inevitably short-term because this moment of conjuncture, in which the elimination of Robespierre enjoyed mass support,

---

59  Bronislaw Baczko, "Thermidorians," in F. Furet and M. Ozouf (eds.), *A Critical Dictionary of the French Revolution*, Cambridge: Harvard University Press, 1989, 412.

60  Robespierre, "Sur la guerre," January 2, 1792, *OC*, VIII, 83.

or at least minimal mass opposition, obscured the fundamentally elite bourgeois politics of Thermidor. Following the rise to power of the Committee of Public Safety and then the acceleration of the Terror—and the increasingly radical violence to which the Revolution turned—the post-Terror relationship itself only came to rest on a superficial relative peace between "the people" and elites, based in a common desire for revenge. That peace could never last. Not only was it dependent on a new cycle of largely anti-Jacobin violence, but, just as they always had, elites understood the people to have no stakes in a stable peace in and of itself. For them, the masses—and this was of course the problem Robespierre had identified in the Revolution all along—had "nothing to lose." They were always ready to explode. That was how all the trouble had started. Revolution had derailed the Revolution.

Consequently, if there was a bourgeois variation on self-denial in Thermidor, it was what we would now call distinctively liberal: knowing that revolutionary democracy handed power to benighted plebeians—and convinced that was the source of the problem—the Thermidorian Convention organized around a categorical rejection of mass politics. Instead, it turned to a model of "government of the nation by the best," men (all men) who, by property and education, had a stake in a stable social order. Politics and political society became a quasi-professional realm, one which required expertise, training. It seemed the only way to bring the Revolution to a close. This turn was not merely strategically expedient, but was also as much a product of Enlightenment reason as any other feature of revolutionary ideology and practice.

For our purposes, the essential lesson of the Thermidorian reabsorption of the Revolution is not, therefore, to be found in constituent power's paradoxical act of self-negation. Rather, Thermidor is important because it marks a categorical rejection of the possibility of an honorable poverty in the emerging bourgeois-liberal order: the negation of one constituent class by the power of another, and modern liberalism's constitution—in its very origins—in mass disfranchisement. For the Thermidorians, the Terror exposed honorable poverty as dangerous mythology, all the more destructive because the poor themselves had come to believe it. In the new order, there could be no right to necessity, no equality to which liberty must accommodate itself. The poor—"the people," the mob, the rabble, [*la canaille*]—had no honor, and there was no honor in poverty.

Robespierre might have berated them for their "delirious" fear that the Revolution made it possible that "people who have nothing to lose will then be able, like us, to exercise the rights of citizens." He may have ridiculed them for their "arrogant" denial that for the poor,

> the rough clothes that cover me, the humble room I buy for the right to retire and live in peace, the modest wage with which I feed my wife, my children; all this, I admit, is far from lands, mansions, carriages; all of it amounts to nothing perhaps, to those accustomed to luxury and opulence, but it is something to humanity: it is sacred property, without doubt as sacred as the brilliant domain of wealth.[61]

But in the eyes of the bourgeois of Thermidor, history had proved him disastrously wrong and their fears fully justified.

The idea or promise of an honorable poverty thus became a kind of abandoned terrain or no-man's-land after the Revolution. It was the ground from which everyone fled: Robespierre and his allies went one way, to a revolutionary violence that would erase poverty by eliminating counterrevolution and purifying the nation, while the ex-revolutionary bourgeoisie went another, to a narrowly defined honor among the propertied and educated "community of the free."

### Trust in "The People"?

Alain Badiou and Slavoj Žižek both argue that the stakes in these politics—"confidence in the masses" (Badiou) or "trust in the people" (Žižek)—are at the very heart of revolutionary ideology. Žižek is quick to acknowledge that much rests on what exactly we mean by

---

61  Robespierre, "Sur le marc d'argent," *OC*, VII, 164.

"the people," but both he and Badiou use the term just as Robespierre did—to describe a seamless whole. (Recall that Robespierre used the pronoun "it," not "they.")[62]

Yet because they both, like Negri, set out to reveal what they posit as the "truth" of the people's revolutionary potential, Badiou and Žižek repress two crucial questions that, however much we might try to wish them away, seem hard to avoid, both politically-theoretically and in the actual historical unfolding of revolutionary moments. First: to whom is the injunction to "trust in the people" addressed? One reading would suggest it is addressed to the people. The people should trust in the people! I do not believe this is accurate. In fact, Badiou's and Žižek's addressees, those enjoined to trust in the people, are not *of* the people. They are, rather, those who would not, in general, trust in the people: those who see themselves as above, or at least distant from, the people. They are not those who hate the people, or who refuse the very idea of the people, but those who would manage the people, who want to secure the people's freedom, but cannot trust the people to do so. They are Keynesians, or radicals harboring a secret Keynesianism.

Second: Trust in the people unquestioningly? No matter where they lead us? It is true that any dedication to an honorable poverty implies a trust in the people, but what is less clear is which comes first: honorable poverty, or trust in the people? Is the former the best basis for the latter, or vice versa? Even Robespierre frequently contradicted himself on this question. Do we trust the people simply because of their inherent "dignity," their "natural goodness [*bonté naturelle*]"?[63] Or do we ensure the people are trustworthy by recognizing necessity, guaranteeing everyone "something to lose or preserve"? "It's far better to render poverty honorable than to outlaw opulence; the cottage of Fabricius has nothing to envy of the palace of Crassus."[64]

---

62 Alain Badiou, *Logics of Worlds*, New York: Continuum, 2009, 23; Slavoj Žižek, *The Parallax View*, Cambridge: MIT Press, 2009, 379. Robespierre referred to "the people [*le peuple*]" with the pronoun *il*, which in this context means "it," not "he."

63 Robespierre, "Sur le marc d'argent," *OC*, VII, 164, 167.

64 Robespierre, April 24, 1793, *OC*, IX, 459: "*il s'agit bien plus de rendre la pauvreté*

In other words, do we embrace a kind of revolutionary faith in the incontrovertible truth of the will of "the people," or do we work with the notion (as Robespierre occasionally said, and the Thermidorians took as fact) that only those recognized as having an adequate stake in society can be trusted to construct and maintain it? That liberals have opted for the latter since the very birth of liberalism in the revolutionary era is one of the illiberal truths of liberalism. The story of that choice—which since Robespierre is a choice always made in the shadow of the Terror—and the brutal manner in which individuals and groups and large portions of the world have been denied a stake is what Domenico Losurdo calls the "counter-history" of liberalism.[65]

I am purposefully avoiding the word "reform" or "reformism" to describe this stance, through which the "community of the free" gradually embraces those granted enough of a stake in civilization to be deemed worthy of freedom or "trust." Reformism in some form might very well describe a common dynamic in liberalism, but in itself the concept is substantively empty. It is neutral as to political aims, ideology, or institutional organization. All it assumes is that they are reasonably fixed; whatever the politics, so long as one remains within its own self-determined limits, any adjustment is reformist. Its ideological "mass," as it were, is nil. This is why the standard IMF term for the capital-friendly policy conditions imposed by its lending is "reforms," while some on the left can accuse insufficiently radical others of "reformism."[66] The term can do all this work because it says so little. If reaction and revolution

---

*honorable, que de proscrire l'opulence; la chaumière de Fabricius n'a rien à envier au palais de Crassus."* Fabricius was a celebrated third-century BCE Roman consul, lauded in Dante's *Purgatory*: "Oh good Fabricius, you chose to possess virtue with poverty instead of great wealth with iniquity" (Canto XX, 25–27, trans. W. S. Merwin, New York: Knopf, 2001, 193). Crassus, a consul of the first century BCE (and, with Caesar and Pompey, a member of the triumvirate) is commonly thought to have been the richest person in the Roman Empire. He was also, as Robespierre knew, the leader of the army that crushed Spartacus's slave rebellion in 71 BCE.

65  Losurdo, *Liberalism*.

66  This is to say nothing of the way the term became a tool for critical dismissal on the left.

are indeed moments in a dialectic, "reform" can tell us very little about its development. Indeed, I have a suspicion it is barely involved.

The political path obscured or oversimplified by this oppositional framing—the Hegelian or Keynesian path—is commonly mischaracterized as "reformist." But it is definitely not. It is an immanent critique of both liberalism and radicalism at the same time. This path, a dialectical or quasi-dialectical development, drops out of view when we parse history into reaction, revolution, and their mediation in "reform." If a dialectical sensibility is any help here, it is not through an analysis of some supposedly "synthetic" reformism. Instead, it is because of its capacity to at least remind us of a political path that, however successfully or unsuccessfully, attempts to overcome ("sublate," as Hegel's *aufgehoben* is often translated) the opposition with which the Revolution appears to leave us: bourgeois Stability versus radical Terror and Truth; roll back the revolution or follow it through to the bloody end. If both these paths are genetically infrarevolutionary—in other words, if they arise immanent to the revolutionary dynamic—the critique that embodies their dialectical outcome is necessarily postrevolutionary. It is only conceivable retrospectively, after history has mapped a revolutionary terrain.

This is the Keynesian vista, and from it both original paths appear doomed. On the radical side, the legacy of the Terror seems to delegitimize every way forward. Who in their right minds would "trust in the people" after that? On the reactionary side, inequality and endless accumulation constantly threaten the social fabric and lead to nothing but dictatorship or chaos and disorder, or both. From within the revolution, it seems, the way forward leads to Stalin, the way back to feudalism.

The alternative Keynesians posit to escape this trap becomes visible for those whom this vista enables what they take to be an understanding of the world as it "actually" is. Their eyes are not clouded by radicalism, liberalism, or conservatism. They see through the flimsy historical foundations of a meritocracy of the victors. They recognize the "modern community's" "arbitrary and inequitable distribution of wealth and incomes."[67] They accept, reluctantly, the historical and political legitimacy of both reaction and revolution. They "understand" both impulses and suggest that their supersession—not a compromise—lights the only possible route to honorable poverty in a bourgeois order.

If the history of the revolution is the trajectory of a political dynamic that rocketed skyward only to plummet back to earth by the gravity of Terror and reaction, honorable poverty is its zenith. It is the peak of a development that liberalism and radicalism together make possible, and Keynesianism is the political project to isolate that instant, to defy the gravity of uncertainty, fear, and ideology in a political economy that does not have to fall to earth. It is an effort to shorten the temporal units of history and thus deny the effective force of the long run. It is, as it were, an asymptotic politics, promising to forever approach, instant by instant, a prosperous shared stability. It refuses the radical "illusion" that civilization is compatible with equality—and thus rejects the idea that one can rid a civilized world of poverty—but it holds out the prospect of a poverty by which the poor are not dishonored, because they are not responsible for it.

This prospect hinges on the categorical rejection of an essential component of liberal ideology—the principle of scarcity. The legitimacy of the Revolution is founded, as Robespierre said, in the fact that scarcity is neither inevitable nor natural. It is socially produced, and as such, both morally indefensible and politically disastrous. For the Keynesian this is not an endorsement of radical redistribution. Far from it. But it is a rejection of the liberal proposition that a necessary corollary of meritocracy is the threat of starvation. Keynes would have agreed wholeheartedly with Robespierre that if freedom of trade required "bayonets to calm fears or appease hunger," then we have missed the "real principle": "For my own part, I believe that there is social and psychological justification for significant inequalities of incomes and wealth, but not for such large disparities as exist to-day."[68]

---

67  John Maynard Keynes, *Collected Writings*, vol. VII, Cambridge: Cambridge University Press, 1971–1989, 372.

68  Ibid., 374.

If capitalist society rejects a more equal distribution of incomes and the forces of banking and finance succeed in maintaining the rate of interest somewhere near the figure which ruled on the average during the nineteenth century (which was, by the way, a little *lower* than the rate of interest which rules today), then a chronic tendency towards the underemployment of resources must in the end sap and destroy that form of society.[69]

The possibility of an honorable poverty then—one in which having less, perhaps even almost nothing, still carries dignity—demands an attack on scarcity, in the interests of a social stability in which all have an interest. But it is not merely that "we" (the privileged subject implicit in liberal discourse, those whom Badiou and Žižek admonish to "trust in the people") have an interest in "their" subsistence for our own sakes. Rather, the concept of an honorable poverty assumes what Robespierre also knew: that there was no Reason in, and no reason for, "the people" having "nothing to lose":

> These people of whom you speak are, apparently, men who live, who subsist in the midst of society, without any means to live and subsist. So if they are provided with those means, they have, it seems to me, something to lose or preserve.[70]

If the liberalism of the classical era—epitomized by Keynes's theoretical nemesis Ricardo—dismisses this possibility, it dismisses honorable poverty as well. Keynesianism, in contrast, is constituted in part in an effort to carve out a space for it, a space liberalism denies it. In this sense, at least, it is genuinely—if asymptotically—more hopeful and utopian than the radical Left usually admits.

However, if Keynesianism is an immanent critique of liberalism's understanding of scarcity, it is at the same time a critique of the revolutionary imperative to trust in the people. No Keynesian, Keynes included, trusts in the people on principle. For Keynesians, the

---

69   Keynes, *Collected Writings*, vol. XIV, 132.
70   Robespierre, "Sur le marc d'argent," *OC*, VII, 164.

people themselves, in their ignorance, bitterness, and despair—however justifiable—are their own (and everyone's) worse enemy. Keynesians adopt without question the liberal perspective that civilization is an elite bourgeois project. This is why an illiberal honorable poverty is so essential to the Keynesian program. It is also why Keynesianism is a distinctively postrevolutionary politics and political economy. It is only possible after the Revolution, since it is a product of neither one "side" or the other, but of an analysis of the failures and truths of both.[71] It aims to walk the tightrope from which Thermidor fell one way and Robespierre the other.

---

71   Arguing against the common assumption that G. E. Moore shaped Keynes's mature ideas, David Andrews says that Keynes's effort to see the truths in apparently incommensurable ideas marks him as a "Coleridgean" (and links this quality in Samuel Taylor Coleridge to Hegel also); David Andrews, *Keynes and the British Humanist Tradition*, London: Routledge, 2010, 11–16, 126–31.

CHAPTER 5

# Freedom After Revolution

This is how Hegel comes to be crucial to the development of the Keynesian vista: through his fundamental contribution to the struggle to come to grips, *conceptually*, with the French Revolution and with the post-Robespierre, post-Thermidorian moment. In his political philosophy, elaborated most fully in the *Philosophy of Right* (1821), he lays out both the rationale for, and the conceptual and institutional implications of, Keynesianism's postrevolutionary reason.[1] For Hegel, this task was necessitated by the vacuum in European political imagination, especially after the fall of Napoleon, which he and many others understood as the closure—long past the point of no return—of the Revolutionary era. That vacuum seemed to open a chasm into which Europe, and Germany in particular, threatened to tumble, swallowed up either by the Scylla of a delusional but resurgent feudal absolutism that history rendered destined to fail, or by the Charybdis of the social disorder created by the *tabula rasa* politics he associated with Jacobin "popular sovereignty." Both terrified him.

The solution, as Hegel saw it, lay in holding on to those threads of the social fabric, woven by history and custom, which allowed for communities to persist and thrive, while also embracing the new

---

1   G. W. F. Hegel, *Elements of the Philosophy of Right*, trans. H. B. Nisbet, Cambridge: Cambridge University Press, 1991. (Hereinafter cited as *PhR*.)

dynamics unleashed by the unfolding of freedom that defined modern life as such. The dream of rolling political life back to tradition ("positivity") was in his eyes both foolish and impossible.[2] But so too was the *ab nihilo* construction of a "new society" or a "new man." He was thoroughly "anti-utopian."[3] As he said of the Revolution:

> when these abstractions are invested with power, they afforded the tremendous spectacle, for the first time we know of in human history, of the overthrowing of all existing conditions within an actual major state and the revision of its constitution from first principles and purely in terms of *thought*; the *intention* behind this was to give it what was *supposed* to be a purely *rational* basis. On the other hand, since these were only abstractions divorced from the Idea, they turned the attempt into the most terrible and drastic event.[4]

The problem the Revolution posed, then, was on what basis to ground freedom; it could not remain abstract or, in Hegel's terms, "one-sided." Concrete (or more-than-one-sided) freedom must also recognize necessity.

This chapter and the next examine in some detail Hegel's thoughts on freedom and necessity in the wake of the Revolution. The manner in which events had unfolded in France seemed to many to demonstrate conclusively that the two were forever in contradiction. Freedom had, it seemed, denied necessity, only to discover its irrepressibility, while necessity had not only negated freedom but had in fact obliterated it in the name of a supposedly more "virtuous" freedom. Hegel too could see the logic of this argument, but (like

---

2  Terry Pinkard, *Hegel: A Biography*, Cambridge: Cambridge University Press, 2000, 407.

3  J. J. Drydyk, "Who Is Fooled By the 'Cunning of Reason'?" *History and Theory* 24: 2, 1985, 152.

4  Hegel, *PhR*, §258R. Forgive the gendered "new man," but to say "person," "human," or "individual" would misconstrue Hegel's undeniably gendered thoughts on the matter.

Keynes), while he was always aware "the world was in danger of falling apart right before his eyes," he absolutely refused its inevitability.[5] "His thought as a whole is cunning; it hopes to achieve victory over the superior power of the world, about which it has no illusions."[6] Modern governmentality, he argued, had the conceptual and institutional tools to overcome this tendency.

## Hegel and (the) Revolution

I am far from the first to argue that Hegel's work can only be understood in the context of (the French) Revolution. Joachim Ritter claims that "there is no other philosophy that is a philosophy of revolution to such a degree and so profoundly, in its innermost drive, as that of Hegel," and Charles Taylor maintained that "Revolutions are only understood and justified by reason *ex post facto* . . . [and] Hegel's philosophy is as it were a defense of the Revolution after the event."[7] There is, in addition, a small but growing series of studies arguing that the Haitian Revolution was also essential to his thinking.[8] But while we have come to recognize the centrality of revolution to Hegel's thought—in the broad sense of revolution mobilized in Chapter 3—what one might call the "Adorno problem" remains

---

5   Pinkard, *Hegel*, 633.

6   Theodor Adorno, *Hegel: Three Studies*, trans. Sherry Weber Nicholsen, Cambridge: MIT Press, 1993, 42–43.

7   Joachim Ritter, *Hegel and the French Revolution*, Cambridge: MIT Press, 1982, 43; Charles Taylor, *Hegel*, Cambridge: Cambridge University Press, 1975, 425. The following account is greatly informed by Ritter and Taylor, and also by Manfred Riedel, *Between Tradition and Revolution: The Hegelian Transformation of Political Philosophy*, trans. W. Wright, Cambridge: Cambridge University Press, 1984; Eric Weil, *Hegel and the State*, trans. Mark Cohen, Baltimore: Johns Hopkins University Press, 1998; Rebecca Comay, *Mourning Sickness: Hegel and the French Revolution*, Stanford: Stanford University Press, 2011; and Slavoj Žižek, *Less Than Nothing: Hegel and the Shadow of Dialectical Materialism*, London: Verso, 2012, especially 240–64.

8   Susan Buck-Morss, "Hegel and Haiti," *Critical Inquiry* 26, 2000, 821–65; Sybille Fischer, *Modernity Disavowed: Haiti and the Cultures of Slavery in the Age of Revolution*, Durham: Duke University Press, 2004, 24–33; Nick Nesbitt, *Universal Emancipation: The Haitian Revolution and the Radical Enlightenment*, Charlottesville: University of Virginia Press, 2008, 113–24.

relatively underexamined. Which is to say that the question is not just how revolution shaped Hegel's thought, but how Hegel's thought shaped revolution and our conception of it.[9] Because, as Hannah Arendt put it, all the revolutionaries of the nineteenth and twentieth centuries, "even if they did not learn their lessons from Marx (still the greatest pupil Hegel ever had) and never bothered to read Hegel, looked upon revolution through Hegelian categories."[10]

No one has argued more powerfully, more insistently, than Hegel that the revolution was one of ideas.

> As long as the sun has stood in the firmament and the planets have circled around it, it has never [before] been known for man to stand on his head, that is on his thoughts, and construct reality in accordance with them.[11]

But it is crucial to note that his views are not captured by the common dismissiveness with which he is accused of "idealism." The term "idealist" can characterize his thought in a historically specific manner, in which ideas emerge and change in the midst of inescapably politicized and material worlds. The Revolution, he said, embodied the contradictory truths of enlightenment rationalism, and in so doing, it both realized its world-historic potential and exposed its inevitable and deadly limits.[12]

Hegel's judgment, however, is not condemnation, but rather a measured assessment of the consequences for the world of the thought through which it unfolds. Despite two centuries of mischaracterization as an "organicist" mystic, at no point does Hegel write off the capital-R Reason on which modernity is to be founded.

---

9    Adorno, *Hegel*, 1: "arrogance echoes in the loathsome question of what in Kant, and now Hegel as well, has any meaning for the present . . . The converse question is not even raised: what the present means in the face of Hegel."

10    Hannah Arendt, *On Revolution*, New York: Penguin, 2006, 44.

11    Quoted in Riedel, *Between Tradition and Revolution*, 40.

12    For a recent account that emphasizes the Revolution's idealist sources, see Jonathan Israel, *Revolutionary Ideas: An Intellectual History of the French Revolution from the Rights of Man to Robespierre*, Princeton: Princeton University Press, 2014; Hegel is briefly mentioned on 333–34.

Nowhere are the justly celebrated liberty of the individual and the emergence of a "civil society" beyond the sway of the state disavowed. On the contrary, Hegel credits Kant and Rousseau with placing the identity of freedom and reason at the heart of modern life: "[m]an is not free, when he is not thinking."[13] With enlightenment came science and the "discovery of the laws of Nature"; "all miracles were disallowed." This knowledge is what "received the name of *Reason*. The recognition of the validity of these laws was designated *enlightenment [Aufklärung]*," perhaps the supreme achievement of historical development: "a glorious mental dawn. All thinking beings shared in the jubilation of this epoch."[14]

Yet, as for all things in Hegel's eyes, these welcome contributions cannot be contained in one "moment" of time and space, nor can their evolving meaning be determined by their origins. His critique of Kant and Rousseau—and, therefore, of the revolutionary world they helped constitute—rests on the claim that, for all its merits, "modern reason foundered on the rock of reality."[15] Contrary to what Kant and many Kantians since have emphasized, the problem with "pure reason" is not that our concepts are inadequate to a world we can never fully grasp.[16] The problem is that, however "transcendentally" constructed, the enlightenment Reason of Kant and Rousseau is one-sided. Refusing (for very different reasons) the inevitability of Hobbes's version of "human nature" (the base drives that, if not subdued, generate a desperate "state of nature"), they both posit modern subjectivity as a product of the rational will alone.

---

13  G. W. F. Hegel, *The Philosophy of History*, trans. J. Sibree, New York: Dover, 1959, 439. (Hereinafter cited as *PhH*.)

14  Ibid., 440–41. For Hegel, however much Haiti and colonialism matter to the era in which political economy consolidated as a "modern science"—Haiti, for example, was the source of a significant fraction of the French bourgeoisie's wealth—they did so explicitly as a response not to colonialism, but to the French Revolution. When Hegel wrote that the "important question of how poverty can be remedied is one which agitates and torments modern societies especially," and thus that political economy is the science of "modern societies," he did not understand Haiti as a modern society.

15  Arendt, *Human Condition*, 301.

16  Immanuel Kant, *Critique of Pure Reason*, Cambridge: Cambridge University Press, 1998, 377: The problem with the "pure reason" espoused by Leibniz is that "nothing is allowed to the thing beyond what is contained in the concept."

Kant, Hegel said, argued that since Reason is limited in its capacity to understand the world in its fullness, unable to see beyond phenomena, the only truth Reason can wholly know is imminent to the subject himself or herself. The only thing completely subject to the imperatives of a fully rational will is human subjectivity. The rational will is thus anchored in a "radical moral autonomy"; objective comprehension cannot be anything more than subjective perception.[17] Consequently—and this for Hegel is Kant's great failure—the "is" becomes the "ought." The result is that the identity of freedom and thought is realized in a universalizing moral code produced not in the social world (with others in the times and places where it must be put to work) but in the abstract reflections of the autonomous, inward-looking subject.

To Hegel, then, Kant's and Rousseau's enlightenment produced a woefully inadequate conception of human interaction, stuck in the realm of abstraction—only half a truth, one might say. Despite his still-common dismissal as an idealist (a term which obscures as much as it clarifies in Hegel), he posited that reason can find no purchase when it does not connect with a grounded community's ethics, histories, and ways of living. These inform social worlds that are by definition historically and geographically embedded, but also dynamic, differentiated, and subject to multiple influences. Thus, however well-intentioned, the Kantian effort to discover a perfectly consistent, rational, and universal Truth in the mind of each and every individual is not only impossible, but also virtually certain to fail disastrously. Purposefully rejecting any consideration of actuality, what Keynes called "the world in which we actually live"—because its truth was supposedly beyond our intellectual reach—Kant could never provide anything but an "empty formalism."[18]

As Charles Taylor puts it, Hegel believes Kant's moral autonomy was "purchased at the price of vacuity." Formal abstraction means his account can only stay at the "edges of politics." It can only function as a moral guardrail, "setting limits beyond which states or

17   Taylor, *Hegel*, 369–70.
18   Hegel, *PhR*, §135.

individuals should not tread."[19] It outlines the formal contractual social bond between free-thinking autonomous individuals, but it cannot give the social life any content, it cannot account for the world in which people have no choice but to actually live. As Hegel sees it, only politics—which we might call reason at work in the "real world"—can do that. Freedom is not the exercise of individual moral autonomy. On the contrary, it is nothing if not a "structure of social interaction"; it can only exist in a "true and proper ground" which is always already social.[20] The priority of the concrete in this sense is what leads Hegel to reject Kant's elevation of *Moralität* (rationally correct morality) over *Sittlichkeit* (ethics grounded in custom).

### Morality, Custom and Freedom

Those familiar with the ABCs of Hegel will recognize *Sittlichkeit* as one of his keywords; we might be forgiven for sometimes thinking it is the be-all and end-all of his political theory, a kind of Holy Grail in which the Particular recognizes itself in the Universal, the Universal embraces the Particular, and all is One in The Notion. Although there are elements of truth to that interpretation, it is more likely to lead to misunderstanding. *Sittlichkeit* (literally, "ethical-ness") is often translated as "ethical life," but that cannot do it justice, since it fails to emphasize what we might call the irreducible "groundedness" attached to *Sitten*. Indeed, German has a perfectly good word for "ethics" in the common English sense of "principles of action"— *Ethik*—and Hegel does not use it. *Sitten* means "mores" as they hold meaning through the social customs of a particular community. In German, for example, the phrase "dos and don'ts" is *Sitten und Unsitten*; the colloquial equivalent of "When in Rome, do as Romans do" is "*Andere Länder, andere Sitten*."[21] *Sittlichkeit* is not about being

---

19    Taylor, *Hegel*, 370, 376.
20    Hegel, *PhR*, §71.
21    Literally, "other lands, other ways."

Right or Just in the light of abstract Reason, but about being true to, and morally committed to, an actually existing history and geography, a community and its way of life.

In other words, *Sitten* is at least as close to the English idea of "convention," or even "cultural norms," as it is to "ethics." This is the *Sittlichkeit* Hegel endorses against an unmoored Kantian moral Right.

> "*Sittlichkeit*" refers to the moral obligations I have to an ongoing community of which I am part. These obligations are based on established norms and uses, and that is why the etymological root in "Sitten" is important for Hegel's use. The crucial characteristic of *Sittlichkeit* is that it enjoins us to bring about what already is . . . [T]he common life which is the basis of my *sittlich* obligation is already there in existence. It is in virtue of its being an ongoing affair that I have these obligations; and my fulfillment of these obligations is what sustains it and keeps it in being.[22]

Kant, however, "cannot escape from the dualism of inner morality and the outer reality facing it.[23] He gets hung up on the "ought," and cannot, as it were, follow through. With Hegel, in *Sittlichkeit* the gap between "is" and "ought"—*Sein* and *Sollen*, a difference inscribed in the very foundations of Kantian Reason—is denied.[24] To put it perhaps a little too simply, Hegelian reason is rationality that holds for the dynamic reality it confronts. Reason that can only hold in a world that *ought* to be can hardly make sense of, and may well wreak havoc upon, the world that actually *is*.

Consequently, for Hegel the inescapable task of modern life is "the political realization of freedom," that is, freedom grounded in the concrete practices of social life.[25] On these grounds, the failure of the French Revolution lay in the fact that the revolutionaries

---

22   Taylor, *Hegel*, 376.

23   Ritter, *Hegel and the French Revolution*, 158; compare with Györg Lukács, *History and Class Consciousness*, Cambridge: MIT Press, 1971, 161.

24   Taylor, *Hegel*, 376.

25   Ritter, *Hegel and the French Revolution*, 47.

eventually fell for what Stathis Kouvelakis calls "the Kantian political illusion": the blind pursuit of a sublime "absolute freedom," dislodged from history and geography. That is to say, for Hegel "the French Revolution was Kantian."[26] Havoc—disorder, violence, fanaticism— is Hegel's ultimate assessment of the Terror, the outcome of the Revolution's attempt to reconstitute, by any means necessary, the actual on the basis of pure Reason. The Terror thus represents a complete inversion of the Revolution's original principles.

Hegel associates this disastrous turn with forces unwittingly unleashed by Rousseau. Rousseau's great achievement, giving him a place among the great thinkers of freedom, was "to put forward the *will* as the principle of the state," a principle in which thought is both form and content, "which is in fact *thinking* itself."[27] In other words, Rousseau's contribution to modernity is to show that the state is neither "natural" nor "arbitrary," as absolutism would have it. It is a vehicle of social purpose, the means to collective freedom. This great contribution, however, is marred by a terrible error. Rousseau misunderstood the essentially distinct ontological status of the universal dimension of the collective. He did not recognize that the "general will" is more and other than the aggregate of many identical wills. Rousseau—and the revolutionary Jacobins after him—confused the universal element of the social fabric with the mere "*common element*" of all individual wills. The universal or general on this account is nothing "above," "better," or even "other" than the enumerated serial multitude, and the "general will" is nothing more than an accumulated homogeneous mass, an aggregate of all consensual wills.

This precipitates a political calamity. For what binds the collective is thus no "higher" or distinct social interest. It is just a set of simple individual "contracts," based on the arbitrary will and opinions of the many and on the "express consent" of each counterparty. Each individual constituent seeks, through the contract, the realization of a formal Kantian freedom with no concrete grounding in life as it is

---

26  Stathis Kouvelakis, *Philosophy and Revolution: From Marx to Kant*, trans. G. M. Goshgarian, New York: Verso, 2003, 26.

27  Hegel, *PhR*, §258R.

actually lived. By 1794, even though they are not Kantians, the one-sidedness of Kant's Pure Reason is the only "freedom" of which the revolutionaries can conceive: "what was *supposed* to be a purely *rational* basis . . . turned the attempt into the most terrible and drastic event."[28] Thus, formal freedom, for Hegel, is the historically limited origin of what the French Revolution achieved as well as all it failed to achieve. It marks the Revolution as simultaneously a "glorious mental dawn" and as the origin of blood-soaked Terror. On one hand, it is the point at which humanity "had advanced to the recognition of the principle that Thought ought to govern spiritual reality"[29]; on the other, Thought remained "without execution," the basis of an "absolute freedom" with no ground in the concreteness of social life.[30]

Hegel is at pains to point out that these developments were by no means challenges that communities must inevitably face, as each must go through a phase of terror in some twisted stage of modernization. Rather, they are the product of particular histories and geographies: *Sitten* are necessarily the grounds of concrete freedom, and they also present it with its most intractable challenges. The particularly "terrible" path traced by the Revolution was for Hegel largely attributable to the fact that it was *French*. The Germans had of course also experienced Enlightenment—it is Kant who is often credited with designating it *Aufklärung*—but in contrast to the French, among the Germans "formal freedom" in the shape of the "*Kantian* Philosophy" "assumed no other form than that of tranquil theory." Without the "tranquil confidence" bequeathed to Germany by the Protestant Reformation, rendering it "so far advanced in Thought," the French fell victim to the Kantian illusion, and could not resist the desire to give formal freedom "practical effect."[31]

---

28    Hegel, *PhR*, §258R; compare with Hegel, *Phenomenology of Spirit*, trans. A. V. Miller, Oxford: Clarendon Press, 1979, §§582–95. (Hereinafter cited as *PhS*.)

29    Hegel, *PhH*, 440.

30    Hegel, *PhR*, §71.

31    Hegel, *PhH*, 443–44. This account draws on Kouvelakis, *Philosophy and Revolution*, 26. Habermas has long adopted this Hegelian assessment of the Revolution as his own. Indeed, one expects it might be one of the main reasons Hegel has attracted so

This is an almost paradigmatic instance of "idealism" as the term is usually thrown at Hegel. He argues that "from this inner revolution there emerges the actual revolution of the actual world."[32] In the French effort to realize in society the principle of Kantian "radical moral autonomy," philosophy was the "impulse" for the Revolution.[33] The problem is that in France, freedom was thus grounded in *Moralität*, not *Sittlichkeit*; "only abstract Thought, not the concrete comprehension of absolute Truth—intellectual positions between which there is an immeasurable chasm."[34] In other words, the principle of *Moralität*, a product of Enlightenment, suggests that freedom and society—into which humans freely enter—rest solely on a reason whose only basis is human will.

For Hegel, this attempt to realize "absolute freedom" is doomed to become its opposite. His argument as to why this is the case is fascinating, at least partly because it does not seem so far-fetched today. The inversion comes about because, insofar as individuals must enter into society entirely of their own will, society must be solely and equally the product of its members' radical exercise of liberty. Everything in it must constantly be made "from scratch," since all dimensions of society must therefore be a product of the equal participation of all and must constantly be subject to universal decision. Such a society categorically rejects anything Hegel calls "positive," that is, already existing or given. All social structures must be the product of a kind of "total democracy," a social unanimity that must hold if no citizen's freedom or radical autonomy is to be

---

much of his attention over the years. Jürgen Habermas, "Appendix I: Popular Sovereignty as Procedure," in *Between Facts and Norms: Contributions to a Discourse Theory of Law and Democracy*, trans. William Rehg, Cambridge: MIT Press, 1998, 489: "the instrumentalism underlying a practice that directly attempts to realize theory has had disastrous effects. Robespierre already set up an opposition between revolution and constitution: the Revolution exists for war and civil war, the Constitution for victorious peace."

32   Hegel, *PhS*, §582.

33   Alan Ryan tells us that it "goes without saying" that "Hegel in effect stalks Kant throughout the *Philosophy of Right*"; Alan Ryan, *The Making of Modern Liberalism*, Princeton: Princeton University Press, 2012, 540; Comay, *Mourning Sickness*, 95: "Hegel's critique of Kant is merciless and unremitting."

34   Hegel, *PhH*, 446; see Taylor, *Hegel*, 368.

infringed. No "silent assent, or assent by representative" is allowed in this system, only a claim to the existence of a totalizing "general will," a maximally homogenous social fabric that thinks and wills as one.[35]

The substantive emptiness of absolute freedom leads inevitably to a conception of liberty severed from the differentiated social fabric of real human communities. Individuals come to associate themselves not with the "particular spheres" in which they live, but with "the general purpose." Their work is the "universal work." In this condition, difference loses its social value, which instead consists in the unity of the individual with "the universal consciousness and will." But with the abolition of difference, "the vanished independence of real being," an illusion of pure universality hangs like "the exhalation of a stale gas, of the vacuous *Être suprême* [supreme Being]."[36] The general will cannot accept difference, it demands sameness. Robespierre himself is supposed to have said, "*il faut une volonté UNE* [We must be of *one* will]."[37] But this universal will, in the attempt to make itself actual and impose itself on the world, can achieve nothing positive. It demands total participation from all, but individual deeds are not universal by definition. No one can share completely in someone else's actions. As pure universality, then, "there is left for it only *negative* action; it is merely the *fury* of destruction."[38]

This completely abstracted universality has no basis in "the ethical and real world of culture." It is an abstraction that understands itself as existing solely in two equally abstract forms: a "simple, inflexible

---

35  Hegel, *PhS*, §584.

36  Ibid., §§585–86.

37  Taylor, *Hegel*, 403–10. This phrase—"*il faut une volonté UNE*"—is central to Arendt's critique of Robespierre (and of his "student" Marx) in *On Revolution*. It has been frequently requoted, always citing Arendt as the source. The quotation's provenance, however, is very unclear. It took me a long time to trace the passage to its source (Arendt does not provide one herself), which turned out to be a rare collection of unpublished papers supposedly gathered from the houses of Jacobin leaders after their executions. Whether Robespierre wrote or said it, we do not and cannot know; see Maximilien Robespierre, *Papiers inédits trouvés chez Robespierre, Saint-Just, Payan, etc., supprimés ou omis par Courtois*, 2ᵉ tome, Paris: Baudouin Frères, 1828, 15.

38  Ibid., §§586.

cold universality," and "the discrete, absolute hard rigidity and self-willed atomism" of individual self-consciousness.[39] The destruction of the given world in the pursuit of absolute freedom is thus also the negation of any difference between these two extremes, of the very substance of sociality and individuality—difference. The result is a disaster. As Hegel famously says:

> The sole work and deed of universal freedom is therefore *death*, a death too which has no inner significance or filling, for what is negated is the empty point of the absolutely free self. It is thus the coldest and meanest of all deaths, with no more significance than cutting off a head of cabbage or swallowing a mouthful of water.[40]

In absolute freedom the individual self loses all its content, all its "determinations"; the "complexities of existence" in a "valid *external* world" vanish.[41]

And in death—"this flat, common monosyllable"—is "contained the wisdom of government," which is of course doomed by the very logic of its being.[42] For the very fact that it is government as such asserts "government" as a particular will, which is by its very nature opposed in its particularity to the universal will. It must therefore be overthrown, yet any who take its place are immediately guilty themselves. Suspicion becomes the principle of public life, and just being suspected ("mere disposition") equivalent to guilt.[43] According to Hegel, this commitment, which finds its original inspiration in Kant and its justification in Rousseau's theory of the "general will," is the Terror: "The principle of virtue" (the identity of the individual and the general will)

> was set up as supreme by Robespierre, and it can certainly be said that this man took virtue seriously. Now *virtue* and *terror* prevailed;

---

39   Hegel, *PhS*, §§594, 590.
40   Ibid., §594.
41   Ibid., §590.
42   Ibid., §591.
43   Hegel, *PhH*, 426.

for subjective virtue, whose rule is based purely on disposition, brings the most terrible tyranny in its train.[44]

Those suspected of a lack of virtue are liquidated, until that moment in 1794 when the Terror expends its final energies on its own architects.

The historical "accuracy" of this account of the Terror is irrelevant. What matters are the lessons it teaches. The terrible connection it illuminates between freedom and death stood for Hegel as the most significant challenge to modernity and enlightenment. How was it that a historically "legitimate" revolution for bourgeois liberty—a "glorious mental dawn" for the self-expansion of reason and freedom that he took to be the purpose of history—how had this run so completely out of control, leading to an "illegitimate" and illiberal unfreedom previously unimaginable?

In this instance, at least, Hegel is just like the "defunct economists" Keynes considers at the end of *The General Theory*, of whom "practical men, who believe themselves to be quite exempt from any intellectual influences, are usually the slaves."[45] For Hegel, this catastrophe always threatens to corrupt bourgeois liberalism, and it is anxiety over this corruption that founds the Keynesian critique. That potential corruption originates at the very heart of liberal freedom, the modern "civil society," in which liberalism and capitalism simultaneously produce and realize their promises and their perils.

## After Revolution: Hegel on Liberalism

Hegel traced liberalism's origins to the Revolutionary era because he understood it to be, like the Revolution, a product of modern, absolute freedom. Hegel's critique of liberalism is thus based on the

---

44   G. W. F. Hegel, *Political Writings*, Cambridge: Cambridge University Press, 1999, 218; see also Arendt, *On Revolution*, 64.

45   John Maynard Keynes, *Collected Writings*, vol. VII, Cambridge: Cambridge University Press, 1971–1989, 383.

Revolution and on the Terror in particular. Its ideological consolidation began in revolution, and its more mature, postrevolutionary form was marked indelibly by the experiences of revolution. Thus, like revolution itself, liberalism was for Hegel both a reason to celebrate and a reason to fear, an ambiguity that has troubled almost all attempts to understand his relation to liberalism. He was simultaneously openly sympathetic to liberal concerns, but refused the "pure" categories upon which it eventually came to depend. It is impossible to say he was categorically antiliberal, let alone a "revolutionary" or a "radical," but he was not quite a liberal, either. The problem, as the most astute readers of Hegel remark, is that like Keynesianism more broadly, his thought cannot be placed squarely inside or outside the liberal camp.[46]

Hegel's lifetime virtually coincided with what he took to be the birth of the modern age. It began with the American War of Independence (he was born in 1770) and ended with the founding of the bourgeois constitutional monarchy that followed the July Revolution of 1830 (he died in 1831). He thus lived through what he considered to be the moment liberalism was constituted in the act of severing itself from Revolution, and the question of liberalism's politics was still open for most of his life. His great historical-political contribution to the concept of liberty was thus to question liberals' efforts to fix its meaning in some transcendental firmament, to struggle with the contradiction internal to freedom, the unfreedom immanent to its sociality.[47] He understood this problem as thoroughly modern in two senses: first, because freedom is the founding

---

46 Jacques d'Hondt, *Hegel en son temps*, Paris: Éditions Sociales, 1968; Karl-Heinz Ilting, "Hegel's Concept of the State and Marx's Early Critique," in Z. A. Pelczynski (ed.), *The State and Civil Society: Studies in Hegel's Political Philosophy*, Cambridge: Cambridge University Press, 1984; Taylor, *Hegel*; Ritter, *Hegel and the French Revolution*; Solange Mercier-Josa, *Entre Hegel et Marx: Points Cruciaux de la Philosophie Hégélienne de Droit*, Paris: L'Harmattan, 1999; Eric Weil, *Hegel and the State*; Comay, *Mourning Sickness*; Kouvelakis, *Philosophy and Revolution*; Domenico Losurdo, *Hegel and the Freedom of Moderns*, Durham: Duke University Press, 2004; Michael Feola, "Truth and Illusion in the Philosophy of Right: Hegel and Liberalism," *Philosophy and Social Criticism* 36: 5, 2010, 567–85.

47 Feola, "Truth and Illusion," 575.

principle of modernity; and second, because in freedom's diremp-
tion, made manifest in the Revolution, its internal oppositions and
instability reflected the fundamental condition of all things modern.
Hegel's legacy—and Keynes's too—is the result of a life dedicated to
the belief, half-hope and half-conviction, that reason could overcome
or "sublate" this opposition, not merely theoretically or ideally, but
concretely, in the "real world." A real revolution, but without
revolutionaries.

At the turn of the nineteenth century, the bourgeois assessment of
the Revolution's shortcomings was basically that it had ended up
depending too much on the unreasonable assumption that the
masses were reasonable. That assumption put too much liberty in the
wrong hands. The struggle of the emerging bourgeoisie to capture
freedoms long enjoyed by the aristocracy turned into a battle to eradicate any trace of the existing social fabric—*Sittlichkeit*—in the interests of universal liberty, and in that moment the die was cast. As soon
as the mob was granted a voice, and its material conditions of existence became a "political" question—something we could do something about, an object of struggle—all was lost.

The reaction on the part of conservatives like Savigny and von
Haller, with whom Hegel is sometimes mistakenly grouped, was to
reject democracy or universal liberty as mere euphemisms for
chaos.[48] They looked back nostalgically at the usefully rigid social
order of the *ancien régime* and their comfort at the top of it. But
Hegel was no conservative.[49] Like Keynes, he was a sworn enemy of
the cult of tradition or nostalgia, of the idea that the important questions can always be answered with the norms and formalities of the

---

48   Hegel, *PhR*, §257. Friedrich Carl von Savigny (1779–1861) was a key contributor
to the historical school of jurisprudence, a conservative movement that formulated the
problem of law as the gradual consolidation of a people's culture and spirit, and thus not a
legitimate subject of Enlightenment rationalist critique. Karl Ludwig von Haller (1768–
1854) was a Swiss reactionary and friend of the aristocracy who opposed the conception of
the state that emerged from the Revolution; he favored something akin to a "small state"
social order led by the landed elite.

49   Taylor, *Hegel*, 424; J. R. Archer, "Oakeshott on Politics," *Journal of Politics* 41: 1,
1979, 154: "Certainly Oakeshott has reconciled Hegel with Burke which deserves as much
applause as the standing of Hegel on his head."

past. He mocked all claims that a theory or institution had value because it reflected "the wisdom of our ancestors."[50] Until his death, he rejected entirely the conservative effort to roll back history, to recreate a social order in which the Revolution was impossible. And yet, by the middle of the nineteenth century, liberals like Rudolph Haym had somehow twisted his words and actions into evidence that his *Philosophy of Right* was one long justification for the restoration of Prussian absolutism.[51]

But the truth is otherwise. Any honest engagement with Hegel discovers a consistent opponent of absolutism and a critic of existing political structures.[52] This is impossible to see if we do not bother to consider what those existing political structures were. Even today, it is too easy to forget that the social and political–economic context in which he lived was for all intents and purposes the moment of truth for European modernity—not the "beginning," if we could ever identify one, but the point of no return.

Take, for example, his famous 1806 letter to his friend Immanuel Niethammer, in which he described seeing Napoleon enter Jena as watching History on horseback.[53] Superficially, this is easily taken as an endorsement of imperial autocracy, which is to completely misunderstand what Napoleon meant at the time. In the early nineteenth century, Germany was effectively the last stronghold of feudalism in western Europe—indeed, Prussian feudalism seemed to be

---

50  Hegel, *Political Writings*, 237; compare with Jürgen Habermas, "On Hegel's Political Writings," in *Theory and Practice*, trans. John Viertel, Boston: Beacon Press, 1973, 174–75. It is worth noting that liberalism is basically the idea—in contemporary capitalist democracies—that the important questions can always be answered with the norms and formalities of the present.

51  Rudolph Haym, *Hegel et Son Temps: Leçons sur la Genèse et le Développement, la Nature et la Valeur de la Philosophie Hégélienne*, Paris: Gallimard, 2008 [1857].

52  Pinkard, *Hegel*; Losurdo, *Hegel and the Freedom of Moderns*.

53  "[T]he day the French occupied Jena and the Emperor Napoleon penetrated its walls . . . I saw the Emperor—this world-soul [*Weltseele*]—riding out of the city on a reconnaissance. It is indeed a wonderful sensation to see such an individual, who, concentrated here at a single point, astride a horse, reaches out over the world and masters it"; Hegel to Friedrich Immanuel Niethammer, Jena, October 13, 1806, in Hegel, *The Letters*, trans. Clark Butler and Christiane Seiler, Bloomington: Indiana University Press, 1984, 114.

reinvigorating itself.[54] The German states were a collection of fiefdoms caught between a quasi-imperial absolutist Prussia and the political instability and intrigue of a Holy Roman Empire to which all were formally beholden. The whole world was sacrificed to petty regional loyalties, traditional hierarchies, lordly caprice and hereditary wealth. In the thrilling if blood-curdling shadow of world-historical transformations like the French Revolution, the American War of Independence, and the accelerated liberalism of Britain following the English Revolution of a century earlier—not to mention the Haitian Revolution that unfolded over the 1790s and early 1800s—Hegel and other anti-absolutist intellectuals were in the permanent grip of what Marx would later call the "German *misère*": the experience of existing in a space and time that history was leaving behind. It seemed as if the progress of reason and freedom was embracing everywhere but Germany, which was instead trapped in a frozen zone, impervious to monumental developments elsewhere.

This was the state of mind in which Hegel welcomed the "anti-Robespierre" Napoleon, "a King for the Revolution."[55] This is the lens through which he viewed his own world, the world that Bonaparte appeared to be sweeping away with the historical force of the Revolution behind him (it was essential that he was French)—a world of petty minor monarchies, the fickle territorial politics of the Holy Roman Empire, the tyranny of the Prussian military, and the whole edifice of hereditary aristocratic privilege. Napoleon might have been an Emperor by then, but he was far better than a Prussian Kaiser or a Duke of Württemburg. Hegel saw the coming of this "world-soul" as the arrival of the political institutions of modernity in backward Germany: the Napoleonic legal code (which promised greater *de jure* equality before the law), the end of feudal property, representative assemblies that included the bourgeoisie, and, most

54   Perry Anderson, *Lineages of the Absolutist State*, London: New Left Books, 1974, 271–72.

55   Patrice Guéniffey, *Bonaparte*, trans. Steven Rendall, Cambridge: Harvard University Press, 2015, 628, 575.

important of all, the French experience of liberty as it was born in the crucible of the Revolution.[56]

Even his *Philosophy of Right*, arguably more measured than the *Phenomenology of Spirit*, and often taken (by those who have never read it) as one long obeisance to absolutism, is filled with sharp critique of the politics of its moment. It was first published only two years after the German Confederation's Karlsbad Decrees of August 1819, which rolled back the reforms gradually instituted over the decade following Prussia's defeat by Napoleon in 1807.[57] Hegel supported the reforms enthusiastically. Although not all of them were realized, the proposals were quite radical—in a word, *liberal*: to strip the Prussian nobility of hereditary control of the army and bureaucracy, to institute bicameral Estates, and to establish a constitutional (as opposed to the existing, absolutist) monarchy. Karlsbad reasserted absolutist privilege with a vengeance, and any desire on Hegel's part to appear perhaps a little less oppositional is unsurprising. Yet the *Philosophy of Right* nonetheless describes a state that looks nothing like the feudal relic Friedrich Wilhelm IV and his conservative allies were desperately trying to resurrect.

To appreciate his nonconformity, consider one of the most famous examples of his supposed endorsement of the Restoration: the preface to the *Philosophy of Right*. (I choose it because it is so frequently misunderstood.) There we find Hegel's notorious declaration that "what is rational is actual; and what is actual is rational."[58] This is commonly taken to epitomize his sycophancy to the throne, as if he were saying something like "Everything is as it ought to be, and if the existing order is feudal absolutism, it is redeemed in its very existence." As it happens, we know from Hegel's more journalistic political writings, letters, and lectures that he definitely did not believe he

---

56  Hegel, *PhH*, 456 n.4.

57  These reforms, known as the Stein-Hardenberg reforms (named after two key actors, Karl von Stein and Karl August von Hardenberg), were central to efforts to modernize the Prussian state following the defeat by Napoleon. Their effectiveness was extremely limited.

58  Hegel, *PhR*, 20.

lived in the best of all possible worlds.[59] So he is either practicing self-censorship (a real possibility, admittedly) or he is saying something different. Maybe, as some have suggested, he is even attempting both: to say in "code" what he "really" means.[60]

But one need only take Hegel at his word—his monumental *Logic* of 1812 had already worked through each of the key terms in great detail—to get closer to what he is trying, a little awkwardly, to say.[61] The claim that the "actual is rational" is in fact an attack on precisely the idea that the "ought" has anything at all to do with knowledge. For Hegel, actuality is not equivalent to "empirically existing" or what he calls the "positive." Instead, it is closer to something like "true essence," the "actual" historical dynamics beneath the contingent surface of the world.[62] Since, for him, history is the product of reason unfolding, the actual in this sense must of course be rational. It is tautological.[63]

The rational-actual tautology is thus not a defense of the status quo, but a critique of the claim that philosophy has the capacity to issue instructions to the world on how things ought to be. The point of investigating "actuality" is not to prescribe based on "mere reality or positivity"—"trivial, external and transitory objects, institutions, conditions, etc."—but to uncover the dynamics and direction of historical movement.[64] *Philosophy of Right* takes up this task for modern politics and goes on to describe the historical unfolding of reason, in the form of freedom in an "ethical state" that looks almost nothing like Hegel's Prussia.

Moreover, as Losurdo and others have demonstrated meticulously, the assertion that the "actual is rational" in Hegel's sense is not merely

---

59    Pinkard, *Hegel*.

60    On these questions, see Losurdo, *Hegel and the Freedom of Moderns*, 3–14.

61    G. W. F. Hegel, *Science of Logic*, London: George, Allen & Unwin, 1969.

62    "For science has to do only with the Idea, which is not so impotent that it only ought to be without actually being; hence philosophy has to do with an actuality of which those objects, institutions, conditions, etc. are only the superficial exterior." (Hegel, *PhR*, 390, n.22).

63    As he writes later in the *Philosophy of Right* (§270), "True actuality is necessity; what is actual is necessary in itself."

64    G. W. F. Hegel, *Encyclopaedia of the Philosophical Sciences in Basic Outline, Part 1. Science of Logic*, Cambridge: Cambridge University Press, 2015 [1830], §6, 36.

anticonservative; it is in fact essential to the revolutionary tradition. Uncovering the ways in which the rational becomes actual is precisely and necessarily the goal of a long line of radical theoreticians. Luxemburg, Lenin, and Gramsci explicitly commend Hegel's insight on this point. Marx, who despite his almost obsessive engagement with the text never mentions the rational-actual phrase, is not so far from its logic in much of his revolutionary writing.[65] The *Manifesto* is, if nothing else, the result of a radical embrace of Hegel's position, of what he famously called the "cunning of Reason."[66] This is not merely a revision of Adam Smith's invisible hand, or of de Mandeville's Fable of the Bees; instead, one can also hear echoes of this stance in Martin Luther King's claim that the "arc of the moral universe is long, but it bends toward justice."[67] All we need to remember is the overwhelming tumult of Hegel's time to understand that saying the actual is rational is in no way an endorsement of how things have "always" been, how they are, or how reactionaries say they "should be."

Hegel embraced the Revolution; indeed, he drank a toast to it every year on July 14, the anniversary of the storming of the hated Bastille.[68] But he felt a responsibility to explain its place in history, for its destructive force seemed to many incompatible with modernity, the progress of freedom and reason. It was not only reactionaries who were blind to the rationality of the actual and instructed the world on how it "ought" to be.

---

65    Losurdo, *Hegel and the Freedom of Moderns*, 32–38.

66    Hegel, *PhH*, 32-33; Hegel, *Science of Logic*, 746.

67    Joshua Cohen, "The Arc of the Moral Universe," *Philosophy & Public Affairs* 26: 2, 1997, 91-134. See Martin Luther King, Jr., *A Testament of Hope: The Essential Writings of Martin Luther King, Jr.*, James Washington (ed.), San Francisco: Harper & Row, 1986, 141, 207, 277, 438. King was likely paraphrasing Theodore Parker, a 19th-century Unitarian.

68    Pinkard, *Hegel*, 451. According to Slavoj Žižek (*In Defense of Lost Causes*, London: Verso, 2008, 208): "one should never forget that Hegel's critique is immanent, accepting the basic principles of the French Revolution (and its key supplement, the Haitian Revolution)." Losurdo reminds us that "every revolution in the history of humanity was celebrated by Hegel, despite his reputation as an incorrigible defender of the established order"; Losurdo, *Hegel and the Freedom of Moderns*, 99. Franz Rosenzweig, in *Hegel and the State*, however, argues for a less complex role for the revolution in Hegel's thought, that is, "pure fear of revolution"; quoted in Habermas, "On Hegel's Political Writings," 189.

## Freedom, Abstract and Concrete

Hegel's account of the Revolution's historical actuality tells us a great deal about his diagnosis of his own age of emergent liberal capitalism. He took the Revolution as a moment in which the world was given a tool it desperately needed but could not yet understand and had no idea how to use properly; a gun in the hands of a child. The Terror taught modernity that modern liberty is much more complicated and subtle than it appeared in the utopian pronouncements of someone like Rousseau. Freedom unleashed as an unmediated force in the world would only become its opposite. But it was irrefutable in Hegel's mind that the freedom endorsed by his liberal contemporaries represented historical progress, and there was no reason why, if approached in its full complexity, the unfolding of universal freedom was impossible. Indeed, insofar as freedom was for Hegel the object of reason, universal freedom was realizable, although there was no guarantee that the road toward it would be smooth, safe, or short.

Hegel's lectures on the philosophy of history trace freedom and reason into the depths of what we might euphemistically call the "unreliable" histories of the world to which he had access and found himself attracted—most of them racist, Eurocentric, and misogynistic. Unfortunately, these absurd racial logics and the overcooked exoticism of the "anthropology" on which some of the *Philosophy of History* is based are its best-known features. Without in any way excusing this dimension of the lectures, of most interest for present purposes is Hegel's explanation of the end of feudalism, a process which, as we know, had yet to work itself out in the Germany in which he wrote. There we find both further evidence of his rejection of the historical "actuality" of the German status quo and a subtle analysis of liberalism.

Unlike most liberals—and this is crucial to Hegel's critique—Hegel refuses to posit freedom as an abstraction. For him that is impossible and meaningless. He is compelled to put some meat on liberty's bones. "Why did this principle of Freedom remain merely formal? And why did the French alone, and not the Germans, set about realizing it?"[69] Hegel says that Germany's freedom was a legacy of the Reformation: liberty was construed not as "license," but as independence and rational "obedience to the laws of the state" in which "man is free, for all that is demanded is that the Particular should yield to the General. Man himself has a conscience; consequently the subjection required of him is a free allegiance."[70] Germany's special relation to modernity is due to Protestantism, in which, in contrast to French Catholicism, there is "a tranquil confidence in the [Honourable] Disposition of men"—not the masses— which is the "fountain of all equitable arrangements that prevail with regard to private right and the constitution of the State."[71]

In France, on the other hand, the changes associated with the rise of modern liberty were

> necessarily violent, because the transformation was not under- taken by government. And the reason why the government did not undertake it was that the Court, the Clergy, the Nobility, the Parliaments themselves, were unwilling to surrender the privileges they possessed, either for the sake of expediency or that of abstract Right.[72]

Consequently, while the Revolution marks the "glorious mental dawn" at which humanity recognized the priority of Reason, it also initiated the disaster of the many and the all becoming "the govern- ment" in absolute freedom.[73]

This is the history that makes Hegel, in contrast to most liberals, eager to highlight the oppressive uses to which "liberty" has been put in the interests of the "community of the free." Noting that it was the byword of feudal lords in the struggle against the crown, he points out that the

---

69   Hegel, *PhH*, 443.
70   Ibid., 423.
71   Ibid., 444–45.
72   Ibid., 446–47.
73   Ibid., 447–51.

barons of England extorted the Magna Charta from the King; but the citizens gained nothing by it, on the contrary they remained in their former condition. Polish Liberty too, meant nothing more than the freedom of the barons in contraposition to the King, the nation being reduced to a state of absolute serfdom.[74]

The concept of liberty is too often illusory, or a ruse: "we must always be careful to observe whether is it not really the assertion of private interests which is thereby designated."[75]

These are the simultaneously volatile possibilities, hopeful and terrifying, that modern liberty brings to the world. Hegel calls "Liberals" those of his post-Revolutionary contemporaries who somehow, foolishly, remain beholden to the dogma of abstract freedom, even though (and unlike Rousseau or even Robespierre) they have the benefit of knowing how the story turns out. Ignoring the chaos it has unleashed, they refuse to see the double-edgedness of this sword:

> Not satisfied with the establishment of rational rights, with freedom of person and property, with the existence of a political organization in which are to be found various circles of civil life each having its own functions to perform, and with that influence over the people which is exercised by the intelligent members of the community, and the confidence that is felt in them, "*Liberalism*" sets up in opposition to all this the atomistic principle, that which insists upon the sway of individual wills; maintaining that all government should emanate from their express power, and have their express sanction. Asserting this formal side of Freedom—this abstraction—the party in question allows no political organization to be firmly established. The particular arrangements of the government are forthwith opposed by the advocates of Liberty as the mandates of a particular will, and branded as displays of arbitrary power.[76]

---

74    Ibid., 429–30.
75    Hegel, *PhH*, 429–30.
76    Hegel, *PhH*, 452.

To be branded a "liberal" by Hegel, then, is faint praise. As Hegel's own political development hopefully makes clear, there is nothing to be celebrated in *Liberalism*'s irreducible, often calamitous, instability, through which the

> will of the Many expels the Ministry from power, and those who had formed the opposition fill the vacant places; but the latter having now become the Government, meet with hostility from the Many and share the same fate. Thus agitation and unrest are perpetuated.[77]

Hegel knew full well, however, that the modern concept of freedom was irrevocable, and he was glad for it. The genie could not be put back in the bottle; there was no going back now. The question, then, was what would become of it, since it could clearly engender both catastrophe and glory. His answer was that freedom had to be confronted and realized in the "world in which we actually live," and the path to glory, if it were discoverable, required a transformation of the sociality of the communities realizing their liberty: "For it is a false principle that the fetters which bind Right and Freedom can be broken without the emancipation of conscience—that there can be a Revolution without a Reformation."[78]

The emancipation of conscience was therefore not merely the task of many atomistic particulars, but a problem for *Sittlichkeit* itself. These dynamics defined the dialectical force of modernity, they posed the question "modern communities" were condemned to ask themselves: this "collision, this nodus, this problem is that with which history is now occupied, and whose solution it has to work out in the future."[79] The answer, clearly, could not be liberalism, or not only. There was too much at stake.

---

77  Hegel, *PhH*, 452. See also Pinkard, *Hegel*, 197, 609.
78  Hegel, *PhH*, 453.
79  Ibid., 452.

# CHAPTER 6

# Necessity and the Rabble

Hegel learned from Robespierre that the problem of freedom can never be abstracted from the question of necessity or human "needs." Necessity thus stands as liberalism's greatest material, political, and conceptual obstacle. In its committed one-sided abstraction, liberalism categorically denies the purchase of necessity on political life and thought. Unlike most liberals since, Kant is very clear on how complete this separation must be:

> Do freedom and natural necessity in one and the same action contradict each other? And this we have answered sufficiently . . . since in freedom a relation is possible to conditions of a kind entirely different from those in natural necessity, the law of the latter does not affect the former; hence *each is independent of the other, and can take place without being disturbed by the other.*[1]

When he later formulated *Ius necessitatis* in the wake of the French Revolution, Kant perceived the very core of revolutionary politics in what Arendt declared the "most irrefragable of all titles" for Robespierre: necessity.[2] In Arendt's eyes, when Robespierre brought

---

1  Immanuel Kant, *Critique of Pure Reason*, Cambridge: Cambridge University Press, 1998, 545 (emphasis added).
2  Hannah Arendt, *On Revolution*, London: Penguin, 2006, 49.

compassion for those unable to escape necessity—the poor—to the political "market-place," he irrevocably destabilized politics as a category of modern social life, and in so doing created the conditions of possibility for what we now call political economy, the science of government.

> [We now] find it difficult to realize that according to ancient thought on these matters, the very term "political economy" would have been a contradiction in terms: whatever was "economic," related to the life of the individual and the survival of the species, was a non-political, household affair by definition.

We cannot see, Arendt assures us, that a "classless society" is in truth a "non-political ideal."[3]

The shared origins of political economy and Keynesianism lie here, at the confrontation between liberal freedom and necessity. As Foucault might have said, political economy is, at its core, almost a social oncology, first fully elaborated in the midst of the postrevolutionary European moment, in the truly desperate attempt to diagnose the mass dynamics unleashed at the end of the eighteenth century:

> It is indeed as though the forces of the earth were allied in benevolent conspiracy with this uprising, whose end is impotence, whose principle is rage, and whose conscious aim is not freedom but life and happiness. Where the breakdown of traditional authority set the poor of the earth on the march, where they left the obscurity of their misfortunes and streamed upon the market place, their *furor* seemed as irresistible as the motion of the stars, a torrent rushing forward with elemental force and engulfing a whole world.[4]

---

3   Ibid., 71; Hannah Arendt, *The Human Condition*, Chicago: University of Chicago Press, 1958, 29; Hannah Arendt, "On Violence," in *Crises of the Republic*, New York: Harcourt Brace, 1972, 151.

4   Arendt, *On Revolution*, 103.

## *Notrecht* and Civil Society

Hegel's political philosophy was in many ways an attempt to embrace political economy as a philosophy, to understand the implications of necessity—of labor, needs, poverty, scarcity—for philosophy and political life. He named the problem of necessity *Notrecht*, the right or law [*recht*] of necessity [*Not*], and took it to mark the most fundamental rebuke to the one-sided abstraction of "freedom" at the heart of Enlightenment thought. As Arendt glosses it, in "the happy days of Enlightenment," it seemed like only despotism stood between humanity and freedom, but after the French Revolution, it appeared there was "no release" from "the force of history and historical necessity":

> "all those who, throughout the nineteenth century and deep into the twentieth, followed in the footsteps of the French Revolution saw themselves not merely as successors of the men of the French Revolution but as agents of history and historical necessity, with the obvious and yet paradoxical result that instead of freedom, necessity became the chief category of political and revolutionary thought.[5]

However eager Arendt is to lay the blame for this "perfidy" at Robespierre's feet, the history of *Notrecht* stretches further back than the Jacobins. Hegel might have formulated it with Robespierre and his comrades in mind, but he probably had Kant's *Ius necessitatis* and some lessons from Hobbes in mind, too. In *Leviathan*—which is in many ways a set of propositions concerning a very similar problem, the relation between order, security, and prosperity—Hobbes named and justified the condition Hegel later called *Notrecht*:

> If a man by the terrour of present death, be compelled to doe a fact against the Law, he is totally Excused; because no Law can oblige a man to abandon his own preservation. And supposing

---

5   Ibid., 42–43.

such a Law were obligatory; yet a man would reason thus, *If I doe it not, I die presently; if I doe it, I die afterwards; therefore by doing it, there is time of life gained*; Nature therefore compels him to the fact.

When a man is destitute of food, or other thing necessary for life, and cannot preserve himselfe any other way, but by some fact against the Law; as if in a great famine he take food by force, or stealth, which he cannot obtaine for mony or charity; or in defence of his life, snatch away another mans Sword, he is totally Excused, for the reason next before Alleged.[6]

Hegel's *Notrecht*, while certainly echoing Kant, cleaves much closer to Hobbes's account. For Kant, while the "motto of necessity is, 'Necessity has no law,'" it presents itself not as an irrepressible challenge or critical exception to right, but as an antinomy: necessity has no law, "but there can never be any case making the unjust and wrong justifiable before the law."[7] In other words, just as Kant says that for the sake of reason we must act according to the fiction that each individual is autonomous and uniquely responsible for his or her own acts—knowing all the while that is a fiction—here we must, for the sake of the same reasoned order, deny the legitimacy of *Ius necessitatis*, knowing all the while that its truth puts the lie to the law, its origins prior to any question of legitimacy.[8] For Kant, despite his recognition of its moral rationale and his well-earned reputation as a Jacobin sympathizer, "*revolution is against the law* (!)."[9]

In contrast, Hegel defends the poor—for they are almost always

---

6 Thomas Hobbes, *Leviathan*, Penguin: London, 1968 [1651], 345–46.

7 Immanuel Kant, *The Metaphysics of Ethics*, 3d ed., trans. J. W. Semple, Edinburgh: T. & T. Clark, 1886.

8 Kant, *Critique of Pure Reason*, 544; Kojin Karatani, *Transcritique: On Kant and Marx*, Cambridge: MIT Press, 2005, 116–17.

9 Rebecca Comay, *Mourning Sickness: Hegel and the French Revolution*, Stanford: Stanford University Press, 2011, 37. Comay appends the exclamation mark.

the ones who are subject to *Notrecht*.[10] Like Hobbes, he "totally Excuses" the poor:

> *In extreme danger* and in collision with the rightful property of someone else, this life may claim (not in equity, but as a right) a *right of necessity* [*Notrecht*]; for the alternatives are an infinite injury to existence with total loss of rights, and an injury only to an individual and limited existence of freedom, whereby right as such and the capacity for rights of the injured party, who has been injured only in *this* specific property, continue to be recognized.[11]

For Hegel, necessity is a question of "life" itself, as Arendt says. But, at least in his eyes, she is wrong to suggest that this question is opposed to, or other than, that of freedom. Revolution's "conscious aim"—"life and happiness"—is not against or unconcerned with freedom. It is *prior* to freedom. To inquire or even wonder about freedom before, or disengaged from, necessity is at best a meaningless exercise and more likely a calamity.

> [Life] as the totality of ends, has a right in opposition to abstract right. If, for example, it can be preserved by stealing a loaf, this certainly constitutes an infringement of someone's property, but it would be wrong to regard such an action as common theft. If someone whose life is in danger were not allowed to take measures to save himself, he would be destined to forfeit all his rights; and since he would be deprived of life, his entire freedom would be negated.[12]

We cannot even understand freedom, let alone experience it, without necessity constantly (and necessarily) impinging upon our thoughts and actions. Conversely, the problem addressed by *Notrecht* is always,

---

10   Hegel does not follow up on what we might now recognize as an Agamben-esque argument regarding *Homo sacer*, who, existing outside the law is neither subject to nor subject of it.

11   G. W. F. Hegel, *Elements of the Philosophy of Right*, trans. H. B. Nisbet, Cambridge: Cambridge University Press, 1991, §127. (Hereinafter cited as *PhR*.)

12   Ibid.

ultimately, the problem of freedom. Revolution—Arendt's "upris-ing"—is the product of the unity of necessity and freedom breaking the surface of history, leaving it impossible to ignore any longer.

The necessity at issue, however—that upon which real freedom hinges—has two crucial features. First, it is concrete. Hegel may be commonly called an "idealist," but his political philosophy is poorly characterized as such.[13] "Materialist," at least as Marx used the term, sometimes seems closer to the truth, although that too falls short. In truth, while the *Philosophy of Right* has an idealist arc in its overall frame—"the actual is rational"—the politics upon which it is founded have a very uneven relationship to idealism, at least as it was formulated by Hegel's predecessors like Fichte or Schelling.

> [N]ecessity reveals the finitude and hence contingency of both right and welfare—of the abstract existence of freedom as distinct from the existence of the particular person, and of the sphere of the particular will as distinct from the universality of right. Their one-sided and ideal character is thereby posited.[14]

Hegel's point is that necessity foils false claims regarding the metahis-torical universality of freedom and right. Until they have a material content in "life," they are one-sided and empty.

Second, the necessity in question has a very specific temporality: the short run. While in the longer view there are "many prerequisites for the preservation of life," these provide no grounds for *Notrecht*, for the future is so uncertain that the category of "necessity" has little or no purchase.[15]

---

13   "Hegel, straddling the French Revolution and the Restoration, joined the two moments of philosophical life, materialism and spiritualism, dialectically. Hegel's successors destroyed this unity, returning to the old materialism with Feuerbach and to the spiritual-ism of the Hegelian right"; Antonio Gramsci, *Prison Notebooks*, vol. II, ed. and trans. Joseph Buttigieg, New York: Columbia University Press, 1996, 143.

14   Hegel, *PhR*, §128.

15   Indeed, for Hegel it is a *retro*spective category by definition, because any phenom-ena's necessity can always only be grasped after the fact. This is part of his point in the famous remark about the Owl of Minerva (philosophy), who takes flight at dusk, only able to make sense of the day in its last light, when it is already done.

The only thing that is necessary is to live *now*; the future is not absolute, and it remains exposed to contingency. Consequently, only necessity of the immediate present can justify a wrong action, because its omission would in turn involve committing a wrong—indeed the ultimate wrong, namely the total negation of the existence of freedom.[16]

The recognition of immediate necessity is a prerequisite to concrete freedom.

The key question, then, for the state and for political economy—the question, in fact, to which the emergence of political economy is an answer—is this: What forces produce this necessity? What conditions generate situations in which necessity supersedes right and property, and what can be done to prevent them? Hegel's answer to these two questions—one about causes and the other about solutions—is the subject of the two most oft-studied sections of the *Philosophy of Right*, "Civil Society" and "The State." The first theorizes the dynamics animating a thoroughly modern nonstate realm and shows how, despite its remarkable wealth production, it must simultaneously produce poverty, "deprivation and want."[17] The second describes the institutional and conceptual basis for a state best suited to overcoming and ultimately abolishing civil society's immanent self-destructiveness.

## Civil Society

Hegel's civil society has attracted more attention over the last two centuries than any other element of his political philosophy. And for good reason, because in many ways it announced modernity itself. While Kant had used the same phrase (*bürgerliche Gesellschaft*), and Bodin and others had elaborated a *societas civilis*, Hegel's civil society presupposes "a complete break with this tradition. To this extent one

---

16   Hegel, *PhR*, §127.
17   Hegel, *PhR*, §185.

might say that before Hegel the concept of civil society in its modern sense did not exist":

> What Hegel made the times aware of with the phrase "civil society" was nothing less than the result of the modern revolution: the emergence of a depoliticized society through the centralization of politics in the princely or revolutionary state and the shift of society's focal point toward economics, a change which this society experienced simultaneously with the Industrial Revolution and which found its expression in "political" or "national-economy."[18]

This is the process by which the political and civil conditions of European society were separated, and in the subject of each of its members emerged the distinction between bourgeois and *citoyen*, private citizen and citizen of the state, standing side by side.[19]

Hegel's civil society is thus explicitly historicized both as an idea and as a dimension of social life. The resulting analysis shares elements with its predecessors yet also goes beyond them. While Hegel's civil society is, like most others', implicitly "closed" insofar as it is spatially contained by the limits of sovereign authority, it is neither the ultimate end of political life (à la Hobbes), nor the necessary unity of atomistic individuals (à la Rousseau).[20] It is, rather, the second of three moments in the unfolding idea of *Sittlichkeit*: the family, civil society, and the state. It is therefore not yet that for which we aspire—real freedom—but neither is it a step backward from Rousseau's primordial purity. It is the necessary "stage of difference" of "self-sufficient individuals" in the movement of humanity toward Spirit. Civil society is the product of the disintegration of the first moment (family; "the natural ethical spirit") as the organizing principle of social life, and the

---

18    Manfred Riedel, *Between Tradition and Revolution: The Hegelian Transformation of Political Philosophy*, trans. W. Wright, Cambridge: Cambridge University Press, 1984, 147–48.

19    Hegel, *PhR*, §263; Riedel, *Between Tradition and Revolution*, 142; Terry Pinkard, *Hegel: A Biography*, Cambridge: Cambridge University Press, 2000, 483–84.

20    Hegel, *PhR*, §§187R, 194R, 303R.

precondition of the third (the state; "the actuality of the ethical idea").[21]

Despite the "stagist" framing, the family–civil society–state progression does not unfold as a clear linear development inside some preexisting territory. The way civil society "passes over" into the state is complex: civil society "intervenes between the family and the state, even if its full development occurs later than that of the state."[22] The relation between the state and civil society is thus dynamic, and it is not always clear what features of social life belong where, or whether they are in motion or part of both civil society and the state simultaneously.

These complexities result from the development of civil society itself. The emerging primacy of self-sufficient individuals as what we might call political-economic subjects drives its movement out of the disintegration of the family. According to Hegel, this leads to an understanding of "formal universality," an acknowledgment of something like "equal rights as citizens" enjoyed by all as "children" of civil society.[23] This equality, however, is merely formal, not "actual" in its content. Its "formalistic view of freedom," which Hegel associates specifically with liberalism, sanctions massive material inequalities between subjects through juridical equality in "the right of property" and leads civil society to develop an "external order" to ensure property rights: the (implicitly territorially contained) "external state."[24] The external state is not yet the "actuality of ethical life." It is rather the closest thing in Hegel to what we usually mean by "the state" today, that is, the Weberian state, and Hegel is in no way its champion.[25] Instead, in the unfolding of *Sittlichkeit*, the external state "withdraws and comes to a focus in the end and actuality of the

---

21   Ibid., §§181, 157, 257.

22   Stathis Kouvelakis, *Philosophy and Revolution: From Marx to Kant*, trans. G. M. Goshgarian, New York: Verso, 2003, 41; Hegel, *PhR*, §182.

23   Ibid., §238.

24   G. W. F. Hegel, *Political Writings*, Cambridge: Cambridge University Press, 1999, 219; Hegel, *PhR*, §§157, 208, 183.

25   Gareth Stedman Jones, "Hegel and the Economics of Civil Society," in S. Kaviraj and S. Khilnani (eds.), *Civil Society: History and Possibilities*, Cambridge: Cambridge University Press, 2001, 17.

substantial universal and of the public life which is dedicated to this—i.e. in the constitution of the state." Which is to say that civil society finds its ultimate end in the state, but (at least to Hegel's knowledge) a state unlike any that exists.[26]

Civil society itself contains a familiar Hegelian triad:

A. The mediation of need and the satisfaction of the *individual* through his work and through the work and satisfaction of the needs of *all the others*—the system of *needs*.
B. The actuality of the universal of *freedom* contained therein, the protection of property through the *administration of justice*.
C. Provisions against the contingency which remains present in the above systems, and care for the particular interest as a *common* interest, by means of the *police* and the *corporation*.[27]

Recognizing that each moment deserves detailed discussion on its own, here I focus on the account as a whole. Hegel argues that civil society, an "immense power which draws people to itself and requires them to work for it, to owe everything to it, and to do everything by its means," is a distinctively modern social formation.[28] Emerging in the context of a consolidated, if unstable, system of modern sovereign nation-states, civil society is *bürgerliche Gesellschaft*; it is bourgeois by definition. In fact, a better translation would read "bourgeois-civil society," without suggesting the possibility of nonbourgeois forms; civil society is a historically specific category.[29] "In civil society, each

---

26  Gillian Rose, *Hegel contra Sociology*, London: Verso, 2009, 96; Domenico Losurdo, *Hegel and the Freedom of Moderns*, Durham, NC: Duke University Press, 2004, 62; Joseph Buttigieg, "Gramsci on Civil Society," *boundary 2* 22: 3, 1995, 30; Norberto Bobbio, "Gramsci and the Conception of Civil Society," in Chantal Mouffe (ed.), *Gramsci and Marxist Theory*, London: Routledge & Kegan Paul, 1979, 22.

27  Hegel, *PhR*, §188.

28  Ibid., §238.

29  Ibid., §190R. Some argue that Hegel was writing specifically about England: Peter Thomas, *The Gramscian Moment: Philosophy, Hegemony, and Marxism*, Amsterdam: Brill, 2009, 176; Stedman Jones, "Hegel and the Economics of Civil Society," 126; Jan Rehmann, "'Abolition' of Civil Society? Remarks on a Widespread Misunderstanding in the Interpretation of 'Civil Society,'" *Socialism & Democracy* 13: 2, 1999, 1–18.

individual is his own end, and all else means nothing to him." Echoing Hobbes's emphasis on mutual interdependence, the "selfish end" (in Hegelian, "particularity in itself") is unrealizable "without reference to others; these others are therefore the means to the end of the particular," and "subjective selfishness turns into a contribution towards the satisfaction of the needs of everyone else."[30] The "formal freedom" of this "system of needs" is the liberal actualization of particularity in itself: "particularity passes over into universality."[31] In civil society, self-interest is the one interest we share.

Here we hear echoes of the English political economy Hegel is reading, for civil society is precisely that realm in which the "invisible hand" is supposed to do its work. Indeed, anticipating Foucault's analysis of governmentality and civil society, Hegel locates the origins of political economy in the effort to understand the laws governing the "mass of contingent occurrences" produced by the pursuit of self-interest that constitutes civil society.[32] But relative to Smith or de Mandeville, Hegel has less faith in "private vice" as a source of "publick virtue" (a skepticism he shared with James Steuart, whose political economy was more important to Hegel than that of Smith, Say, or Ricardo).[33] He

---

30   Hegel, *PhR*, §§182A, 199. By the time he was writing the *Philosophy of Right*, Hegel had been struggling to understand the bourgeois for decades, a figure whose structural position he also identified in ancient Rome. As he put the same problem in 1802: "The status of this class is accordingly determined by the fact that its province is possession in general and the justice which is possible in this context, that it at the same time constitutes a coherent system, and that, as a direct consequence of the elevation of the relation of possession to formal unity, each individual who is inherently capable of possession is related to all the others as a universal entity, or as a citizen in the sense of a *bourgeois*"; Hegel, *Political Writings*, 150–51, 292 n.73.

31   Hegel, *PhR*, §186.

32   Michel Foucault, *The Birth of Biopolitics: Lectures at the Collège de France, 1978-1979*, New York: Picador, 2008, 291–98; Michel Foucault, *The Essential Foucault*, New York: New Press, 2003, 234–35; Hegel, *PhR*, §189A.

33   On Steuart's influence on Hegel, see Raymond Plant, "Hegel and Political Economy—II," *New Left Review* I: 104, 1977, 107; Mark Neocleous, "Policing the System of Needs: Hegel, Political Economy, and the Police of the Market," *History of European Ideas* 24: 1, 1998, 43–58, 49–50; see also Paul Chamley, *Économie Politique et Philosophie chez Steuart et Hegel*, Paris: Librarie Dalloz, 1963; Dominique Carboret, "The Market Economy and Social Classes in James Steuart and G. W. F. Hegel," in Ramón Tortajada (ed.), *The Economics of James Steuart*, London: Routledge, 1999, 57–75. Arguably, if his *Theory of Moral Sentiments* is read alongside *The Wealth of Nations*—the latter was intended to

develops a subtler, and less sanguine, critique of the resulting social dynamics.

There are certainly moments in which he concedes that bourgeois civil society's remarkable commercial self-expansion justifies its self-congratulation. Sometimes he even sounds like a liberal champion of capitalism as a full-employment machine: "The endless multiplication of the needs of others is a lasting general resource for everyone"; and "No one can take a bite of bread without thereby providing bread for others."[34] Indeed, and unsurprisingly, Hegel finds in this organic mutual social interdependence a virtually spiritual force of integration:

> Needs and means, as existing in reality, become a *being* for *others* by whose needs and work their satisfaction is mutually conditioned. That abstraction which becomes a quality of both needs and means also becomes a determination of the mutual relations between individuals. This universality, as the *quality of being recognized*, is the moment which makes isolated and abstract needs, means, and modes of satisfaction into *concrete*, i.e. *social* ones.[35]

But if the recognition of needs is akin to the anticipation of demand, this is what we now know as "effective demand." The manner in which the system of needs generates exchange-based interdependence, and the way in which liberals theorize that achievement, obscures contradictions that belie its supposed harmonious

---

complement, not overwrite, the former—then Smith is much closer to Hegel and Keynes than to classical liberalism; Gilles Dostaler, "Néoliberalisme, keynésianisme et traditions libérales," *La Pensée* 323, 2000, 71–87.

34  G. W. F. Hegel, *Vorlesungen über Rechtsphilosophie*, Band I, ed. Karl-Heinz Ilting, Stuttgart: Frommann-Holzboog, 1973, 313; Band III, 614; compare with "this mediation of satisfaction by the labor of all constitutes the general resources"; Hegel, *Sämtliche Werke*, Band 8, ed. Hermann Glockner, Stuttgart: Frommann-Holzboog, 1964, §524. All quoted and translated in Joel Anderson, "Hegel's Implicit View on How to Solve the Problem of Poverty: The Responsible Consumer and the Return of the Ethical to Civil Society," in Robert R. Williams (ed.), *Beyond Liberalism and Communitarianism: Studies in Hegel's Philosophy of Right*, Albany: SUNY Press, 2001, 188.

35  Hegel, *PhR*, §192.

self-regulation. Hegel sees no guarantee that all will be well-integrated in market-based sociality. The "right of particularity"—which all enjoy in the "formal freedom" of civil society—is by no means an "equalizer":

> The possibility of sharing in the universal resources—i.e. of holding particular resources—is, however, conditional upon one's own immediate basic assets (i.e. capital) on the one hand, and upon one's skill on the other; the latter is in turn itself conditioned by the former, but also by contingent circumstances.[36]

Formal equality *qua* "citizens" or "persons" does not cancel out

> inequality of human beings in civil society—an inequality posited by nature . . . —but in fact produces it out of the spirit itself and raises it to an inequality of skills, resources, and even of intellectual and moral education.[37]

Left to itself, bourgeois civil society makes lived inequality worse, insofar as it takes nature's caprice regarding to whom we were born, our access to resources and "capital," and raises it up as social infrastructure (an argument echoing Rousseau in the second part of *Discourse on Inequality*).[38] Civil society thus becomes a "spectacle of extravagance and misery as well as of the physical and ethical corruption common to both." No specific group, class, or individuals are to blame for this outcome: the realm of the bourgeois can only "establish itself and develop its full activity by way of its confusion and superseding of one confusion by another."[39] It is the result of the particular seeking its own ends in an unequal, and uncertain, world.

An attempt to undo this condition—for example, by putting the "direct burden of support" for the "increasingly impoverished mass"

---

36   Ibid., §200.
37   Ibid., §200R.
38   Jean-Jacques Rousseau, *Discourse on the Origin of Inequality*, Toronto: Dover, 2004 [1755].
39   Hegel, *PhR*, §185; Hegel, *Political Writings*, 150.

on the wealthy—"would be contrary to the principle of civil society and the feeling of self-sufficiency and honour among its individual members." Moreover, the astounding productivity of modern civil society means that solutions to poverty whereby "livelihood might be mediated by work (i.e. by the opportunity to work)" are no better. They would only "increase the volume of production; but it is precisely in overproduction and the lack of a proportionate number of consumers who are themselves productive that the evil consists, and this is merely exacerbated by the two expedients in question." Ultimately, then, and perhaps the greatest contradiction of all—a paradox in the midst of plenty—it is civil society's unprecedented riches that render it incapable of self-regulation: "despite an *excess of riches*, civil society is *not wealthy enough*—i.e. its own distinct resources are not sufficient—to prevent an excess of poverty and the formation of a rabble."[40] Keynes called this problem the "curse of Midas," a classically inspired turn of phrase Hegel would have appreciated.

## The Rabble: Poverty without Honor

The rabble is a key figure in Hegel's political philosophy. It is a historical actor and a specter, conjuring up both the *sans-culottes* of Paris 1793 and the menacing "people" Robespierre habitually recalled to chasten the Convention; it is both the revolutionary force and the looming threat of revolution. To say, as I have, that Hegel's thoughts on political and political economic matters are shaped by the revolution more than anything else is also to say that the rabble, as actor and specter, haunts his every word in the *Philosophy of Right*.

The rabble is not some premodern mass that has yet to be absorbed by civil society. It is a product of civil society, a modern phenomenon. And, since the rabble is the inevitable precipitate of an unregulated bourgeois civil society enjoying its "freedoms"—which generates as much "deprivation and want" as it does riches—it is the

---

40  Hegel, *PhR*, §245.

inevitable outcome of the neglect of necessity. "Rights to a livelihood are real rights, and they must necessarily be respected to prevent a rabble from emerging."[41] For Hegel, history made it clear, as Robespierre said, that *Notrecht* can only be denied by bayonets and that is bound to fail sooner or later. For all involved, from the rich to the poor, neither freedom nor justice would result.

> Every human being has a right to demand a livelihood from society, so also must society protect him against himself. It is not just starvation which is at stake here; the wider viewpoint is the need to prevent a rabble from emerging.[42]

It is crucial to emphasize here that the rabble is constituted almost entirely by the poor, and it is constituted *involuntarily*. The poor are not "naturally" rabble. No individual "chooses" to join the rabble in any sense of "free choice"; he or she is driven there by the specific experience of poverty in bourgeois civil society, in which productivity "increases in an unendingly large proportion to consumer need, and thus in the end even those who work hard cannot earn their bread." The rabble is condemned to demand its subsistence.[43]

---

41  Hegel, *PhR*, §§243, 238.

42  Ibid., §240. For these same reasons, the rabble is for Hegel one of the principal drivers of European colonialism. In passages most famously associated with David Harvey's account of the capitalist nation-state's "spatial fix"—but also noted before Harvey by Rosa Luxemburg and Albert O. Hirschman, among others—Hegel describes the colonies as a social safety-valve for the rabble; Ibid., §246, 248R: "This inner dialectic of society drives it—or in the first instance *this specific society*—to go beyond its own confines and look for consumers, and hence the means it requires for subsistence, in other nations which lack those means of which it has a surplus or which generally lag behind it in creativity, etc . . . Civil society is driven to establish colonies. The increase of population alone has this effect; but a particular factor is the emergence of a mass of people who cannot gain satisfaction for their needs by their work when production exceeds the needs of consumers." See also Ibid., §§247–48; compare with Rosa Luxemburg, *The Accumulation of Capital*, trans. A. Schwarzschild, London: Routledge, 2003; Albert O. Hirschman, "On Hegel, Imperialism, and Structural Stagnation," *Journal of Development Economics* 3, 1976, 1–8; David Harvey, "The Spatial Fix: Hegel, von Thünen, and Marx," *Antipode* 13: 3, 1981, 1–12.

43  *Vorlesungen*, IV, 612, 614; quoted and translated in Anderson, "Hegel's Implicit View on How to Solve Poverty," 188, 192; Frank Ruda, *Hegel's Rabble: An Investigation into Hegel's Philosophy of Right*, London: Continuum, 2011, 145.

To be of the rabble, then, is in practice to be the opposite of free. As individuals, the poor are alienated,

> left with the needs of civil society and yet—since society has at the same time taken from them the natural means of acquisition, and also dissolves the bond of the family in its wider sense as a kinship group—they are more or less deprived of all the advantages of society.[44]

A "large mass of people sinks below the level of a certain standard of living," and

> that feeling of right, integrity, and honour which comes from supporting oneself by one's own activity and work is lost. This leads to the creation of a *rabble* [*Pöbels*], which in turn makes it much easier for disproportionate wealth to be concentrated in a few hands.[45]

But if the poor are not "naturally" rabble, it is equally important to Hegel's account that the problem is not poverty per se, but rather the "disposition associated with poverty," that is, "inward rebellion against the rich, against society, the government, etc." This, not relative poverty, is the real "evil": "that the rabble do not have sufficient *honour* to gain their livelihood through their own work."[46]

> The emergence of poverty is in general a consequence of civil society, and on the whole arises necessarily out of it. Poverty is a condition in civil society which is unhappy and forsaken on all sides. The poor are burdened not only by external distress, but also by moral indignation . . . The poor are subject to yet another division, a division of emotion between them and civil society. The poor man feels excluded and mocked by everyone, and this gives

---

44   Hegel, *PhR*, §241.
45   Ibid., §244.
46   Ibid.

rise to an inner indignation. He is conscious of himself as an infinite, free being, and thus arises the demand that his external existence should correspond to this consciousness. In civil society it is not only natural duress against which the poor man has to struggle. The poor man is opposed not only by nature, a mere being, but also by my will . . . In this position, where the existence of freedom becomes something wholly contingent, inner indignation is necessary. Because the individual's freedom has no existence, the recognition of universal freedom disappears. From this condition arises that shamelessness that we find in the rabble. A rabble arises chiefly in a developed civil society.[47]

Which is to say: Robespierre returns through the dialectic of modernity. *Bourgeois civil society—liberalism—renders honorable poverty categorically impossible.* In *"this specific society,"* there is no honor in poverty, and the poor are, by definition, without honor.[48]

There are two further features of Hegel's rabble that merit some attention at this point, as both come to serve a more significant function in Keynes's own Keynesianism, an intervention in a world even further defined by the separation of civil society and the state, the bourgeois from the *citoyen*. The first, as briefly hinted above, is that the rabble is constituted almost entirely by the poor—but not completely. In his later lectures, Hegel also mentions the possibility of what we might call a "rich rabble."[49]

[The] rabble disposition also appears where there is wealth. The rich man thinks that he can buy anything, because he knows himself as the power of the particularity of self-consciousness. This wealth can lead to the same mockery and shamelessness that we find in the poor rabble.[50]

---

47  Hegel, *PhR*, 453n.
48  Hegel, *PhR*, §246.
49  Ruda dubs it the "luxury-rabble"; see *Hegel's Rabble*, 41.
50  Hegel, *PhR*, 454n.

This is something of a distraction; clearly the problem of the rabble is overwhelmingly the result of modern poverty, just as it is clear that the rabble is the reason the "important question of how poverty can be remedied is one which agitates and torments modern societies especially."[51]

And yet, the rich rabble also matter, perhaps disproportionately, relative to their number in a given society. Frank Ruda suggests—and Žižek agrees—that "gamblers" exemplify Hegel's rich rabble, those who do not work but instead rely "on the contingent movement of bourgeois economy" in arenas like the stock market.[52] In that sense, they too are outside the interdependent "system of needs" that constitutes bourgeois civil society (in their case, by choice). Like the poor rabble, a product of modern political-economic dynamics, the rich rabble are also a postrevolutionary variation on premodern feudal–aristocratic parasitism: the rentiers, those who live off the wealth of civil society but contribute nothing to it by their labor. In other words, today we would call the rich rabble "finance capital," and if Hegel were alive, its growing influence on bourgeois civil society might have caused him great concern—if nothing else, it certainly would have surprised him. He expected the dialectic of modernity to lead—and to be led, by the ethical state—in a different direction.

The second feature worth noting is that with the emergence of the rabble, as agent and specter, the temporality of necessity is fundamentally altered. "Earlier," Hegel says, "we considered *Notrecht* as something referring to a momentary need." But with the constitution of the rabble in an "increasingly impoverished mass," and the socialization of what might otherwise be an atomized or (to use Sartre's term) "serial" experience of dishonor, "distress no longer has merely this momentary character. In the emergence of poverty the power of particularity comes into existence in opposition to the reality of freedom."[53] In other words, once civil society has a rabble on

---

51　Ibid., §244; Ruda, *Hegel's Rabble*, 133.
52　Ibid., 132; Slavoj Žižek, *Less than Nothing: Hegel and the Shadow of Dialectical Materialism*, London: Verso, 2012, 436.
53　Hegel, *PhR*, 453 n.4.

its hands, it is potentially already too late—merely attempting at that point to suppress the problem by meeting its needs will not necessarily be enough. The "rabble-mentality," the product of poverty combined with a collective feeling of exclusion and dishonor, cannot be dependably neutralized by the exercise or acknowledgement of *Notrecht* alone. The necessity determining *Notrecht* is transformed in the rabble from a moment of desperate need to a structural condition.

This in turn demands a reconsideration of the role and reason of the state's very mode of government. It must not only "unify," in the sense that the particular (the individual) must understand itself as an element of the universal (the state), in direct relation to it, as the standard accounts of Hegel's ethical state always (rightly) emphasize. The state must also be both anticipatory and pharmaceutical, that is, it must constantly monitor the present with its relation to the future in mind and be ready to diagnose problems and administer solutions to meet immediate necessity. And it must do so in the knowledge that uncertainty troubles both such efforts:

> Now even if the possibility exists for individuals to share in the universal resources, and even if this possibility is guaranteed by the public authority, it remains—apart from the fact that such a guarantee must always be incomplete—open to contingencies of a subjective kind. This is increasingly the case the more it takes such conditions as skill, health, capital, etc. for granted.[54]

Modern government thus requires a science of these relations—of the present to the future, and of diagnosis to prescription: political economy. The state is the only institution that can ensure the poor "sufficient honour," and political economy is the means to that end.

---

54   Ibid., §237.

# CHAPTER 7

# The State and the Masses

H ow is the state to provide the poor with "sufficient honour"? What role does political economy play in its provision, and why is it so essential to "modern societies"? After Foucault, we might frame these questions in terms of the centrality of political economy to "governmentality." But it is not widely recognized that he was far from the first to ask them on these terms: in 1821, reflecting on the problem of material poverty and the rabble, Hegel diagnosed *in media res* what Foucault recognized with hindsight a century and a half later:

> Political economy is the science which starts from this view of needs and labour but then has the task of explaining mass-relationships and mass-movements in their complexity and their qualitative and quantitative character. This is one of the sciences which have arisen out of the conditions of the modern world.[1]

---

1    G. W. F. Hegel, *Elements of the Philosophy of Right*, trans. H. B. Nisbet, Cambridge: Cambridge University Press, 1991, §189R. (Hereinafter cited as *PhR*.) This is not the only point on which Hegel directly anticipates Foucault. For example, in his 1802 discussion of the German Constitution, Hegel considers the shift in the exercise of state power during the era Foucault identifies as the transition from the "state of justice" to the "state of government": "[t]his transition from the state of overt power to that of calculated power was not, of course, accomplished all at once." In his examination of the question of crime in civil society—i.e. as object of biopolitics—Hegel remarks: "crime is no longer an injury merely to a subjective infinite, but to the universal cause whose existence is inherently stable and

For Hegel, the distinctively modern confrontation between free-dom and necessity is the state's *raison d'être*, and political economy is how the modern state thinks. A substantial part of the distinctiveness or innovation of Hegel's philosophical enterprise lies in his effort to incorporate and come to terms with the meaning of political econ-omy and "the economic" as a category of modern life. In contrast to Kant, who tried to completely exclude political economy from prac-tical philosophy, it was "the impotence of the ought" that motivated Hegel to study political economy.[2] When he did so, he found it provided him "with a frame of reference for a completely altered conceptual deduction."[3]

The conceptual alteration shapes two principal dimensions of Hegel's approach to the problem of *Recht*—of law and right, freedom and necessity—in other words, of government. First, Hegel does not see political economy as just another (if somewhat vulgar) way of grasping the modern condition. Instead, it is for him a specifically *modern* way of understanding modernity. It is, one might say, the way in which modernity comes to understand itself; in Habermas's words, "writing in the wake of political economy," Hegel realized it "unmasked" the fact that production, not law, held society togeth-er.[4] After the Enlightenment, and especially after the Revolution, *Recht* is always necessarily, if not only, a political-economic relation. Second, political economy provides modern government with what has been called a "spectator's" view of "the whole realm of human action."[5] It is something of a bird's-eye view on history, the

---

strong. This gives rise to the viewpoint that an action maybe a *danger* to society." See G. W. F. Hegel, *Political Writings*, Cambridge: Cambridge University Press, 1999, 49; Hegel, *PhR*, §218.

2  Jürgen Habermas, *Between Facts and Norms: Contributions to a Discourse Theory of Law and Democracy*, trans. William Rehg, Cambridge: MIT Press, 1998, 57.

3  Manfred Riedel, *Between Tradition and Modernity: The Hegelian Transformation of Political Philosophy*, trans. W. Wright, Cambridge: Cambridge University Press, 1984, 8, 44.

4  Habermas, *Between Facts and Norms*, 45.

5  Hannah Arendt, *On Revolution*, New York: Penguin, 2006, 42–43. Arendt actually labels this "spectatorial" stance Hegel's "political fallacy," but she then goes on to say: "this fallacy is relatively difficult to detect because of the truth inherent in it, which is that all stories begun and enacted by men unfold their true meaning only when they have come to

perspective that allows us, for example, to isolate a "system of needs" in the dispersed, anarchic sociality of production-distribution-consumption. In postrevolutionary modernity, *Recht* is always, if not only, an aggregate, *mass* relation.

For Hegel, then, what Marx called political economy's fully developed "final shape"—the early nineteenth-century work of David Ricardo and Thomas Malthus, for example—is indeed bourgeois, as Marx said. But it is never "vulgar," as Marx also often said. It emerges contemporaneously with bourgeois-liberal civil society, not as a simple alibi for that society but rather as a result of its contradictions. This political economy is postrevolutionary by definition, and, unsurprisingly, constructed more or less consciously as an antirevolutionary science, born of the desire to maintain some stability in the process of change and, in so doing, to rescue modernity in ways that may be "truer" to its concept—concrete freedom. In other words, the point is not to elaborate a reason that justifies the abstract ethics of the modern liberal-commercial order, but rather to understand the relations that constitute that order, so that the state can construct the necessary material and institutional foundations for its legitimacy.

## Hegel on Political Economy

To grasp how Hegel embraced political economy, it is perhaps helpful to take a close look at the paragraph (§236) in the *Philosophy of Right* where he emphasizes its governmental-regulatory implications most directly. The argument directly precedes his account of the rabble. It very clearly points to the implications of *Notrecht* for the Smithian "circular flow" of the system of needs and derives the consequently essential role of the state. Here it is in full, including later

---

their end, so that it may indeed appear as though only the spectator, and not the agent, can hope to understand what actually happened in any given chain of events." Ultimately, it is clear that the "fallacy" of a spectatorial account of "what actually happened"—to which she falls victim as much as any other thinker—are not the real problem for Arendt. What draws her ire is that it is *Hegel* whose spectatorial categories come to shape revolutionary consciousness, and not those of someone less critical and less "pitying," like Thomas Jefferson.

remarks (added by Hegel) and additions (*Zusatz*, student transcriptions from Hegel's lectures):

> The differing interests of producers and consumers may come into collision with each other, and even if, *on the whole*, their correct relationship re-establishes itself automatically, its adjustment also needs to be consciously regulated by an agency which stands above both sides. The right to regulate individual matters in this way (e.g. by deciding the value of the commonest necessities of life) is based on the fact that, when commodities in completely universal everyday use are publicly marketed, they are offered not so much to a particular individual as such, as to the individual in a universal sense, i.e. to the public; and the task of upholding the public's right not to be cheated and of inspecting market commodities may, as a common concern, be entrusted to a public authority.— But the main reason why some universal provision and direction are necessary is that large branches of industry are dependent on external circumstances and remote combinations whose full implications cannot be grasped by individuals who are tied to these spheres by their occupation.
>
> > Remark: At the opposite extreme to freedom of trade and commerce in civil society are public arrangements to provide for and determine the work of everyone. These included, for example, the building of the pyramids in ancient times, and other enormous works in Egypt and Asia which were undertaken for public ends, and in which the work of the individual was not mediated by his particular arbitrary will and particular interest. This interest invokes the freedom of trade and commerce against regulation from above; but the more blindly it immerses itself in its selfish ends, the more it requires regulation to bring it back to the universal, and to moderate and shorten the duration of those dangerous convulsions to which its collisions give rise, and which should return to equilibrium by a process of unconscious necessity.
> >
> > Addition: The aim of oversight and provisions on the part of the police [*Polizei*] is to mediate between the individual and the

universal possibility which is available for the attainment of individual ends. The *Polizei* should provide for street-lighting, bridge-building, the pricing of daily necessities, and public health. Two main views are prevalent on this subject. One maintains that the *Polizei* should have oversight over everything, and the other maintains that the *Polizei* should have no say in such matters, since everyone will be guided in his actions by the needs of others. The individual must certainly have a right to earn his living in this way or that; but on the other hand, the public also has a right to expect that necessary tasks will be performed in the proper manner. Both viewpoints must be satisfied, and the freedom of trade should not be such as to prejudice the general good.[6]

Two things are worth mentioning right away, because they shape everything that follows. First, the as-yet-unnamed state is political economy's protagonist from the beginning. The very first sentence of the paragraph establishes the inability of civil society to self-regulate, even if, from an aggregate perspective, it appears to do so "automatically." Hegel is not suggesting that correct relationship *will* re-establish itself; he is saying that *even if it does*— there is no guarantee at all, and elsewhere he makes it clear he thinks such a development so unlikely or rare as to be a distraction—the liberal market economy always "needs to be consciously regulated by an agency which stands above" the collision between producers and consumers. Again, this is wisdom Hegel learned from James Steuart, the most important influence on his understanding of market society. For Steuart, maybe even more than for Hegel, "the market is permanently on the verge of collapse." The problem is that modern economies are just too complicated to be expected to work smoothly. Their component parts cannot be left to the caprice of the market, but must take form "according to a determined proportion." Which is to say that Steuart, like Hegel after him, assumes an authoritative "statesman at the head of government, systematically conducting every part of it"

6    Hegel, *PhR*, §236.

so the market can provide "liberty" while also operating for the "general good."[7]

The second thing to note is that the problem of necessity raises its irrepressible head immediately: the regulator-state or "agency which stands above" is required first and foremost because of the constant potential for problems in the market-based distribution of the "commonest necessities of life." These necessities—Robespierre's *denrées*, the material realm of *Notrecht*—are where the rubber hits the road, as it were, for Robespierre but also for Hegel and Keynes. The distributional challenge is only one side of the problem of poverty— there is also the curse of dishonor—but it is the first priority, and addressing it or not is the difference between a secure footing for civilization and disorder. At the level of state power, this is equivalent to the difference between direction and domination, universality or pure "outward" force.

In political economy as *savoir* and *connaissance*, the modern state has at its disposal the tools to explain, and thus consciously regulate, "mass-relationships and mass-movements in their complexity and their qualitative and quantitative character." Barring such oversight, markets tend to operate according to a liberal conception of "commercial freedom" completely unmoored from the customary principles of morality or justice grounded in actually existing communities. In abstracting from the inescapable substance of material life, commodities essential for life are rendered formally equivalent to nonessential luxuries, and their concrete actuality is denied. As Robespierre said, in the real world of necessity, indigo and wheat are not equivalent. A similar problem holds in that the supply of necessities, like other commodities, is offered on a "mass" basis to a "mass" of undifferentiated consumers, an anonymous "public," whose internal dynamics like relative deprivation are of no concern to free commerce. Without the state, the quality of these essential goods is no single agent's responsibility.

---

7    Mark Neocleous, "Policing the System of Needs: Hegel, Political Economy, and the Police of the Market," *History of European Ideas* 24: 1, 1998, 49–50; see also Chapter 6, n.33.

But, Hegel writes, it is not just these features that make political economy and its attendant regulatory capacities so important to modern communities. The "main reason why some universal provision and direction are necessary" is the dependence of much of the modern economy, and thus modern life, "on external circumstances and remote combinations whose full implications cannot be grasped by individuals who are tied to these spheres by their occupation." The state, again, is the sole agent that can see the "general interest" and address these challenges, coordinating investment and protecting the community's circular flow from the inescapable uncertainties and contingencies that characterize the bourgeois liberal market-based mode of resource allocation.

Hegel's appended remark in paragraph §236 follows out the logic of this argument. Clearly, he says, one might take the above as a rationale for an almost "total" state, in which everyone is accorded his or her proper economic place by way of "public arrangements to provide for and determine the work of everyone." But that would be to forget that here we are talking about the postrevolutionary world. As far as Hegel is concerned, the modern centrality of the individual subject—particularity—may not be unmediated, but it is irrevocable. The state that refused it would be little more than a variation on what many, including Hegel, have unfortunately characterized as "Oriental despotism." Even if it were an appropriate alternative, Hegel considered it untenable in postfeudal Europe.

And yet, even if Hegel insists we must embrace—enthusiastically, even—the advent of a particular experience of individual freedom on the historical stage, that does not mean he believes we must accept its abstract logic uncritically. Indeed, as his critique of liberalism makes perfectly clear, Hegel regards such uncritical acceptance as at least as great a danger as despotism. It is the celebration of "particular interest" or "selfish ends" that threatens *Sittlichkeit* most immediately, because its unfettered pursuit (in the name of "freedom of trade and commerce") leads again and again to precisely those "convulsions" that bourgeois civil society is by its nature entirely unprepared to manage. The more "commerce" opposes itself to regulation "from above," the more self-interested it becomes, "the more it requires regulation to bring it back to the universal."

The universal is thus a "resource" for all, and the objective of both regulation and the provision of necessities is simultaneously to produce it and to ensure its secure footing. The chief regulator and provider is the *Polizei*, which for Hegel is close to what we would now call "public administration" in the "public interest."[8] In the German tradition from which Hegel drew the term, the primary focus of the *Polizei* was the "abolition of disorder." He assigns it responsibility for a set of tasks that could almost have been drawn word-for-word from Smith's account of the state's role in *The Wealth of Nations*: "street-lighting, bridge-building, the pricing of daily necessities, and public health."[9] Again, there is no reason in Hegel's mind (or Keynes's, certainly) for state intervention to be an all-or-nothing affair, as if the question must be decided on Manichean terms, either absolutism or *laissez-faire*. "Although particularity and universality have become separated in civil society, they are nevertheless bound up with and conditioned by each other."[10] The question is thus a rather pragmatic matter: the individual is free to make a living as he or she chooses, but the provision of necessities and public goods must not be sacrificed on the altar of liberal dogma: "the freedom of trade should not be such as to prejudice the general good."

## Poverty and Honor

"The general good" is not only enjoyed generally; it is also always a particular phenomenon. The general good is realized in recognizing that the right of individual persons "means not only that contingencies which interfere with this or that end should be cancelled

---

8    I use the original *Polizei* to avoid any confusion arising from "police." It is not an agency to prevent crime and punish criminals, but one that "polices" in the sense of "policing the limits": "[w]ithout policing, the market cannot exist"; Neocleous, "Policing the System of Needs," 53.

9    Hegel, *PhR*, §236.

10    Ibid., §184.

[*aufgehoben*] and that the undisturbed security of persons and property should be guaranteed, but also that the livelihood and welfare of individuals should be secured." In other words, it is in the interest of the universal that "particular welfare" be "duly actualized."[11] This requires both the provision of necessities (that is, acknowledging *Notrecht* and securing the welfare of the poor) and the promise of "that feeling of right, integrity, and honour which comes from supporting oneself by one's own activity and work." These are the only conditions in which a modern society can avoid the emergence of a rabble and attendant disorder.

But because the "emergence of poverty is in general a consequence of civil society, and on the whole arises necessarily out of it," in a social formation in which the bourgeoisie is hegemonic, "inner indignation is necessary" for the poor.[12] This is what Hegel means when he writes that a "rabble arises chiefly in a developed civil society." It is precisely when bourgeois civil societies' market-based arbitrariness and contingency dominate that the potential for the creation of a rabble is greatest. The closer liberalism comes to *laissez-faire* purity, the more likely it is to implode. The only answer is to construct a different hegemony, one that dialectically overcomes civil society's contradictions while preserving the modern individual liberty of which it is both cause and effect. This is possible via a set of nonbourgeois political-economic and social institutions that can bridge the chasm between civil society's individual freedoms and the state's general good.

Interestingly, Hegel takes the provision of necessities to be rather unproblematic. He offers some brief suggestions on tax regimes and endorses Robespierrist price controls on what we would now call "wage goods," but in general he assumes that any state worthy of the name will have the capacity to make these arrangements. Again, however, it is not just material deprivation and want that is the problem. It is not enough to merely feed the poor; society must also allay the "rabble mentality" to which poverty disposes them, the dishonor

---

11    Ibid., §230.
12    Ibid., 453n.

to which they are constantly subject. This is why "the important question of how poverty can be remedied is one which agitates and torments [*bewegende und quälende*] modern societies especially."[13]

And yet: it is absolutely essential, at this stage in the argument, to emphasize that Hegel is in no way proposing the provision of necessities or price ceilings as a "solution" to poverty. The point is not to rid modern societies of poverty, which he understood as an impossible task. Substantive inequality is imposed by nature.[14] Modern poverty may be a product of bourgeois civil society, but poverty per se is transhistorical. Consequently, while "remedy" is the standard translation for Hegel's infinitive *abzuhelfen*—hence "how to remedy poverty" might be more grammatically accurate—we would be wrong to regard "cure" as synonymous with "fix." Hegel does not believe poverty can be eliminated or cured. He believes the "rabble mentality" can be subdued, even overcome in the becoming-ethical state, but poverty will not disappear as a consequence. "To remedy" is best understood here as "to treat," that is, to manage, care for, or tend to. The question of poverty per se is not amenable to a cure. When Hegel declares it "agitates and torments modern societies especially," he does not mean that poverty is greater, more terrible, or more widespread than it was in premodern societies. He means, rather, that relative to earlier ages, for modernity the question of poverty, particularly mass poverty, is especially agonizing, even haunting.[15] Hence the emergence of political economy as a science of government, a distinctively modern knowledge and way of knowing focused on the problem of the age.

In short, the question for Hegel is precisely the one Robespierre wrestled with in 1792: the possibility of honorable poverty in a liberal order. And, like Robespierre, Hegel comes to the conclusion that insofar as bourgeois liberalism renders the state and the "general good" subordinate to the commercial order of civil society and the

---

13    Ibid., §244A.
14    Ibid., §244A, 453n.
15    Jean-Claude Bourdin, "Hegel et la «question sociale»: société civile, vie et détresse," *Revue germanique internationale* 15, 2001, 168–69.

abstract freedom of self-interest, honorable poverty in a liberal order is impossible. But if he agrees with Robespierre that bourgeois civil society is not the answer, in contrast to him—indeed, in direct response to the terrorist legacy of Robespierre the *"homme à princ-ipe"*—Hegel refuses the revolutionary critique. Instead, he proposes the peaceful "disorganization of civil society," a gradualist revolution without revolution under the guise of much wiser, more pragmatic and experienced *"hommes d'état."*[16]

## The Structure of the Ethical State

The principal means to this end are two sets of institutions: the *Polizei* (mentioned above) and the *Korporation*, Hegel's term for any nonstate association or society formally recognized by the state.[17] It serves as a sort of intermediate point between civil society and the ethical state, in which the *Korporation* member's particularity expresses itself as a universal end for the first time, in the "inherent likeness of such particulars, as the quality *common* to them all." Because Hegel emphasizes the realm of labor in his account, there are moments in the *Philosophy of Right* when it almost seems as if the *Korporation* is merely a medieval guild.[18] Yet professional and trade

---

16   Hegel, *PhR*, §255R; Hegel, *Political Writings*, 265, 269. In a critique of the Jacobins in "On the English Reform Bill," Hegel (using the French in the original) writes of the "antithesis between the *hommes d'état* [men of state or statesmen] and *hommes à principes* [men of principle] which at once emerged quite starkly in France at the beginning of the Revolution." The problem, he says, is that *hommes à principes* like Robespierre "can gain a foothold all the more easily because the principles themselves are, as such, simple in charac-ter, so that they can be grasped quickly even by the ignorant; and since these principles can in any case claim, by virtue of their universality, to be adequate for all, they are sufficient to enable anyone with some facility of talent and some energy of character and ambition to attain that effect on the reason of the masses (who are equally inexperienced in such matters). Conversely, it is not so easy to acquire the knowledge, experience, and business routine of the *hommes d'état*, although these qualities are equally necessary for applying rational principles and introducing them to actual life"; Ibid., 265.

17   I use Hegel's German *Korporation* for the same reason I use *Polizei*—because the standard meaning of the English translation ("corporation") is far enough from what Hegel has in mind as to be unhelpful.

18   Hegel, *PhR*, 455 n.2: As the editors of *Philosophy of Right* suggest, Hegel seems to have had "mixed feelings" about the guild system. He supported the Stein-Hardenberg reforms of 1808 to 1812—at that time, the most radical internal challenges ever posed to

associations are not the only bodies that fulfill the role of *Korporation*; churches and municipal governments do as well.[19] The *Korporation* has powers recognized by the state (such as membership and apprenticeship), which give it "the right to assume the role of a *second* family for its members," a role civil society as a whole cannot perform since it "is more remote from individuals and their particular requirements."[20]

From the perspective of the individual member, however, perhaps the primary political-economic function of the corporation is this: it ensures that his or her "livelihood is *guaranteed*." In other words, Hegel says, the *Korporation* promises its members "*secure* resources"; necessary livelihood and "capability" are "*recognized*" for each individual. Consequently—and this is why the *Korporation* is so essential to Hegel's political vision, specifically with respect to modernity's tendency to produce a rabble—the "member of a *Korporation* has no need to demonstrate his competence and his regular income and means of support—i.e. the fact that he *is somebody* . . . Thus, he has *his honour in his estate*."[21]

This, ultimately, is what it means to have honor: to be "somebody," and to be secure in somebody-hood. That security is provided by the *Korporation*, but the honor resides in "*belonging to an estate* [*Ständ*]"—a broad social position Hegel contrasts with class [*Klasse*].

---

Prussian absolutism—which (among other changes) abolished guild monopolies in favor of "free enterprise." At the same time, however, he viewed the decline of the guild system as a *result* of the bourgeois pursuit of self-interest the reforms endorsed: "According to the principle of atomicity, each cares merely for himself and does not concern himself about anything in common; it is left to each whether he is destined for a certain social estate, without considering the utility of his choice from a political point of view; since, according to those who want it this way, someone whose work no one approves will go into another trade. This principle gives such a person over to contingency. Our standpoint of reflection, this spirit of atomicity, this spirit of finding your honour in your individuality and not in what is common—this is destructive, and has caused the corporations to fall to pieces"; Ibid., 455 n. 2.

19    "[T]he member of civil society, in accordance with his *particular skill*, is a member of a corporation whose universal end is therefore *wholly concrete*, and no wider in scope than the end inherent in the trade which is the corporation's proper business and interest"; Ibid., §251; §§270R, 288.

20    Ibid., §252.

21    Ibid., §253.

The term "estate" had of course been in common use in prerevolutionary France to name the nobility, clergy, and the people (the first, second, and third estates, respectively). Hegel, however, understands the postrevolutionary polity as radically transformed (a declining aristocracy having lost its taken-for-granted primacy, and the "people" no longer an undifferentiated mass).[22] As he understood it, in modern civil society the estates constitute the social division of labor and thus determine the political-economic categories of citizenship; they are a crucial means by which the selfish ends of particularity are overcome in the development of a consciousness of the universal.[23] Membership in an estate is the only way in which the citizen can enjoy the "stability," "rectitude," and "recognition" in which honor consists, and, because the estate, like civil society, is not itself a formal or legal category, the *Korporation* is the means by which such membership is secured. Both the poor-rabble and the rich-rabble lack this honor:

> When complaints are made about that luxury and love of extravagance of the professional classes which is associated with the creation of a rabble, we must not overlook, in addition to other causes (e.g. the increasingly mechanical nature of work), its *ethical* basis . . . If the individual is not a member of a legally recognized

22    Hegel is not at all clear on who belongs to what estate in the new bourgeois order. In particular, the membership of the second estate, the "estate of trade and industry," is vague. "It has the task of *giving form* to natural products, and it relies for its livelihood on its *work*, on *reflection* and the understanding, and essentially on its mediation of the needs and work of others. What it produces and enjoys, it owes chiefly to *itself* and to its own activity." This is intended to distinguish the second estate from the first, the peasantry, which is "more inclined to subservience"; the second estate is "inclined to freedom." Through the lens of more recent social categories, exactly who comprises the "second estate" is never resolved. Are they bourgeois capitalists? Artisans? Industrial workers? All three or some combination thereof? One might argue that this lack of clarity as to who exactly the freedom-inclined beneficiaries of bourgeois civil society are has since become essential to liberals, since it suggests that either we are all entrepreneurs, or that at the very least bourgeois interests are everyone's interests. In other words, with Hegel, the second estate sometimes seems to be equivalent to society in general. See Ibid., §204.

23    This conceptualization of the estate owes a great deal to Steuart; see Dominique Carboret, "The Market Economy and Social Classes in James Steuart and G. W. F. Hegel," in Ramón Tortajada (ed.), *The Economics of James Steuart*, London: Routledge, 1999, 57–75.

corporation (and it is only through legal recognition that a community becomes a corporation), he is without the *honour of belonging to an estate*, his isolation reduces him to the selfish aspect of his trade, and his livelihood and satisfaction lack *stability* . . . Within the corporation, the help which poverty receives loses its contingent and unjustly humiliating character, and wealth, in fulfilling the duty it owes to its association, loses the ability to provoke arrogance in its possessor and envy in others; rectitude also receives the true recognition and honour which are due to it.[24]

Thus, along with the family, the *Korporation* constitutes the "ethical [*Sittliche*] root of the state." But unlike the family—which Hegel takes as a prior, transhistorical constraint on modern individual self-interest—the *Korporation* is based squarely in civil society, in the "system of needs." It alone ensures honor. In a market-based society, it is not enough to create informal or unrecognized collectives, not directly linked to and recognized by the state, for it is only through these linkages that the "individual citizen" can have a (necessarily indirect) share in the "universal business of the state." The *Korporation* is thus the only way "to provide ethical man with a universal activity in addition to his private end." Without it, all we have is "decline into a miserable guild system."[25]

Hegel's *Korporation* is thus a means by which to achieve many institutional objectives at once and to subdue bourgeois civil society's contradictions and their tragic consequences in the form of the rabble (by overcoming them). The *Korporation* promises to realize these goals by recognizing the priority of immediate necessity—providing subsistence—and allocating all citizens to an appropriate place in the circulating system of needs. In so doing, it eliminates the uncertainty and "contingency" with which the modern subject—the poor especially—is afflicted, and stability and honor are established as both a buffer against civil society's "principle of atomicity" and as

24   Hegel, *PhR*, §§207, 253.
25   Ibid., §§255, 255R.

a means by which to participate productively in the modern market economy. In other words, the *Korporation* is nothing less than Hegel's solution to the problem of under- and unemployment. It does not promise the end of poverty—an impossibility—but rather the end of the alienation of the poor that leads to the emergence of the rabble. Along with the "sanctity" of the family, "the honour attaching to the *Korporation* are the two moments around which the disorganization of civil society revolves."[26] It is the means by which the "sphere of civil society thus passes over into the *state*."[27]

This disorganization of civil society is the key to escaping the havoc permanently percolating in modernity. In civil society, "separation is the determining factor," and thus "[e]verything depends on the unity of the universal and the particular within the state . . . The state is the sole precondition of the attainment of particular ends and welfare."[28] If, however, "the state is confused with civil society," then it is realized only as a coercive night-watchman for which "the security and protection of property and personal freedom, *the interest of individuals as such* becomes the ultimate end."[29] For Hegel, this is liberalism, the direction in which post-Revolutionary Europe seemed to be headed, and it would be a disaster. So too, however, would be a condition in which the state was realized as a mere contract among individuals, as representing the abstract "*common element*" of all contracted individual wills, and subject to the same arbitrariness as the single individual will upon which it is modeled. This is exactly what led to the Terror, because

> when these abstractions are invested with power, they afforded the tremendous spectacle, for the first time we know of in human

---

26   Ibid., §255R.

27   Ibid., §256.

28   Ibid., §263, 261A. In the words of Shlomo Avineri, the "state becomes necessary at the moment when society seems to be heading for disruption and chaos: it is the re-integration of the self into itself as a universal being after economic life has particularized, atomized and made its activity into an abstraction"; Shlomo Avineri, *Hegel's Theory of the Modern State*, Cambridge: Cambridge University Press, 1972, 99.

29   Hegel, *PhR*, §258R.

history, of the overthrowing of all existing conditions within an actual major state and the revision of its constitution from first principles and purely in terms of *thought*; the *intention* behind this was to give it what was *supposed* to be a purely *rational* basis.[30]

But Hegel, who understood the irreducible force of *Notrecht*, "did not dwell on the sacred and inviolable nature of the contract."[31] Such principles and abstractions were Kantian—*Sollen*, not *Sein*. They had no basis in *Sittlichkeit*, the world in which we actually live, and consequently "they turned the attempt into the most terrible and drastic event."[32]

The state enjoys its superordinate position because it is the knowledge of *Sittlichkeit*, social life itself, unfolding in the world. It has the privileged capacity to know "actuality," not merely the persons and things in the world, but their proper ethical relations, locations, and functions.[33] This means that unlike all the subordinate moments in modern societies (family, civil society, *Korporation*), the state is "*manifest* and clear to itself," it "thinks and knows itself and implements what it knows in so far as it knows it." Indeed, the principle of the state is "*thinking* itself."[34] This is why "the interest of the family and civil society must become focused on the state": because "the essence of the *modern* state" is that the universal necessarily has "the complete freedom of particularity and the well-being of individuals" as its proper content.[35] Here Hegel tries to go beyond Hobbes, for

---

30    Ibid.

31    Domenico Losurdo, *Hegel and the Freedom of Moderns*, Durham, NC: Duke University Press, 2004, 70.

32    Hegel, *PhR*, §258; see also Hegel, *Phenomenology of Spirit*, trans. A. V. Miller, Oxford: Clarendon Press, 1979, §§582–95. We find echoes of this assessment in Max Weber, *Economy and Society*, vol. 2, Berkeley: University of California Press, 1978, 1209–10: "This charismatic glorification of 'Reason', which found a characteristic expression in its apotheosis by Robespierre, is the last form that charisma has adopted in its fateful historical course." Robespierre, said Weber, presided over a "*Führer Demokratie*"; *Economy and Society*, vol. 1, 268.

33    Hegel, *PhR*, §270A: "A hand which has been cut off still looks like a hand and exists, but it has no actuality."

34    Ibid., §§257–58.

35    Ibid., §260A.

whom the particular and the universal always remain separate, married in the state only as a matter of necessity, so that the particular might persist in security. With Hobbes, subjection to the state is a sacrifice on the part of the individual so that he or she may maintain his or her particularity. For Hegel, the point is that this moment is overcome, and the particular comes to find its substance in the universal. Hobbes's is a theory of civil society and the "external state," whereas what Hegel offers is the state proper.[36]

It is essential to Hegel's account, however, that state-rationality is not misconstrued as having tapped into a vein of abstract truth that provides it with a universalizable set of rules or doctrines upon which all "proper" states operate. On the contrary, the state is the "nervous system"; the principle of the state is not Truth but "*thinking*," Reason operating concretely as a mode of government: "The state is not a work of art; it exists in the world, and hence in the sphere of arbitrariness, contingency, and error, and bad behaviour may disfigure it in many respects."[37] This is the world, riven with radical uncertainty, in which we actually live, the one in which bourgeois civil society "sets particularity at liberty" and the state "brings it back to universality."[38] This is Hegel's definition of what Keynes calls the "social interest," and only the state can realize it.

---

36   Ibid., §289A: "[c]ivil society is the field of conflict in which the private interest of each individual comes up against that of everyone else." This is further evidence of the way in which for Hegel (as for Keynes), the destructive atomization Hobbes associated with the state of nature is in fact not "natural" *qua* primordial, but a product of modernity itself. The chaos with which Hobbes associated nature is the reason he turned from an abstract "Reason" to "reckoning," or practical reason. As Charles Taylor argues, the social obligation engendered by the rejection of "nature" and the emphasis on "prudence" led Hobbes to his contractarian conception of society. Hegel too "fully endorses the modern rejection of the meaningful order of nature." Charles Taylor *Hegel*, Cambridge: Cambridge University Press, 1975, 367–68. However, Hegel also refuses the contractual solution in favor of a state that unifies the universal and the particular. Hegel's state, like Hobbes's, is clearly relatively autonomous from civil society—necessarily *distinct* from it, but unlike Hobbes's, it is never *separate* from it. Charles Taylor, *Hegel and Modern Society*, Cambridge: Cambridge University Press, 1979, 74.

37   Hegel, *PhR*, §§263, 258A.

38   Ibid., §260.

It is obvious to Hegel that the supra-institutional functions of a state that must be "the seat of knowledge" cannot be entrusted to just anyone: "those who know ought to govern."[39] Democracy or "popular sovereignty" is a bad idea, "one of those confused thoughts which are based on a *garbled* notion of the *people*." Hegel might have celebrated the modern emergence of individual liberty, but he was in no way a democrat in the "rule of, by and for the people" sense. Those who operate society's "nervous system" must clearly have an enlightened orientation—to the universal itself.[40]

The members of this "universal class" are in some sense ahead of their time. They are already operating with a knowledge and "political disposition" of which the masses are deemed incapable.[41] They see through what Keynes called the "colossal muddle": beyond civil society's stumbling path from confusion to confusion and through the common "confusion" of civil society with the state. They understand that the regulation and provision of necessities that modern societies' stability demands are themselves entirely dependent on the state's stability. The state must, therefore, do its best to give itself the only secure foundation available—the welfare of its subjects.[42] The "universal class" is the techno-philosophical bureaucratic elite that manages these relations. It facilitates a supersession of the Fable of the Bees through a constitutional order in which private vice is no longer public virtue despite itself (the vulgar version of Smith's circular flow), but the distinction itself disappears as the private interest finds its self-conscious realization in public virtue.

---

39  Hegel, *PhH*, 476.

40  Hegel, *PhR*, §279; see also §273 and Terry Pinkard, *Hegel: A Biography*, Cambridge: Cambridge University Press, 2000, 606–608. "On the English Reform Bill" of 1832, Hegel's last explicitly political contribution, is (among other things) a critique of the extension of the franchise in Britain on precisely these grounds; Hegel, *Political Writings*, 234–70. Instead, he clearly endorsed a constitutional monarchy, in which, as the classical distinction goes, the king reigns but does not govern. Government is the province of the universal class. Hegel (*PhR*, §280) says in no uncertain terms that the modern monarch is merely "someone to say 'yes' and to dot the 'i'."

41  Ibid., §268A.

42  Avineri, *Hegel's Theory of the Modern State*, 134: to Hegel the state is "universal altruism."

Much, if not all, of the universal class's capacity to undertake this role is attributable to political economy, the science of modern government; it "has the task of explaining mass-relationships and mass-movements in their complexity and their qualitative and quantitative character." In other words, political economy is useful precisely because the world is dynamic and uncertain: it examines *change*, some of which can be anticipated, but a lot of which cannot. It does not take a snapshot of a fixed set of relationships that allows state-rationality to formulate rules of operation. Rules like that would be useless; the stability of the social order and the guarantee of well-being—the provision of which for Hegel is *the* function of the state—is not maintained by sticking to procedure, but by the unending process of adaptably bringing "back to universality" the constantly changing masses of particularities "set at liberty" by modernity.[43] Moreover, radical uncertainty means that the state's project can in no way merely focus on long-run goals as classical liberalism suggests. There is no political equilibrium in which we can trust, no ultimate natural stability upon which society can rely, hunger will not disappear: "it is necessary to provide for single individuals, and no one should trust a principle according to which 'things will adjust, they will take care of themselves.'"[44]

Even at its most rigidly "classical" and *laissez-faire*, the central role of political economy at the "seat of knowledge" is proof that modern liberal government does not trust that "things will adjust, they will take care of themselves." If it really believed things "will take care of themselves," government would be either idle or unnecessary. And in its mistrust, it exposes itself as Keynesian, always aware that even in the unlikely event that some day "the ocean will be flat again," there is no guarantee the ship will weather the storm.

---

43 Hegel, *PhR*, §270A: "the state actualizes itself and gives its determinations a stable existence."

44 Quoted in Losurdo, *Hegel and the Freedom of Moderns*, 81.

## CHAPTER 8

# A Theory of Political Economy

At the 1989 bicentenary of the storming of the Bastille, London's *Daily Telegraph* published an editorial cartoon reproducing Jacques-Louis David's famous painting *The Death of Marat*, in which the murdered Jacobin revolutionary Jean-Paul Marat slumps over in his bath, clasping a letter introducing his assassin. In the cartoon, though, instead of the note from Charlotte Corday, Marat's lifeless hand holds a book entitled *Yet Another Book About the French Revolution*.[1] The cartoon is funnier than it is fair, but there is something to it. The Revolution has been "done." Its impact on Euro-American political thought, if not quite as well covered as the progress of events, has received only slightly less attention. Why keep returning to it? How much can it still matter, and in any event, hasn't enough been said?

And yet the Revolution's echoes have hardly faded away. On the contrary, its legacy remains immensely important. We continue to struggle with it, and seem fated to do so for a while longer. In the liberal capitalist global North, and perhaps elsewhere as well, it scores our history so deeply that what we call modernity is literally unthinkable without it. Even when we do not call it by name, it shapes, disproportionately, how we think about the world. As with

---

1 Reproduced in William Doyle, *The French Revolution: A Very Short Introduction*, Oxford: Oxford University Press, 2001, 104.

Keynesianism in general (see Chapter 2), this is both a cause and effect of the Eurocentrism that plagues political economy. The French Revolution is crucial to this account not because it was the *only* revolution that mattered in the revolutionary era, but because it was the one that absorbed the attentions of Europe's political economic and philosophical elites—all affluent white men who, unfortunately and with devastating effect, are nonetheless both the origins and the original thinkers of the problems at hand. For precisely this reason, it is worth briefly returning to the Revolution to see how Hegel's political thought led him from the Terror to political economy. Resetting the Revolution at the origins of political economy will also allow us to connect Keynes directly to it.

Just as it was for those long-dead white men, a substantial part of the Revolution's political significance in the centuries since lies in its apparently unresolvable ambiguity (for convenience, let us say it ended with Bonaparte's *coup d'état*, on November 9, 1799, better known as 18 Brumaire, Year VIII). On one hand, for those "moderns" who have come after, it stands as perhaps the decisive moment in the death of absolutism and the *ancien régime*. On these grounds, the Revolution is for all intents and purposes the inaugural moment of modernity in Europe. The "French people" threw off the yoke of centuries, toppling a brutal and stifling order in the name of *liberté, égalité, et fraternité*. If we want evidence that history is unqualified progress, at least some of the time, it seems to be here. Even some of its harshest critics, like Edmund Burke and Thomas Carlyle, took it as an inevitable series of events; Carlyle went so far as to see it as a bloody but necessary step in the right direction.[2] For all but the most nostalgic aristocrat, it is impossible not to be thankful, and for many it is impossible not to be inspired.

On the other hand, as anyone with a passing familiarity with the course of events knows, at anything finer grained than a clunky progressivism or conservatism, the Revolution's lessons and legacies

---

2  Raymond Williams, *Culture and Society, 1780–1950*, London: Penguin, 1961, 24, 30; Thomas Carlyle, *The French Revolution*, London: Continuum, 2010 [1837], 61.

are far more complex. Those like Robespierre who undid the old order often did so viciously and by terrible means. Many thousands of innocents were slaughtered. It is not difficult to sympathize with the claim that the revolutionaries proved true Keynes's certainty that when we let violence out of Pandora's box, it cannot be contained, and—aside from the (slightly comforting) hope that it eventually turns on those who unleashed it, finding its more or less deserved end—the results are bound to be horrific.[3] In its climactic instantiation in the last stages of the Terror and Thermidor, the Revolution effectively ate itself. In so doing, it prepared the ground both for the return of the king in Napoleon's bellicose liberal imperialism and for the civil unrest that plagued France (and many of its neighbors) at least until the founding of the Third Republic in the 1870s.

## Revolution and Liberal Ambivalence

In retrospect, it is certainly possible to take sides in this struggle and condemn one party or the other. A "radical" who rues the Revolution's ultimate "betrayal" by the bourgeois traitors of Thermidor shares with the conservative a one-sided assessment of its legacy. Whether they deem the Revolution inevitable or not, it was either a promise or a disaster; it could not be both. But the positions defining this opposition—condemnatory and celebratory—are in fact not the most common reactions; an outright denunciation of the Revolution would jar today's "reading public" as readily as the title of Sophie Wahnich's *In Defence of the Terror*.[4]

Instead, a deep-seated ambivalence prevails with regard to the Revolution because ambivalence is partially constituted in the politics that has become increasingly hegemonic in western Europe and North America since Hegel's time. Liberalism might have been

---

3  Keynes, "A Short View of Russia," *CW*, IX, 267; Gilles Dostaler, *Keynes and his Battles*, Cheltenham: Edward Elgar, 2007, 89.

4  Sophie Wahnich, *In Defence of the Terror: Liberty or Death in the French Revolution*, London: Verso, 2012.

germinating, or consolidating, or inchoate in the decades before 1789. But as Hegel shows, modern liberalism (inside and outside France) is at least partly a *result* of the French Revolution. No French Revolution, no liberalism. Arendt's unremitting disappointment that modern liberalism did not somehow instead emerge in the crucible of the American War of Independence—which those we now call "liberals" endorsed almost unanimously—is founded in an impossible revisionism.[5] As Habermas explains it, Arendt's hope is that by drawing upon the "heritage" of the American Revolution (as opposed to the French), "we could emerge from the shadows of *terreur*." But, they are not interchangeable: in contrast to

> the American Revolution, which was, so to speak, the *outcome* of events, the French Revolution was *carried forward* by its protagonists in the consciousness of a revolution . . . One could even say that the bourgeois revolutions—the Dutch, English, and American—became aware of themselves *as* revolutions only in the French Revolution.[6]

In a way that the American Revolution—better described as the American War of Independence—never did, events in France engendered a "radically this-worldly, postmetaphysical concept of the political," oriented to the world in which we actually live—a consciousness "expressed in the conviction that a new beginning could be made . . . an uncoupling of the present from the past."[7]

Liberalism was from its inception founded on a complex and unstable but thoroughly genetic relationship with the Revolution, and whatever the differences between the contradictory claims of modern liberals, from Hayekian libertarians to Habermasian social democrats, they share an inability to get over it. On one hand, the Revolution is utterly essential to liberals' own account of their

---

5  Hannah Arendt, *On Revolution*, New York: Penguin, 2006; see especially 83ff.

6  Jürgen Habermas, "Appendix I: Popular Sovereignty as Procedure," in *Between Facts and Norms: Contributions to a Discourse Theory of Law and Democracy*, trans. William Rehg, Cambridge: MIT Press, 466.

7  Ibid., 466–67.

identity because the historical emergence of the social relations and institutional structures they affirm is tied directly to it. Property-based, proceduralist, individualist meritocracy, organized by the abstract order of representative democracy, is at least partly a product of the French Revolution. On the other hand, they regret the Revolution's "radical" side—its violence, dogmatism, and mass mobilizations—and dismiss any suggestion that such rupture might ever be necessary again. It is as if past revolutions have taught modern liberals all they need to know about how unnecessary one might be in the future. In fact—Arendt in particular epitomizes this tendency—the dismissal of revolution's post-Revolutionary necessity has evolved into outright antagonism, so much so that twenty-first century liberalism is at least partially defined by an acritical rejection of the French and every other revolution, in the hope that we have indeed reached the end of history.[8]

Although some might take as axiomatic Arendt's assessment of the French and American revolutions as "liberal revolutions," this bourgeois variation on the Marxian category "bourgeois revolution" obscures important relationships. The French Revolution was not exactly a liberal "event," as if the force behind it was an evolving consensus on the truth or necessity of ideas and arrangements we now call "liberal." That is the liberal story, but, as Arendt surely knew, it is not true. As a mode of political-economic thought and organization in the process of consolidation, liberalism had its pre-Revolutionary prophets, certainly (John Locke, Adam Smith, and others).

---

8    As the *über*-free marketeer, anti-Keynesian, and Nobel Prize-winner Robert Lucas hilariously announced in 2003, "the central problem of depression prevention has been solved, for all practical purposes, and has in fact been solved for many decades." All that remains is to provide the masses with "better incentives to work and save." See Robert Lucas, "Macroeconomic Priorities," *American Economic Review* 93: 1, 2003, 1. It is tempting to include Francis Fukuyama's *The End of History and the Last Man*, New York: Free Press, 1992, in a list of arrogant neoliberal foolishness, but it would not be fair. In the quarter-century since, Fukuyama recanted the reactionary teleology and distanced himself from the absurd neoconservative claims to omniscience it has since come to epitomize. Better to recall to the less eschatological claims of Habermas, "Appendix I: Popular Sovereignty as Procedure," 468: "The Revolution dismisses its dissidents, who no longer rebel against anything except the Revolution itself."

But the Revolution is not so much evidence of liberalism *avant la lettre* as one of its key determinations.

In the Euro-American political tradition, before the term "liberalism" was coined in the early 1800s, differentiation in emancipatory politics was not articulated by the relation or opposition between "liberal" and "radical."[9] Indeed, there was a time—the Prussia of the Restoration in which Hegel completed his *Philosophy of Right* is a case in point—when to be "liberal" was "radical," at least as we use the latter term today. Inside the revolutionary dynamic of the era, then, what unfolded was in many ways a struggle over what liberalism would become, a fight between revolutionaries over who would enjoy the liberty Revolution promised: freedom for all, or freedom for some? To the extent that we can describe a "radical" emancipatory politics at the time of the French Revolution, what little meaning the term "radical" might have describes those who prioritized the "who" question (who shall enjoy membership in the "community of the free"?) over the "how" of emancipation (what are the appropriate and justifiable procedures of social reconstruction in the interests of liberty?). That, by the end of the Napoleonic era, the "how" had completely displaced the "who" among liberals is proof of the bourgeoisie's Kantian victory.

In the Euro-American "West" today, despite many challenges, the victorious have extended their ideological territory. The liberal conception of emancipation as a formal question, properly posed only in the rational *agorae* of Supreme Court decisions or draped in "veils of ignorance," is now hegemonic across virtually all political fora. As Keynes himself said, even self-described conservatives are entirely liberal in this sense.[10] The question for all of them is not "who are 'we,' and who among us remains unfree?" Instead, it is "what are proper or acceptable paths from unfreedom to freedom?" All other paths are denounced more vehemently than unfreedom itself.

---

9  The origin of "liberalism" in its modern meaning lies in post-Napoleonic Spain, when *los liberales* gathered at the *cortes* of Cadiz (1810–1813) to formulate the short-lived 1812 Constitution (in opposition to *los serviles*, who called for the restoration of the Bourbon monarchy under Ferdinand VII).

10  Keynes, "Democracy and Efficiency," *CW*, XXI, 491–500.

This procedural formalism underwrites the never-ending liberal obsession with "extremism"—the epithet thrown at anyone whose politics refuses to prioritize means over ends, the how over the who of freedom—and goes some way toward explaining liberals' total refusal to deal with "extremes": they have no conceptual resources to do so. It is also the logic behind modern liberal democracies' institutionalized neglect of injustice in favor of endless fretting over the legitimacy of the means by which it might be redressed. Yes, liberals acknowledge, horrible crimes have stained and sustained the past— slavery, colonialism, gendered violence, and oppression—but how can we "undo" history? Sorry, but what's done is done. Like it or not, we're all in this together.[11]

This mode of conceptualizing the problem of liberty propounds a judgment of both the present and its possibilities and the past and the lessons it has to offer. The Revolution itself has provided virtually endless terrain for such efforts. As much or more than Russia in 1917, the French experience is held up as proof that radical zeal has terrible consequences. After more than two hundred years, the Terror and Robespierre remain paradigmatic, synonymous in the western imagination with the horrors that unfold from an uncompromising commitment to revolutionary universalism—in other words, the perils of prioritizing freedom's "who." The standard account suggests that this commitment is disastrous—not, it might seem, without historical basis. Unsurprisingly, this leads to the same conclusions as the critique of "extremism"; the political priority of ends over means, we are told, will always lead to violence and terror. When that rule takes a populist cast, even the sages cannot last. Robespierre's politics of the blade finally and inevitably turned on him.

This is the reason that in the historiography of the Terror, the most interesting debates do not revolve around "empirical" details, like individual or group animosities and alliances. There are certainly lots

---

11  For a fascinating account of this dynamic, focused on Canadian settler colonialism's historical erasure via "reconciliation" and "recognition," see Glen Coulthard, *Red Skin, White Masks: Rejecting the Colonial Politics of Recognition*, Minneapolis: University of Minnesota Press, 2014.

of histories that recount the events and conflicts that led to the Girondins' end in mid-1793, for example, or the personal animosities that developed within the Committee of Public Safety before Robespierre's fall. But what almost everyone is actually interested in is the "causes" of the Terror and its "justifiability," then and since. These questions in fact bleed together. The search for causes is really about what led some revolutionaries to understand the Terror as a legitimate instrument of social transformation, while an important aspect of the problem of legitimacy is motivated by the related "historicist" obligation to understand why the Terror "made sense" to *la Montagne* and its (shifting and heterogeneous) urban and peasant sometime-allies.[12]

The questions of causality and legitimacy attract all this interest for the obvious reason that since the very instant it "ended," the Terror has been inseparable from a presentist compulsion to defend or condemn. In the eyes of some historians, for whom "presentism" is a sin, this has engendered a fundamental flaw in the historiography of the Revolution, because so many have taken to telling the story for their own "political purposes."[13] It seems to me, however, that such "purposes" are both inevitable and invaluable. They give history the only kind of meaning it can have—in the present. Indeed, today the Terror matters less for its "true" causes or its relative legitimacy at the time than for the lessons its observers believed they learned from it. The Terror remains important to modern politics not because of what "actually" motivated or justified it, but primarily because of the ways it shaped political thinking in the decades and centuries following.[14]

For even if the French Revolution had faded from view for many— its historical status as revolutionary archetype diminished by that of

---

12  *La Montagne* was the nickname of Robespierre's Jacobin faction in the Constituent Assembly (up to summer 1792) and the Convention (from September 1792 to his arrest twenty-two months later). It refers to their location in some of the highest benches (on the left side) of the rooms in which delegates met.

13  A similar historiographical hubbub surrounds the question of whether slavery caused the American Civil War. For decades, racists insisted slavery had little to do with it, while progressives insisted emancipation was a key factor.

14  Habermas, "Appendix I: Popular Sovereignty as Procedure," 464–67; Slavoj Žižek, *In Defense of Lost Causes*, London: Verso, 2008, 157–58.

the Bolsheviks of 1917 or the Chinese in 1949—the analyses of its contemporaries who tried to come to grips with it, and those whose entire worldview was fundamentally structured by it, continue to shape how we think about politics. As long as politics are impinged upon by the work of (for example) Jean-Jacques Rousseau, Immanuel Kant, and Edmund Burke, not to mention Hegel and Marx—or anyone whose thought has been shaped by their work—the French Revolution will remain a "contemporary" event.

This may seem an "idealist" way of framing the problem. Surely there are "material" ways in which the Revolution shapes our lives, institutionally, geopolitically, and so on. But the most important of these "material" factors is arguably the fundamentally "idealist" tenor of the Revolutionary age—anyone who believes ideas make the world go around will act in the world more or less according to ideas. Indeed, if Gramsci has not already convinced us, the whole epoch is a lesson in the colossal errors to which the materialist-idealist opposition leads.[15] As Lucio Colletti never tires of pointing out in his critique of Marxian "clerisy," the dogmatic Leninist commitment to materialism in the battle against idealism (only the "shame-faced" are unwilling to choose a side, says Lenin) is itself an unadulterated idealism.[16] How else could one explain why the opposition matters at all? If materialism holds unconditionally, the "battle of ideas" between materialism and idealism means nothing. In truth, the

---

15    All thought must "go beyond the traditional conceptions of 'idealism' and 'materialism' . . . As for the expression 'historical materialism,' greater stress is placed on the second word, whereas it should be placed on the first: Marx is fundamentally a 'historicist'"; Antonio Gramsci, *Prison Notebooks*, vol. II, trans. Joseph Buttigieg, New York: Columbia University Press, 1996, 153. Contrast this with Lenin: "The question then is, are there more comprehensive concepts with which the theory of knowledge could operate than those of being and thinking, matter and sensation, physical and mental? No. These are the ultimate, most comprehensive concepts, which epistemology has in point of fact not surpassed . . . One must be a charlatan or an utter blockhead to demand a 'definition' of these two 'series' of concepts of ultimate comprehensiveness which would not be a 'mere repetition': one of the other must be taken as primary"; V. I. Lenin, *Collected Works*, vol. 14, Moscow: Progress Publishers, 1972, 146.

16    Lucio Colletti, "A Political and Philosophical Interview," *New Left Review* I: 86, 1974, 28; Lucio Colletti, "Marxism and the Dialectic," *New Left Review* I: 93, 1975, 9–12; Lenin, *Collected Works*, vol. 14, 292.

Terror is violent proof that however much life shapes consciousness, history is impossible if consciousness does not bite back. Even the most cursory reading of Robespierre's stirring speeches to the Convention cannot help but impress upon us the degree to which his politics is an "ideal" construction that did nothing if not shake his world to its foundations. The Terror was the result of ideas simultaneously produced by and "materialized" in specific historical conditions—imperfectly, certainly, but there is no other way. That is how history works.

## The Postrevolutionary Origins of Political Economy

Because of this very dynamic, the Revolution, and perhaps especially the Terror, are important because of the way they were both a product of, and contributed to, the formation of modern political thought in the form of "political economy." Among all the Revolutionary era's legacies, this must be one of the most important. If political economy is the science of liberal government, as Hegel (and later Foucault) show so convincingly, then this—crisis in the *relation* between the governors and the governed—is the paradigmatic problem for properly *political* economy. Recall Hegel's description:

> Political economy is the science that starts from this view of needs and labour but then has the task of explaining mass-relationships and mass-movements in their complexity and their qualitative and quantitative character. This is one of the sciences which have arisen out of the conditions of the modern world.[17]

Keynesianism is clearly not equivalent to political economy in the Hegelian sense. Rather, Keynesianism is distinctive in the qualitative function it accords political economy in its critical constellation, what we might call its emphasis on the properly *political* purposes of

---

17   G. W. F. Hegel, *Elements of the Philosophy of Right*, trans. H. B. Nisbet, Cambridge: Cambridge University Press, 1991, §189R. (Hereinafter cited as *PhR*.)

political economy. In the classical and neoclassical tradition, political economy is a quantitative endeavor, a descriptive input–output *tableau* of stocks, flows, and prices. For Keynesianism, the necessity of political economy to modernity originates in necessity itself: needs, work, poverty, order, government. Its conceptualization of the structures upon which these necessities hang, and if and how they might be managed, altered, or eliminated, has determined what range of relations between society and the individual, between government and its subjects, between the state and civil society, is considered possible. These relations include those that determine distribution— the classical focus of political economy—but also those that involve production, population, regulation, technique. This is of course not to say that political economy can answer any question asked of it, but it is to say that any question asked of it will be addressed in a manner that puts these dynamics front and center. What it does well is identify the manner in which "political" (in other words, "interested") forces shape the modes of, and relative gains from, "economic" distribution—what "politics" decide "who gets what and how much."

What political economy does much less well, yet cannot help but obsess over, is how "economic" distribution shapes both living politics and the political as a category of social life: what form political action takes; how different groups mobilize (or not); what counts as "political," and how legitimation proceeds (or not). It cannot help but obsess over these questions because these are what it really, truly wants to answer. Political economy is not a "neutral" fact-gathering mission (despite the posturing going on in some economics and political science departments, where "political economy" is reduced to the investigation of more or less "distorted" market-driven allocation, or, at best, modeling the effect of "interests" on "economic" dynamics or policy).[18] The point is not merely to know "who gets what and how much." Almost everyone does indeed want to know

---

18   See, for example, Jeffry Frieden, "Invested Interests: The Politics of National Economic Policies in a World of Global Finance," *International Organization* 45: 4, 1991, 425–51; or Allan Drazen, *Political Economy in Macroeconomics*, Princeton: Princeton University Press, 2000.

that, but only because we want to know what that might say about what political economy cannot tell us: what the "facts" might mean, what we can *expect*, and what we might do in light of those expectations.

This urge—to know, or be able to anticipate, what the present means for the future—is the urge that political economy tries to satisfy, the origin and function of the political economy of which Hegel speaks. One of Keynes's great contributions in *The General Theory* (see Chapters 10 and 11) was explicitly to make the future the focal point of political economy. Not that it had been unimportant before him; it was (in Foucault's words) a knowledge and way of knowing (*savoir et connaissance*), one that consolidated as the panicked elites and state institutions of post-Revolutionary western Europe sought frantically to figure out what, if anything, was about to go sideways: what the hell was going on with the "masses," and what to do about it. That political economy could not ultimately provide them with more than part of what they sought is obvious: it can survey and perhaps even "explain" the distributional conjuncture—"mass-relationships and mass-movements in their complexity and their qualitative and quantitative character"—but it can never know with certainty the political meaning or implications of any given moment. Keynesianism's unrepentant lack of precision is merely an honest acknowledgement of this truth: "I accuse the classical economic theory of being itself one of these petty, polite techniques which tries to deal with the present by abstracting from the fact that we know very little about the future."[19]

When Hegel identified its crucial importance, when it first took a fully developed form with Keynes's classicals—Say, Steuart, Smith and Ferguson, Ricardo and Malthus in particular—political economy was in the midst of a struggle for its soul. Would it be founded on the sanguine, long-run-oriented abstractions of Ricardian faith (No tariffs! No poorhouses!) or circumspect short-run Malthusian caution (a few tariffs, maybe some poorhouses)? "Malthus," Keynes

---

19    J. M. Keynes, "The General Theory of Employment, *Quarterly Journal of Economics* 51, 1937, 215.

wrote, "is dealing with the monetary economy in which we happen to live; Ricardo is dealing with the abstraction of a neutral monetary economy."[20] *Sein* versus *Sollen*. As far as Keynes was concerned, Malthus—whose theory of "gluts" and "effective demand" underwrote Keynes's conception of sub-full employment conditions—was the only sane choice.[21] The "Ricardian victory," with its naïve abstractions, was "vainly" and "vehemently opposed" by Malthus. Nevertheless, it convinced political economy it could "safely neglect the aggregate demand function," and in so doing, "constrained the subject for a full hundred years in an artificial groove":

> Ricardo conquered England as completely as the Holy Inquisition conquered Spain. Not only was his theory accepted by the city, by statesmen and by the academic world. But controversy ceased; the other point of view completely disappeared; it ceased to be discussed . . . You will not find [the great puzzle of Effective Demand] mentioned even once in the works of Marshall, Edgeworth and Professor Pigou, from whose hands the classical theory has received its most mature embodiment.[22]

To Keynes, the "aggregate demand function," that is, effective demand, is *the* analytical core of political economy. To neglect it is to neglect the very point of political economy for government: to understand "mass-relationships and mass-movements in their complexity and their qualitative and quantitative character." In his eyes, it is impossible not to feel "that the almost total obliteration of Malthus' line of approach and the complete domination of Ricardo's for a period of a hundred years has been a disaster to the progress of economics. Time after time," Keynes writes, "Malthus is talking plain sense, the force of which Ricardo with his head in the clouds wholly fails to comprehend."[23]

---

20    Keynes, "Thomas Robert Malthus," in *CW,* X, 97.

21    Thomas Malthus, *Principles of Political Economy, Considered with Their View to a Practical Application*, London: W. Pickering, 1836, 141, 144, 179.

22    Keynes, *CW,* X, 87; Keynes, *CW,* VII, 32–33;.

23    Ibid., 98. English political economists Thomas Malthus and David Ricardo were early nineteenth century contemporaries and correspondents. They are often held to have

The most crucial difference between Malthus and Ricardo lies here, in their differential faith in the eschatology of equilibrium and the certainty it promised.[24] Virtually all the classical political economists, Smith, Ricardo, and Malthus among them, took both the market and poverty to be "natural" and "nature" to be the normative order. Nature, being unalterable, was not subject to critique, scientific or ethical. Ricardo thus concluded that the goal of "politics" should be to encourage the long-run *telos* of *laissez-faire*. Malthus, in contrast, felt certain that this entirely ignored the fact that:

> the progress of society consists of irregular movements, and that to omit the consideration of causes which for eight or ten years will give a great *stimulus* to production or population, or a great check to them, is to omit the causes of the wealth and poverty of nations—the grand object of all enquiries in Political Economy.[25]

As Keynes saw it, all one needed was to return to the world in which we actually live to "comprehend the real significance of the vaguer intuitions of Malthus."[26] Malthus believed that in (what he also called) "the actual state of things," it was foolhardy to imagine that Ricardo's "uniform progress" was in any way inevitable. Moments of "stagnation" like the years that followed the Napoleonic Wars (1815–1820) demanded intervention:

---

together established what Marx called political economy's fully developed "final shape." Although, from the perspective of radical political economy, their similarities often seem to outweigh their differences, their respective analyses of, and policy recommendations concerning, an emergent liberal economic order, often contrasted greatly. They remain a point of reference for scholars.

24   Keynes quotes at length from their correspondence in 1817 to show that they understood that this was the fundamental basis of their differences. As Ricardo put it: "you always have in your mind the immediate and temporary effects of particular changes, whereas I put those immediate and temporary effects quite aside, and fix my whole attention on the permanent state of things which will result from them"; quoted in Keynes, *CW,* X, 97.

25   Malthus to Ricardo, in David Ricardo, *The Works and Correspondence of David Ricardo*, vol. VII, ed. Piero Sraffa, Cambridge: Cambridge University Press, 1951–73, 120.

26   Quoted in Keynes, *CW,* X, 88.

the employment of the poor in roads and public works, and tendency among landlords and persons of property to build, to improve and beautify their grounds, and to employ workmen and menial servants, are the means most within our power and most directly calculated to remedy the evils arising from the disturbance in the balance of produce and consumption, which has been occasioned by the sudden conversion of soldiers, sailors, and various other classes which the war employed, into productive labourers.[27]

Keynes was always adamant that there were two distinct Malthuses: the eighteenth-century author of the essays on population, attacking the radical claims of William Godwin and Thomas Paine, and justifying the unavoidable suffering of the poor; and the modern, nineteenth-century political economist of *Principles of Political Economy*, focused on the problem of unemployment.[28] But even in Malthus's first incarnation, Keynes believed that he had ultimately recognized that it is the political question we cannot answer that matters in the end. If mass poverty, scarcity, and inequality are inevitable, then all we can (and must) do is contain the range of poverty's political implications, and that requires us to mitigate it, even if we run "against nature" in doing so.

We are required to intervene because the crucial feature of any existing economic order is not its (long run) approximation to

---

27    Malthus to Ricardo, quoted in Ibid., 98, 102.

28    Ibid., 105–106, 94: Malthus "passed over completely in surroundings and intellectual outlook from the one century to the other . . . [T]he first edition of the *Essay* belonged to a different world and a different civilization." Keynes was very defensive of his attachment to Malthus, who he felt was disproportionately associated with the terrible implications of the essays on population. As a reader of both his early and later work, I would say that it is indeed sometimes hard to believe they share the same author. The complexity of this legacy has allowed readers—and one can hardly say unfairly—to know radically different Malthuses, and use them for a wide array of purposes. For example, to read the chapters on Malthus in two widely used English textbooks on the history of economic thought is to discover, in one, a hateful defender of landed aristocrats' parasitic privileges, and in the other, an incisive, scientific critic of *laissez-faire* doctrine. See E. K. Hunt and Mark Lautzenheiser, *History of Economic Thought*, 3d ed., Armond, NY: M. E. Sharpe, 2011, 65–90; Ingrid Rima, *Development of Economic Analysis*, 7th ed., London: Routledge, 2009, 124–41.

nature but its (short run) legitimacy. Since nature in no way enjoys popular legitimacy just because it is natural, this problem will not solve itself. Where there is need, there must also be seen to be justice.[29] If the latter does not make sense of the former, the social order is insecure. Political economy is useful for government only insofar as it can identify the minimum conditions for legitimacy. This is why even the early Malthus advocated teaching political economy to the poor: so that they would understand the inescapability of their fate—which "no possible form of society could prevent"—and thus the blamelessness of the bourgeois order.[30] It was in this frame that he proposed his notorious principle of population, which was primarily intended as "a body-blow against popular radicalism."[31]

As foolish and repugnant (and Thatcherite) as some of Malthus's early conclusions were, therefore—such as his insistence that parishes must not alleviate housing crises among the poor, because "if he cannot get subsistence from his parents on whom he has a just demand, and if the society do not want his labour, has no claim of *right* to the smallest portion of food, and, in fact, no business to be where he is"—Keynes nevertheless did not hesitate to write that if "only Malthus, instead of Ricardo, had been the parent stem from which nineteenth-century economics proceeded, what a wiser and richer place the world would be to-day!"[32] His reasons for resurrecting Malthus are not solely because he got his "economics" right—recognizing the problem of effective demand in his attack on Say,

---

29   Freud, again: "The first requisite of civilization, therefore, is that of justice"; Sigmund Freud, *Civilization and Its Discontents*, trans. James Strachey, New York: Norton, 1961, 47.

30   Thomas Robert Malthus, *An Essay on the Principle of Population*, Harmondsworth: Penguin, 1970, 77: "But though the rich by unfair combinations contribute frequently to prolong a season of distress among the poor, yet no possible form of society could prevent the almost constant action of misery upon a great part of mankind, if in a state of inequality, and upon all, if all were equal." It is worth noting that these words are from the first edition, published in 1798. By the sixth edition (1826), Malthus had removed them.

31   David McNally, "Political Economy to the Fore: Burke, Malthus and the Whig Response to Popular Radicalism in the Age of the French Revolution," *History of Political Thought* 21: 3, 2000, 436.

32   Keynes, *CW,* X, 100–101; Malthus is quoted on 105.

emphasizing the short-run, and so forth. From a Keynesian perspective, Malthus had at least two other great merits. First, his appropriately intuitive vagueness matched Keynes's own pragmatic epistemology. It may be a very anti-Ricardian and even un-scientific position to take, but if the object of one's study, "the causes of the wealth and poverty of nations—the grand object of all enquiries in Political Economy," is not clearly definable, then a precise study cannot be an accurate study.

His second reason for endorsing Malthus is political. Despite the early Malthus's naïve assumption that elites could somehow *decide* if *Notrecht* held (the unemployed have "no claim of *right* to the smallest portion of food"), and despite his aristocratic misconception of the force of necessity, Keynes believed Malthus had asked the right question. He clearly understood that necessity mattered, even if, in his upside-down world, he misconstrued what to do about it. Indeed, the hinge of Malthus's entire project in the essays on population was the scarcity of "necessaries." If Robespierre's *denrées* were too abundant, he argued, then the population spiral was inevitable. Consequently, only if they were made scarce was the progress of wealth possible. Keynes, too saw the tragic necessity of poverty as essential to modernity. Like Malthus, he saw that bourgeois civil society made it clear that the poor has "no business to be where he is." Where Malthus discovers in a cruel necessity the key to modern political economy, Keynes discovers its tragic flaw, the persistence of which is the irresistible force of history itself. On the question of whether the later Malthus had turned his world right-side up or if Keynes had done it for him, Keynes was both certain and convincing:

> In the second half of his life [Malthus] was preoccupied with the post-war unemployment which then first disclosed itself on a formidable scale, and he found the explanation in what he called the insufficiency of effective demand; to cure which he called for a spirit of free expenditure, public works, and a policy of expansionism . . . A hundred years were to pass before there would be anyone to read with even a shadow of sympathy and

understanding his powerful and unanswerable attacks on the great Ricardo.[33]

On this reading, the vast temporal gap between Malthus and Keynes stems from Keynes's conviction that Malthus was the last political economist. Even though, like a good post-Marshallian "business-man," Keynes spoke mostly of "economics" when describing the field of knowledge to which he contributed, his own conversion in the early 1930s from adamant free-trader to Keynesian meant he did not for the most part understand his mature work as a product of the disciplinary tradition. He framed *The General Theory* explicitly as his (successful) attempt to escape the discipline's conceptual and theoretical hold on his mind. In doing so, he claimed not to have founded a "new economics"—he always denied having founded macroeconomics, saying that it had merely been dormant for a century—but to have returned it to the ground, and set it along the path, from which it had started in the first place.

Regarding the century between, he was spare with his praise. He admired John Stuart Mill, whose *Principles of Political Economy* was published at the moment of the European revolutions of 1848, for his unswerving commitment to the cause of civilization. But Mill's equally unswerving commitment to Benthamite utilitarianism and his fundamental role in "perfecting" the "theory of Ricardian economics" led Keynes to name him on the first page of *The General Theory* as part of the problem to be overcome.[34] Alfred Marshal, the dominant, widely admired—even beloved— figure in Cambridge economics when Keynes was a student, was another with whom Keynes felt empathy on most matters but intellectual. Marshall, whose graphical representation of the supply-demand "scissors" in a "free" market is now ubiquitous, had (like Mill) what Keynes considered a generally appropriate political stance. But his leadership in the construction of Ricardian

---

33   Ibid., 107.
34   Keynes, *CW,* VII, 3.

formalization and abstraction made him Keynes's frequent punching bag.[35]

Hence, in many ways he really did understand *The General Theory* as having reconstructed, on much more secure terrain, wisdom from the age immediately following the French Revolution, the age of Malthus and Hegel. Like all of us, he was surely in some ways unaware of his own influences and wrote his own intellectual history to suit his own purposes. His analytical practice was inevitably less coherent than he imagined. As Joan Robinson puts it, he certainly "carried a good deal of Marshallian luggage around with him and never thoroughly unpacked it to throw out the clothes he could not wear." But nevertheless, as she also says, by

> making it impossible to believe any longer in an automatic reconciliation of conflicting interests into a harmonious whole, *The General Theory* brought out into the open the problem of choice and judgment that the neo-classicals [the Ricardian school] had managed to smother. The ideology to end all ideologies broke down. Economics once more became Political Economy.[36]

These "limits" to what political economy can know, in particular its radical uncertainty regarding the future, obviously constrain all ways of knowing. But the ways in which they come to matter in political economy are also encoded in its genetic liberalism. Political economy claims to provide an impossible knowledge, an illusion it sustains by assuming all it cannot know is a function of what it can. Hence, despite the term "political economy," the separation between politics and economy is immanent and crucial to it. Hegel knew this, of course, as did Keynes.

---

35   Marshall is sometimes said to have created the "positive science" of economics out of the "moral science" of political economy. Joan Robinson, who was close with Keynes and in the middle of all the conflict around *The General Theory*, suggests that much of the vehemence with which Keynes was attacked by those he labeled "classicals" was due less to his critique than to his insufficiently respectful attitude toward Marshall; Joan Robinson, *Economic Philosophy*, London: Penguin, 1962, 76–77.

36   Ibid., 76, 73.

This dedication to the politics-economy separation is not only built into political economy, it is also the feature that most recommended its status as the science of Euro-American post-Revolutionary states and their elites. Yet it is the source of its greatest weakness, too. When tasked with demands it had no capacity to understand, demands that categorically refuse the political-economic separation, it was (and remains) little help. Where the world in which we actually live exposed the separation as idealist mythology—revolution being the most radical instance of all—classical liberal political economy was at best so many fingers in the dyke.

What Keynes and Hegel saw clearly is that a conjuncture when such demands are outstanding is not a "special case," as classical political economy suggests. This is precisely why Keynes called his book *The General Theory*—because liberal classical political economy (like all liberalism) claimed to be universally true for a world that ought to exist, but in fact described only a special (even almost impossible) case. This is why, in reality, when liberal government comes face to face with *necessity*, it "goes Keynesian": acknowledges uncertainty and disarticulation, recognizes imperfection and indeterminacy, and turns away from the long run to the immediacy of the moment: "needs and labour."

## The Consent to Remain Poor

Consequently, actually existing modern political economy is Keynesian—even in those moments when it is most austere, most abstract, most dispassionately liberal. It claims it can light the path to "economic bliss," but in those moments when the question it cannot answer asks itself with sufficient force—by way of mass politics, even looming revolution—its pharmacopeia is immediately made available to put off disaster. It is always a guarantee of a prosperous and enlightened future, the inescapably uncertain promise of which it is constantly ready to sustain by any emergency means necessary. Political economy is how government knows what to do to shush those questions it cannot answer before they can be heard.

In other words, the most fundamental concerns of an always-already Keynesian political economy concern neither the (capitalist) organization of production nor the organization of distribution (a contingent mix of state and market) but the organization of *legitimation*. Keynesianism takes market- and state-mediated capitalist production and exchange relations for granted. That, we might say, is for Keynesians the realm of economics proper. Political economy is mobilized in the service of the political sustainability of these relations, a problem for which we must not assume there is a universally applicable solution, or no need for one at all. The (art and) science of political economy lies in mapping the conditions in which the legitimation appropriate to a given modern community is constructed, that is, that which is already adequate to its *Sittlich*.[37] This is to suggest that twenty-first century austerity is an effect, not a cause, of our current political conjuncture.

To see the absolutely essential ways the form of legitimation comes into play, we can juxtapose two historical propositions we have already seen that get to the heart of Keynesianism and Keynesian political economy: the first, from Robespierre, the second from Keynes. Both address a fundamental challenge to the bourgeois order.

In a pamphlet distributed in April 1791, Robespierre declared:

> If you give the public Treasury a larger contribution than I, isn't it because society has given you greater pecuniary advantages? And, if we want to pursue this, what is the source of the extreme inequality of fortunes that concentrates all wealth in a small number of hands? Doesn't it lie in bad laws, bad governments, and finally in corrupt societies? . . . I envy not at all your advantageous share, since this

---

37   Habermas, "Appendix I: Popular Sovereignty as Procedure,"480: "the flip side of a halfway successful welfare state is a mass democracy in which the process of legitimation is *managed* by the administration." Fred Hirsch discusses a related issue in terms of Keynesianism's "macromorality"; see Fred Hirsch, *The Social Limits to Growth*, London: Routledge, 1977, 125–38. The most astute twenty-first century Keynesian political economists recognize explicitly the need for political economic knowledge that is "ethically" specific to its place and time. See, for example, Dani Rodrik, *Economics Rules: The Rights and Wrongs of the Dismal Science*, New York: Norton, 2015.

inequality is a necessary or incurable evil: but at least do not take from me the imprescriptible property of which no human law can strip me. Let me even be proud of an honourable poverty.[38]

Two years later, speaking to the revolutionary Convention in Paris, he continued to emphasize the legitimation problem:

Doubtless we have no need of a revolution to teach the world that the extreme inequality in fortunes is the source of so much evil and so many crimes; but we are no less convinced that equality of property is a chimera. Me, I think equality is less essential to private wellbeing than to public contentedness: it is more important to render poverty honourable than to outlaw opulence.[39]

Writing a century and a half later, and what might seem a world away, Keynes found himself thinking about very similar conditions: In 1924, in his widely read *Tract on Monetary Reform*, he worried over the fact that

[n]o man of spirit will consent to remain poor if he believes his betters to have gained their goods by lucky gambling. To convert the business man into the profiteer is to strike a blow at capitalism, because it destroys the psychological equilibrium which permits the perpetuance of unequal rewards.

Like Robespierre, the question stayed with him. "For my own part," as he put it twelve years later in *The General Theory*, "I believe that there is social and psychological justification for significant inequalities of incomes and wealth, but not for such large disparities as exist to-day."[40]

Honorable poverty or the consent to remain poor; dignity in the face of "a necessary or incurable evil" or deference to "the

---

38 Maximilien Robespierre, "Sur le marc d'argent," *Oeuvres Complètes,* vol. VII, Paris: Presses Universitaires de France, 1910, 164–65.

39 Robespierre, April 24, 1793, *Oeuvres Complètes,* vol. IX, 459.

40 Keynes, *CW,* IV, 29; Keynes, *CW,* VII, 374.

perpetuance of unequal rewards." Here we confront two equally Keynesian conceptions of political economy, two sides of the coin of poverty in the market order. If honorable poverty is a claim upon the postrevolutionary social contract, the consent to remain poor is postrevolutionary resignation. Keynesian political economy was born in, and has attempted to manage, the tumultuous relation between the two. It has wavered back and forth between them— sometimes promising the former (to "solve the economic problem"), sometimes the latter (to "put off disaster"). But one would be forgiven for feeling that lately, Keynesianism has managed a postrevolution- ary *transition* in the bourgeois order, as Robespierre's demand for an honorable poverty has given way to Keynes's tragic effort to enable the poor to live willingly with their poverty.

Neither Robespierre nor Hegel nor Keynes, however—and this distinguishes them from many of their contemporaries—believe the poor deserve their fate. For each of them, the poor are those unlucky enough to be handed the poverty modernity produces and distrib- utes as inevitably as wealth. Keynesianism is the liberalism of those who (however reluctantly) acknowledge in the arbitrary inequity of poverty the continued historical legitimacy of revolution; this is why and how it makes so much sense to so many whenever "Western civilization" threatens to go off the rails. It is, as I said, simultane- ously an immanent critique of both liberalism and revolution.

You might say this is an impossible stance, and perhaps, in the long run, that is so. But, as Keynes said—and again, his point was not metaphorical—"in the long run we are all dead." It is in the "short run," the infinite moments of deferral in between, that the problem of maintaining "civilization" must be undertaken. A signifi- cant obstacle to understanding what is at stake in political economy, the science of *government*, is that like Keynesianism, it cannot adequately be grasped by means of liberalism's categories, categories that deny, a priori, any relation between freedom and necessity.[41]

41   This is also often said of Hegel; see Domenico Losurdo, *Hegel and the Freedom of Moderns*, Durham: Duke University Press, 2004, 26–31; Charles Taylor, *Hegel*, Cambridge: Cambridge University Press, 1975, 374–87; Joachim Ritter, *Hegel and the French Revolution*, Cambridge: MIT Press, 1982; see also Jay Drydyk, "Hegel's Politics: Liberal or Democratic?"

It might have taken Keynes himself until he was fifty years old to construct the "economic" logic of this relation, but he knew it intuitively long before *The General Theory*. He warned as early as 1919 that civilization's "thin crust" *is* necessity:

> The danger confronting us, therefore, is the rapid depression of the standard of life of the European populations to a point which will mean actual starvation for some . . . Men will not always die quietly. For starvation, which brings to some lethargy and a helpless despair, drives other temperaments to the nervous instability of hysteria and to a mad despair. And these in their distress may overturn the remnants of organization, and submerge civilization itself in their attempts to satisfy desperately the overwhelming needs of the individual. This is the danger against which all our resources and courage and idealism must now co-operate.[42]

## "Bourgeois" Political Economy and "Western" Civilization

I would like to close this account of political economy with a brief reflection on its relationship to colonialism. It is not an easy subject to address in passing. Nevertheless, when I spoke of these ideas while writing this book, the question arose several times, partly, I think, because we do not have a great deal to go on. All we know is that there *must* be a relation.

I believe the first words of Aimé Césaire's *Discourse on Colonialism* of 1955 provide one place to begin:

---

*Canadian Journal of Philosophy* 16: 1, 1986, 99–122; and especially Michael Feola's excellent 2010 article "Truth and Illusion in the *Philosophy of Right*: Hegel and Liberalism," *Philosophy and Social Criticism* 36: 5, 2010 567–85. I would go so far as to say that the hegemony of liberal categories in the Euro-American theoretical imagination has distorted an understanding of many not properly classifiable as liberal/not liberal, for example Hobbes, Smith, Hegel, Walter Lippman, José Ortega y Gasset, and Hannah Arendt.

42   Keynes, *CW,* II, 144.

A civilization that proves incapable of solving the problems it creates is a decadent civilization.

A civilization that chooses to close its eyes to its most crucial problems is a stricken civilization.

A civilization that uses its principles for trickery and deceit is a dying civilization. The fact is that the civilization we call "European," "Western" civilization, shaped as it has been by two centuries of bourgeois rule, is incapable of solving the two major problems to which it has given rise: the problem of the proletariat and the colonial problem; that Europe is able to justify itself neither before the court of conscience nor before the court of reason . . .[43]

This is, among other things, a critique of political economy. It is an indictment of Europe's (and America's) increasingly tenuous attempts to buy time, to manage the unmanageable injustices it has wrought. This is still the object of political economy—again, distinguishing properly political economy from an "economics" posited as the analysis of budget-constrained optimization and more or less competitive price determination. Whatever its internal differences, today's political economy—that, for example, of the *Financial Times*, the *Economist*, of Piketty, Stiglitz, Krugman, and, ultimately Keynes—remains the anxious precipitate of revolution. Keynesianism is liberalism's most significant theoretical and political development in the face of revolutionary menace.

---

43  Aimé Césaire, *Discours sur le colonialisme*, Paris: Éditions Présence Africaine, 1955, 1 (my translation):

Une civilisation qui s'avère incapable de résoudre les problèmes que suscite son fonctionnement est une civilisation décadente.

Une civilisation qui choisit de fermer les yeux à ses problèmes les plus cruciaux est une civilisation atteinte.

Une civilisation qui ruse avec ses principes est une civilisation moribonde.

Le fait est que la civilisation dite «européenne», la civilisation «occidentale», telle que l'ont façonnée deux siècles de régime bourgeois, est incapable de résoudre les deux problèmes majeurs auxquels son existence a donné naissance: le problème du prolétariat et le problème colonial; que, déférée à la barre de la «raison» comme à la barre de la «conscience», cette Europe-là est impuissante à se justifier; et que, de plus en plus, elle se réfugie dans une hypocrisie d'autant plus odieuse qu'elle a de moins chance de tromper.

This book emphasizes the way the French Revolution in particular shaped both Keynesianism's and political economy's problematic. In both cases, this originary influence is at once a cause and an effect of the Eurocentrism that has plagued political economy and the Keynesian critique (see Chapter 2).

There were, to be sure, other revolutions on Europe's mind, as Susan Buck-Morss and others remind us. In her celebrated 2000 paper "Hegel and Haiti," Buck-Morss argues that the famous lordship and bondsman dialectic in Chapter 4 of Hegel's *Phenomenology of Spirit*—one of the most influential formulations of the problem of freedom in the history of philosophy—is not principally a reflection on ancient slavery or feudalism, but on the Haitian Revolution of 1791–1804.[44] Nick Nesbitt has followed this up in passages in the *Philosophy of Right*, reinforcing Buck-Morss's argument that even though Haiti and Haitian slaves' world-historical realization of freedom are not identified in his work (Haiti is mentioned only once), "Hegel knew."[45] If so, this means that among other things, much of what we understand to be the European "Reason" and liberalism from which Keynesianism emerged was constructed not only in light of the history of colonialism and slavery, but of the history-*making* of the colonized themselves. Buck-Morss and Nesbitt are, as it were, doing detective work to "prove" Césaire was right when, fifty years ago, he said that to "study Saint-Domingue is to study one of the origins, one of the sources, of contemporary Western Civilization."[46] How could it be otherwise? Whether

---

44    G. W. F. Hegel, *Phenomenology of Spirit*, trans. A. V. Miller, Oxford: Clarendon Press, 1979, 104–38; Susan Buck-Morss, "Hegel and Haiti," *Critical Inquiry* 26, 2000, 821–65. The debate concerning the historical basis of Hegel's lordship/bondsman dialectic is long and fascinating. See George Armstrong Kelly, "Notes on Hegel's 'Lordship and Bondage,'" *Review of Metaphysics* 19: 4, 1966, 780–802; Andrew Cole, "What Hegel's Master/Slave Dialectic Really Means," *Journal of Medieval and Early Modern Studies* 34: 3. 2004, 577–610.

45    Nick Nesbitt, *Universal Emancipation: The Haitian Revolution and the Radical Enlightenment*, Charlottesville: University of Virginia Press, 2008, 113–24; Buck-Morss, "Hegel and Haiti," 844.

46    Aimé Césaire, *Toussaint L'Ouverture: La révolution française et le problème colonial*, Paris: Présence Africaine, 1961, 21.

Buck-Morss and Nesbitt are right to find Haiti barely concealed in Hegel—and there are several who have cast doubt on the matter—the larger postcolonial point that the West and its Reason are more than trivially a product of its other can hardly be impugned.[47]

And yet, while the force of these other, non-European histories are finally recognized as the sociohistorical, cultural force they were, attention to a genetic colonialism has been remarkably scarce in the history of political economy, a field even more prone to the "partial blindness among seas of perspicacity" that Buck-Morss impugns in the history of philosophy.[48] We should be grateful to brilliant critics like C. L. R. James, Paul Gilroy, and Buck-Morss for helping us to see the fundamental role of the developments like the Haitian Revolution in the history of the theory and practice of North Atlantic liberalism. But this has hardly improved our vision of the history of political economy, even among the very critics who have opened our eyes to the Eurocentric clouds in which many heads were stuck.[49]

In fact, in an important and thoroughly justifiable effort to emphasize the rich and complex political and ethical worlds outside Europe and its settler-colonial satellites, perhaps political economy has been purposefully neglected? Take, for example, David Scott's privileging of the discursive realms of philosophy and political theory, a privilege that in some ways reproduces the liberal separation between politics and the grubby "economic" world of necessity:

the narrative of revolution is inseparable from the larger narrative of modernity and inseparable, therefore, from those other cognitive and ethical-political categories that constitute and give point

---

47   See, for example, Anders Stephanson's sharp critique of "Hegel and Haiti," "The Philosopher's Island," *New Left Review* II: 61, 2010, 197–210.

48   Buck-Morss, "Hegel and Haiti," 825.

49   C. L. R. James, *Black Jacobins: Toussaint L'Ouverture and the San Domingo Revolution*, New York: Vintage, 1963; Paul Gilroy, *The Black Atlantic: Modernity and Double Consciousness*, London: Verso, 1993.

to that narrative—categories such as "nation," "sovereignty," "progress," "reason," and so on.[50]

One would expect that a more "universal history"—to use Buck-Morss's term for her method of "provincializing Europe"—would show that the Transatlantic "narrative of revolution" is inseparable not only from the lofty "cognitive and ethical political categories" animating the great philosophies of freedom, but also from categories like "needs and labour," poverty, wealth, and distribution. There are, however, few if any accounts that make this case. There are thousands of excellent analyses of the political economy of colonialism, development, postcolonialism, and so on, but we still have neither a *Black Jacobins* nor a "Hegel and Haiti" for political economy.[51]

It bears emphasis here that for Hegel, Keynes, and Césaire, "contemporary Western Civilization" is a *post-Revolutionary* phenomenon. Certainly, as Marx said, western Europe is "the homeland of political economy," and it is true that it began to solidify as knowledge in the pre-Revolutionary era, in the work of Smith, Quesnay, Say, and the other Physiocrats.[52] This is the mid-eighteenth-century political economy from which Foucault generalizes its role in liberalism. But it is surely impossible that political economy weathered the revolutionary earthquakes without significant change. Political economy after the Terror learned much from the Physiocrats, and obviously from Smith, but it was nonetheless radically transformed. Its political purposes changed, and its urgency became paramount. It came into being as a "discipline" with revolution on its mind.

---

50   Susan Buck-Morss, *Hegel, Haiti, and Universal History*, Pittsburg: University of Pittsburg Press, 2009, 107–19; David Scott, *Conscripts of Modernity: The Tragedy of Colonial Enlightenment*, Durham: Duke University Press, 2004, 89.

51   The most compelling histories of political economy—which in my view would include David McNally, *Political Economy and the Rise of Capitalism: A Reinterpretation*, Berkeley: University of California Press, 1988; and Donald Winch, *Riches and Poverty: An Intellectual History of Political Economy in Great Britain, 1750–1834*, Cambridge: Cambridge University Press, 1996—suggest that the social forces shaping its ideas were almost entirely European, the French Revolution foremost among them.

52   Karl Marx, *Capital*, vol. I, New York: Vintage, 1976, 931.

This is why I would rearrange Foucault's chronology and, in doing so, dispute—or at least open up—his influential conception of what it is political economy does. Marx aptly characterized the physiocratic mode Foucault emphasizes as little more than "political arithmetic."[53] It is a very long way from Quesnay's *Tableau Économique* to what Marx called political economy's "final shape"— that is, the "modern," distinctively *post*-revolutionary, knowledge and "way of knowing" with which Hegel is concerned. Consequently, from the beginning of the nineteenth century, political economy is not, or not only, the form through which liberal government becomes "aware that it always risks governing too much," as Foucault claims. It is not, or not only, the "self-limiting governmental *ratio*" that "if there is a nature specific to the objects and operations of governmentality, then the consequence of this is that governmental practice can only do what it has to do by respecting this nature."[54] Foucault can only make these declarations because his conception of liberalism leads him to mischaracterize or undercharacterize political economy. Since the beginning of the eighteenth century, political economy has been just as importantly about how to govern more rather than less.

Indeed, we must go further still: the history of Keynesianism demonstrates that the defining lesson "modern" political economy teaches government is that it must not only always be prepared to govern more and differently and quickly, but that even when it does so, it can never provide a "solution." The defining lesson modern political economy teaches is tragic: there is no solution—the world, as Malthus put it, is both imperfect and "imperfectible." Liberal capitalism involves, even produces, the poverty, the looming disorder—the revolutionary or chaotic popular menace—that threatens it and with which it must constantly be ready to deal. As Keynes said, a principal function of political economy is always, consequently, "to put off disaster," to "buy time."[55] If, however, like Foucault one

---

53    Karl Marx, *Contribution to a Critique of Political Economy*, 1970, 54.

54    Michel Foucault, *Birth of Biopolitics: Lectures at the Collège de France, 1978–1979*, New York: Picador, 2008, 17, 16.

55    Wolfgang Streeck, *Buying Time: The Delayed Crisis of Democratic Capitalism*, trans. Patrick Camiller, London: Verso, 2014.

categorizes Keynes (for example) as a "nonliberal" and Keynesianism as "nonliberal" "interventionism" in the face of a "crisis of liberalism," it is harder to see this, and harder to see the fundamental role revolution played in the formulation of political economy and its earthy, "pragmatic" categories.[56]

This emphasis on wary sensitivity and agile response to popular unrest is built into political economy's very foundations, even into the Ricardian heritage Keynes wrote off as naïvely abstract and unworldly.[57] Writing on Ireland, for example, Ricardo recommended "timely concessions to the people":

> Reform is the most efficacious preventative of Revolution, and may in my opinion be at all times safely conceded . . . I think the disaffected would lose all power after the concession of Reform. Reform may be granted too late, but it can never be too soon.[58]

Moreover, the valence of revolution for political economy was not entirely conservative. Ricardo himself suggested that "the fear of insurrection, and of the people combining to make a general effort, are the great checks on all governments." It is only the "fear which the government and the aristocracy have of an insurrection of the people that keeps them within the bounds which now appear to arrest them."[59]

Yet we must remember that these seemingly radical pronouncements remain of a piece with much of Keynes's account of Ricardo. This is the logic of supply and demand and long-run equilibrium transported to the realm of state–civil society relations, a radically different understanding of social life than Keynes's (or Malthus's) more pragmatic, immediate distrust of some natural tendency toward social harmony. This, if Keynes is correct, is certainly what motivated the later Malthus to advocate poor relief and protectionist

---

56  Foucault, *Birth of Biopolitics*, 69–70, 218.
57  William Dixon, "Ricardo: Economic Thought and Social Order," *Journal of the History of Economic Thought* 30: 2, 2008, 235–53.
58  Ricardo, *Works*, vol. VIII, 49-50.
59  Ricardo, *Works*, vol. VIII, 133; Ricardo, *Works*, vol. V, 497.

legislation: a recognition that if his principles of population were indeed at work, it was perhaps unlikely the poor would accept quietly their culling by starvation: "when the people found themselves . . . entirely disappointed . . . massacre would in my opinion go on till it was stopt by military despotism."[60] The objective is to render revolution unnecessary or just not worth the trouble. In all cases the point of classical political economy was to prevent revolution, to "put off disaster." It truly was the science of "Western Civilization."

Perhaps this is obvious. Yet, while political economy is a product of "Western Civilization" and therefore also of colonialism, it emerged as a tool of domestic popular management, not primarily a tool for the organization of colonialism, although it was of course useful for such purposes. It is, rather, an elite governmentality developed to make sense of and coordinate the social order of the "modern communities" of western Europe and North America. Like Keynesianism itself, its interests in, and internalization of, dynamics in the rest of the world are almost entirely a reflection of its introverted orientation to its own "homeland." When Hegel and Keynes were writing, political economy had little interest in communities it did not deem "modern" or (as Ricardo and Malthus phrased it, "improved"), except insofar as they impinged upon resources in which Euro-American government was interested. The purpose of political economy was and has always been to manage the trajectory of liberal modernity, not so much in the interests of capital, as in that of "Western Civilization."

---

60    Dixon, "Ricardo," 250–51. As Ricardo wrote to James Mill, somewhat more delicately, "the only prospect we have of putting aside the struggle . . . between the rich and the other classes, is for the rich to yield what is justly due"; quoted in Dixon, "Ricardo," 251. At least on home soil. Unsurprisingly, the same risk of disorder in the colonies required, in the minds of some, a different analysis. They attacked "the total failure of the attempt to introduce Free Labour at Sierra Leone, in Hayti" . . . "in the agriculture of the West India colonies there is . . . no choice. It is slave labour, or none." As one advocate of the West Indian lobby in Britain wrote, Ricardo's advocacy of free trade and free labor would "ruin the whole body of West Indian proprietors [and] convert a body of slaves . . . into a set of lawless banditti, revelling in blood"; quoted in Michael Taylor, "Conservative Political Economy and the Problem of Colonial Slavery, 1823–1833," *The Historical Journal* 57: 4, 2014, 977, 985.

Pick up most any standard development economics text today, and you will discover that things have hardly changed. Virtually all of it warrants extraordinary skepticism. The best of it—the work of Lance Taylor or Albert Hirschman stands out—is as Keynesian as political economy gets; indeed, Hirschman said development economics was a child of Keynesianism.[61] The worst of it is so ill-suited to the multiplicity of other- and more-than liberal capitalist histories and geographies in the world that it either obsesses over the fragment of "the economy" that looks like what it already thinks it knows, or it flounders about like an IMF officer on a three-day mission to Mauritania to "restructure" its economy in the badly drawn image of a machine the Fund thinks it has the expertise to operate. When it (development economics or the IMF) finds it does not—virtually always—it denounces local "corruption" and "misaligned incentives," ill-defined property rights and "incomplete markets."

That political economy has little capacity to deal with noncapitalist social formations is not to impugn the excellent work done on the political economy of development, from Rosa Luxemburg on down. But that work is all an imposition by political economy's homeland on the world beyond it. There is arguably no such thing as a noncapitalist political economy and no such thing as a nonliberal political economy that is neither disingenuous nor cynical. In both cases the classical capitalist or liberal subject is imputed to worlds of which he or she is certainly not "representative" and may

---

61    Lance Taylor, *Structuralist Macroeconomics: Applicable Models for the Third World*, New York: Basic Books, 1983; Lance Taylor and Rudiger von Arnim, *Modeling the Impact of Trade Liberalization: A Critique of Computable General Equilibrium Models*, London: Oxfam International, 2006; Albert O. Hirschman, *The Strategy of Economic Development*, New Haven: Yale University Press, 1958; Albert O. Hirschman, "How the Keynesian Revolution Was Exported from the United States, and Other Comments," in Peter Hall (ed.), *The Political Power of Economic Ideas: Keynesianism Across Nations*, Princeton: Princeton University Press, 1989, 347–59. For powerful critiques of development economics, see for example Arturo Escobar, *Encountering Development: The Making and Unmaking of the Third World*, Princeton: Princeton University Press, 1995; Jayati Ghosh, "Microfinance and the Challenge of Financial Inclusion for Development," *Cambridge Journal of Economics* 37: 6, 2013, 1203–19; Gillian Hart, "Development/s after Neoliberalism: Culture, Power, Political Economy," *Progress in Human Geography* 26: 6, 2002, 812–22.

even be absent entirely. If we are generous, we might say Keynesianism's Eurocentrism is partly structured in the pragmatic acknowledgment of this insuperable truth. On these grounds, the French Revolution is most important in the history of Keynesianism's and political economy's simultaneous emergence because they could not and did not try to understand events like the Haitian Revolution.

We need not be so kind. More likely, and more often, Keynesianism and political economy are largely a product of Euro-American imperial self-absorption. The French Revolution is the founding moment of two centuries of Keynesianism because unlike the Haitian or Bolivarian revolutions, it was the one that appeared immediately to threaten the "civilization" it was assumed had yet to be constructed elsewhere. And unlike the French Revolution, because these "peripheral" developments were not understood to require the reconstruction of popular legitimacy, but more the reassertion of imperial coercion, the problems were not primary subjects of political economy as science of liberal government. Keynes and Keynesians have always felt a vague and sometimes even urgent sympathy for the plights of the rest of the world, but ultimately, beyond the possibility that disorder elsewhere might impinge upon "civilization," they do not really care.

PART 3

# Keynes

# CHAPTER 9

# How to Read *The General Theory* I

By the time he had formulated the theoretical framework of *The General Theory*, Keynes regarded himself as something of a radical in his own way.[1] In reversing the Ricardian victory, he believed he had taken the wind out of classical economics' sails, with (he presumed) enormous analytical and political consequences. The classical tradition was by his measure a crucial pillar in modernity's disastrous status quo:

> That it could explain much social injustice and apparent cruelty as an inevitable incident in the scheme of progress, and the attempt to change such things as likely on the whole to do more harm than good, commended it to authority. That it afforded a measure of justification to the free activities of the individual capitalist, attracted to it the support of the dominant social force behind authority.[2]

These are not the words of an earnest missionary for liberal capitalism.

And yet that is frequently how his critics on the Left characterize Keynes. Perhaps this is quasi-defensible in a polemic, in which the

---

1 For a detailed, chapter-by-chapter summary of *The General Theory*, please see *A Companion to* The General Theory, available for download at versobooks.com.

2 Keynes, *CW*, VII, 33.

point is to hold Keynes up as representative of what "Keynesianism", tacitly assumed to be equivalent to the "welfare state" or "social democracy," became. But it is a significant mistake if the point is to reach an understanding of Keynes and the Keynesian critique. The radical histories are thus not necessarily the place to begin an examination of *The General Theory*, because their point is rarely to critically understand it; instead, the point is often to either dismiss it or to hold it up to the mirror of *Capital* and enumerate the ways in which the latter analytically outperforms or anticipates the former.[3]

There are certainly a few very powerful Left critiques of Keynesian economics from which to draw; examples include the work of Paul Mattick, Geoff Pilling, and Michael Roberts. Antonio Negri and Massimo De Angelis in particular have made crucial contributions to this literature, because they not only examine Keynes's economics but also attempt to historicize it, helping us to understand what flaws it might contain as well as where it (and those flaws) came from and why. Both recognize that it is not enough to merely point out that Keynes came to "save capitalism" to explain either the theoretical structure of *The General Theory* or, more important, its crucial relationship, then and now, to the wider social field of liberal capitalism.[4]

I would not want to suggest there is no utility in the analytical take-down of Keynes and Keynesianism—to attempt to show how as economics it was *not* a breakthrough, that its categories like investment are ahistorical or abstract, that Keynes's own politics were much more cautious than it might seem, and so forth.[5] But I would

---

3  For example, Chris Harman, "The Two Faces of John Maynard Keynes," *Socialist Review*, November 2008: "Today's new converts to Keynesianism in the US, British and European governments aim, as Keynes did, to save capitalism from itself. That means they are going to make the rest of us pay in order to keep capitalists happy."

4  Antonio Negri, "Keynes and the Capitalist Theory of the State post-1929" [1968], in *Revolution Retrieved: Writings on Marx, Keynes, Capitalist Crisis and New Social Subjects*, London: Red Notes, 1988; Massimo De Angelis, *Keynesianism, Social Conflict and Political Economy*, London: Palgrave, 2000. For an extended engagement with Negri, see Chapter 15.

5  This, for example, is the particular contribution of Geoff Pilling, *The Crisis of Keynesian Economics: A Marxist View*, London: Croom Helm, 1986.

suggest that the persistent political power of the ideas laid out in *The General Theory* are not undone by these critiques, and our understanding of that power is not much better developed because of them. Such efforts, however meaningful "scientifically," are based on the assumption that if you demonstrate to people that they are empirically "wrong," they will just change their minds. They assume that if we can trump Keynes with a "truer" theory that exposes its failures, nostalgic or deluded reformist third-way advocates will abandon their faith in business or the capitalist state. However desirable that outcome might be, it cannot be our only approach for at least two reasons. First, assuming the goal is to delegitimize Keynes in the eyes of the Left, it has, for decades or even centuries, been a spectacular failure, especially but not only in moments of crisis. Second, it abandons what seems (to me) to be the much more important question of why a Keynesian sensibility, and the Keynesian critique of liberal capitalism, continue to matter so much to so many. If we take this as a relevant ideological characteristic of the world, as I think we should, then we must acknowledge that like all ideology, it can neither be understood nor undone by a set of reasoned proofs that it is mistaken.

These critics have done a good job of identifying Keynesianism's theoretical and policy limits, and I will not cover those arguments in detail here. Instead, I think it best to return to the intellectual circle in which Keynes wrote his *magnum opus*, to understand the way in which it developed in the midst of vociferous debate not merely between proponents and opponents of *laissez-faire*, but among the opponents themselves. For example, we might arguably begin with the most brilliant, creative, and (ultimately) Left-oriented of Keynes economist-contemporaries and colleagues, Joan Robinson. She was a key member of Keynes's "circle" when he was writing *The General Theory* and did better than almost anyone, often in pithy turns of phrase, to make sense of the substance of his thought. But in the end leaving it to Robinson would be inadequate for the simple reason that she drank too much of the Keynesian Kool-Aid. She was, at least from the 1930s to the 1950s, a true Keynesian in the "economics of Keynes" sense. She knew *The General Theory*'s arguments, perhaps better than Keynes did himself, because she believed much of it so thoroughly (if believed is the right word). In a series of supremely well-written books, she both contributed to the construction of Keynes's book and fleshed out its implications for monopoly and competition, pricing, and more, offering essential and original critique, additions, and theoretical innovations along the way.[6] But Robinson was wrong, too, and on important counts. In particular, she was a true Keynesian in her tortured misunderstanding of Marx. It is true that, in contrast to Keynes himself, she actually read Marx's writings.[7] But it is clear that she did not, and perhaps could not, understand him in the way she "got" Keynes.

I find it difficult to forgive her for this and take it as symptomatic of a Keynesian way of reading. Marx had far more to offer than Robinson understood, perhaps especially to the reading of Keynes. For one thing, like Keynes, he was far more of a "realist" than he is given credit for. Indeed, there is a pragmatism to his thought, a realistic assessment of the facts-of-the-matter, that is almost entirely missed, even sometimes by his "orthodox" acolytes. Keynes was a pragmatist if nothing else, and so too was Hegel.[8] That is perhaps the biggest shocker: Hegel was so *not* what he is conventionally thought to be that sometimes it seems hard to even begin talking about it without being dismissed from the start. But Hegel's sensibility was so thoroughly worldly that, as we have seen, his caricature is laughable. To read his political writings is to discover someone who thought long and hard about how the world "actually" worked,

---

6   See, in particular, the following works by Joan Robinson:, *The Economics of Imperfect Competition*, London: Macmillan, 1933; *Essay in the Theory of Employment*, London: Macmillan, 1937; *An Introduction to the Theory of Employment*, London: Macmillan, 1937 (a very clear explanation of *The General Theory*); and *The Accumulation of Capital*, London: Macmillan, 1956.

7   Joan Robinson, *An Essay on Marxian Economics*, 2nd ed., London: Macmillan, 1966.

8   Hegel once wrote in his journal, "Reading the morning paper is the realist's morning prayer"—and as we know from Buck-Morss, among others, Hegel was an avid newspaper reader. He was in fact a strongly pro-Napoleonic newspaper editor (of the Bamberger *Zeitung*) in 1807–1808, after the publication of the *Phenomenology of Spirit*. See Terry Pinkard, *Hegel: A Biography*, Cambridge: Cambridge University Press, 2000, 240–47.

someone who might even be described as "cynical" enough to appreciate that one should not expect too much of it. At times he seems to have wanted to be the Machiavelli of his age, and although he never achieved it, he was certainly Machiavellian.[9] Indeed, it is not only in his political writings that this predominates. Read his "idealist" philosophical works after his essays on the English Constitution or the German Republic and a different Hegel emerges. Hegel himself offered the best account of the "idealism" to which he adhered: "Once the realm of ideas is revolutionized, actuality will not hold out."[10] Keynes could not have agreed more.

The pragmatism of these thinkers is greatly underexamined. The question that underlies any pragmatism, no matter how historically suppressed, is this: what is it for? Why be "pragmatic"? Why reject pure principle or be "realistic"? What conditions demand this orientation? And in these three cases—Hegel's, Marx's, and Keynes's—these questions are a way of asking what they understood to be the range of the "actually" possible, and within that range, what they thought best, and what we might honestly expect ourselves to achieve. On this, the three differ in substance if not in form. Concerning that which Keynes and Hegel sought to realize—a world without revolution—Marx sat on the other side of the fence. But he was no less "realistic" about its possibilities, a fact in no way impugned by a history that shows him to have been wrong in important ways. Being "realistic" has nothing to do with turning out, in hindsight, to have been "right": as Hegel said, "plans and theories have a claim to reality in so far as they are *practicable*, but their value is the same whether they exist in actuality or not."[11] Nevertheless, to find what exactly lies at the heart of the "realism" to which almost every common sense appeals to is to uncover what is actually at stake, to

---

9   G. W. F. Hegel, *Political Writings*, Cambridge: Cambridge University Press, 1999, 81: *The Prince* is "a distinguished and truthful conception produced by a genuinely political mind of the highest and noblest sentiments."

10   Letter to Niethammer, quoted in Pinkard, *Hegel*, 270. The snide critique of Schelling's "identity" philosophy in the *Phenomenology*, as the "night in which all cows are black" is about as aggressive a "real-world" critique as one can find in German Idealism.

11   Hegel, *Political Writings*, 16.

determine what drives reality's apostles to abandon the realm of abstract principle for the gritty and compromised acceptance of the world in which we actually live.

Keynes once said, in a discussion of Malthus, that "economics is a very dangerous science," and this gritty and compromised acceptance of the world is partly what he means.[12] By "descending" to earth from abstraction, economics and political economy are transformed from a set of propositions about the normative structure of the world to a set of descriptive claims about the world. These theories are "dangerous"—political—by definition. They attempt to capture the world or fragments of it, to shape our concepts of the world so that we change how we approach it—analytically, politically, governmentally.

But the pragmatic realist cannot avoid infusing his or her theories with the structure of feeling in which he or she is embedded. This too is "dangerous," for it cannot help but transmit that structure of feeling across time and space. We tend to hypostatize our worldview, so that it seems a product of the world and not of our necessarily ideologically inflected perspective on it. An anxious political economy can easily come to appear to be a political economy of a world that is by nature eternally anxious. Keynes's reaffirmation in 2008 was at least partly a product of the structure of feeling in which he worked: when you feel like you are on a precipice, those that wrote on a similar precipice in the past make a lot of sense. The question it is difficult to raise, however, is where exactly the precipice resides: in you or in the world.

## Keynes Is Our Hegel

Marx read Hegel most closely with these concerns on his mind, at a time when Hegel had been dead for a decade, and the *Philosophy of Right* was being widely taken up by the forces of reaction, turning Hegel's post-Revolutionary critique of liberalism and revolution into

---

12   Keynes, *CW,* X, 91.

a very un-Hegelian defense of conservative restoration. Marx's most explicit and sustained engagements with Hegel's political thought— the "Contribution to a Critique of Hegel's Philosophy of Law" and "On the Jewish Question"—were thus the product of a particular conjuncture.[13] On the one hand, Hegel, who had long mattered to him enormously, was being stood on his head by the authorities. On the other, he found himself in a moment of calm in a period of personal and political crisis. Married in June 1843, he settled into his mother-in-law's home in Kreuznach, eighty kilometers southwest of Frankfurt, for five months prior to a move to Paris (where Marx would become bound to his other life partner, Friedrich Engels). But his failure to establish a university career (and thus maintain some social status and standing in the eyes of his wife's family) and the Prussian state's newfound repressive energies generated endless questions, which seemed to lack solid answers. If the development of Marx's political thought has a discernable trajectory we might retrospectively impose—something many have attempted—Kreuznach marks not so much a fork in the road as a fraught threshold before a point of no return.

The manuscripts he wrote in Kreuznach are in no way anomalous in the progress of his life's work; tracing his path with the privilege of hindsight, there is little that is not easily fit into a superficially coherent, if bland, story of transition from youthful philosopher to mature political economist. Yet, while Marx's burgeoning radicalism sparkles in their pages, there is also a sense in the Kreuznach writings that his mind is still very unsettled, that his categories and concepts have shaken off much conventional wisdom but have not yet developed the coherence that might allow them to protect themselves, as it were. It is as if they have a direction but no destination, and as such their unfolding happens on some precarious but productive terrain common to both where he was heading and where he had been. To say that his ideas in Kreuznach "hover between liberalism and

---

13   Karl Marx, "Contribution to the Critique of Hegel's Philosophy of Law" and "On the Jewish Question," in *Marx-Engels Collected Works*, vol. 3, New York: International Publishers, 1973 [1843-1844], 3–129, 146–74.

socialism" is not exactly true—they are not in fact "between" commitments, but are rather stretched across a whole range of commitments—but it does give some sense of their restlessness.[14]

To engage Hegel wholeheartedly in this synaptic state of mind—
not, I think, an uncommon way to engage Hegel (he might well
induce it)—is like trying to follow the flight of a snowflake in a bliz-
zard. There are moments when you lock on, and watch the movement of the single idea with exhilarating clarity, its independence
and its part in the whole both almost magically illuminated. There
are moments, too, when you try and try again, but all you can catch
is the flurry of movement as a whole, unable to latch on to any one
thing. And there are also those moments when you discover you have
been in an unreflective stupor for several minutes, missing anything
interesting that might have happened. Any glance through the notes
that make up the "Contribution to a Critique," an almost manic
collection of verbatim quotations from the section on the state in the
*Philosophy of Right*, interrupted by insightful commentaries both
celebratory and damning, communicates the eagerness with which
Marx is searching almost desperately for *something* in Hegel's text: a
way through or a tunnel to the other side of a system that makes
perfect sense but simply cannot be true.

Marx seems to have more moments of clarity than many of us,
perhaps, but all three experiences shape how Hegel came to matter to
him. So too, of course, did the other ideas with which he was then
engaged, especially Ludwig Feuerbach's—so much so that these texts
are sometimes described as the product of a mind that does not yet
qualify as truly "Marx": since Feuerbach's critique of Hegel "only"
made it to materialism—not quite historical materialism—a "merely"
Feuerbachian Marx is deemed unfinished, immature, either too
liberal or insufficiently radical.[15] While the effort to demote those

---

14   Norman Fischer, "Marx's Early Concept of Democracy and the Ethical Bases of
Socialism," in John P. Burke, Lawrence Crocker and Lyman Legters (eds.), *Marx and the
Good Society*, Cambridge: Cambridge University Press, 1981, 59.
15   On this account, most famously associated with Louis Althusser, Marx does not
become Marxist until two years later, with the "Theses on Feuerbach," in *Marx-Engels
Collected Works*, vol. 5, New York: International Publishers, 1973 [1845], 3–5.

aspects of Marx's thought judged inadequate to Marxism is only one more fortification in the increasingly irrelevant kingdom of orthodoxy, whether or not Marx of Kreuznach was yet worthy of his name is immaterial (no pun intended). The point, rather, is that Feuerbach elaborated a critique of idealism that so captured Marx that it became more than just a lens through which he read; it became for him the true, if unintended, internal structure of Hegel's thought.

That critique is that idealism "inverts" the real relation between thought and being, between philosophy and human life, rendering the material world a product of thought. The person becomes the worldly realization of personality, the subject the realization of subjectivity. In his Kreuznach writings, Marx sees this subject/predicate inversion everywhere in Hegel's *Philosophy of Right*. He pounces with indignation at every hint of its "mystification": the state is not a "mystical subject," as Hegel would have it, incarnated in its subjects, and the sovereign is not the incarnation of the Idea of sovereignty. This is an inverted world. In reality, subjects are the basis of the state, and sovereignty is "nothing but the objectified mind of the subjects of the state."[16]

After a while, it becomes tempting to take this move as a bit of a gimmick, to get a little defensive of Hegel. But the substance of the critique—that Hegel's is a seamless account of what is for all intents and purposes an upside-down world—is nonetheless essential to Marx's analysis of the very real power of Hegelian political philosophy. For at no point does he suggest that it is "untrue" or "unrealistic." On the contrary, that is the problem: it is true, it is realistic. Mystification is not deception, nor is it fabrication. Indeed, it is precisely this recognition on Marx's part—that what mattered was not ultimately a question of being correct or incorrect in one's account of the constitution of social life, but of the power of that account to capture what was true to its moment—that marks Marx's transition in Kreuznach from philosophical to political critique. "Marx turned Hegel against himself; he elaborated a Hegelian critique of Hegel."[17]

---

16  Marx, "Contribution to the Critique of Hegel's Philosophy of Law," 24.

17  Stathis Kouvelakis, *Philosophy and Revolution: From Marx to Kant*, trans. G. M. Goshgarian, New York: Verso, 2003, 236.

This is the sense in which I propose that *The General Theory* should be read. While I cannot bring Marx's insight to that reading, and I do not think a paragraph-by-paragraph close reading of *The General Theory* is appropriate to the task, I am convinced that Keynesianism's eternal return calls for the sensibility that animated Marx's engagement with Hegel in Kreuznach. The only way we will understand *The General Theory* and its many and varied lives is to approach it with this sensibility: recognizing that what matters is not whether Keynes is right or wrong, vague or precise, but the conception of "modern" social life at the heart of *The General Theory*. If we can understand some of that, we will be in a much better place to understand why Keynesianism has such a hold on liberal capitalism in its moments of angst. This is what I mean when I say that Keynes is our Hegel. The fact that he has such affinity with the Hegelian conception of post-Revolutionary politics, and the importance of political economy therein, only makes this effort all the more important.

This is also why it is so crucial to read Keynes again at this moment. What goes by the label "Keynesianism" today, almost all of which is more-or-less technical post-World War II economics, is not a good way into *The General Theory*, nor is it necessarily an adequate representation of the Keynesian critique of modernity. In fact, while excellent work on Keynesianism's broader relevance and complexity has appeared recently, from the pen of Robert Skidelsky in particular, most of what is available on the economics side of things would actually make a very poor introduction to *The General Theory*.[18]

## "The Economics of Keynes"

The relation between post-World War II "Keynesian economics" and its foundational text is much more uneven and distant than many assume (see Chapters 12 and 13). The welfare state, or crisis-oriented

18    Robert Skidelsky, *Keynes: The Return of the Master*, London: Penguin, 2009; Robert Skidelsky, *Keynes: A Very Short Introduction*, Oxford: Oxford University Press, 2010.

fiscal policy through "automatic stabilizers" and deficit spending, are today all considered essential features of Keynesianism, even though they are almost entirely absent not only from *The General Theory* but from virtually all Keynes's work. Attacks on the limits of "state intervention" or the "mixed economy" elaborated by critics on both the Left and Right is not, ultimately, a critique of Keynes; both mischaracterize the political economic theory and objectives to which he was committed.[19]

Postwar "Keynesianism" is widely conflated with the "economics of Keynes," I think, at least partly for the simple reason that Keynes is hardly read anymore. His writing is mostly remembered for its witticisms: "In the long run, we are all dead"; or "it is worse, in an impoverished world, to provoke unemployment than to disappoint the rentier."[20] One receiving a lot of airtime recently runs:

> Speculators do no harm as bubbles on a steady stream of enterprise. But the position is serious when enterprise becomes the bubble on a whirlpool of speculation. When the capital development of a country becomes the by-product of the activities of a casino, the job is likely to be ill-done.[21]

Interestingly, these snippets actually give us a better sense of Keynes's motivation to challenge the "classical" political economy of his teachers than any list of postwar "Keynesian" policies. Classical economics, the school of thought that had dominated capitalist governance at least since the mid-nineteenth century, built the theoretical rationale for the invisible hand of high liberal *laissez-faire*. In the years after World War I, Keynes came to reject this common sense. He and others advocated state intervention and public works

---

19   See for example Friedrich Hayek, *A Tiger by the Tail: The Keynesian Legacy of Inflation*, London: Institute of Economic Affairs, 1972. For a compelling critique of the idea of a "mixed economy" that tries not to reduce Keynes to its simple frame, see Paul Mattick, *Marx and Keynes: The Limits of the Mixed Economy*, Boston: Porter Sargent, 1969.

20   Keynes, *CW*, IV, 65; *CW*, IX, 75. (*CW*, IV is *A Tract on Monetary Reform* of 1924.)

21   Keynes, *CW*, VII, 159.

throughout the 1920s.[22] Neither he nor they needed *The General Theory* to make this case: the policies we call "Keynesian" are all basically "logical" reactions to falling profits, unemployment, and social unrest, and many—though by no means most—orthodox economists (for example, Frank Knight, Jacob Viner, and Paul Douglas) advocated them at the time. As with the crisis following the Lehman Brothers' bankruptcy in 2008, the calls for, and necessity of, state provision of some aid for the present and some hope for the future had little relation to the poverty or injustices visited upon the masses. It was about saving civilization; the masses' welfare was merely a means to an end. Keynes made this point repeatedly throughout his career, beginning with his denunciation of the Versailles Treaty for imposing a reparations scheme that, by "degrading the lives of millions of human beings" would "destroy, whoever its victor, the civilisation and progress of our generation." This is the same sensibility that led him to an equally energetic denunciation of the return to the gold standard—that "barbarous relic"—for its likely effect on the "psychological equilibrium" of the "man of spirit" that "permits the perpetuance of unequal rewards."[23]

The stakes in the success of this legitimation project are literally existential. Without careful attention to civilization's "thin and precarious crust"—which we can now recognize as necessity itself—the rabble promised upheaval and irrationalism. When Keynes said "in the long run we are all dead," this is what he had in mind. Clearly, what had been economics' classical "common sense" was no longer sensible. The situation demanded new analytical tools, capable of confronting a problem of such enormous scale and scope.

---

22   The classical approach, despite its geographically uneven hegemony in Europe and North America from the early 1800s, had come under attack before Keynes, and market fundamentalism, to the extent that it ever organized state policy, had been "temporarily" suspended many times—for example, 1858 (United States, then Europe), 1873 (United Kingdom), 1907 (United States), 1914 (all over), and 1923 (Germany).

23   Keynes, *CW,* II, 142, 170; *CW,* IV, 24. Alternatively, as he wrote in "The End of *Laissez-Faire*," "capitalism, wisely managed, can probably be made more efficient for attaining economic ends than any alternative yet in sight, but that in itself is in many ways extremely objectionable"; *CW,* IX, 294.

*Liberal "Realism"*

An understanding of Keynes and Keynesianism thus demands a much more fundamental engagement with a current of reflexively critical liberalism in modern political economy.[24] Keynes's theory of capitalism is elaborated from a self-consciously "realistic" epistemological stance, at once pragmatic and intuitionist. He constantly reminds his readers that in contrast to classical orthodoxy, his ideas reflect "the world in which we actually live" and concern "how the economy in which we actually live works."[25] This actually existing capitalism is driven by expectations, because capitalism's motor is entrepreneurial investment, and investment is solely a function of relative expected yield. These expectations are always more or less radically uncertain. The likelihood of future outcomes can never be precisely or even probabilistically determined, and the more significant the event, and the further into the future, the more and more uncertainty we must admit. Consequently, virtually all aims or claims to precision in economic analysis are false, and they are close to absurd when we look any distance into the future. Keynes's well-known distaste for fancy mathematics reflects these intuitions, which he took to be a much more appropriate theoretical basis for a practical engagement with the world. As another witticism commonly attributed to him goes, "It is better to be vaguely right than exactly wrong."[26]

The *Treatise on Money* of 1930 was Keynes's first attempt to formulate a properly scientific justification for the interventionist intuition in the face of unemployment. But the failures of its "magic formula" prescription for capitalism's failures—cheap money—were evident to him even before it appeared in print.[27] *The General Theory's*

---

24   Massimo de Angelis, *Keynesianism, Social Conflict and Political Economy*, Basingstoke: Macmillan, 2000.

25   For example, Keynes, *CW,* VII, 13, 19, 24 n.3.

26   These are in fact the words of Carveth Read, *Logic: Deductive and Inductive*, London: Grant Richards, 1898, 272. Keynes's variation is considerably less succinct. He said it is better "to see the truth obscurely and imperfectly rather than to maintain error reached indeed with clearness and consistency and by easy logic on hypotheses inappropriate to the facts"; *CW,* VII, 371.

27   Roger Backhouse and Bradley Bateman, *Capitalist Revolutionary: John Maynard Keynes*, Cambridge: Cambridge University Press, 2011, 88–93; Peter Clarke, *The Keynesian Revolution in the Making, 1924–1936*, Oxford: Clarendon Press, 1988, 75.

contribution—and this was its express purpose—was instead to develop the most coherent and useful theory of market-based civil society and its relation to the state in modern capitalism. It illuminated the economic mechanisms on which modern communities actually relied (*Sein*), not those on which they should rely (*Sollen*).

The first step in this project was the dismantling of what Keynes called "Say's Law," after the pre-Revolutionary French Physiocrat Jean-Baptiste Say. Keynes credits Say (whose name, like Keynes's own, has come to be associated with ideas not entirely his own) with the proposition that, given a flexible price system like that assumed by classical and neoclassical economists, changes in supply will always be met with corresponding changes in demand so as to enable full employment of all factors of production. Keynes argued that this "law," commonly summed up by the claim that in conditions of *laissez-faire* "supply creates its own demand," was the fundamental assumption of "classical economics," the orthodoxy that had held sway from the early nineteenth century to Keynes's day. In economics today, Say's Law lives on in the assumption that markets are "perfect."[28]

Although one might not know it, given its continued centrality to classical and neoclassical orthodoxy—evidence of what can only be described as a quasi-religious commitment to willful ignorance—Keynes destroyed the logic of Say's Law in *The General Theory*. Contrary to common misconceptions, however, his argument was not simply that in real markets, prices do not in fact instantaneously adjust, preventing markets from clearing (that is, market participants lack the information necessary to make these adjustments or do not

---

28    Paul Sweezy writes that Keynes's "greatest achievements were freeing economics from the tyranny of Say's Law and exploding the myth of capitalism as a self-adjusting system which reconciles private and public interests"; Paul Sweezy, "Keynesian Economics: The First Quarter Century," in Robert Lekachman (ed.), *Keynes' General Theory: Reports on Three Decades*, New York: St. Martin's Press, 1963, 305.

In light of this achievement, it might be hard to explain the continuing dominance of the myth of self-adjustment and complete markets. According to Keynes, the victory of "the Ricardian economics," even though it so plainly contradicted common sense, was due to its prestige (it made no sense to the uninitiated), its virtue (it was austere, rigid, and "unpalatable"), and its beauty (in its "consistent logical superstructure"); Keynes, *CW,* VII, 33.

have technical and institutional frameworks to make them quickly enough). As Keynes and most orthodox economists recognize, that is of course true. The allowance for these "frictions" is often all that is needed to categorize a modern economic model as "Keynesian." But if that were the source of the problem, then Keynes's critique would be fairly trivial, and orthodoxy would still be the best medicine, since the policy lesson would be the same it offers for every market misfire: Do everything in your power to remove obstacles to price flexibility.

Keynes isolated much more powerful dynamics that put the lie to Say's Law. At the most general level, he argued that it could not hold because of the inevitable uncertainty that pervades a "monetary production economy," that is, a modern capitalist economy, in which production is dependent upon investment through monetary flows. He demonstrates this in a series of logical steps. First, he shows that if it were true that all markets always clear, then if an individual or firm wished to "save" money, at a systemic level those savings must be considered "spent" as investment, since presumably the market for investible funds also clears. In other words, modern banking, whether "savers" wish it or not, must enable all savings to find a way into investment, since demand for investment flows are met by supply of those flows. In this case, the classical theory says that the price that adjusts to produce equilibrium in the "loanable funds" market is the interest rate, which shifts so as to ensure that the amount saved is exactly the amount invested. In other words, Say's Law asserts that because all income is either consumed (spent directly) or saved (and so spent indirectly), "the whole of the costs of production must necessarily be spent in the aggregate."[29]

Keynes's second point is to ask if this is how real markets might be expected to work. Decisions to save are clearly separate from investment decisions. They are not motivated by the same economic forces. Is it not the case that there are times when people feel uncertain about the future? When they might choose to hold money out of circulation to prepare for unforeseen events or take advantage of sudden opportunities, or simply because they are unsure what "the

---

29   Ibid., 26.

economy" will do in the future and want to be prepared if they need to act quickly? If so, then these decisions to save will not lead to investment, and "the whole of the costs of production" will *not* "necessarily be spent in the aggregate."

Keynes suggested that this uncertainty, which he called "liquidity preference," would change both with unexpected events, good or ill, and with what modern economists call the business cycle, rising when prospects seemed bleaker, declining when they improved. People tend to worry less about rainy days when skies are sunny. In the theoretical structure of *The General Theory*, liquidity preference is an essential pillar because it, not a saving-investment supply-demand equilibrium, determines the interest rate. If liquidity preference describes the general level of caution, or the relative desirability of liquid assets, then the interest rate—the price a borrower must pay money holders for access to their money-capital—is a direct function of that caution. If uncertainty is high, then the interest rate will have to reach a level high enough to encourage money holders to over-come their liquidity preference, throw (some) caution to the wind, and lend. This demands a confidence in adequate returns from investment not only on the part of the lenders, but also on the part of borrowing entrepreneurs, who of course have to be optimistic enough to believe that the rate of interest on repayment will be lower than the eventual rate of return on the investments for which the money was borrowed.

Moreover, said Keynes, the level of investment is not a product of the Say's Law saving-investment supply-demand dynamic, either. It is not determined by the level of saving—banks produce money for investment demand; they have no need for a dollar saved to lend a dollar. Nor is it determined solely by the rate of interest, but rather by what Keynes called the "marginal efficiency of capital"—the expected rate of profit. Investors will only invest when they antici-pate returns they deem adequate. Anticipated and adequate returns will of course depend upon potential investors (who will vary in their optimism, their experience, their information, what they consider adequate, and so on) but it seems foolish to plan on investment if expected returns are less than the rate of interest.

If so, then when the economic outlook is dim, liquidity preference will increase, but cash will not necessarily flow to investment opportunities if they do not appear to offer a reasonable rate of return. If liquidity preference is anything other than zero—that is, if there is any reason to feel uncertain about the future and hold cash—then "the whole of the costs of production" will not "be spent in the aggregate" and Say's Law cannot hold. If it does not, then even with perfectly flexible prices (which never in fact exist anyway), a market equilibrium is not necessarily a "full employment" equilibrium. In fact, given that it is hard to imagine a complex capitalist economy in which liquidity preference is effectively zero (in which there is no uncertainty) for all participants, the basic Keynesian "fact" is that economies may find equilibria—Keynes never disavows the metaphysics of equilibrium—but they will always be more or less suboptimal. Though there is no one to blame, there must therefore be resources unused by the economy, their productive capacity untapped. Which means that policies based in orthodox economics, which assume that leaving the market alone will allow it to pull in all available resources at market-clearing prices, are useless. Classical economics "has nothing to offer."[30] It is inadequate to "the world in which we actually live."

### A Theory of Actually Existing Capitalism

Keynes thus explicitly intended *The General Theory* as a critical theory of "actually existing" capitalism, the reality that falls short of classical, all-engines-firing, *laissez-faire* utopia. This theory of liberal civil society is Hegelian: it consists in the identification of a set of immanent, mutually reinforcing relational dynamics that make capitalism much less stable than classical economics or political economy would have us believe. These factors constitute a systemic logic, its components so interlocked that identifying any single one as primary is a false choice.[31] To simplify, though, one might argue that the root of

---

30  Ibid., 260.
31  Indeed, the structure of *The General Theory*'s argument, constantly tracking back and forth, referring to ideas not yet discussed and reworking others already introduced,

Keynes's critique is the unavoidable fact of qualitative uncertainty, as opposed to quantifiable risk: as another of his famous witticisms goes (this one from 1937), regarding the most important of future events (wars, political shifts, etc.), "We simply do not know."[32] For Keynes, this is not a capitalist problem; it is an inescapable, transhistorical, fact of life.

Since capitalism is a "monetary production economy," the relation between uncertainty and money—and the particular uses to which capitalism puts it—make all the difference.[33] Money is not, as the classicals have it, merely a convenient means of payment with no "real" long-run economic effects. In a monetary economy, uncertainty has a specifically *monetary* effect: money is a store of value, and when uncertain people choose to put something aside for a rainy day, or just in case a good deal comes along, they put aside money, and that makes money different than any other commodity. The preference for money or moneylike things over less fungible assets is how liquidity preference manifests itself, as a signal of "confidence."

Keynes was far from the first person to think about the economic effect of confidence or uncertainty. But he identified two crucial aspects of this tendency for people's sense of uncertainty, and therefore their liquidity preferences, to shift or oscillate—movements that are transmitted to the rate of interest. First, the reasons for the oscillations are themselves uncertain—since we cannot know the future, *a fortiori* we cannot know the future degree of liquidity preference—and thus we cannot predict with any certainty future rates of interest. Second, the "sentiments" (to use today's terminology) that determine liquidity preferences are not very diverse. They tend, rather, to

---

shows Keynes's struggles with causal priority. This problem is very much like that with which Marx struggled in his (Hegelian) account of the circulatory moments in the relations of production; see especially the 1857 Introduction to Karl Marx, *Grundrisse*, New York: Vintage, 1973.

32   Keynes, *CW,* XIV, 114.

33   Keynes, *CW,* XIII, 408; Luigi Pasinetti, "J. M. Keynes's 'Revolution'—The Major Event of Twentieth-Century Economics?" in Luigi Pasinetti and Bertram Schefold (eds.), *The Impact of Keynes on Economics in the 20th Century*, Cheltenham: Edward Elgar, 1999, 12; Augusto Graziani, *The Monetary Theory of Production*, Cambridge: Cambridge University Press, 2009.

produce herd behavior, to shift together, due to what Keynes called "mass psychology." And mass psychology is self-reinforcing, especially in modern markets, even for those who would "rationally" choose not to go along with the crowd. You might feel like everyone is an idiot to be selling all their stocks, but if you don't do the same, the "logic" of your reasoning is no guarantee against your investments plummeting in value when everyone else's does.[34]

For Keynes, the effects of these dynamics on investment were the most important destabilizers in capitalism, primarily because of their impact on current and expected interest rates. Like most other bourgeois of his age and ours, Keynes always held up the entrepreneuriat as the true engine of modern prosperity. If there is a *primum mobile* in capitalism, it is entrepreneurial "investment demand," the businessperson's desire to take advantage of opportunities for productive investment.[35] In Keynes's account, even saving is a function of investment—completely reversing the classical notion that saving must precede investment, he argued that saving is the *ex post* result of wealth accumulation generated by investment. Investment begets saving, not the other way around. But if liquidity preference rises with uncertainty, then money holders will hoard cash, interest rates will rise, and investment will be constrained. And without vigorous investment demand, capitalism is out of joint. The solution was not, therefore, price adjustment, or, more specifically, wage reduction, as the classicals said. Lowering wages in a "free market" would only increase uncertainty, push prices down and interest rates up, and make matters worse. Who would borrow, invest, and hire workers in such conditions?

In this account, unemployment is a product of the way capitalism works, a true crisis tendency. And, as Keynes said at the close of *The General Theory*, "it is certain that the world will not much longer tolerate the unemployment which, apart from brief intervals of excitement, is associated—and, in my opinion, inevitably

---

34  "Worldly wisdom teaches that it is better for reputation to fail conventionally than to succeed unconventionally" (Keynes, *CW*, VII, 158).

35  Unsurprisingly, for Keynes entrepreneurs were always business*men*.

associated—with capitalistic individualism."[36] What *The General Theory* provides is mostly a diagnosis of this condition, and only hypothetical suggestions for a "prescription." What Keynes thought might be done is only described in broad terms, mostly in the last three chapters that make up Part VI of the book, "Short Notes Suggested by the General Theory." Even in this part of the text there is almost nothing about specific policies, institutional structures, or modes of distribution. Virtually every policy or institutional relationship we commonly call "Keynesian" today goes unmentioned. If they are to be found anywhere, it is in his pre-*General Theory* writings. Keynes wrote *The General Theory* as a "revolutionary" reconstruction of economic theory, not as a guidebook for the path to abundance.

There is, however, a subtext to the analysis that points, or at least gestures, to a theoretically grounded "economic bliss" (in contrast to the pep rally version in the "Grandchildren" essay of 1930 discussed in Chapter 1), a first-cut suggestion as to how to "solve the economic problem":

> My goal is the ideal; my object is to put economic considerations into a back seat; but my method at this moment of economic and social evolution would be to advance towards the goal by concentrating on doing what is economically sound.[37]

As the "Grandchildren" essay demonstrates, Keynes believed in a "posteconomic" world long before he developed *The General Theory*. From his perspective, it all made sense: here we had the British and other "modern communities," with wealth, technology, and knowledge absolutely unimaginable even a few decades before. These communities had productive capacity beyond anyone's wildest imagination, and, he thought, people were better off and healthier than ever before (like most Keynesians, he was not big on reflecting on colonialism and imperialism). When things stagnated, it was not for

---

36    Keynes, *CW,* VII, 381.
37    Keynes, *CW,* XXI, 34.

lack of technology, labor power, or knowledge. Materially—in the forces of production, we might say—almost everything was in place.

The one thing that seemed to be missing, however (and usually when we most need it), was sufficient capital. In 1930, no one could get their hands on it. But how, with wealth like never before, could capital be scarce? Why must we make ourselves poor? It seemed absurd[38]:

> For the resources of Nature and men's devices are just as fertile and productive as they were. The rate of our progress towards solving the material problems of life is not less rapid. We are as capable as before of affording for every one a high standard of life—high, I mean, compared with, say, twenty years ago—and will soon learn to afford a standard higher still. We have not been deceived. But to-day we have involved ourselves in a colossal muddle, having blundered in the control of a delicate machine, the working of which we do not understand.[39]

The result, he said, was the ironic "Fate of Midas":

> [T]he richer the community, the wider will tend to be the gap between its actual and its potential production; and therefore the more obvious and outrageous the defects of the economic system . . . If in a wealthy community the inducement to invest is weak, then, in spite of its potential wealth, the working of the principle of effective demand will compel it to reduce its actual output, until, in spite of its potential wealth, it has become so poor that its surplus over its consumption is sufficiently diminished to correspond to the weakness of the inducement to invest.[40]

---

38   These concerns are the source of his constant and vehement opposition to the gold standard, framed most famously in "The Economic Consequences of Mr Churchill" of 1925; Keynes, *CW,* IX, 207–30.

39   Ibid., 126.

40   Keynes, *CW,* VII, 31. The reasoning is as follows: the marginal propensity to consume is weaker in wealthy communities, and the inducement to invest is lower because the community already has a lot of capital, so interest rates have to adjust ("fall rapidly") to make the marginal efficiency of capital closer to $r$, and encourage productive capital-asset investment, as opposed to debt purchase or speculation (not that they are always separate).

With *The General Theory*, Keynes believed himself to be providing a user's guide to the "delicate machine" that is the modern capitalist economy. The "scarcity theory" of capital it laid out exposed the way in which its daily operation consistently generated the apparent paradox of "poverty in the midst of plenty." The reason, he argued, was that "capital has to be kept scarce enough" that return on its investment will be deemed acceptable by capitalists. Capital must be "kept scarce" to the point at which "we" become sufficiently impoverished so as to make profitable investment worthwhile.[41] As Thomas Piketty put it recently, arguing precisely the same "stagnationist" point, "[t]oo much capital kills capital."[42]

The questions to which Keynes turned emerged logically from this account: What determines investors' judgments of acceptable rates of return? What makes investment seem worthwhile? His answer: again, the rate of interest. The idea that capitalists are interested in investment to make some material contribution to the world, or to be "productive" in some honorable way, is a bourgeois myth: it is a fundamental error, he wrote, to believe that capital is "productive," or "that the owner of wealth desires a capital-asset *as such*, . . . what he really desires is its *prospective yield* . . . [T]here is always an alternative to the ownership of real capital-assets, namely the ownership of money and debts."[43] Consequently, the expected return on investment, the "marginal efficiency of capital," cannot fall below the rate of interest. If it does, who will invest?

So, to make capital less scarce, to induce investment, interest rates must fall. Not because this renders borrowing less expensive (although that is helpful), but because we must regulate capitalist "free market" pricing dynamics, to reduce the rate of return with which entrepreneurial investment must compete. Ultimately, Keynes said, the

---

41    Ibid., 30, 215, 217. In other words, scarce enough to produce a rabble; the rabble is a product of the fallacy of composition inherent in competitive ("individualistic") capitalism, and the condition in which it coalesces is the same condition that is necessary for profit. The rabble is the "unintended" consequence of the organization of life by the rule of value.

42    Thomas Piketty, *Capital au XXIᵉ siècle*, Paris: Seuil, 2013, 336 (my translation).

43    Keynes, *CW*, VII, 212.

scarcity theory of capital demonstrates that "there are no intrinsic reasons for the scarcity of capital" in modern capitalism. Indeed, he thought it perfectly reasonable to expect "modern communities" to be capable "of depriving capital of its scarcity-value within one or two generations." There is no reason for us to be poor; indeed, "it is to our best advantage to reduce the rate of interest to that point . . . at which there is full employment."[44] Low interest rates are the essential precondition for economic bliss—not, as commonly thought, back-to-work programs, fiscal stimulus, tax cuts, unemployment insurance, and so on: most of these are not even mentioned.

This is his critique in a nutshell. The way capitalism works leaves some holding the short straw—that is, with no means to make a living—and there is no guarantee that if they wait a little while, someone will come along and welcome them aboard. To keep the engine moving, these disequalizing mechanisms of economic disfranchisement must be mitigated in "the social interest." All the more "technical" aspects of Keynes's economics—effective demand, propensities to consume, multipliers, and so on—are, as we will see, functional pieces of this explanation.

---

44  Ibid., 375–77.

# CHAPTER 10

# How to Read *The General Theory* II

Perhaps the most important contribution of New Keynesian economics to Keynesianism's theoretical edifice—especially if importance is judged by its impact on the mainstream discipline of economics—is its studious attention to the operation of the "delicate machine's" even more delicate wiring: prices. According to New Keynesians—a group in which we would include some of the most influential "policy-oriented" economists of the last quarter-century, like Joseph Stiglitz, Janet Yellen, Lawrence Summers, and Paul Krugman—the persistent trouble with the *laissez-faire* design of the capitalist machine is principally attributable to the limits of an actually-existing price system.

Like the classical economics that drew Keynes's fire, modern neoclassical microeconomics and its macroeconomic variations (monetarism, new classical economics, real business cycle theory, and so on) are founded upon a theory of price that for the most part assumes away the complications of the world.[1] According to this

---

1 For an accessible critique of these schools of macroeconomics, see Robert Skidelsky, *Keynes: The Return of the Master*, New York: Penguin, 2009, 29–51; for a more technical variation, see Lance Taylor, *Reconstructing Macroeconomics: Structuralist Proposals and Critiques of the Mainstream*, Cambridge: Harvard University Press, 2004, 199–231. For a historical account of the relations between these mainstream schools and New Keynesian economics, see Roger Backhouse and Mauro Boianovsky, *Transforming Modern Macroeconomics: Exploring Disequilibrium Microfoundations, 1956–2003*, Cambridge: Cambridge University Press, 2013, 160–70.

theory of the world, information—which is absolutely crucial because it is what enables each of us to base our decisions on the optimum potential gain associated with any particular decision or plan—is transmitted principally through prices. For classicals, neoclassicals, and New Classicals, prices are *the* determinants of both rational microeconomic action and efficient macroeconomic resource allocation. Hence these economists' antipathy to any "distortion" of what they take to be "natural" competitive market pricing—for example, minimum wage policies, state subsidies, or welfare benefits.

These theories also presume, for the most part, that the comparative knowledge that economic agents learn from prices—X is more expensive than Y, borrowing from Bank A is cheaper than from Bank B—is instantly available to everyone, always and everywhere. Indeed, more extreme variations (in the work of Milton Friedman's "life-cycle" models, or Eugene Fama's "efficient market hypothesis," for example) assume that prices are not only instantly known to agents, but that all relative prices over the entire course of one's lifetime, or even forever, are also known, a proposition labeled "perfect foresight." Now, almost every real-life economist readily admits these assumptions are not born out in the world in which we actually live. But unpredictable time lags, uncertainties, qualitative judgments, and nonoptimizing decisions—not to mention culture, history, and accident—make the abstractions of formal modeling, upon which most modern economists rely, extraordinarily unwieldy, even impossible. Hence, even when such "frictions" are acknowledged, they are not treated as the rule, but are theorized as exceptional, departures from how an economy and its price system *should*—if it were not human, I suppose—function. The actually-existing economy is thus taken to be a distorted instantiation of an abstract, Kantian frictionless norm, and its "failures" are judged, and bemoaned, relative to *Sollen*, not *Sein*.

New Keynesians, like Keynesian economists of all stripes, begin from the premise that modern monetary economies demand a commitment to the marvels of the price system to which human institutions and behavior are inevitably inadequate. In contrast to how things work according to the formal models of so-called "fresh-water" economists, actual prices are plagued by rigidities or "sticki-ness": they neither change fast enough due to information problems or institutional inertia, nor do they rise or fall when they "should" because signals are misrecognized, contradictory, or flatly rejected, as when workers refuse a wage cut, thereby (supposedly) preventing their class-fellows from finding jobs.[2] This produces not only "market failures"—in other words, "missing" or imperfect markets—but an inherent stiffness and delayed response in the market, like a human body with sore joints, or a nervous system that can only tell the brain a finger is burning after it has been in the fire for a long time.

### Expectations, Investment and Effective Demand

The recognition that markets' inevitable imperfections shape the economic operation of "the world in which we actually live" is one of the main things New Keynesians like Krugman claim to have learned from *The General Theory* (indeed, it is largely why they call them-selves New *Keynesians*), and there is much in its pages to justify this claim. Part I (Chapters 1–3) contains Keynes's evisceration of Say's Law, the proposition (see Chapter 9) that if prices are sufficiently responsive, then it is by definition true that (a) any good produced for sale on the market will find a buyer; and (b) in the aggregate, those productive forces put toward unprofitable endeavors will not lie idle, but will be reassigned, generating full employment equilibrium.

Keynes claims that with the exception of a few "brave heretics," Say's Law tacitly underwrites the entirety of classical economics. The classicals are thus a remarkably diverse group; by Keynes's estimation

---

2    Orthodox or mainstream economics are sometimes called "freshwater" because the institutions at the center of their development (the Universities of Chicago and Minnesota, for example) are inland, whereas Keynesianism received a warmer welcome at "saltwater" sites like Harvard, MIT, and Berkeley.

they run from David Ricardo to Samuel Bailey, Karl Marx, and John Stuart Mill and from William Jevons, Alfred Marshall, and Dennis Robertson to Keynes's influential Cambridge colleague Cecil Pigou. Their common error, he argues, is the indefensible assumption that market equilibria are full-employment equilibria. Of course, the diverse interests of those grouped as classicals meant that they did not all assess this "truth" in the same manner. Jevons and Marx, says Keynes, both believed Say's Law, but "[t]he system bred two families—those who thought it true and inevitable, and those who thought it true and intolerable."[3] Part I of *The General Theory* is dedicated to showing that in *laissez-faire* conditions, such a proposition sits somewhere between extremely doubtful and absurd.

*The General Theory*'s exposure of the myth of Say's Law, and its demonstration of the virtual inevitability of sub-full employment *equilibria* (not just temporary disequilibria, that is, exceptional departures from the Kantian norm), is the crucial step on the way to one of Keynes's most famous contributions, the theory of "effective demand." Effective demand is the centerpiece of Keynes's attempt to grasp how the volume of employment is actually determined in "the economic society in which we actually live."[4] It is a straightforward equilibrium concept, determined by the intersection of supply and demand schedules. In that sense, it fits nicely with classical epistemology. Yet, because Keynes rejects the classical assumption of full employment and instantaneous price adjustment, effective demand describes the aggregate forces that produce a macroeconomic equilibrium that is not a priori assumed to clear all markets. This—the isolation of an originary inequality or gap—is a crucial difference. One might even say it is the seed from which the entirety of *The General Theory* is cultivated.

---

3  Keynes, *New Statesman & Nation,* November 10, 1934, *CW*, XXVIII, 32. The ad hoc nature of the "classical" category drew fire from Keynes's critics like Dennis Robertson, who charged (and Keynes later admitted) that he seemed to "clap that label *opprobrii causa* on to the vacuous countenance of some composite Aunt Sally of uncertain age"; Bertil Ohlin, Dennis Robertson, and Frank Hawtrey, "Alternative Theories of the Rate of Interest: Three Rejoinders," *Economic Journal* 47: 187, 1937, 436.

4  Keynes, *CW,* VII, 3.

In the colloquial understanding of Keynesianism today, it is commonly thought that effective demand describes the level of "real" purchasing power-backed demand in an economy. In other words, it is thought that while "true" demand might be $X$, but realized or "effective" demand is $< X$, simply because people do not have the wealth or incomes to act on and thus realize their "true" demand. This definition of "effective demand" would seem to fit with the colloquial or "welfare state" understanding of Keynesianism in general, because fiscal stimulus or unemployment insurance, for example, is thus explained as an attempt to help aggregate demand overcome household budget constraints.

But this is not what Keynes means by "effective demand," and the difference matters a great deal for an understanding of *The General Theory* and post-World War II Keynesian economics. For Keynes, effective demand is an explicitly expectational variable; it describes a current state of things determined by past expectations of a future state of things. His reasoning is as follows: entrepreneurs make production decisions in light of expected demand—they are producing now for sales in the future—and taken together, these decisions determine the total volume of output at any point in time. As a result, past entrepreneurial *expectations* regarding future demand determine current aggregate supply. As an economist might put it, factors of production, including labor, are employed at time $t$ to meet expected demand at time $t + 1$. The level of output (supply) in the economy at any one moment thus reflects the sum total of firms' prior estimations of demand that can be supplied at acceptable rates of return.

This process determines the aggregate supply schedule. Interestingly, it is also entrepreneurial expectations—not the expectations of those to whom they sell—that determine aggregate demand. Aggregate demand is also an expectational variable, "the proceeds which entrepreneurs expect to receive from the employment of $N$ men." If entrepreneurs anticipate that the cost of supplying the market by employing $N$ workers is less than the "proceeds" (revenue) they expect production will bring in, then they will tend to increase $N$ until the expected price of supplying the goods is equal to the revenues expected from selling them, that is, aggregate demand. The point at which the aggregate demand schedule intersects with the aggregate supply schedule is, Keynes says, "the effective demand."[5]

The aggregate demand function, therefore, is not "objectively" determined by unmediated market forces, technology, and the like. Like all Keynes's quantities, it is heavily influenced by what he called "psychology." Effective demand—which, it is worth emphasizing, is *always* a macroeconomic measure, the aggregate of all firms' production decisions—is a function of entrepreneurs' expectations on two fronts: it is the sum of both "the amount the community is expected to spend on consumption" and "the amount which it is expected to devote to new investment." It is "effective" because it is the level of demand that most matters for the economy as a whole, since it is the level businesses anticipate and thus "actually" organize themselves to meet. The "real" level of demand at any moment only matters after the fact, because expectations of the future are influenced by previous periods and are adjusted in their light.[6] It seems it is not just Minerva who needs an owl to try to make some sense of the world after the day is done. Demeter, who we might think of as the goddess of production, is just as necessarily retrospective, her wisdom just as uncertain until after the fact.

Keynes was certainly not the first to note the effect of expectations on entrepreneurial activity, so he is at pains to point out the difference between the conclusions of the theory of effective demand and those to which expectations-oriented classical economics lead. The distinction might appear to be a "technical matter," but it matters. Keynes argues that although classical economics had long recognized the importance of the "state of mind of the businessman" (in the words of Cecil Pigou, whom Keynes targets as representative of classical economics), expectations' real force has been completely disguised by classicals' commitment to Say's Law, which is assumed to hold for all levels of employment and output. In other words, the

---

5  Ibid., 25.
6  Ibid., 29.

classical position tacitly assumes that a sub-full employment level of effective demand is unstable by definition. If everything offered is purchased, competition alone will ensure that both supply and demand continue to rise, in step, to the point of full employment. Which is to say that in the classical theory, all talk of expectations or confidence is meaningless, because expectations ultimately do not matter: even when the state of confidence is low, market dynamics will push us back to full capacity on their own. What we "expect" is moot. If this were true, then a theory developed with the express purpose of explaining changes in the volume of employment—like *The General Theory*—would be a waste of time: the gaps between actual employment and all-engines-firing are merely temporary disequilibria to be erased by markets' tendency to full employment.

Keynes introduces two crucial "psychological" variables to allow him to specify the mechanisms by which a capitalist economy produces "unique," less-than-full employment equilibria, conditions in which there is no necessary tendency for the economy to right itself, let alone lead us "back" to full employment (as if we were ever there in the first place). First, he posits a "fundamental psychological law," which states that taking habits, current conditions, and expectations of the future at any one place and time as given, the "community" in aggregate has a tendency to consume less than the full amount of any increase in income. In Keynesian language, the marginal "propensity to consume" (the proportion of any additional income that is consumed) is always less than unity. When incomes rise, we will not spend it all, but instead hold on to some fraction of the increment.

Consequently, when overall employment and hence "community" income increases (driven by entrepreneurs' expectations of demand), it will not be possible for entrepreneurs to dedicate all increased employment to producing consumption goods and services, since consumers will spend only a portion of the aggregate increase in income, as determined by the propensity to consume. Thus, if an increase in income $X$ generates consumption demand $Y < X$, then the gap $X - Y$ created by the shortfall means that some part of increased employment must be put to work on something other than satisfying consumption demand; put to work, that is, supplying the other side of effective demand: investment demand. Otherwise, any increase in employment will always be temporary, because entrepreneurs will not earn the returns that make the higher level of employment worthwhile and will reduce employment as a consequence. Keynes's conclusion is that if we take any particular community's propensity to consume as more or less given in the short run—fixed by consumption habits, savings propensities, institutional and technological constraints, and so forth—then employment depends upon the level of investment. If incomes are increasing, then investment demand must be sufficiently vibrant to employ resources in excess of that required by consumption demand.

Yet even the merest glance at the history of capitalism makes it clear that investment is by no means consistently vibrant. Its timing and volume is, rather, highly uneven and uncertain, determined by the second of Keynes's "psychological" variables, the "inducement to invest." This is obviously a function of business expectations, specifically regarding anticipated yield. Keynes claims that for any given entrepreneurial opportunity, inducement to invest, and consequently the actual level of investment, ultimately depend on the relationship between the rate of expected return on investment (the "marginal efficiency of capital") and the interest rate that corresponds to the time horizon associated with the investment. For example, if the investment is expected to provide a return over ten years, then assuming a consistent level of perceived risk, the interest rate to which it will be compared will be the highest possible rate on lending for up to ten years' duration—in practice, this usually means comparing it with the highest possible yield on a ten-year bond.

According to Keynes, investment decisions are determined by the difference, if any, between the return businesses can expect from investing in "productive activity" and the return they can expect from lending money (by purchasing corporate or government debt) relative to their desire to hold cash for speculative or precautionary reasons (their liquidity preference). In other words, levels of both the marginal efficiency of capital and the long-run interest rate are subject to the volatility of uncertain expectations. If, in the extreme case, the return on lending is higher for all feasible investment horizons, there is no inducement to invest. If the marginal efficiency of capital is higher than that interest rate which compensates the risk of not holding cash, then there is some inducement to invest, which will increase with both the size of the premium over the interest rate and the level of investors' confidence in their judgments concerning the future.

These ideas allow Keynes to foreshadow the "essence of the General Theory of Employment" early in the book and demonstrate clearly the fundamental role of expectations therein: the level of employment in equilibrium depends upon the aggregate supply schedule (partly a function of employers' expectations regarding what level of employment they should undertake), the community's propensity to consume (partly a function of consumers' expectations regarding the future), and the volume of investment (partly a function of investors' confidence). Given these determinants, a situation satisfying Say's Law, the classical assumption that supply is always equal to demand, is neither "normal" nor even likely. It is, on the contrary, a potential but highly improbable "special case." A level of effective demand involving full employment *might* result from "self-regulated" markets, but there is no reason to expect it and very good reason to doubt it:

> Thus—except on the special assumptions of the classical theory according to which there is some force in operation which, when employment increases, always causes [investment] to increase sufficiently to fill the widening gap between [aggregate supply and the demand for consumption goods]—the economic system may find itself in a stable equilibrium with $N$ at a level below full employment, namely at the level given by the intersection of the aggregate demand function with the aggregate supply function.[7]

---

7   Ibid., 30.

### Suboptimal Equilibria in Suboptimal Markets

Keynes believes his theory—a "general" as opposed to "special" theory—explains the "paradox of poverty in the midst of plenty." For if effective demand is insufficient, the level of investment and hence the level of employment will come "to a standstill *before* a level of full employment has been reached."[8] Ultimately, the classical theory, in its adherence to a probably unrealizable Say's Law, is a normative account of "the way in which we should like our Economy to behave," not an explanation of why it behaves the way it actually does. Classical economics describes an "ought," not an "is."[9]

Keynes's astonishment at the continued commitment to Say's mythology is echoed by today's New Keynesians like Joseph Stiglitz and Janet Yellen (Chair of the US Federal Reserve). Not only do Keynes's arguments provide a devastating critique of the market-clearing ideas that continue to dominate economics, but New Keynesians find further support for their position in these passages of *The General Theory* because, unlike the "post-Keynesian" account, theirs is ultimately grounded in a deep faith in the power of the market as a resource allocation mechanism. And, despite the claims of those who want to recuperate the radical in him, Keynes seems to share this faith, at least in principle. He obviously *does not* reject the assumption that classical equilibrating mechanisms—Léon Walras's famous "*tatônnement*"—are determinant in the last instance.[10] Indeed, he too situates equilibrium at the core of political-economic ontology. Supply and demand *do* determine the volume of employment in *The General Theory*. The problem as Keynes sees it is not

---

8   Ibid., 30–31.

9   Ibid., 34. Keynes's emphasis on the priority of demand is sometimes mistaken as a mere reversal of the causal direction of Say's Law (for example, in the idea that the "Keynesian maxim" is "if demand is right supply will look after itself"); John Allett, *New Liberalism: The Political Economy of J. A. Hobson*, Toronto: University of Toronto Press, 1981, 261. I hope it is clear from this account of *The General Theory* that this incorrectly represents Keynes's ideas. Like Hegel before him, there is very little that Keynes thought would "look after itself"—certainly not something so complex and uncertain as aggregate supply.

10   See, for example, Bernard Maris, *Keynes, ou l'Économiste Citoyen*, 2nd ed., Paris: Sciences Po, 2007, 6, 65–67.

equilibrium theorizing per se. Rather, the problem is that market dynamics produce equilibria that are almost never characterized by full employment.

Consequently, it is important to him to explain sub-full employment in a manner generally consonant with mainstream, economically "rational," supply-and-demand thinking. Just like his New Keynesian acolytes, he claims that (in theory at least) the liberal market economy's price system gets it right: *if* the world were as the classicals say, and workers accepted a lower wage, employment would increase. But, he says, in the "actual world," this never works.

These problems do not reside in the price system, as if it were flawed in its very design. They arise, rather, because real human institutions and informational limits prevent the price system from doing what in theory it has the potential to do. It is our own imperfections, rigidities, and irrationalities that cause the problems. Keynes, like the new Keynesians, clearly argues that in principle (in the world as he would like it to be) the market is the perfect institution. Yet we must accept that it is not and do our best to cope with its limits. Classical liberals have the wrong expectations, because they misrecognize their normative propositions as positive theory. They misperceive the "natural" state of human communities and thus do not recognize that we would only be able to even attempt to implement *laissez-faire* after having consciously produced a second nature, a world in which it makes sense.

Keynes substantiates this argument by focusing on two postulates upon which, he claims, the classical theory of employment must necessarily rest. The first concerns classical thinking on the demand for labor, which assumes that the real wage equals the marginal product of labor. That is, workers will be employed until the real value of the wage of the last worker hired is equal to the marginal product of his or her labor. Workers in search of employment will find it as long as employers can pay them less than the additional returns expected from adding workers to the production process; when employing additional labor no longer promises sufficient additional return, hiring stops. The second postulate is the basis for the classical theory of labor supply. It asserts "that the utility of the wages when a given volume of labour is employed is equal to the marginal disutility of that amount of employment."[11] The working class continues to supply its labor to employers as long as real wages compensate it for the hassles associated with additional work (giving up control of one's time, inability to take care of other responsibilities like children, and so on). When the wage drops below that point, workers will no longer accept it, since it will have reached a level deemed inadequate to compensate for the disutility of wage work.

Together, the two postulates describe the supply and demand schedules or "curves" in the classical labor market. The similarity between classical economics and the neoclassical economics of today is evident in the fact that these postulates, and the supply-demand "scissors" they describe, remain the rudiments of most economics education. The first postulate describes a downward-sloping demand schedule: the higher the wage, the less workers hired. The second proposes an upward-sloping supply schedule: the lower the wage, the less labor offered on the labor market. The (equilibrium) volume of employment in the economy is determined by the schedules' intersection.

Keynes claims that while the first postulate is acceptable (a point on which he later wavered), the second must be rejected, because it is incompatible with the glaring reality of what Keynes, always on the lookout for cracks in the social order, calls "involuntary unemployment."[12] Classical theory tells us that unemployment is voluntary, ultimately because of workers' collective or individual unwillingness to accept lower wages (in other words, the marginal disutility of labor is unreasonably high). Keynes's critique is straightforward, derived, he says, from "the facts of experience": in the middle of the Great Depression, it is ridiculous to suggest (as the second postulate does) that if a worker is unemployed, it is because he or she is refusing to work at the going wage. With millions of

---

11   Keynes, *CW,* VII, 5.

12   "Men are involuntarily unemployed if, in the event of a small rise in the price of wage-goods relatively to the *money-wage, both the aggregate supply of labour willing to work for the current money-wage* and the aggregate demand for it at that wage would be greater than the existing volume of employment"; Ibid., 15.

workers more than willing to work at the going wage, or even for a lower wage (this is his definition of being involuntarily unemployed), the second postulate is absurd.

While Keynes focuses his attack on the classical theory of the labor market in particular, his point is also to show that Say's Law governs classical thinking concerning the employment of all factors of production. This logic applies to the wage relationship and to other markets, the most important being the capital market, the supply of and demand for investment opportunities. In this arena, Say's Law posits that the supply of capital (income) always equals the demand for capital. Thus, any income not consumed or directly invested by income-earners (savings) ultimately gets invested indirectly, whether the earner wishes it or not; if it did not, then the capital market would not be operating in "full employment" conditions. In other words, taking for granted the universal intermediation of an undiscussed financial sector and an instantly flexible interest rate (the price of capital), classical economics according to Keynes asserts that any income "saved" by one earner will eventually find its way to someone who will borrow it to invest.[13] There is no hoarding, no accumulating of cash, and no shortage of investment demand. Capital is fully employed by assumption.

The limits to the classical model are exacerbated by the fact that it pairs the full employment assumption with one of monetary neutrality—the proposition that in the long run the level of the money supply and nominal prices have no effect on the economy in aggregate. If money is neutral, changes in the money supply will propagate evenly across the economy, affecting money prices alone, and leaving "real" and relative prices unchanged—a 50 percent increase in the money supply will, after an adjustment period, merely mean that all prices will rise by 50 percent, meaning relative and real prices

---

13    Like almost all economic considerations of the ways in which savings are transformed into loanable capital, Keynes's account does not even hint at the mechanics of the process, except to suggest that it is supposed to occur via bank intermediation, but he does not say how. To his credit, he is a critic of these ideas; his opponents offer no clearer explanation.

will be the same as before the increase in the money supply.[14] Which is to say that with respect to the labor market, classical economists assume away any distinction between real wages and "money wages" in equilibrium, and, furthermore, assume that economic agents see through the veil of inflation and operate solely in response to "real" prices, wages, and interest rates.

The second classical postulate—that the utility of wage earnings is exact compensation for the disutility of wage work—is thus a combination of two subpostulates. The first is that workers respond only to changes in the "real" wage and enter and leave the labor market not on the basis of nominal wage rates, but on the level of purchasing power that compensates for the disutility of employment. The second—a quite remarkable assumption, when stated explicitly—is that not only do workers respond to real wages and prices but that they enjoy a collective capacity to purposefully lower real wages. If they did not, then when workers discovered that real wages overcompensated them for the disutility of work and were therefore "too high," they would not be in a position to reduce them until all workers were employed. Even if we take the first subpostulate seriously, without this second subpostulate full employment would be impossible, because in a context (like the 1930s) in which the utility associated with a given wage income exceeded the disutility of employment, workers would be unable to lower the real wage to a point adequate to full employment equilibrium.[15]

In one of *The General Theory*'s most important and original arguments, Keynes shows that in the real world, both these ideas are wrong: workers are not, at least in the short run, focused on real wages, and, even if they were, and were willing to accept reduced real

---

14    Long-run monetary neutrality remains a key assumption of much orthodox macroeconomics; it is a crucial reason for widespread (though by no means unanimous) opposition among economists to monetary "stimulus," since if money were in fact neutral (it is not), in the end the only legacy of such stimulus would be inflation. This, in basic outline, is the standard critique of the "Keynesian" Phillips curve (the "trade-off" policy-makers face between unemployment and inflation).

15    This second subproposition underwrites the common claim that workers' "excessive" wage demands cause unemployment.

wages (which clearly many were in the 1930s), there are good reasons to doubt they could lower them anyway. First, "within a certain range the demand of labour is for a minimum money-wage and not for a minimum real wage . . . [W]hether logical or illogical, experience shows that this is how labour in fact behaves." Moreover, Keynes goes on to argue that most wage bargains are motivated by concerns over relative wages. Because wage struggles are usually about money-wages, workers are fighting not for a piece of capital's pie, says Keynes, but for a larger piece of the "aggregate real wage" relative to other segments of the labor force. Real wage reductions that impose declining purchasing power on all workers are not usually resisted "unless they proceed to an extreme degree." Mild to moderate inflation, even in the price of wage goods, rarely leads to labor upheaval, and insofar as this holds, workers are "instinctively more reasonable economists than the classical school."[16]

Indeed, if labor did not in fact behave in this manner and acted according to the motivations attributed to it by classical economics, it would severely destabilize modern capitalist economies. Employment decisions are not made in the long run temporality of monetary neutrality, and if they are made on the basis of real wages, then any change in prices other than the wage would require a shift in the labor supply curve in response, as workers in aggregate adjusted to the new real wage. Moreover, as the Great Depression demonstrates, it is obvious that workers often *will* accept a cut in money wages: "Labour is not more truculent in the depression than in the boom—far from it. Nor is its physical productivity less. These facts from experience are a *prima facie* ground for questioning the adequacy of the classical analysis."[17]

The problem is that even if they accept money-wage cuts—the only kind of cuts employers can make, since that is what they pay, and the only kind of cuts workers can accept, since that is how they are paid—workers cannot determine their real wages. Keynes bases this claim in both economic theory and empirical features of modern

16   Keynes, *CW*, VII, 14.
17   Ibid., 9.

capitalism. On the theoretical side, recall the first postulate, the one Keynes accepts: the wage is equal to the marginal product of labor. If this equality holds, then when money wages decline because workers accept wage cuts, real wages are "inevitably rising in the same circumstances on account of the increasing marginal return to a given capital equipment when output is diminished." In other words—and I feel compelled to point out the tenuousness of this argument, which he later recognized—Keynes is saying that as wages are cut, the returns to production per unit of labor will increase, allowing producers to lower prices, thus negating the effect of the wage cut by restoring real wages to the level at which they stood before the money-wage cuts.

The second factor that limits labor's capacity to determine the real wage is far more meaningful: the "traditional theory maintains, in short, *that the wage bargains between the entrepreneurs and the workers determine the real wage.*" This, he says, is "not obviously true"—an understatement, to say the least: it is just plain false.[18] There are many forces that make it impossible for wage bargains to determine the real wage—not least of which are the difficulties, in a "free market," of coordinating labor and capital across many sectors so as to arrange an economy-wide real wage cut, which will require not only a shift in wage rates, but the relative stability of the price level. Businesses must reduce prices less than wages (otherwise the real wage will not decline), despite declining purchasing power and falling aggregate demand (and the likelihood of a debt-deflation spiral), and they must maintain this stance over time. And this is to say nothing of the fact that the second postulate, by assuming full employment, not only says workers can determine the real wage in principle but that they can determine the specific real wage *appropriate to full employment equilibrium*, that is, the wage at which the labor market will "clear" and all willing workers find jobs. Only if this is true—and it is not, and never has been—could we dismiss the fact of involuntary unemployment. Even in the context of strict corporatist state oversight of wage bargaining, this would be almost

---

18   Ibid., 11–12.

unimaginable, and in a "self-regulating" labor market in which capital dominates a segmented working class, the suggestion is laughable.

Which is to say that as long as the classical theory of employment dominates how these problems are understood—and to a significant extent, it still does, at least in economics departments and economic policymaking—we are unable to see what might be done regarding involuntary unemployment, because classical theory does not acknowledge that it is even possible.

# How to Read *The General Theory* III

The principal objective of all varieties of Keynesianism, including Keynes's own, is always formulated in relation to classical and neoclassical orthodoxy: a scientific theory more adequate to the world than that it attempts to supplant. The theory of involuntary unemployment epitomizes this approach. Falsifiable empirical "facts" about the world "in which we actually live" sustain the logic of the Keynesian position: in modern capitalist markets, structural rigidities and unrealizable institutional capacities and informational requirements mean *laissez-faire* simply cannot deliver on its promises. The limits to capitalism are endemic to the mode of production itself, because it is always populated by agents so constrained.

Today this positivist framing dominates because most self-described Keynesians avoid an explicitly *political* argument for Keynesianism. They tell us we should commit to Keynesianism not because it is more just, egalitarian, or ethical—although they might think so—but for the simple reason that it is truer, its explanation of how the world works more rational and logical than classical and neoclassical dogmatism. They maintain that Keynesianism is just better science, the crowning achievement of centuries of economic reason. As any reader of Paul Krugman's *New York Times* editorials knows, we should all be Keynesians *because* we are civilized moderns, with access to a true science of the world as it actually operates.

(Indeed, for Krugman, anyone who is not his kind of Keynesian is deluded.) This account happily accepts the orthodox motivational assumptions of *homo economicus*, and in that sense is as beholden to Ricardo, de Mandeville, or the vulgarized "invisible hand" as any "freshwater" neoclassical. The problem Keynesian science shows is that the world and the bodies and minds with which we must live inevitably impinge upon this idealized behavioral infrastructure. To Keynesians, Keynesianism is thus the enlightened recognition of the worldly fetters on and of human nature.

Keynes's argument for his theory (like Krugman's) was often couched in a similar disdain for orthodoxy's willful blindness to the "facts of experience." But he was much quicker to defend it as an enlightened politics, because he believed Keynesianism explained both the causes and the political implications of involuntary unemployment—and thus of poverty. *The General Theory* explained the forces that produce involuntary unemployment, the means through which it could be addressed, and—most important—the political-economic reasons it *must* be addressed. Although rarely framed as such by today's Keynesians, this more than any particular illuminated Truth helps explain the ongoing appeal of Keynesian thinking across decades of increasingly frequent crisis. In sharp contrast to both the smooth progress mythologized by classical and neoclassical theories and the dire diagnoses of some varieties of radical analysis, Keynesianism aims to provide a nonrevolutionary pharmaceutical science, of and for crisis.[1]

Indeed, one might define Keynesian reason as the scientific form of a political anxiety endemic to modernity.[2] It is always a product of, and is sustained by, those terrible moments when liberalism's and capitalism's shared *salto mortale*—the impossible commitment to the idealist separation of what Poulantzas called the economic and political "regions" of the lifeworld—is exposed as an act of raw political

---

1   On these grounds, Thomas Piketty's *Le Capital au XXIᵉ Siècle* (Paris: Seuil, 2013) is the most faithful and most significant contribution to Keynesianism since Keynes; see Chapter 14.

2   Raúl Prebisch, *Introducción a Keynes*, México: Fondo de Cultura Económica, 1947, 9–10.

will.[3] This is not necessarily to say that Keynesianism is the name we give the program to resecure the "regional" separation, although much of post-World War II "Keynesianism" might justifiably be so understood. At one level it was largely a technocratic attempt to demonstrate that problems commonly "mistaken" as political are in fact problems of economic management. And yet, Keynesianism is also always a more or less explicit acknowledgement that the politics-economy separation is ultimately untenable, a necessary but tempo-rary-at-best artifact of politics alone.

Keynesianism is therefore the political economy of those who know that modernity is defined by both a commitment to the separation between political and economic life and a recognition of that separation's irreparable fragility. Modernity produces, by definition, the very forces that make the separation unworkable, thus threatening the security of the world itself. Which is to say that Keynes, like Hegel, worked out his political economy for a post-Robespierre, postrevolutionary world that is basically Hobbesian: as he wrote just after *The General Theory* appeared, the "average man" "wants peace, and he cares about nothing else."[4] Because humanity "loves peace more than it hates Fascism," Keynesianism is civilization's only hope.[5] Like Hobbes's political theory, it is the political economic "correlative of the inherent instability of a community founded on power."[6] We should be Keynesian because we are civilized, yes, but largely because if left to "self-regulate," "individualistic capitalism" is at root *un*civilized,

---

3  Nicos Poulantzas, *Political Power and Social Classes*, London: New Left Books, 1973, 57–58.

4  Keynes, *CW*, XXVIII, 52.

5  Keynes, Letter to the editor, *New Statesman & Nation*, August 29, 1936, in *CW*, XVIII, 55.

6  Hannah Arendt, *Origins of Totalitarianism*, New York: Harcourt, Brace, 1951, 143. Arendt says that Hobbes "depicts the features of man according to the needs of the Leviathan. For argument's and conviction's sake, he presents his political outline as though he started from a realistic insight into man, a being that 'desires power after power,' and as though he proceeded from this insight to a plan for a body politic best fitted for this power-thirsty animal. The actual process, i.e., the only process in which his concept of man makes sense and goes beyond the obvious banality of an assumed human wickedness, is precisely the opposite"; *Origins of Totalitarianism*, 140–41.

even *anti*-civilization, leading to radically uncertain, contradictory, and arbitrary outcomes.

That said, Keynes's Hobbesianism has a distinctive and crucial Hegelian dimension. As noted in Chapter 2, the modern "economic society in which we actually live" is not one carved out of a prior "state of nature" and to which we risk crisis-induced "return." Instead, "modern communities" produce the very *bellum omnia contra omnes*, the rabble potential, they must overcome.[7] The "Warre of all against all" is not a precapitalist past but a product of the core dynamics of modernity.[8] Civilization is under threat not despite but rather *because* of liberal capitalism. Individuals are not driven by utility maximization and Mandevillean "Fraud, Luxury and Pride," but by fundamental uncertainty in the face of the future. To Keynes, classical economics' conception of human motivation was a relic of its high liberal origins: "nothing short of the exuberance of the greatest age of the inducement to investment could have made it possible to lose sight of the theoretical possibility of its insufficiency."[9]

This is the reason Keynes (unlike most self-identified Keynesians) emphasizes the absolutely essential function in his theory of the "fundamental psychological law"—that in a "modern community" the marginal propensity to consume is always less than unity, which is to say that the community will not consume all of a given increase in income. This "law" is incompatible with orthodox macroeconomics, committed as it is to the mythology of "rational

---

7   Keynes, *CW,* VII, 317, 3. Some claim this is also Hobbes's argument; C. B. MacPherson, *The Political Theory of Possessive Individualism, Hobbes to Locke,* Oxford: Oxford University Press, 1962, 99–100; C. B. MacPherson, "Introduction," in Thomas Hobbes, *Leviathan,* Penguin: London, 1968, 9–63; Neil Davidson, *How Revolutionary Were the Bourgeois Revolutions?* Chicago: Haymarket Books, 2012, 19–23.

8   Thomas Hobbes, *De Cive, or, On the Citizen,* Cambridge: Cambridge University Press, 1998 [1642], 12.

9   Keynes, *CW,* VII, 353. Indeed, little elicited Keynes's disdain more quickly than "Benthamite" claims regarding maximization as a universal motor of individual action; Ibid., 81; "Some Economic Consequences of a Declining Population," *Eugenics Review,* April 1937, in *CW,* XIV, 124. He would have enjoyed Marx's quip that "Mr. Bentham was a genius in the way of bourgeois stupidity"; Karl Marx, *Capital,* vol. I, New York: Vintage, 1976, 759.

expectations" and the perfect knowledge and foresight that under-
gird dynamic stochastic general equilibrium modeling.[10] For
Keynes, economic action is not usefully considered "rational" or
"irrational," at least in the sense economists give the terms.
Certainly, the law assumes people are "self-interested," but this
produces more complex and contingent behavior than constrained
optimization. A radically uncertain future is axiomatic, always and
everywhere. No coping mechanisms we devise to deal with this
aspect of the human condition can undo it. Once we recognize that
"individual judgment is worthless" in the face of a "future about
which we know so little," questions of self-interested optimization
lose purchase, and rational expectations' omniscience appears
absurd.[11]

## The Fetish of Liquidity

This is why liquidity—the ability to readily buy or sell an asset at a
relatively small transactions cost—is so crucial to Keynes's conceptual structure. He focuses on investment, which he considers the
engine room of capitalism, arguing that an obsession with "the anticipation of impending changes" is an "inevitable result" of capitalist
"investment markets organised with a view to so-called 'liquidity'"—
in other words, organized with a view to holding one's wealth in
money or near-money form. In the realm of investment, changing
preferences for liquidity are the most important effect of ineradicable, individualized, self-interested uncertainty in the economic
"region" of modern social life:

> Of the maxims of orthodox finance none, surely, is more *anti-
> social* than the fetish of liquidity, the doctrine that it is a positive
> virtue on the part of investment institutions to concentrate their

10   Keynes, *CW,* VII, 96–97; John Maynard Keynes, "The General Theory of
Employment," *Quarterly Journal of Economics* 51: 2, 1937, 220.
    11   Ibid., 214, 221.

resources upon the holding of "liquid" securities. It forgets that *there is no such thing as liquidity of investment for the community as a whole.* The social object of skilled investment should be to defeat the dark forces of time and ignorance which envelop our future.[12]

The political core of Keynesianism, and its importance in Keynes's time and our own, lies here, in the centrality of this mode of analysis to modern politics. It describes liberal capitalism as simultaneously a virtuous circle of wealth production and as a vicious circle of political and social disintegration. The "fetish of liquidity"—the product of a deadly combination of fear and opportunism in a capitalist monetary economy—leads inexorably to hair-trigger obsession with "anticipating impending changes."[13] Unsurprisingly, this generates those changes and in particularly volatile form. Money and money-like assets make a more or less liquid position not only easy to realize but imperative for any single potential investor, leading to a communitywide prisoners' dilemma. Each individual, in search of a means through which to make the best of the uncertainty for himself or herself, makes the non-cooperative choice, for "there is no such thing as liquidity of investment for the community as a whole." Driven by what Keynes called the "precautionary" and "speculative" motives to liquidity, money holders act directly against the "social interest," feeding off and intensifying the very "dark forces of time and ignorance which envelop our future," forces we should instead be focused on defeating:[14]

The actual, private object of most skilled investment to-day is "to beat the gun," as the Americans so well express it, to outwit the crowd, and to pass the bad, or depreciating, half-crown to the other fellow . . . There is no clear evidence from experience that the investment policy which is socially advantageous coincides with that which is most profitable. It needs *more* intelligence to

---

12   Keynes, *CW,* VII, 155 (emphasis added).
13   Ibid.
14   Ibid.

defeat the forces of time and our ignorance of the future than to beat the gun.[15]

Keynes—quite reasonably, it seems to me—thinks the classical position on liquidity preference is ridiculous. The idea that Say's Law means that not spending is as good for effective demand as consumption is "absurd, though almost universal." This "fallacy" persists despite the obvious fact that "since the expectation of consumption is the only *raison d'être* of employment, there should be nothing paradoxical in the conclusion that a diminishing propensity to consume has *cet. par.* a depressing effect on employment."[16] The effect of diminishing employment levels on liquidity preference is straightforward and will only exacerbate the downswing: as rising unemployment and declining aggregate demand reinforce each other, liquidity preference will rise as uncertainty increases and confidence falls. The result—the necessary *increase* in interest rates, to overcome the reluctance to lend money—just makes matters worse.

Keynes attributes the classical "fallacy" to the misconception discussed earlier (Chapter 10), that what a wealth owner wants to obtain with his or her money is a "capital-asset *as such*." This, Keynes says, is bunk. What he or she really seeks is the capital asset's expected yield. People invest not to enjoy the ownership of productive equipment or enterprise, but for monetary return—profit—and if anticipated returns from investment seem too low or unpromising, most will simply do something else with their money. Moreover, there is no "practical" escape from these "psychological" conditions in the hope that people who desire to accumulate wealth will still choose to invest no matter how low the expected return, as long as it is the highest available. This is not so. If the rate of interest exceeds the marginal efficiency of capital but is not high enough to overcome the "fetish of liquidity," wealth holders will continue to hold; if it exceeds that level, they will choose debt purchase, not productive investment.

---

15   Ibid., 155–57. See also Pascal Combemale, *Introduction à Keynes*, Paris: La Découverte, 1999, 81.

16   Keynes, *CW,* VII, 211.

Now, the mere desire of wealth owners to be wealthier clearly has no necessarily positive effect on the marginal efficiency of capital at all. Nor, however, does an asset's productivity. Productivity will factor into investment decisions but will induce investment only in a situation in which increasing productivity is expected to meet adequate effective demand. Investment ultimately depends not on productivity, but on two explicitly expectational variables: only a level of effective demand at a future date that improves the marginal efficiency of capital elicits investment. "Productivity" is not what attracts investment: "It is much preferable to speak of capital as having a yield over the course of its life in excess of its original cost, than as being *productive*."[17] Capital's "yield over time" has an entirely contingent relationship to both its productivity and the labor through which it was produced.[18] It is determined, rather, by its *scarcity*, that is, the extent to which there is some demand for its

---

17    Ibid., 213.

18    Ibid., 214. The status of labor in Keynes's account is sometimes confused, not least because of an often misunderstood claim: "I sympathise, therefore, with the pre-classical doctrine that everything is *produced* by *labour* . . . It is preferable to regard labour . . . as the sole factor of production, operating in a given environment of technique, natural resources, capital equipment and effective demand"; *CW*, VII, 213–14. Some Marxists have interpreted this as proof of Keynes's affinity for Marx's supposed "labor theory of value." This theory, at least as it is commonly understood, posits labor as the producer of all value in the world. This is a significant misunderstanding of Keynes. It also reflects a misunderstanding of Marx; see Diane Elson, "The Value Theory of Labour," in Diane Elson (ed.), *Value: The Representation of Labour in Capitalism*, Atlantic Highlands: Humanities Press, 1979, 115–80; Moishe Postone, *Time, Labour and Social Domination: A Re-Interpretation of Marx's Critical Theory*, Cambridge: Cambridge University Press, 1993; Geoff Mann, "Value After Lehman," *Historical Materialism* 18: 4, 2010, 172–88.

Keynes's point is not that an asset's value is determined by its "labour-content"; nor did he claim that all value is produced by labor. Keynes maintained that it is useful, in the short run, to take every *thing* as produced by labor alone, to take the volume of employment as the one variable in the context of a given (fixed) factor environment. This is not a labor theory of value, but a pragmatist's theory of a "monetary production economy." Keynes may link these arguments explicitly to "preclassical" thinking, but his thinking on value was thoroughly classical (a category that on these grounds cannot include Marx), no different than that of orthodox post-Jevonians like Marshall or Pigou, for whom the theory of value is nothing more than the theory of relative price determination. For Keynes, the relation of labor to value is indeterminate, if it has any meaning at all; value is the form yield takes; see Maurice Dobb, *Theories of Value and Distribution Since Adam Smith: Ideology and Economic Theory*, Cambridge: Cambridge University Press, 1975, 214–15.

services in excess of its owner's.[19] Indeed, capital must be scarce because otherwise its yield would be too low to compete with the rate of interest on money. If capital like machinery, for example, were not scarce, it would yield much less, and therefore attract much less demand as an investment. It can always be *materially* productive, regardless of its scarcity.[20]

This argument is absolutely crucial to an understanding of *The General Theory*: scarcity is neither natural, nor an objective supply-side constraint (as per the standard summary of economics as the study of the distribution of scarce goods among competing uses). Scarcity is a necessary social condition of capitalist political economy. Without scarcity, modern "individualistic capitalism" does not work. Consequently, according to Keynes, scarcity is socially produced, so as to generate prospective and real yield.

On one level, this seems obvious: scarcity always has both absolute and relative dimensions, and relative scarcity, supply relative to demand, is clearly a product of social relations. That is what marketing is all about. But Keynes's theory of capital elides this distinction, because what matters for him is not the social production of the "experience" or "perception" of scarcity, but of material scarcity per se—necessity—whether relative or absolute. To ensure that investment in many classes of assets is profitable, capitalism must create and reproduce their scarcity.

We do not generate the required scarcity only by straightforward means, like quotas or seasonal restrictions to prevent overproduction, although in certain markets these are important tools. Instead, scarcity is more importantly produced in more subtle ways, as a necessary if unintentional consequence of the capitalist search for

---

19   Suzanne de Brunhoff, *The State, Capital, and Economic Policy*, London: Pluto, 1978, 79. The quantity of value is also, but not only, a function of scarcity; in addition, the direction and level of spending matter.

20   If Keynes had been at all aware of the debate between Rosa Luxemburg and Mikhail Tugan-Baranovsky on effective demand (it seems he was not), he would have come down squarely on Luxemburg's side; Michał Kalecki, "The Problem of Effective Demand with Tugan-Baranovsky and Rosa Luxemburg," in *Selected Essays on the Dynamics of the Capitalist Economy*, Cambridge: Cambridge University Press, 1971, 146–55.

yield. We develop, say, an "optimum amount of roundaboutness" in production, to supply the markets in time and space that we expect consumption demand will support.[21] Or, as the financial dynamics that helped trigger the collapse of 2007–8 suggest, we multiply asset classes to generate new realms of scarcity. Production can only be organized so as to make a profit in light of effective demand, and such conditions may not require it to be so organized, nor capital so abundant, as to produce full employment at any one instant or across time. In addition, we cannot avoid this problem by assuming (or hoping) that when current demand is not forthcoming, full employment will be organized so as to meet future demand. There will always be suboptimal equilibria and disequilibria in real markets.

Of all the factors of modern capitalist production that must be kept scarce, the most important, in Keynes's view, is capital itself. But this is not to say that Keynes saw this as an inevitable condition in capitalism. Indeed, it is misleading to say that the "assumption that capital is scarce, or inadequate, informs Keynes's entire argument."[22] Keynes does not "assume" that capital is scarce—in economic terms, this would be the equivalent of assuming quasi-full capacity, a "full employment"-like assumption that risks leading to conclusions as naïve as those of the classical economists. On the contrary, anticipating the recent empirical work of Thomas Piketty, Keynes argues that in the variety of capitalism that had dominated since the mid-nineteenth century, and had run up against its own limits in the Great Depression, capital had a tendency to do exactly the opposite—to become terribly abundant.[23] Such abundance is ultimately intolerable. Consequently, capital is *made* scarce because it must be scarce. Otherwise, profit, and thus investment, seem impossible, killing effective demand. Because of the "fetish of liquidity," capital

---

21   Keynes, *CW*, VII, 217.

22   Victoria Chick, *On Money, Method and Keynes: Selected Essays*, London: Macmillan, 1992, 22.

23   Piketty, *Capital*, 223–314.

has to be kept scarce enough in the long-period to have marginal efficiency which is at least equal to the rate of interest for a period equal to the life of the capital, as determined by psychological and institutional conditions.[24]

Indeed, if we assume (as Keynes did) that some proportion of the population are savers and that negative interest rates are impossible (both of which have turned out not to be true), then if capital were to become so abundant that its marginal efficiency were zero (meaning additional investment would produce negative yields), any effort on the part of employers to maintain the existing level of employment (which requires both employment in investment goods production and positive investment equal to savings) would produce negative returns. The only way out of the situation is that "the stock of capital and the level of employment will have to shrink until the community becomes so impoverished . . . and the standard of life sufficiently miserable to bring savings to zero."[25]

This situation will arise even sooner than we would like to hope, says Keynes, because it is naïve to assume that zero marks the de facto lower bound on interest rates, that the only fixed floor is that interest rates cannot be negative. In modern capitalism, "institutional and psychological factors" generally determine a rate of long-term interest considerably above zero. Keynes suggests that if we take this "reality" into account—and it is true that even in our era of negative rates, there is still no instance of a negative long-term rate of interest—things look even more difficult. For if so, the marginal efficiency of capital will be less than the interest rate long before it reaches zero, to say nothing of the effects on liquidity preference in such a context,

---

24    Keynes, *CW,* VII, 217.

25    Ibid., 217–18. Recall that saving is for Keynes an *ex post* function of investment: "Increased investment will always be accompanied by increased saving, but it can never be preceded by it. Dishoarding and credit expansion provides not an *alternative* to increased saving, but a necessary preparation for it. It is the parent, not the twin, of increased saving." If so, a massive fall in investment will drastically reduce saving, even to zero. See John Maynard Keynes, "The Process of Capital Formation," *Economic Journal* (September 1939), in *CW,* XIV, 281.

and therefore the chances of creating and maintaining a condition of full employment are even further diminished.

This means that even when the technical conditions of production are capable of sustaining a level of employment and welfare far above what they presently provide, in conditions of *laissez-faire*, the rate of interest is "the villain of the piece" because it is unlikely to decline to a level at which existing capital might realize its investment potential—and thus its capacity to provide employment.[26]

## The Scarcity Theory of Capital

*The General Theory* labels these arguments the "scarcity theory": an abundance of capital is a *problem* for capitalism, one that must be constantly overcome.[27] It explains the paradox through which an accumulation of wealth materially adequate to the needs of the community will in fact "interfere" with a "reasonable level of employment" and associated standards of life. Again, Keynes frames the problem in Hegelian terms: "[w]e reach a condition where there is no shortage of houses, but where nevertheless no one can afford to live in the houses that there are"—in other words, an "excess of riches" cannot prevent an "excess of poverty."[28]

Because the rate of interest has a positive lower bound in *laissez-faire* conditions, capital must be scarce enough in the long run to render the marginal efficiency of capital sufficiently high to compete with it. And because there is no force in capitalist markets to guarantee this outcome, we consequently face the "awkward possibility" that, as capital accumulates (resulting in a declining marginal efficiency), crisis-induced poverty is a more likely outcome for "modern communities" than the generalized prosperity we might associate with "abundance." This is because under the conditions associated

26   John Maynard Keynes, "Saving and Usury," *Economic Journal* 42: 165, (March 1932), in *CW,* XXIX, 16.

27   Keynes, *CW,* VII, 215.

28   Ibid., 322.

with *laissez-faire*, a marginal efficiency of capital approaching or equal to zero necessarily requires "that proportion of unemployment which ensures zero saving."[29]

Keynes believes this is the fate that befell the United States and Britain with the Great Depression.[30] In both cases, national economic development led to a situation in which capital was so abundant its marginal efficiency fell faster than the interest rate.[31] The diminished investment this engendered required a massive social adjustment: the production of "impoverishment" capable of reducing aggregate savings to zero. The negative effect on progress of this "law of motion" is the reason why, given identical technical conditions, a relatively capital-poor community may be better off than a capital-rich community, because the poorer one will maintain returns on investment that enlist a higher level of employment for longer— although upon catch-up, it too will suffer the "fate of Midas."

On the surface, the "scarcity theory" of capital is by no means radical. It is one variation on a "secular stagnation" theory with a long history, and it was, unsurprisingly, hotly debated in Keynes's time. These discussions considered a range of dynamics that might plausibly have put the world on the path to Great Depression, like the close of the colonial frontier, declining population growth, and technical change. Keynes's thoughts on stagnation are wide-ranging and sometimes inconsistent, but there are two essential points in his analysis that distinguish it. First, whatever these contingent drivers identified by other diagnoses, Keynes was adamant that the Great Depression did not have to happen. Even if to some it appeared inevitable in retrospect, there was no "necessity" to it, in the sense that the political and economic knowledge and institutions existed to avoid it and could quickly and easily have been put to work. Second, the causes of stagnation are not, ultimately, historically specific conjunctures like the end of the frontier, but

---

29  Ibid., 219.

30  Again, Piketty's work, embedded in a much more historically compelling empirical framework, nonetheless broadly confirms Keynes's assessment (see Chapter 14).

31  Keynes, *CW,* VII, 219–20.

lie, on the contrary, in the structural dynamics of modern capitalism itself.

Together, these claims form the basis for Keynes's most urgent
proposition regarding stagnation, scarcity, and crisis: that the capital-
ism-begets-poverty trajectory that led to the Great Depression (let us
call it Trajectory 1) will continue to play out only if we continue to
leave the forces driving capital accumulation entirely to the market.
If the rate of investment and the propensity to consume are "deliberately controlled in the social interest," then the predicament is escap-
able (let us call this Trajectory 2). Trajectory 2 is what Keynes calls
"the only practicable means of avoiding the destruction of existing
economic forms in their entirety," the only way around "the problem
of unemployment"—a problem it "is certain that the world will not
much longer tolerate."[32]

In *The General Theory*, Keynes does not connect this analysis to
anyone other than his hero Malthus. But the problem of scarcity that
lies at the heart of the opposition between Trajectory 1 and Trajectory
2 haunts modern political thought.[33] C. B. MacPherson finds its
roots in Hobbes, and Nicholas Xenos traces its evolution in modern
liberalism from Hume and Smith through to Keynes and Rawls.[34]
Indeed, one might argue that the technocracy Keynes proposes is
akin to Hobbes's more radically sovereign power—a connection
Keynes himself later acknowledged.[35]

In other words, the fear of Trajectory 1 motivates the tradition of
modern anxiety in the capitalist "West" or global North, a tradition
whose theoretical elaboration is developed fully and explicitly in
Hegel's analysis of civil society. It is traceable, if in less systematic
form and sometimes just in traces, across a range of otherwise diverse
thinkers, from Hobbes, Kant, and Malthus to John Stuart Mill,

---

32   Ibid., 381.

33   Keynes, *CW,* X, 99–100.

34   C. B. MacPherson, *Democratic Theory: Essays in Retrieval*, Oxford: Clarendon,
1973, 17–18; Nicholas Xenos, "Liberalism and the Postulate of Scarcity," *Political Theory*
15: 2, 1987, 225–43.

35   Sterling Lamprecht, "Review of *Hobbes and His Critics*, by John Bowle," *Political
Science Quarterly* 67: 4, 1952, 612.

Émile Durkheim, and Max Weber. But it culminates in a more or less Hegelian analysis of modern bourgeois civil society whose crucial institutional forms—capitalist markets and private property—propound an atomistic individualization in fundamental contradiction with the complex interdependence of developed political economies and a robust conception of sociality.

By this account, civil society is the realm of "difference" in which self-interest is the only interest we share. The relentless accumulation of riches in civil society, through the circular flow of a Smithian "system of needs," produces remarkable, unprecedented, and increasingly concentrated wealth—but at the same time, because it cannot find a productive place for all, cannot produce an adequate consumer base for its output. Expanding "impoverished masses" thus fall further and further out of the political community that underwrites civil society—bourgeois liberal citizenship and its "community of the free."

Keynes asks the same question Hegel and others asked as capitalism consolidated itself in post-1789 Europe: can civil society address this tendency to produce poverty on its own terms? Does it have the conceptual and political resources to heal the fatal flaw in itself? The answer is No. It cannot and does not. In Hegel's explanation, this failure is due to a mismatch between the political-economic relations of modernity and the consciousness its produces. To support the poor with "welfare," not requiring them to work, violates civil society's fundamental principle—"the feeling of self-sufficiency and honour among its individual members."[36] The precipitate of this process is precisely the mass threat to civilization that Hegel calls the "rabble"—the soil of unreason, bitterness, and violence, the "anti-people."

Civil society's inability to realize its ideal means it cannot provide a place of honor for all in the "moral" and economic system upon which it is built. Those left behind carry civil society's ethic and expectations, but its persistent failure to allow them to live according

---

36  G. W. F. Hegel, *Elements of the Philosophy of Right*, trans. H. B. Nisbet, Cambridge: Cambridge University Press, 1991, §245. (Hereinafter cited as *PhR*.)

to these standards breeds the "rabble mentality."[37] This is Keynes's "paradox of poverty in the midst of plenty," civil society's indecent "scandal," its inescapable shadow.[38]

Much of modern political and economic theory is built upon the fear of a rabble that constantly threatens bourgeois society.[39] There are two principal questions addressed by the range of thought that fear elicits. First, is this defining threat to modern civilization a regrettable but unavoidable fact of life—"true and inevitable," as Keynes says—or something that history can overcome? The classical political economy of Ricardo and Malthus take the former position, Hegel the latter. Second, does the threat of the rabble arise exogenously, from outside civil society (as it does, for example, for Kant), or is it in fact a product of modernity itself (as it is for Hegel)? Keynes, as we know, answers with Hegel on both counts: poverty and the rabble are neither inevitable nor eternal, nor are they exogenous threats to "modern communities," but products of those communities' internal dynamics.[40]

Deprivation and want are "boundless" because the poverty with which we are concerned is both absolute *and* relative and "arises necessarily out of" civil society. The potential for breakdown immanent to civil society is partly a function of material need, of a lack of the means for basic survival, but it is also inherent in social relations that dishonor the poor.

> Poverty itself does not reduce people to a rabble; a rabble is created only by the disposition associated with poverty, by inward rebellion against the rich, against society, the government, etc . . . This

37    Solange Mercier-Josa, *Entre Hegel et Marx: Points Cruciaux de la Philosophie Hégélienne de Droit*, Paris: L'Harmattan, 1999, 89–90; G. W. F. Hegel, *PhR*, §245, note to §244, 453.

38    Giovanni Mazzetti, "Capitalismo e «Welfare»: Involuzione a Sinistra," *Critica Marxista* 3: 4, 2006, 97.

39    MacPherson, *Possessive Individualism*; Stathis Kouvelakis, *Philosophy and Revolution: From Marx to Kant*, trans. G. M. Goshgarian, New York: Verso, 2003; Davidson, *How Revolutionary Were the Bourgeois Revolutions?*

40    For example, Immanuel Kant, *Political Writings*, Cambridge: Cambridge University Press, 1992, 80–82, 98, 108–9; Mercier-Josa, *Entre Hegel et Marx*, 91; Kouvelakis, *Philosophy and Revolution*, 21.

in turn gives rise to the evil that the rabble do not have sufficient honour to gain their livelihood through their own work, yet claim that they have a right to receive their livelihood.[41]

Keynes, like Hegel before him, understands the escape from the inevitability of absolute scarcity as among the greatest achievements of modernity.

Yet scarcity persists, as Hobbes, Smith, and others suggest, because moderns' "unlimited desire" makes relative poverty inevitable and ineradicable.[42] Indeed, poverty is the defining problem of "modern societies especially."[43] A dogmatic "free-market" liberal commitment to civil society's "autonomy" means that when capitalism fails to deliver the goods, as it often clearly does, "the social interest" is abandoned. The poor are left to descend to an indignant rabble, and civilized society pays the price. Recall Keynes's words from the 1924 *Tract on Monetary Reform*:

> No man of spirit will consent to remain poor if he believes his betters to have gained their goods by lucky gambling. To convert the business man into the profiteer is to strike a blow at capitalism, because it destroys the psychological equilibrium which permits the perpetuance of unequal rewards . . .[44]

## The "Thin Crust" of Civilization

The logical infrastructure of this argument—the forces, categories, and relationships it posits—defines the realm of anything properly called Keynesian. Keynes's lifework, from his critique of Versailles to his plans for a post-World War II global clearing bank and international trade organization, was an attempt to understand the mechanisms that tend to turn liberal capitalism into a casino and thus to

---

41  Hegel, *PhR*, §244R.
42  Xenos, "Liberalism and the Postulate of Scarcity," 225–26.
43  Hegel, *PhR*, §244R.
44  Keynes, *CW*, IV, 29.

devise a means to protect the "psychological equilibrium" on which social order depends. Whether it deserves the "revolutionary" honorific he gave it or not, the diagnosis of the slump he developed (insufficient effective demand) is far more sophisticated—and Hegelian—than is commonly recognized. Like Hegel, Keynes is not trying to show that we do not spend enough to keep the engine running, but to understand why this condition must arise "endogenously" in capitalism, its *political* significance, and what to do about it.

Keynes's fear is definitively modern—the "insecure footing" upon which bourgeois society places civilization. Keynes did not see himself as riding to the rescue of liberalism or capitalism for their own sakes any more than Hegel did. He saw himself as riding to the rescue of civilization, and the utopian quality of his rescue plan in many ways challenges the historical hierarchies of bourgeois civil society. But he believed that the only answer was a radically renovated liberalism, because what we would now call liberal capitalism was the form civilization took—to undo it would by definition be to undo civilization.

And for Keynes, the Russian Revolution, German and Italian fascism, and widespread unrest during the 1920s and 1930s suggested that civilization might very well be undone by the very operation of bourgeois civil society. This is the fear that motivates *The General Theory*. But the problem it poses is not one of culpability. Keynes "does not blame the bourgeoisie for being bourgeois" any more than Hegel does.[45] Rather, he sees the bourgeois as a perfectly sensible product of a mode of social organization that prioritizes private accumulation over public good, one based on the erroneous assumption that the former necessarily leads to the latter. This leads to the "very usual confusion" in capitalist civil society between what is good for the individual and what is good for the collective. As Keynes put it in a 1942 radio address, "each individual is impelled by his paper losses or profits to do precisely the opposite of what is desirable in the general interest."[46]

---

45   Laurence Dickey and H. B. Nisbet, "General Introduction," in G. W. F. Hegel, *Political Writings*, Cambridge: Cambridge University Press, 1999, xxix.

46   Keynes, The Listener (BBC), April 2, 1942; Keynes, *CW*, XXVII, 266, 20, 480; see also Keynes, *CW*, VII, 20, 85, 131, 293.

As Hegel said, this "confused situation can be restored to harmony only through the forcible intervention of the state."[47] The state is the sole institution that has the capacity to see beyond this confusion. This is not to say, however, that its role is to somehow inoculate civil society, to make it possible to just ignore the poverty endemic to modern communities. On the contrary, while the state itself is the only solution, it too is threatened by poverty and the poor.[48] The way to avoid the perils of Trajectory 1 is to use the state to manage civil society's contradictions through the expertise of a Hegelian "universal class," enlightened technicians with the knowledge and power to identify "the social interest," to see beyond particularity and construct a state in which the universal and the particular no longer conflict. They are the "very few" who maintain civilization by way of "rules and conventions skillfully put across and guilefully preserved."

Consequently, the question every Keynesian is always trying to answer is: What causes "poverty in the midst of plenty"? Why, "despite an *excess of wealth*," is civil society "*not wealthy enough*"? What is to be done about those the system produces and then disavows—the rabble, the involuntarily unemployed? Modernity has generated the most productive societies the world has ever known, historically unprecedented abundance. How is it possible we remain *not wealthy enough*? As Joan Robinson explained it in 1962:

The foundation of a comfortable standard of life is a decent house. A family requires, above everything, a reliable health service and the best possible education; but growing wealth always leaves us with a greater deficiency in just those things. It is not an accident that it should be so . . . [W]hen, as a nation, "we have never had it so good" we find that we "cannot afford" just what we most need.[49]

---

47   Hegel, *PhR*, §185.

48   Ibid., §265: "If their welfare is deficient, if their subjective ends are not satisfied, and if they do not find that the state as such is the means to this satisfaction, the state itself stands on an insecure footing."

49   Joan Robinson, "Latter Day Capitalism," *New Left Review* I: 16, 1962, 46.

From a narrowly "economic" perspective, New Keynesians like Krugman identify the state's work in the "social interest" with the maintenance of a specific level of consumption. They understand any structural inadequacy through the principle of effective demand and Keynes's critique of Say's Law. Supply does not automatically solicit sufficient demand, prices do not adjust instantaneously, and thus some are abandoned on the margins of the economy. Post-Keynesians agree but they insist that the problem is not that the state or irrational agents lead to "rigidities" and "imperfections" that hinder markets' potential to efficiently allocate resources via the price mechanism. Instead, they argue, no actually-existing price mechanism could ever accomplish the goals assigned to it—not because of information asymmetries or nominal rigidities, but because we live with inescapable uncertainty and make production and especially investment decisions on that irreducibly unstable basis. Effective demand is thus highly indeterminate: it is what producers expect demand to be at a certain future period, and thus the demand for which they "really" produce. There is no reason to expect this will lead them to use all their capacity or recruit all available labor and resources, and they almost never do. As a result, there will always be some unused productive capacity in the economy, including labor power, which is by definition "involuntarily" unemployed.

Post-World War II Keynesianism in general, therefore, takes Keynes to be suggesting that the role of an invigorated "interventionist" state is to stimulate aggregate demand through expansionary monetary and fiscal policy. Keynes's own diagnosis, however, is founded on a critique (however sympathetic) of such mechanistic underconsumptionist thinking. It focuses instead on underallocated and misallocated *investment*, and of the role of the state in a radical remedy of this condition.[50] "Free" markets are suboptimal not

---

50   Keynes, *CW*, VII, 324–26. For Robinson, this was to a significant extent a "public goods" question: "Capitalist industry is dazzlingly efficient at producing goods to be sold in the shops, and, directly or indirectly, profits are derived from selling. The services to meet basic human needs do not lend themselves to mass production: they are not an easy field for making profits, especially as, with our egalitarian democratic notions, they have to be

because they put insufficient purchasing power in the hands of consumers, but because civil society's internal dynamics do not lead capitalist entrepreneurs to produce "what we most need," or a productive, honorable place for all. This is not a New Keynesian "market failure"; this is how the system "actually works."

Keynes proposes a very Hegelian solution to this puzzle. At the heart of modern capitalist civil society, he says, there lies the absolute necessity for that poverty no "man of spirit" will accept for long. Modern communities plant the seeds of their own collapse. Yet Trajectory 1, revolution *with* revolution, is not inevitable. It is not a product of nature or God or the laws of economic development. It is a social and historical product, a "terrible muddle" we create ourselves, and one we can undo. Trajectory 2, revolution *without* revolution, is realizable *if* reason prevails, if the principal determinants of economic activity are "deliberately controlled in the social interest."[51] If a community can establish a long-term rate of interest consistent with full employment, and if the state organizes investment—plans it, not undertakes or mandates it—then

> a properly run community equipped with modern technical resources, of which the population is not increasing rapidly, ought to be able to bring down the marginal efficiency of capital in equilibrium approximately to zero within a single generation . . . [T]his may be the most sensible way of gradually getting rid of many of the objectionable features of capitalism. For a little reflection will show what enormous social changes would result from a gradual disappearance of a rate of return on accumulated wealth.[52]

---

offered irrespective of means to pay. Consequently they must be largely provided through taxation. To supply goods is a source of profit but to supply services is a 'burden upon industry'"; "Latter Day Capitalism," 46.

51  Keynes, *CW,* VII, 219. Keynes insists on a distinction between state-coordinated investment (which he advocates) and state-controlled (which he does not); see *CW,* XXI, 87, 345.

52  Keynes, *CW,* VII, 376.

This is the celebrated "euthanasia of the rentier," an echo in *The General Theory* of Hegel's glee at the demise of feudal aristocracy.[53]

If this can be achieved—and all Keynesians hold that only inherited ways of thinking prevent it—then we can have a "best of all possible worlds" that preserves the best features of other possible worlds once thought incompatible. It is not guaranteed, of course—if it were, the anxiety at the heart of Keynesianism would disappear. But pragmatic reason is the only thing that can take us there.

However, despite his emphasis on expert-based technocratic managerialism, Keynes does not thereby seek to render politics some "postpolitical" conflict-free zone. As discussed in chapter 2, Keynesian reason recognizes in bourgeois civil society—despite what Hegel called its "political nullity" and economic contradictions—the potential of a realm of free citizen interaction, the "bourgeois public sphere" that Arendt idealized and Rawls and Habermas spent much of their careers trying to recapture in thought experiments.[54] The trouble lies in the fact that in a "modern community" the political so easily gets contaminated by leakages from what Keynes called the "economic problem" and Arendt called the "social question": poverty. Trajectory 2 is the only answer: overcoming the contradictions of civil society by means of Keynes's "wise Government" by "statute and custom and even by invoking the sanctions of moral law," to fundamentally reconfigure the destructive self-interested ideology of modern capitalism, and to shift the realm of modern political liberty from the private to the public sphere.[55] Only this can deliver sufficient honor to the impoverished that they can be reliably depended upon to "consent to remain poor."

---

53  Terry Pinkard, *Hegel: A Biography*, Cambridge: Cambridge University Press, 2000, 244–46.

54  Hegel, "On the Scientific Ways of Treating Natural Law, on its Place in Practical Philosophy, and its Relation to the Positive Sciences of Right," in *Political Writings*, 150.

55  Keynes, *CW,* VII, 351.

# PART 4

# After Keynes

## CHAPTER 12

# Keynesian Political Economy and the Problem of Full Employment

It is well-known that the massive state investment and economic planning required by World War II gave Keynes both ample opportunity to promote his ideas and an attentive audience for them. But by early 1942, the bureaucracies of some of the Allied nations were feeling sufficiently optimistic to turn their attention to the world after the war. Keynes himself was working with the British Exchequer in an ill-defined advisory role—one biographer describes his assignment as being "just Keynes"—when he received some draft chapters of a report entitled *Social Insurance and Allied Services*.[1] The document, later known as the Beveridge Report and arguably the welfare state's founding document, described a postwar Britain in which state-coordinated full employment, social insurance, and a national health service would ensure the end of capitalism's indiscriminate volatility and instability. Keynes told Beveridge he read the chapters with "wild enthusiasm." How "wild" he really was we cannot be sure—he was as prone to overstated praise as he was quick on the attack—but in any event he seems to have had no interest in the institutional structure or politics of the welfare state that now bears his name. When the ideological battle lines were drawn following the

---

1  Donald Moggridge, *Keynes*, London: Macmillan, 1976, 121.

report's publication in December 1942, he was studiously quiet, neither for nor against.[2] What he was concerned about was its affordability.

His silence is probably at least partially attributable to the "socialist" bent of both Beveridge and his plan. But Keynes's initial enthusiasm is easily understandable in the wake of the troubled 1920s and 1930s and the populist authoritarianisms to which he believed they led. As Beveridge put it, quoting Charlotte Brontë in the frontispiece to his *Full Employment in a Free Society* of 1944, "misery generates hate," and the war was for Keynes only the latest addition to the overwhelming evidence that was true.[3] As such, any argument that the state could indeed "afford" to address the problem of misery was welcome. It was another contribution to the project Keynes had begun the previous decade with *The General Theory*.

For the Great Depression had made unemployment the political *and* economic problem of the age. It demanded a radical reconfiguration of social science and state policy, and for the first time, it had made joblessness a national question.[4] It was certainly of interest to economists before Keynes's time, but its place at the core of modern macroeconomics was cemented by *The General Theory*; indeed, macroeconomics is unthinkable without it. After the Depression, and after Keynes, unemployment became the single most important indicator of social welfare in liberal capitalist states and remained so until the late 1970s (at which point it obviously did not disappear; rather it was trumped, in the eyes of the state and elites, by inflation).

2 Robert Skidelsky, *John Maynard Keynes, 1883–1946: Economist, Philosophy, Statesman*, London: Pan Macmillan, 2003, 708–10.

3 William Beveridge, *Full Employment in a Free Society*, London: George Allen & Unwin, 1944. The quotation is from *Shirley* (1849), Brontë's novel of the Luddite movement. In full, it succinctly describes Hegel's rabble: "Misery generates hate: these sufferers hated the machines which they believed took their bread from them: they hated the buildings which contained those machines: they hated the manufacturers who own those buildings."

4 John Garraty, *Unemployment in History: Economic Thought and Public Policy*, New York: Harper & Row, 1978; Clair Brown, "Unemployment Theory and Policy, 1946–1980," *Industrial Relations* 22: 2, 1983, 164–85; Geoff Mann, "Unemployment," in Eric Arneson (ed.), *Encyclopedia of U.S. Labor and Working Class History*, vol. 3, New York: Routledge, 2007, 1399–1403.

Keynesian economics' long-standing, if uneven, influence is surely due in great measure to the fact that *The General Theory* represents the first systematic political economic framework oriented to the analysis of unemployment. After World War II, no one thinking or writing about unemployment in the industrialized capitalist part of the world could ignore his work, and there were (and are) a lot of people thinking or writing about unemployment.[5]

In that impending postwar moment in the Euro-American capitalist core, when the state-organized war production that had solved the problem of unemployment was no longer necessary, many (Keynes included) feared the Depression would return. That it did not—on the contrary, that the state helped coordinate the longest economic expansion and the highest employment rates in recorded history—was celebrated as the greatest triumph of political economy the world had ever known. The science of government appeared to have solved the problem of the age. And the benefits enjoyed by "modern communities" as a result extended far beyond higher productivity and consumption. At least as important was the mitigation of a rabble mentality, through the refoundation of what Hegel called the "principle of civil society": the "feeling of self-sufficiency and honour among its individual members." As Beveridge put it, "the greatest evil of unemployment is not physical but moral, not the want which it may bring but the hatred and fear which it breeds."[6]

---

5  This is not to ignore the fact that many outside the industrial-capitalist "West" also engaged with Keynes, Raúl Prebisch perhaps most prominently; see his *Introducción a Keynes* (México: Fondo de Cultura Económica, 1947, 8): "At its core, Lord Keynes's thesis is simple and categorical. The tendency to chronic unemployment is a product of the very wealth of major industrialized communities. *Laissez-faire*, the spontaneous interplay [*juego espontáneo*] of economic forces, is incapable of solving the problem, because there is a serious adjustment problem in the system" (my translation).

6  G. W. F. Hegel, *Elements of the Philosophy of Right*, trans. H. B. Nisbet, Cambridge: Cambridge University Press, 1991, §245; Beveridge, *Full Employment*, 15. A quarter century later, Joan Robinson wrote of the rabble, rich and poor: "The worst part of heavy unemployment was not the waste of potential wealth (and . . . its removal has not been achieved mainly by avoiding waste) but the rotting of individual lives, the damaged self-respect, the desperate egoism and cringing fear on one side and the smug self-deception on the other"; Robinson, "Latter Day Capitalism," *New Left Review* I: 16, 1962, 37.

Yet, if we can describe broad agreement on the historical motivations for Keynesianism, and consequently on Keynesian economists'
quasi obsession with unemployment, there are nonetheless vast
differences in their approaches to unemployment, from work partially
informed by Marx (the theory of the "reserve army of labor" in
particular), to business-as-usual mainstream estimations of the
"natural rate of unemployment."[7]

At first glance, the fact that this range, from neoclassical synthesis
to class analysis, can all fit under the "Keynesian" umbrella might
seem almost absurd. In this chapter and the next, I want to consider
this potential absurdity. How dispersed are the modern varieties of
Keynesianism on the key question of unemployment, and what, if
any, terrain do they share? Taking two sharply contrasting contributions—the work of Michał Kalecki on the one hand, and that of
arguably the most respected New Keynesian of our time, Joseph
Stiglitz, on the other—has much to tell us about the forms the
Keynesian critique can take. If we focus on the specifics, their respective analyses of the same problem, that of the class politics of unemployment, we can see their differences are not due to one or the other
having tapped into "What Keynes Really Meant," or the Truth—for
they could certainly both be True—but are instead a function of the
dialectic of hope and fear that beats at the heart of Keynesianism.

This is why Keynes could give his stamp of approval to many
different, sometimes seemingly incompatible, approaches that
attempted to embrace his ideas. His pragmatism made him much

---

7   On the reserve army of labor, see Karl Marx, *Capital*, vol. 1, New York: Vintage,
1977, 784: "a surplus population of workers is a necessary product of accumulation or of
the development of wealth on a capitalist basis, this surplus population also becomes,
conversely, the lever of capitalist accumulation, indeed it becomes a condition for the existence of the capitalist mode of production. It forms a disposable industrial reserve army,
which belongs to capital just as absolutely as if the latter had bred it at its own cost."

On the natural rate of unemployment, see the founding text, Milton Friedman, "The
Role of Monetary Policy," *American Economic Review* 58: 1, 1968, 8: "The 'natural rate of
unemployment,' in other words, is the level that would be ground out by the Walrasian
system of general equilibrium equations, provided there is imbedded in them the actual
structural characteristics of the labor and commodity markets, including market imperfections, stochastic variability in demands and supplies, the cost of gathering information
about job vacancies and labor availabilities, the costs of mobility, and so on."

less worried about the means by which one found one's way to his conclusions, as long as one found one's way there in the end.[8] This means that although differences in analytical apparatus led to very different recommended interventions, insofar as they recognize (as Joan Robinson puts it) "at the philosophical level, that the mechanisms of a 'free' capitalist system are inherently incapable of regulating themselves," all of them are equally engendered by the post-Robespierre Keynesianism outlined in previous chapters.[9]

## The Impossible Dream of Full Employment

If some postwar Keynesians believed they had found the "solution" to the problem of unemployment, it certainly did not mean it lost its new place at the core of economics and political economy. Even if the problem itself seemed to have disappeared, the utter failure of the "classical" response during the Great Depression, and the hegemony of Keynesianism in the postwar era, meant the disappearance was attributed to that state's obsessive vigilance. This is what Milton Friedman—among the most influential anti-Keynesian economists of the twentieth century—meant when he (not Richard Nixon!) said "We are all Keynesians now."[10] The political and social legacies of the 1930s (populism, poverty, fascism, and radical left movements) so saturated the immediate postwar decades that even libertarian neoclassicals could not avoid being Keynesians. Like Friedman, many non-Keynesians, using classical theories to examine problems other than unemployment, inevitably found themselves asking Keynesian questions about unemployment.

This is the moment at which Kenneth Arrow formulated his famous "impossibility theorem."[11] (He later won a Nobel Prize for

---

8    Robert Skidelsky, *Keynes: The Return of the Master*, London: Penguin, 2010, 102.

9    Robinson, "Latter Day Capitalism," 41.

10    *Time*, December 31, 1965. Friedman later wrote a letter to *Time* (February 4, 1966) to correct what he (quite reasonably) felt was misquotation. What he actually said was this: "In one sense, we are all Keynesians now; in another, nobody is any longer a Keynesian."

11    Kenneth Arrow, *Social Choice and Individual Values*, 2nd ed., New Haven: Cowles Foundation and Yale University Press, 1963. (The first edition appeared in 1951.) Arrow

his formal proof of Walrasian general equilibrium, about as un-Keynesian an effort as one might imagine, at least within the confines of economics proper.) Using the logic of set theory, Arrow was investigating a kind of liberal thought-Utopia: "we ask if it is formally possible to construct a procedure for passing from a set of known individual tastes to a pattern of social decision-making." If so, the resulting "social welfare function" would serve "as a justification for both political democracy and *laissez-faire* economics or at least an economic system involving free choice of goods by consumers and of occupations by workers."[12] In other words, working in a realm of hyperabstraction that might have left Hegel or Keynes slack-jawed, Arrow sought an analytical procedure to realize something like Hegelian ends with Kantian means, to bring the general and the particular together in a way that nonetheless leaves the latter radically autonomous from the former. In this vision, there is no need for the individual to come to understand his or her interest as also the universal interest of the state, no need for an "ethical" transformation. Instead, the status quo of capitalist civil society generates a collective decision that allows every particular to realize its ends simultaneously. There is no dialectically unfolding social totality, just the authoritative technical determination of a social welfare maximizing (market-based) aggregate of independent individual choices—the best of all possible (liberal) worlds.

This too is potentially a very un-Keynesian project. But Arrow's conclusion—that this liberal Promised Land is *impossible*—is the most Keynesian outcome to which it could lead. We might even read it as a logical "proof" of the fundamental Keynesian proposition: even by its own atomistic standards, and even with only

---

actually called it the "general possibility theorem," but since his conclusion—that the theorem proved a social welfare function as he defined it is not possible (p. 60)—it has become known as the "impossibility theorem."

12   It is worth noting that the impossibility of the social welfare function proceeds from it "being required to satisfy certain natural [logical] conditions"; Ibid., 2, 23. See also Amartya Sen, "Rationality and Social Choice," *American Economic Review* 85: 1, 1995, 1–24; Kenneth Arrow and Gérard Debreu, "Existence of an Equilibrium for a Competitive Economy," *Econometrica* 20, 1954, 265–90. The general equilibrium framework is sometimes called "Arrow-Debreu" or "A-D" in honor of Arrow and his coauthor Debreu.

"mild-looking conditions that would seem to reflect elementary demands of reasonableness," liberal capitalist or bourgeois civil society cannot solve its own contradictions.[13] The only methods that can "guarantee the existence of an equilibrium under every possible pattern of individual preferences are dictatorial."[14] In Arrow's words:

> the market mechanism does not create a rational social choice . . . it is not surprising, then, that such ethics can be no more successful than the actual practice of individualism in permitting the formation of social welfare judgments.[15]

Liberalism cannot ground *Sittlichkeit;* its abstract claims to construct a world on the basis of *Sollen* are untenable, even in a thought experiment. Arrow made this very clear: "My own feeling is that tastes for unattainable alternatives should have nothing to do with the decision among the attainable ones; desires in conflict with reality are not entitled to consideration." It is almost as if Arrow stepped behind Rawls's rational "veil of ignorance" a Kantian and came out a Hegelian.[16]

Others, similarly struggling to confront the new situation, were coming to similar conclusions—unintentionally, even reluctantly, becoming Keynesian. Paul Samuelson, for example—he of the "neoclassical synthesis"—was at exactly the same moment formulating a theory of public expenditure and public goods that demonstrated the necessity of some agent of social welfare. Not only was

---

13  Sen, "Rationality and Social Choice," 1; compare with Norman Schofield, "Power, Prosperity and Social Choice: A Review," *Social Choice and Welfare* 20, 2003, 85–118.

14  Anthony Atkinson and Joseph Stiglitz, *Lectures on Public Economics*, Princeton: Princeton University Press, 2015, 254.

15  Arrow, *Social Choice and Individual Values*, 59, 72.

16  Ibid., 73. Later, Arrow makes explicit the connection between Kantian morality and the impossibility theorem (pp. 82–83). Hegel is never mentioned—although we might speculate as to why—but ultimately Arrow concludes that neither the consensus of autonomous individual wills (Kant) nor "ethical absolutism" (Rousseau) can provide an adequate basis for "social ethics" (pp. 84–85). In his enormously influential *A Theory of Justice*, John Rawls took Arrow's work as a serious challenge to his liberal theory of justice, and it unsurprisingly forced him to consider Keynes. See John Rawls, *A Theory of Justice*, Cambridge: Harvard University Press, 1971, 258–84, 298–300.

*everyone* worse off without state provision, but what the state provided (goods from which there was zero expected yield, because they were impossible to privatize) were keystones in the structure of civilization: infrastructure, water, clean air, peace.[17] One could imagine Hegel, were he able to make any sense of it, saying, "I told you so."

In fact, the story of Arrow's impossibility theorem, now seen as the founding contribution to social choice theory, and the related question of public goods, is in some ways a case study in the politics of postwar economics. On the one hand, Arrow's own analysis—what Samuelson called his "mathematical politics"—has been taken up largely by those interested in elaborating the Keynesian conceptual and policy arsenal: economists and other social scientists examining public goods and microeconomists with Keynesian sympathies.[18] These economists—including Amartya Sen, another Nobel laureate and student of Joan Robinson—have challenged the fundamental assumptions of orthodox microeconomics in a manner analogous to the Keynesian effort in macro. They refuse the standard model of individual economic agency and emphasize the ways in which agents' behavior in the world in which we actually live is rarely captured by *homo economicus* and optimization. For instance, Sen has formulated a social choice framework that takes account of what he calls "other-regarding" and "altruistic" preferences that, if it were to bother to respond, would cause mainstream microeconomics significant

---

17    Paul Samuelson, "A Pure Theory of Public Expenditure," *Review of Economics and Statistics* 36: 4, 1954, 387–89. "Primary social goods" is the liberal philosopher John Rawls's term for those goods that a rational person wants whatever else he or she wants. Rawls's categories are less materialist than the examples I propose here: "rights and liberties, opportunities and powers, income and wealth" and "a sense of one's self worth"; Rawls, *A Theory of Justice*, 92. I take this as evidence of his commitment to liberalism, that is, to prioritize abstract moral "goods" over earthly necessity, come hell or high water.

18    Paul Samuelson, "Arrow's Mathematical Politics," in Sidney Hook (ed.), *Human Values and Economic Policy*, New York: New York University Press, 1967, 41–52. Since "Keynesian economics" is by definition macroeconomics, the phrase "Keynesian microeconomics" would seem oxymoronic to economists, who instead speak of the "microfoundations" of Keynesian economics. See, for example, Gregory Mankiw and David Romer, "Introduction," in Gregory Mankiw and David Romer (eds.), *New Keynesian Economics, vol. I: Imperfect Competition and Sticky Prices*, Cambridge: MIT Press, 1991, 16. The question of "microfoundations" is discussed further in Chapter 13.

problems by shaking the behavioral foundations of general equilibrium.[19]

On the other hand, the "impossibility" result elicited a robust reaction among anti-Keynesians. Led by James Buchanan and Gordon Tullock, American economists, and members of Friedman and Hayek's "neoliberal thought collective" the Mont Pèlerin Society, the so-called "public choice school" responded with barely contained outrage at the pomposity of "moral philosophers'" suggestion of any such thing as collective choice or collective rationality.[20] Their critique of Arrow is ultimately founded in what Keynes disdained as "Benthamite calculus": a methodologically individualist utilitarian (or "welfare") denial of both the possibility and the legitimacy of a supra-individual rationality by which a social welfare function might be judged.[21]

That rationality, however—a precondition of the "social interest"—is of course essential to a Hegelian–Keynesian ontology. We might even call it Keynesianism's *Geist* or Spirit. Indeed, anticipating in some ways the argument here, Sen traces the origins of social choice theory to the French Revolution, which, having posed problems for which it did not wait for "a peacefully intellectual solution," drove the post-Revolutionary era to seek ways to avoid such "instability and arbitrariness," just as Hegel himself said.[22] Arrow's analysis readily builds on these earlier efforts, "mathematically" walking

---

19   Amartya Sen, "Rational Fools: A Critique of the Behavioral Foundations of Economic Theory," *Philosophy and Public Affairs* 6: 4, 1977, 317–44.

20   Philip Mirowski, *Never Let a Serious Crisis Go to Waste: How Neoliberalism Survived the Meltdown*, London: Verso, 2013, Chapter 2; James Buchanan and Gordon Tullock, *The Calculus of Consent: The Logical Foundations of Constitutional Democracy*, Ann Arbor: University of Michigan Press, 1962, Chapter 3. If this position recalls Margaret Thatcher's famous dictum "there's no such thing as society," it is because Buchanan and Tullock (like Thatcher) were Hayekians. They would also have agreed with the fuller statement: "there's no such thing as society. There are individual men and women and there are families. And no government can do anything except through people, and people must look after themselves first." The quote is from an interview with *Women's Own* magazine, published October 31, 1987.

21   Keynes, *CW*, VII, 213.

22   Amartya Sen, "The Possibility of Social Choice" (Nobel Lecture, December 8, 1998), *American Economic Review* 89: 3, 1999, 350.

postwar economics, however unwillingly, to the Keynesian precipice and forcing it to look over the edge. With or without a formal "mathematical" apparatus, this is what Keynesianism has been doing since Thermidor.

In fact, some have argued that the immediate legacy of Robespierre's "Arrovian chaos"—the threat of "violence, sufficient to destroy the conditions for existence of economic equilibrium and thus of dynamic equilibrium"—led the post-Revolutionary bourgeoisie to question democracy entirely and laid the grounds for Napoleon's imperial legitimacy.[23] If so, it is further confirmation of the account of Keynesianism in these chapters, for an inescapable problem that Arrow tried to confront is that outside of "*une volonté UNE*," any practicable effort to deal with the impossibility theorem appears necessarily antidemocratic. The only solution—in the language of social choice theory—is "dictatorial."[24] Hegel came to a similar conclusion and endorsed constitutional monarchy; Keynes relied on the vigilant containment of key questions like poverty within the expert halls of the bureaucratic "universal class."[25] As the three chapters in this part of the book show, driven by similar if necessarily differently cast concerns, post-World War II Keynesian economics—the hegemonic economics of its era—could not help but come to similar conclusions.

## Kalecki on the "Political Aspects of Full Employment"

Against the flow of discursive tradition within Keynesian economics since World War II, then, what bears emphasis is less what mode of

---

23    Norman Schofield, "Social Orders," *Social Choice and Welfare* 34, 2010, 510.

24    Arrow, *Social Choice and Individual Values*, 59; Allan Gibbard, "Manipulation of Voting Schemes: A General Result," *Econometrica*, 41, 1973, 587–601; Jean-Jacques Laffont and David Martimort, *The Theory of Incentives: The Principal-Agent Model*, Princeton: Princeton University Press, 2002, Chapter 1.

25    Arrow's Hayekian critic James Buchanan wrote a book with Richard Wagner entitled (not unjustifiably) *Democracy in Deficit: The Political Legacy of Lord Keynes* (Indianapolis: Liberty Fund, 1977).

analysis counts as "truly" Keynesian—formal or not, faithful to the technical details of *The General Theory* or not, and so forth—but rather what modes of analysis Keynesianism can support, the diversity of modern ways of knowing it can animate and sustain. Ultimately, Keynesians are distinguishable not by *how* they come to know what they know (their epistemological or methodological apparatus), but by *what* they know (liberal capitalist modernity produces the seeds of its own destruction) and *why* they know it (reasoned consideration of the concrete "facts of experience").

Michał Kalecki stands near one end of this range of Keynesianisms, and his work can tell us much about the radical potential in Keynes's thought. Kalecki was a Polish economist who, by a series of fateful twists and turns, briefly ended up in Cambridge (with some assistance from Keynes himself) in the late 1930s. Although not so extreme a case as his colleague Piero Sraffa, he is one of those scholars whose extraordinary influence has little to do with the quantity of his scholarly contributions. Like Sraffa, he produced a smaller number of exceptionally powerful interventions. Whether his fellow economists agreed with him or not, his brilliance and humility were widely admired. Indeed, the devotion he continues to inspire among some heterodox economists is such that they will feel offended I have labeled him a Keynesian, since this suggests his achievement was somehow derivative. They might point to the fact that prior to his arrival in Cambridge—and prior to the appearance of *The General Theory*—Kalecki published work in Polish that partly anticipated Keynes's book, and a 1935 article in English is occasionally said to have beaten Keynes to the punch. There even remains a group who claim he was a co-"discoverer" of the "economics of Keynes."[26]

26    George Feiwel, "Kalecki and Keynes," *De Economist* 123: 2, 1975, 164–97; Don Patinkin, *Anticipations of the General Theory? And Other Essays on Keynes*, Chicago: University of Chicago Press, 1982, 62–63; Michał Kalecki, *Selected Essays on the Dynamics of the Capitalist Economy: 1933–1970*; Cambridge: Cambridge University Press, 1971, vii; Michał Kalecki, "A Macrodynamic Theory of Business Cycles," *Econometrica* 3, 1935, 327–44; Robinson, "Latter Day Capitalism," 39; Eprime Eshag, "Kalecki's Political Economy: A Comparison with Keynes," *Oxford Bulletin of Economics and Statistics* 39, 1977, 1–6.

In light of the account of Keynesianism I have developed here, however, we can simply sidestep the problem of "discoverer" status. Whether or not Kalecki co-discovered effective demand with Keynes is no more important to an understanding of Keynesianism than if Hegel beat both of them to it. The biggest and most important difference between Keynes and Kalecki, however, is that the latter had read Marx and been trained in Marxian thinking. Reading his work, it is occasionally possible to see him as a bridge between Keynes and Marx, particularly in his emphasis on the disciplinary necessity for capitalism of a pool of unemployed workers like those Marx included in the "reserve army of labor."

But, if we take a closer look at his most fully developed work—like *Theory of Economic Dynamics: An Essay on Cyclical and Long-Run Changes in Capitalist Economy* of 1954—it is difficult to wedge it into a Marxian frame. If we are forced to apportion the content of his thought, it is more Keynesian than Marxian, even on the question of the reserve army. He is best understood as a Keynesian economist with some radical political sympathies and thus more willing than most to take Marxian ideas seriously.[27]

The influence of these ideas is most visible in his innovative work on a glaring "practical" problem Keynes entirely neglected but that is central to Marxian economics: the degree of monopoly in an economy, a feature associated with "the process of concentration in industry leading to the formation of giant corporations" and the "commercial revolution" through which "price competition is replaced by competition in advertising campaigns, etc."[28] Kalecki argued that trade unions' power to affect the functional distribution of income between capital and labor tends to keep the degree of monopoly

---

27   Suzanne de Brunhoff, *The State, Capital, and Economic Policy*, London: Pluto, 1978, 75–79. This is not to deny that his work in the early 1930s was much closer to Marxism. If he had stopped writing in 1934, rather than three decades later, we would justifiably remember him as basically a Marxist; P. Kriesler and B. McFarlane, "Michał Kalecki on Capitalism," *Cambridge Journal of Economics* 17, 1993, 219–20.

28   Michal Kalecki, *Theory of Economic Dynamics: An Essay on Cyclical and Long-Run Changes in Capitalist Economy*, London: Allen and Unwin, 1954, 17; on Keynes's neglect of monopoly, see Paul Sweezy, "The First Quarter Century," in Robert Lekachman (ed.), *Keynes' General Theory: Reports of Three Decades*, New York: St. Martin's Press, 1964, 309.

down by depressing profit rates, and that there is consequently a tendency for monopolistic power to rise in a "slump" and decline in a "boom."[29] But the degree of monopoly is not only significant in the struggle between workers and bosses over the surplus. It is also self-expansive, insofar as it redistributes income from small to big business, since profits tend to be higher in monopolized sectors. The degree of monopoly thus "has a general tendency to increase in the long run," which, in combination with the fact that in Fordist mass production, innovation is concentrated on the labor process, leads to a diminishing share of income for wage earners relative to capital.[30]

While capitalism's tendency to mass impoverishment is widely (and justifiably) associated with Marxist analysis, the distinctiveness of Keynesianism lies in its theorization of this dynamic, what it means for the social order, and what to do about it. Kalecki was far more Keynesian than Marxian on these fronts: as he said, clearly responding to classical critics of Keynes's "paradox of poverty in the midst of plenty":

> The tragedy of investment is that it calls forth the crisis because it is useful. I do not wonder that many people consider this theory paradoxical. But it is not the theory that is paradoxical but its subject—the capitalist economy.[31]

Like Keynes and Marx, Kalecki was interested in the self-destructive social relations endogenous to the political-economic dynamics of liberal capitalism, but his more strictly economic analysis shares several fundamentals with *The General Theory* in particular. Kalecki too emphasizes both the inevitable "supply-demand mismatch" resulting from uncertainty associated with what Keynes called "expectations"—"capitalists' investment and consumption are determined by decisions shaped in the *past*," as Kalecki puts it—and

---

29 Kalecki, *Theory of Economic Dynamics*, 18. He does note that sometimes the degree of monopoly can fall in a recession, driven by "cut-throat competition."

30 Kalecki, *Theory of Economic Dynamics*, 30, 159.

31 Michał Kalecki, "A Theory of the Business Cycle," in Jerzy Osiatynski (ed.), *Collected Works of Michał Kalecki*, vol. I, Oxford: Clarendon Press, 1991, 554.

(against the "classicals") the dominance of short-run dynamics in economic considerations.[32] His saving-investment function is very like that proposed by Keynes and puts investment, not production, at the center of economic analysis. It rejects the "loanable funds" theory of the interest rate, since "investment 'finances itself'": through a Keynesian liquidity function, "investment automatically brings into existence an equal amount of savings."[33]

In addition, Kalecki's model of the business cycle captures dynamics very much like the "fundamental psychological law" and the "curse of Midas" so central to *The General Theory*. Much as Keynes argued that diminished expected profits (a declining marginal efficiency of capital) required modern communities approaching full employment to "sufficiently impoverish" themselves to reinvigorate entrepreneurial animal spirits, Kalecki's model includes a coefficient of "crucial importance" that indexes both the less-than-full "reinvestment of saving" and the "negative influence upon investment of the increasing capital." Which is to say that when the proportion of savings reinvested is less than unity (merely a variation on the "fundamental psychological law") and further capital accumulation would reduce expected yields (the "curse of Midas"), "the slump is started."[34]

This coefficient alone is sufficient to Keynesianize a model, injecting an inevitable tendency to decline, disorder, and volatility, if only

---

32  Kalecki, *Theory of Economic Dynamics*, 11, 46.

33  Kalecki, *Theory of Economic Dynamics*, 50–55, 73, 88; Michał Kalecki, "Observations on the Theory of Growth," in Jerzy Osiatynski (ed.), *Collected Works of Michał Kalecki*, vol. II, Oxford: Clarendon Press, 1991, 434; Keynes, *CW*, VII, 184–85.

34  Kalecki, *Theory of Economic Dynamics*, 123–25. For those interested in some technical detail, the coefficient is represented (in old-fashioned math, à la Keynes) as $\frac{a}{1+c}$, where $a$ is the proportion of savings reinvested, and $c$ is the accumulation of capital equipment (Keynes's "investment"). When the business cycle reaches its peak, the downturn in the cycle is initiated "because the coefficient $\frac{a}{1+c}$ is less than 1, which reflects the negative influence upon investment of the increasing capital equipment ($c > 0$) and also, possibly, the factor of incomplete reinvestment of saving (if $a < 1$). If there were a full reinvestment of saving ($a = 1$) and if the accumulation of capital equipment could be disregarded (if $c$ were negligible) the system would be maintained at its top level. But, in fact, the accumulation of capital equipment, which with a stable level of economic activity makes for a falling rate of profit, does have a tangible adverse effect on investment ($c$ is not negligible). Moreover, the reinvestment of savings may be incomplete ($a < 1$). As a result, investment declines and thus the slump is started" (125–26).

in the short run, into the heart of a theory of capitalist dynamics. Moreover, Kalecki is carefully Keynesian in showing that the cyclicality implied in the model's emphasis on the short run does not mean that the capitalist dynamic is eventually self-regulating. He points out that, on the contrary, the longer run promises of the classical and neoclassical adherents are by no means guaranteed, since the stimulus produced by capital destruction in a slump will be weaker than that driven by accumulation in a boom (because in a slump, what is destroyed is already idle). This means that "the reserve capital equipment and the reserve army of unemployed are typical features of capitalist economy at least throughout a considerable part of the cycle."[35] In capitalism, involuntary unemployment is the "normal" state of affairs.

Kalecki's "reserve army of unemployed," however, is not necessarily Marx's; and it is not exactly the rabble, either. The reserve army for Marx is an elastic supply of labor, often based in noncapitalist modes of social reproduction like subsistence agriculture or the household, which allows labor supply to shrink and expand to meet the needs of capitalist labor demand. It is "endogenous" only in the strictly economic sense—as a supply factor, its quantities are not exogenously given.[36] The rabble, as we have seen, is an endogenous precipitate of capitalist social relations composed of those so dishonored by that social formation that they are much closer structurally and politically to Marx's *lumpen*. Its existence, qualitatively and quantitatively, is entirely attributable to liberal capitalist civil society. Kalecki's reserve army of *unemployed*—not those capitalism has yet to incorporate, but those it has sloughed off—effectively bridges the

---

35   Ibid., 126, 131. This dynamic is akin to the problem monetary policy-makers sometimes call "pushing on a string." It is easier to influence economic activity negatively (by tightening policy and "slowing" the economy) than it is to stimulate by loosening it. Raising interest rates has an immediate "pinch," whereas in conditions of dormant animal spirits, lowering rates will not necessarily have as ready an impact on investment behavior. Indeed, as almost a decade of basically zero interest rates suggests (beginning in 2008), it can sometimes have almost no impact at all.

36   Stephen Marglin, *Growth, Distribution, and Prices*, Cambridge: Harvard University Press, 1984, 79; Stephen Marglin, "Growth, Distribution, and Inflation: A Centennial Synthesis," *Cambridge Journal of Economics* 8, 1984, 120–21.

two concepts in a manner that speaks to the times in which he worked. In 1943, he theorized the problem of mass unemployment as a Marxian class-political dynamic that generates a Keynesian "economic" outcome; by 1954 he emphasized a Keynesian "economic" dynamic that leads to Marxian "political" outcomes.

## A Keynesian Critique of Keynes

Kalecki's consideration of the problem of unemployment is essential, then, at least partly because it constitutes a fundamentally pragmatic critique of Keynes's politics. Kalecki is compelled by Keynes's explanation of endogenous involuntary unemployment, but he remains unconvinced by Keynes's Hegelian faith in the capacity of the state to produce a sufficiently legitimate "universality" to overcome the distinctively *political* barriers to "full employment" and honor among the masses. Keynes's and his various acolytes'

> assumption that a government will maintain full employment in a capitalist economy if it only knows how to do it is fallacious. In this connection the misgivings of big business about the maintenance of full employment by government spending are of paramount importance.[37]

The problem, according to Kalecki, is that class matters in capitalism, and political economy and economic policy are realms saturated in ideological and political-economic struggle. If it were really just Reason that shaped these realms, the "world in which we actually live" would make little sense: "businessmen in a slump are longing for a boom; why do they not accept gladly the 'synthetic' boom which the government is able to offer them?" The reasons they do not act as rational self-interest suggests they should are evident as soon as we drop the assumption, to which Keynes was normally quite sensitive,

---

37    Michał Kalecki, "Political Aspects of Full Employment" [1943], in *The Last Phase in the Transformation of Capitalism*, New York: Monthly Review Press, 1972, 75.

that the questions of concern can be contained to the economic realm. For Kalecki, the questions are clearly not merely economic, and the reasons for business opposition are evidence of the material, political, and ideological forces at work in the economy.

The reasons are three, all of which are ultimately attributable to liberalism. First, capital—the class composed of capitalists—is opposed to "government interference" on principle. Under *laissez-faire* conditions, capital exercises de facto hegemony: as Keynes showed, "the level of employment depends to a great extent on the so-called state of confidence." Capitalists thus always have "powerful indirect control over government policy: everything which may shake the state of confidence must be carefully avoided because it would cause an economic crisis." When the government "learns the [Keynesian] trick" of increasing employment on its own, "this powerful controlling device" is rendered much less powerful. In other words, writes Kalecki, the "social function of the doctrine of 'sound finance'" is political-ideological: "to make the level of employment dependent on the 'state of confidence.'"[38] This diagnosis of the motives for capitalists' and mainstream economists' endless attacks on government debt remains accurate today. The more the state or other collective agents are prevented from participating in the economy, the more income and wealth generation becomes the business of business alone. To the extent that the public accepts the doctrine of "sound finance"— what in "normal" times would today be called "tight money" and balanced-budget "fiscal conservatism" or in crisis times is called "austerity"—the more capital's hegemony is reinforced.[39]

---

38  Ibid., 76–77.

39  The political stakes in this debate have not diminished one bit since Kalecki's time. Witness, for example, the recent controversy surrounding the work of Carmen Reinhart and Kenneth Rogoff, two of austerity's greatest champions, which proposed a 90 percent sovereign debt-to-GDP ratio as basically a threshold beyond which lies capitalist disaster. This claim, which circulated widely among policy-makers, has since been debunked by Thomas Herndon and colleagues. See Carmen M. Reinhart and Kenneth Rogoff, "Growth in a Time of Debt," *American Economic Review* 100: 2, 2010, 573–78; Thomas Herndon, Michael Ash, and Michael Pollin, "Does High Public Debt Consistently Stifle Economic Growth? A Critique of Reinhart and Rogoff," *Cambridge Journal of Economics* 38, 2014, 257–79.

The second reason capital resists a state-coordinated boom is partly a function of "economic interest"—because public investment supposedly "crowds out" the private sector—but is to an even greater extent "ethical," and ethical in precisely the sense of Hegel's *Sitten*. Public investment or, even worse, subsidized mass consumption (as Hegel put it, addressing the same problem) "would be contrary to the principle of civil society and the feeling of self-sufficiency and honour among its individual members." In Kalecki's words, "here a 'moral' principle of the highest importance is at stake. The fundamentals of capitalist ethics require that 'You shall earn your bread in sweat'—unless you happen to have private means."[40]

The third and final reason capital does not necessarily act as a reasonable Keynesian hope is that, as a class, it is liberal in the dogmatic, myopic sense Keynes and Hegel attacked. It is not sufficiently worried that the emergence of the rabble will lead to a revolutionary "destruction of existing economic forms in their entirety." Its ideological blinders prevent it from seeing that "in the long run we are all dead." On the contrary, it fears the "social and political changes resulting from the *maintenance* of full employment," and is thus concerned to avoid the Keynesian path precisely because it might succeed.[41]

> Indeed, under a regime of permanent full employment, "the sack" would cease to play its role as a disciplinary measure. The social position of the boss would be undermined and the self-assurance and class consciousness of the working class would grow. Strikes for wage increases and improvements in conditions of work would create political tensions. It is true that profits would be higher under a regime of full employment than they are on the average under *laissez-faire*; and even the rise in wage rates resulting from the stronger bargaining power of the workers is less likely to reduce profits than to increase prices, and thus affects adversely only the rentier interests. But "discipline in the factories" and "political

---

40   Kalecki, "Political Aspects of Full Employment," 78.
41   Ibid., 76.

stability" are more appreciated by the business leaders than profits. Their class instinct tells them that full employment is unsound from their point of view and that unemployment is an integral part of the capitalist system.[42]

Capital admits that for many, in the conditions that typify modern civil society, "that feeling of right, integrity, and honour which comes from supporting oneself by one's own activity and work is lost." What it denies is the Hegel–Keynes corollary, that this situation is a *result* of capitalism, not the fault of the poor and unemployed themselves.

In this sense, and this is a product of the reluctantly radical dimension of Keynesianism to which Kalecki is particularly sensitive, capital—both as a set of assets and as a class—is a substantial part of the problem. On the one hand, the necessary scarcity of capital-assets, the precondition of yield, generates an endogenous constraint on the entrepreneurial paradise classical and neoclassical theories posit as the default state of capitalism:

> Many economists assume, at least in their abstract theories, a state of business democracy where anybody endowed with entrepreneurial ability can obtain capital for starting a business venture. This picture of the activities of the "pure" entrepreneur is, to put it mildly, unrealistic. The most important prerequisite for becoming an entrepreneur is the *ownership* of capital . . .[43]

Such ownership is of necessity unevenly distributed. As Piketty has also recently reminded us (see Chapter 14), it is axiomatic that not everyone can be a capitalist, and capitalism is "naturally" disequalizing and destabilizing.

---

42    Ibid., 78. Beveridge makes exactly the same point in *Full Employment in a Free Society*, 22: "Under conditions of full employment, if men are free to move from one employment to another and do not fear dismissal, may not some of them at least become so irregular and undisciplined in their behaviour, as to lower appreciably the efficiency of industry?"

43    Kalecki, *Theory of Economic Dynamics*, 94–95.

Consequently, and contrary to orthodox growth theory, capitalism does not inherently contain in its self-expansion the promise of increasingly well-distributed wealth, because "an increase in the number of paupers does not broaden the market."[44] Again, we return to Robespierre's and Hegel's focus on excessive wealth and poverty side by side. Keynes described a related situation in which we have a glut of houses but few able to afford them, and Kalecki makes a similar point: "increased population does not necessarily mean a higher demand for houses; for without an increase in purchasing power the result may well be the crowding of more people into existing dwelling space."[45]

On the other hand, for these very reasons, Kalecki argues that in a capitalist economy after the Great Depression, it is no longer possible for capital as a hegemonic class to oppose all countercyclical government intervention. "The necessity that 'something must be done in the slump' is agreed to"; in Beveridge's words, "[w]hatever the bearing of full employment upon industrial discipline, one thing is clear. A civilized community must find alternatives to starvation for preservation of industrial discipline and efficiency."[46] But this leaves a very big question unanswered, because in a liberal democracy, the doer of the something-that-must-be-done is at least partly subject to the masses' vicissitudes. In other words, democracy unsettles the businessperson's "confidence," because in "a democracy one does not know what the next government will be like."[47]

To Kalecki, history shows that these political conditions drive capital to push society toward the same end-of-civilization cataclysms that Keynesians expect will be associated with the rabble that

---

44   Ibid., 161.

45   Keynes, *CW,* VII, 322.

46   Kalecki, "Political Aspects of Full Employment," 80; Beveridge, *Full Employment in a Free Society,* 198. For a recent statement-*cum*-admission of this perspective, see David Rothkopf, "Free-Market Evangelists Face a Sad and Lonely Fate," *Financial Times,* February 1, 2012: "21st-century capitalism will look less and less like the economic Darwinism celebrated on Wall Street."

47   Kalecki, "Political Aspects of Full Employment," 79.

capitalism cannot help but produce. The reason is that in a capitalist mode of economic organization, the uncertainties that capital anticipates will be associated with full employment—the resulting popular sovereignty, worker self-assurance, and lack of discipline—has been avoided by one means alone: fascism. Capital tends toward fascism because if under "democracy one does not know what the next government will be like," under fascism "there is no next government . . . One of the important functions of fascism, as typified by the Nazi system, was to remove the capitalist objections to full employment."[48] The "new order" of fascist tyranny maintains both political stability and discipline in the factories.

Indeed, Keynesians—and not just social-democratic "left-Keynesians," but also those closely associated with the "neoclassical" side of the synthesis—readily take this historical "solution" to the problem of the rabble as proof of the Truth of Keynesianism's most fundamental propositions regarding capitalism's threat to civilization. As one of the most prominent post-World War II American Keynesians, Lawrence Klein, remarked:

> [Fascism] is the form that our capitalist society will acquire unless we are successful in bringing about Keynesian reforms or a socialist economy. *If we let nature take its course*, the economic law of motion of capitalism will take us down the same road that Germany followed so recently.[49]

Which is to say, as Keynes himself said, Keynesianism is "the only practicable means of avoiding the destruction of existing economic forms in their entirety"; it is for Keynesians the *only* noncatastrophic

---

48    Kalecki, "Political Aspects of Full Employment," 79. "One of the basic functions of Nazism was to overcome the reluctance of big business to large-scale government intervention . . . Today government intervention has become an integral part of 'reformed' capitalism. In a sense the price of this reform was the Second World War and the Nazi genocide which were the final effect of the heavy rearmament that initially played the role of stimulating the business upswing"; Kalecki, "The Fascism of Our Times" [1964], in *The Last Phase in the Transformation of Capitalism*, New York: Monthly Review Press, 1972, 100.

49    Lawrence R. Klein, *The Keynesian Revolution*, 2nd ed., New York: Macmillan, 1966, 167 (emphasis added).

solution to "the problem of unemployment"—a problem we can be "certain that the world will not much longer tolerate."[50]

According to Kalecki, these dynamics signal precisely the kind of categorical crisis to which Keynesians are so anxiously sensitive, a sensitivity they inherit from liberalism.[51] On this account, fascism, like socialism or communism—indeed, like revolution as such— represents the contamination or even the poisoning of the economic by the political. Unemployment, which "ought" to be a problem addressed by the technical solutions to which the properly economic is supposed to be amenable, becomes the virus that infects the whole social order, as "political pressure replaces the economic pressure of unemployment."[52]

I should be careful not to suggest that Kalecki adopts Keynes's reluctant but tragic bourgeois acceptance of this categorical leakage, as for example, is the case with Arendt or Habermas. Kalecki's own political commitments are sufficiently Left to lead him to accept not only the inevitability but the necessity of significant categorical spillover. But his attention to these dynamics is intimately tied to that part of his analysis that is informed by Keynesianism, and his prognosis for the future of a "modern community" that has recognized the risks capitalism poses to civilization is in many ways quintessentially Keynesian. Once a modern capitalist society accepts the necessity of government intervention in a slump, in the form of both public investment and the stimulation of private investment, the problem of unemployment and poverty becomes a problem which permanently "agitates and torments" them. It becomes, as it were, a fact of everyday life, part of what Kalecki calls a permanent "political business cycle":

> This state of affairs is perhaps symptomatic of the future economic regime of capitalist democracies. In the slump, either under the

---

50   Keynes, *CW,* VII, 381.

51   Alan Ryan, *The Making of Modern Liberalism,* Princeton: Princeton University Press, 2012, 63–90.

52   Kalecki, "Political Aspects of Full Employment," 79–80: "The fascist system starts from the overcoming of unemployment, develops into an 'armament economy' of scarcity, and ends inevitably in war."

pressure of the masses, or even without it, public investment financed by borrowing will be undertaken to prevent large scale unemployment. But if attempts are made to apply this method in order to maintain the high level of employment reached in the subsequent boom, a strong opposition of "business leaders" is likely to be encountered . . . [L]asting full employment is not at all to their liking. The workers would "get out of hand" and the "captains of industry" would be anxious to "teach them a lesson."[53]

Kalecki claims this specifically modern balancing act is made possible by the "Keynesian revolution" in political economy. For it is the advances in economics and economic policy since the 1930s that allow capitalist nation-states to maintain what are, by historical standards, high levels of employment and capacity utilization.[54] This achievement also generates a political "paradox" in which capital consistently resists government intervention in "normal" times while frequently demonstrating, even willingly acknowledging, that in times of crisis that resistance will diminish or even disappear. Hence a political-economic rule becomes cemented into the very foundations of the post-World War II capitalist social order, broadly accepted by both labor and capital: that is, our pursuit of a liberal "economic bliss" depends entirely on the promise that if it comes to it, we will do everything we must, however illiberal, to "put off disaster."

53  Ibid., 83, 82.
54  Włodzimierz Brus, "Preface," in Michał Kalecki, *The Last Phase in the Transformation of Capitalism*, New York: Monthly Review Press, 1972, 61–62.

# CHAPTER 13

# The (New) Keynesian Economics of Equilibrium Unemployment

Kalecki's analysis of full employment leans much less on formal or "mathematical" tools than some of his other work. He was nowhere near as attached to formalism as most twentieth-century economists, but he was relatively technical compared to Keynes. The shift toward the formalization of economic analysis began before Keynes, but in his day it was still possible to contribute professionally to the discipline without the formal apparatus. In the twenty-first century, this is no longer the case and has not been for decades.

I would suggest that the most important aspects of this transformation are not primarily methodological, but epistemological and ontological. The latter are the reasons Keynes was so strongly, if a little inconsistently, opposed to the "mathematization" of economics after Jevons and Walras. The risks he associated with representing economic phenomena as variables or coefficients arose from the way in which they suggest completeness, fixity, and certainty—none of which Keynes thought described much that was meaningful in economic activity. And yet, even by his day formal techniques were the standard mode through which economists tried to come to grips with the world. Consequently, many of those who recognized *The General Theory* as an important (whether revolutionary or not) contribution tried to incorporate it into their worldview by formalizing it using the standard tools of economic analysis. This began immediately upon its publication, in the form of so-called *IS-LM*, a model of the "Keynesian system" originally proposed in 1937 by Keynes's friend John Hicks.[1] Hicks took the principal lesson of *The General Theory* to be that the key question for economists was not what determined prices in conditions of presumed full employment, but what determined quantities (the volume of employment or output, for example) if full employment was not guaranteed. If so, he argued, it was amenable to traditional equilibrium analysis, and we can reconcile Keynes's critique of classical economics with much of the classical approach; thus the article's title: "Mr Keynes and the Classics."

In the post-World War II project of Keynesian economics, there has been little that has been more influential, and more divisive, than *IS-LM*. The model—also known as the "Hicks-Hansen" framework (after Hicks and the refinements of Alvin Hansen, the greatest missionary of Keynesianism in the United States)—frames economic conditions as determined by two macroeconomic curves or "schedules."[2] Each schedule is itself determined by the set of possible equilibria in one of two key "sides" of the economy: the goods/capital market of the "real economy" (where investment demand $I$ meets investment supply $S$) and the money market of "finance," where demand for money (liquidity preference) $L$ meets money supply ($M$). In the 1937 article (which Keynes, somewhat notoriously, vaguely endorsed in a letter to Hicks), and in later work, Hicks posits macroeconomic equilibrium as the intersection of the *IS* and *LM* curves in the output-real interest rate plane.[3]

---

1 John R. Hicks, "Mr Keynes and the Classics: A Suggested Interpretation," *Econometrica* 5, 1937, 147–59; John R. Hicks, *Value and Capital*, Oxford: Clarendon, 1939.

2 Alvin H. Hansen, *A Guide to Keynes*, New York: McGraw-Hill, 1953.

3 Keynes wrote to Hicks, "I found it very interesting and really have next to nothing to say by way of criticism"; Letter of March 31, 1937, in Keynes, CW, XIV, 79.

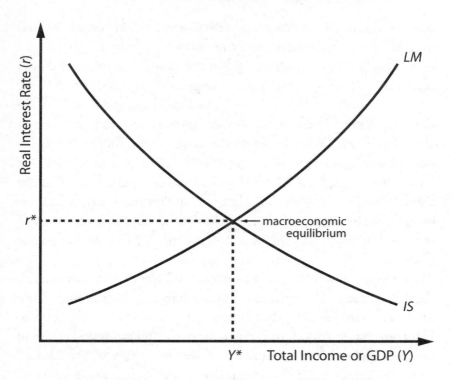

### The *IS-LM* Model of Macroeconomic Equilibrium

Originally formulated by John Hicks in 1937, *IS-LM* models an
economy with "Keynesian" features. The *IS* curve describes the set
of points at which, across the range of real rates of interest ($r$) and
aggregate income ($Y$), investment and saving are in equilibrium.
The *LM* curve describes the conditions for equilibrium between the
demand and supply of money. Macroeconomic equilibrium exists
at the point of intersection of *IS* and *LM*, where income and the
real interest rate have the values $Y^*$ and $r^*$).

The key to understanding the schedules is to remember that any
point along either the *IS* or *LM* curve is itself an equilibrium point
in the relation between the curves' respective components (investment and saving for *IS*, and demand and supply of money for *LM*).
In other words, if you imagine that you could pick either curve up
off the page and turn it sideways to hold it out in front of you like a
telescope, each curve would look like a string of adjacent X-shapes

laid out like vertebrae along a spine. The *IS* or *LM* curves are created by a line connecting the intersections of each X. When you place the curve back on the page, all that is visible is the connecting line, which is the schedule of consecutive equilibria.

To see how this works, take the *IS* curve first. Assume, as Keynes did, that investment is a negative function of the interest rate and that savings are a positive function of income, generated *ex post* by the rising income resulting from investment. The *IS* curve describes the set of equilibria at different real rates of interest and levels of income where investment will equal saving, that is, the combinations of income and interest rate at which investment generates rising income and thus savings to meet its demand.[4] With the real rate of interest *r* on the vertical axis and income or output *Y* on the horizontal axis, the *IS* curve is thus "downward sloping": as the interest rate or cost of capital declines, investment and hence output and income increase. (Inflation would obviously complicate this relationship. Because the rate of interest in question is short-term, it is assumed to equal the nominal rate of interest. This means that inflation is zero, and not a factor.)[5]

With the *LM* curve, Hicks modeled the relation between liquidity preference (which Hicks equated with demand for cash holdings) relative to the money supply.[6] It represents the possible equilibria,

---

    4  Today, *IS-LM* analysis uses the next-period real interest rate on the vertical axis, assuming that higher output in the current period will lead to lower interest rates in the next period (because higher income will lead to greater investment and thus reduce the return to capital).

    5  *Y* represents both income and output because they are assumed to be equal. If it is assumed all output finds a buyer, the nominal value of output in the economy is equal to all the spending in the economy, and that spending comprises the entire economy's income.

    6  The equation of money demand and liquidity preference is arguably another move in classical economics' attempt to excise the novelty of *The General Theory*. The motive for liquidity here loses entirely any trace of the "fetish" Keynes attributed to it and becomes perfectly amenable to absorption into the orthodox theory of the interest rate, so-called "loanable funds" (the interest rate is determined by the supply and demand for existing or "loanable" savings). Given that this became one of the principal points of controversy among economists, and Keynes's insistence that the two theories were very different, it is surprising to many that he did not squash it immediately. See, for example, Josef Steindl, "J. M. Keynes: Society and the Economist," in *Economic Papers*, London: Macmillan, 1990, 292.

for a given level of aggregate income or output, between the desire to hold cash (as opposed to less liquid assets) and the money supply as determined by monetary policy and the banking sector. Liquidity preference is assumed to be primarily a function of the main "motives" Keynes identified: "speculative" and "transactions" demand. The *LM* curve thus describes the interest rate at which the demand for and supply of money is in equilibrium for a given level of aggregate income. The *LM* curve is "upward sloping" because increasing over-all economic activity will in turn stimulate both speculative and transactions demand for liquidity, and the interest rate will adjust to produce equilibrium in the money market.

The point at which the *IS* and *LM* curves intersect is supposed to mark the output and real interest rate at a short-run macroeconomic equilibrium. Although it is rarely stated explicitly, the unit of analysis is implicitly the standard Keynesian unit of the nation-state, since the output measure is usually gross domestic product (GDP) and output is taken to equal income (meaning imports must equal exports). The equilibrium is the point at which investors are happy with the current level of investment, and wealth holders are happy with the level of liquid cash holdings. The interest rate and money supply are assumed to be exogenous, substantially a function of central bank policy. The whole apparatus depends on the assumption that the price level is fixed, because if it was not, it would throw off the relationship between the nominal and real interest rates, shift the real value of output, and render the whole exercise analytically indeterminate. (Hence this approach is sometimes called "fix price.") This is the curse of what economists call "static" analysis. *IS-LM* is also limited by its tacit assumption of a fixed state of expectations. If changed expectations only shifted one curve, then it might helpfully indicate the potential macroeconomic equilibrium in the new conditions. The *IS* curve, for example, might shift outward, meaning the point of intersection with a fixed *LM* curve would increase, indicating an increased demand for money and money supply. But in fact, if expectations change, presumably both the inducement to invest and liquidity preference would shift, making the new situation unclear, and the model much less useful for "real world" application.[7]

*IS-LM* is the ancient offence that set off the angry family feud in which New Keynesians and post-Keynesians (Krugman's "Part 1ers" and "Chapter 12ers") have so long been engaged, with the latter in particular often seeming to exist in a state of permanent outrage.[8] It would astound noneconomists to discover how much ink has been spilled arguing for and against *IS-LM* and later variations like *AS-AD* (aggregate supply-aggregate demand, designed to capture the same relation in a model that can handle changes in the price level).[9] For all the times that New Keynesians have trumpeted Keynes's supportive note to Hicks after he read the paper (and there have been more than a few), there have been even more post-Keynesian textual analyses to show he actually thought it was completely mistaken.[10]

For New Keynesians, *IS-LM* marks the introduction of rigor to Keynes's vague concepts and intuitive, largely nonformal theorizing. It is thus the basis of the celebrated "neoclassical synthesis," a combination of neoclassical equilibrium analysis and the Keynesian rejection of Say's Law, which its adherents believed represented the culmination of all previous economic knowledge. Indeed, they celebrated it as the realization of economics theory's performative dream, a "managed economy which through skillful use of fiscal and monetary policy channeled the Keynesian forces of effective demand into behaving like a neoclassical model."[11] Of course, if the economy could be made to operate like a neoclassical model, then

---

7  D. E. Moggridge, *Keynes*, London: Macmillan, 1976, 174.

8  For a thorough review from the perspective of an important proponent of *IS-LM*, see Don Patinkin, "On Different Interpretations of *The General Theory*," *Journal of Monetary Economics* 26, 1990, 205–43.

9  In *AS-AD* models, the *IS-LM* framework determines the *AD* schedule. Like the *IS* and *LM* curves, the *AD* curve is described by a set of consecutive equilibrium points determined, in this case, by *IS-LM*.

10  Tily accuses "most economists" of taking Keynes's faint praise as "sufficient grounds to ignore his [Keynes's] work entirely"; Geoff Tily, *Keynes Betrayed: The General Theory, the Rate of Interest and "Keynesian" Economics*, London: Palgrave Macmillan, 2010, 251.

11  Paul Samuelson, "A Brief Survey of Post-Keynesian Developments," in Robert Lekachman (ed.), *Keynes' General Theory: Reports of Three Decades*, New York: St. Martin's Press, 1964, 341.

neoclassical economics would be the appropriate way to analyze it. On these terms, Keynesianism experienced its own Thermidor, at least as Negri explained it: it asserts its power paradoxically, only to negate itself.

The neoclassical synthesis suggests that government enjoyed these remarkable powers of manipulation because it understands the position of both curves to be mainly a function of conventional liberal capitalist state policy: the *LM* curve shifts in and out with changes in monetary policy, and the *IS* curve shifts according to fiscal policy (tax and spending). The degree of macroeconomic control this was presumed to enable led many postwar economists to talk about "fine-tuning," as if the curves were thermostats, adjustable as deemed appropriate by the universal class piloting the enlightened state. This is the rock upon which post-World War II American Keynesianism was erected. It is the Keynesianism of a phalanx of influential US Nobel laureates like Paul Samuelson, Robert Solow, James Tobin, and Lawrence Klein, the triumphant Keynesianism that spread from the United States throughout the world; and—or so it is often claimed—the basis of the post-war "Golden Age."[12] Well into the twenty-first century, *IS-LM* remains fundamental to introductory economics education all over the globe and for many stands as the (admittedly simplified) crucible of "Keynesian economics" proper.[13]

For its detractors, however, *IS-LM* is the initial revisionist move in the counterrevolution of "irrelevant" equilibrium economics. It is mere "bastard Keynesianism," the symbol of the "betrayal" of the "economics of Keynes" by "Keynesian economics," and stands

---

12   Hyman P. Minsky, *John Maynard Keynes*, New York: Columbia University Press, 1975, 32–37; Moggridge, *Keynes*, 164–66; Walter S. Salant, "The Spread of Keynesian Doctrines and Practices in the United States," in Peter A. Hall (ed.), *The Political Power of Economic Ideas: Keynesianism Across Nations*, Princeton: Princeton University Press, 1989, 27–52; Albert O. Hirschman, "How the Keynesian Revolution Exported from the United States and Other Comments," in Peter A. Hall (ed.), *The Political Power of Economic Ideas: Keynesianism Across Nations*, Princeton: Princeton University Press, 1989, 347–60.

13   See, for example, the most popular graduate macroeconomics textbook in the English-speaking world, now in its fourth edition: David Romer, *Advanced Macroeconomics*, 4th ed., New York: McGraw-Hill, 2011, Chapter 7.

accused of undoing some of Keynes's most fundamental contribu-tions.[14] Among other sins, it reinforces a strict separation between the real (*IS*) and financial (*LM*) sides of the economy. Despite its emphasis on liquidity preference, it drops Keynes's uncertainty in favor of determinate equilibria, an error Hyman Minsky compared to "*Hamlet* without the prince."[15] It rejects Keynes's flexible analysis of the "world in which we actually live" for a return to rigid formal abstraction. Indeed, for all intents and purposes it resurrects several elements of classical economics Keynes thought he had killed off once and for all—arguably even Say's Law.[16] A recent macroeconom-ics textbook, for instance, tells its undergraduate readers that Keynesians assume that in the long run, "prices and wages fully adjust to clear input and product markets."[17] This is exactly the thinking against which Keynes wrote *The General Theory*.

It would be hard to overstate the importance of *IS-LM* in the disciplinary history of economics. It would also be hard to deny what seem to me to be the irrefutable criticism post-Keynesians have leveled at it—irrefutable, that is, *if* the framework is intended to represent *The General Theory*'s arguments.[18] That is not necessarily the case today, if it ever was; presumably this is why What Keynes Really Meant matters so little to so many contemporary Keynesian economists. In any case, I would suggest it is not worth adding any more to the *IS-LM* literature than the paragraphs above already have.

---

14    Nicholas Kaldor, "The Irrelevance of Equilibrium Economics," *Economic Journal* 82: 328, 1972, 1237–55; Joan Robinson and John Eatwell, *An Introduction to Modern Economics*, New York: McGraw-Hill, 1973, 47; Tily, *Keynes Betrayed*.

15    Minsky, *John Maynard Keynes*, 55.

16    For example, the "loanable funds" theory of the interest rate, which Keynes argued he had corrected with liquidity-preference theory; Lawrence R. Klein, *The Keynesian Revolution*, 2nd ed., New York: Macmillan, 1966, 100; John Maynard Keynes, "Alternative Theories of the Rate of Interest," *Economic Journal* 47: 186, 1937, 241–52, in *CW,* XIV, 201–15.

17    Alan Auerbach and Laurence Kotlikoff, *Macroeconomics: An Integrated Approach*, 2nd ed. Cambridge: MIT Press, 1998, 205.

18    For a systematic dismemberment of *IS-LM* and related orthodoxy, see Minsky, *John Maynard Keynes*, 19–66. Late in life, Hicks did admit that his model was more misrep-resentation than simplification; see John Hicks, "Some Questions of Time in Economics," in A. M. Tang, F. M. Westfield and J. S. Worley (eds.), *Evolution, Welfare, and Time in Economics*, Lanham, MD: Lexington Books, 1976, 140–41.

It is essential to any understanding of postwar Keynesianism, certainly. It crystallizes much of what postwar "Keynesian economics" was all about: the marriage of general equilibrium approaches with "disequilibrium" outcomes—where "disequilibrium" does *not* mean a permanent state of being in the world in which we actually exist, as a reader of *The General Theory* might reasonably assume, but any sub-full employment situation.[19] At the same time, however, *IS-LM* is something of a distraction, leading us down the rabbit hole of endless debates concerning, among other things, the Phillips curve (the inflation-unemployment "trade-off"), savings propensities (the "Cambridge savings equation" and the "Pasinetti inequality" between the proportion saved out of profits and that out of wages), or the compatibility of increasing returns with marginal productivity theory.[20]

It is true that as in its specific instantiation in the *IS-LM* framework, there is much in the neoclassical synthesis that is non- or even

19    See, for example, the enormously influential formulation of the neoclassical synthesis in Don Patinkin, *Money, Interest, and Prices: An Integration of Monetary and Value Theory*, 2nd ed., New York: Harper & Row, 1965. Patinkin writes: "Equilibrium means full employment, or equivalently, unemployment means disequilibrium . . . Keynesian economics is the economics of unemployment *dis*equilibrium" (328, 337–38). This is another version of the common orthodox claim that Keynesian economics is "Depression economics," only useful in a slump and no good for "normal" times. Of course, to call this "disequilibrium economics" makes little sense. For economists, equilibrium is a condition toward which markets "naturally" tend, and Keynes argued that the equilibria toward which they tend are often or almost always below full employment. The claim that anything less than full employment is in "disequilibrium" thus goes directly against the "economics of Keynes." It is worth noting, however, that while some working this vein of economics endorsed *IS-LM*, others rejected it. See, for example, Don Patinkin, "In Defence of IS-LM," *PSL Quarterly Review* 43: 172, 1990, 119–34; and Axel Leijonhufvud, "What Was the Matter with IS-LM," in J. P. Fitoussi (ed.), *Modern Macroeconomic Theory*, Oxford: Blackwell, 1983, 64–89.

20    Keynes always denounced as bunk the tacit orthodox or classical assumption that "the public's readiness to save is independent of the amount of its real income—a man's time preference is a psychological propensity which is irrespective of whether he is rich or poor, so that at a given rate of interest his real savings will be the same irrespective of the amount of his real income." This issue became central to the so-called Cambridge controversy of the 1960s—essentially an extended argument between Keynesians in the United States (MIT and Harvard in Cambridge, Massachusetts) and the United Kingdom (Cambridge University). Keynes, "Professor Pigou on Money Wages in Relation to Unemployment," *Economic Journal* (December 1937), in *CW,* XIV, 264.

anti-Keynesian—again, *if* "Keynesian" refers to "the economics of Keynes." But what is important here is the extent to which the Keynesian critique animates (or not) even some of the most neoclassical of "Keynesian economics." What is important, in other words, is the generalized, and generalizable, hypersensitivity to instability and social breakdown that spans the breadth of the varieties of Keynesianism, whether they are very far from *IS-LM*, as with Kalecki, or are deeply dependent on it, like the New Keynesian model of the labor market discussed in this chapter. Instead of digging further into the technical details, then, I want to use the New Keynesians' formal rapprochement with neoclassical ideas as a way of examining the operation of the Keynesian critique in the evolution of the extraordinarily influential "neoclassical synthesis."

I will, therefore, skip the standard narratives of how Keynes simultaneously conquered Britain and came to America—the home of either "bastard Keynesianism" or the neoclassical synthesis, depending upon the narrator—and the rise and fall (and resurrection) of the American post-Keynesianism of John Galbraith, Hyman Minsky, and James K. Galbraith.[21] That story has been very well told.[22] Here, rather, I want to consider the relation between my account of Keynesianism and the field of orthodox New Keynesian economics that gradually gained prominence during and after the Reagan–Thatcher era.[23]

With respect to the politics of Keynesianism as a postrevolutionary critique of liberal capitalist modernity, the enthusiastic embrace of *IS-LM* does not represent a policy return to classical and neoclassical faith in the markets. Rather, it marks the post-World War II

---

21   Robert Skidelsky, *Keynes: The Return of the Master*, London: Penguin, 2010, 101.

22   For example, Herbert Stein, *The Fiscal Revolution in America*, Chicago: University of Chicago Press, 1969; Byrd Jones, "The Role of Keynesians in Wartime Policy and Postwar Planning," *American Economic Review* 62: 1/2, 1972, 125–33; Salant, "The Spread of Keynesian Doctrines"; Roger Backhouse and Mauro Boianovsky, *Transforming Modern Macroeconomics: Exploring Disequilibrium Microfoundations, 1956–2003*, Cambridge: Cambridge University Press, 2013.

23   This is notable, for example, in the economic staff and advisors with whom Presidents Clinton and Obama surrounded themselves, many of whom are more-or-less neoclassical synthesis-variety Keynesians, for example, Alan Blinder, J. Bradford DeLong, Gregory Mankiw, Carl Shapiro, Joseph Stiglitz, and John Taylor.

consolidation of political economy along the lines Kalecki antici-pated, in the service of a "political business cycle" with a state-insured "floor" below which emergency measures are activated. In other words, even when the "Keynesian–Fordist" Golden Age of the 1950s and 1960s unraveled, the response of nominally Keynesian econom-ics should not be taken as proof—as it so often is—that the Keynesian critique had necessarily been blunted, shouted down, or forgotten and all the Keynesians forced to "go orthodox."

On the contrary, the Keynesian political economy of the post-Keynesian era was founded on the ultimate Keynesian dictum—that at a precipice, we must return to the question of necessity to "put off disaster" in the interests of civilization—which had become common sense. The pairing of punitive austerity and drunkenly accelerated affluence and inequality that has unfolded since the neoliberal victory over the "inflationary" welfare state may have produced a New Gilded Age, but the political economic foundations of its legitimation are *not* merely a repeat of the classical economics that abetted the first Gilded Age.[24] The state reaction to the financial mayhem that followed 2008 was vastly different than the initial response to the Depression of the 1930s. Radically so. The key distinction between the Golden Age and the neoliberal era that followed the supposed death of Keynesianism was not a renunciation of the dictum in favor of permanent austerity, but a change in the ideological location of the precipice. What changed was what is considered to constitute a legitimate "disaster." Remember that the infamous Volcker shock is named after a Keynesian: there is no reason Keynesianism cannot be austere at times—it is a question of legitimacy, a level of suffering the sufferers can sustainably accept.[25]

---

24    Paul Krugman, "Why We're in a New Gilded Age," *New York Review of Books*, May 8, 2014.

25    The "Volcker shock" or "coup" is the popular term for the period 1979–1982, when the United States' Federal Reserve, chaired by Paul Volcker, drove interest rates up in an all-out assault on inflation and (for all intents and purposes) organized labor and the working class in general. Inflation fell from 15 percent in 1980 to less than 3 percent in 1983. It is sometimes seen as the big-bang moment of neoliberalism in the United States. Volcker has recently been a key advisor on financial regulation to President Obama. His proposals for greater regulatory oversight and the reintroduction of some Keynes-era bank-ing rules have received significant attention. He has recently written a very complimentary

## Stiglitz-Shapiro on "Equilibrium Unemployment"

Both Joseph Stiglitz and Carl Shapiro number among the many recent White House Keynesians, and their collaboration gives us a very useful window on the politics of New Keynesian economics. In the mid-1980s (that is, after the monetarist "counter-revolution" pronounced the death of Keynes), Shapiro and Stiglitz published a paper entitled "Equilibrium Unemployment as a Worker-Discipline Device." It had an immediate impact on the thinking of economists and policy-makers on labor markets and unemployment in industrialized capitalism, and the Shapiro–Stiglitz model is now a standard component of economics education, at least in its hegemonic orthodox form.[26]

The Shapiro–Stiglitz account was formulated at the height of the Reagan–Thatcher crusade against organized labor and inflation—framed as the same war on two fronts, because among its other sins, the former supposedly caused the latter—with US unemployment rates higher than at any time since Keynes wrote *The General Theory*. It is in some ways an inverted or mirror image of Kalecki's "Political Aspects of Full Employment" in both its historical context and its reasoning (on Kalecki, see Chapter 12). At perhaps the first moment in capitalist history when workers might reasonably expect a full employment program, Kalecki argues that unemployment is a political product of capitalist opposition to such a program. In contrast, at what was undoubtedly the lowest point in the fortunes of workers and unions in much of post–World War II Euro-America (at least up until that time), Shapiro–Stiglitz come to a similar conclusion regarding the disciplinary role of unemployment but attribute

---

introduction to a 2016 edition of Keynes's *Economic Consequences of the Peace* (New York: Skyhorse).

26  Carl Shapiro and Joseph Stiglitz, "Equilibrium Unemployment as a Worker-Discipline Device," *American Economics Review* 74, 1984, 433–44; republished in Gregory Mankiw and David Romer (eds.), *New Keynesian Economics, vol. 2: Coordination Failures and Real Rigidities*, Cambridge: MIT Press, 1991, 123–42 (page numbers refer to the latter). The continued influence of the Shapiro–Stiglitz model is evident in its central place in the chapter on unemployment in Romer's *Advanced Macroeconomics* textbook (pp. 421–32); see note 14, this chapter.

persistent nontrivial positive rates of unemployment to employers' "rational" but uncoordinated decision-making in light of uncertainty. In their model, unemployment emerges endogenously, as an unintentional and apolitical force that nonetheless keeps workers in order.

Shapiro and Stiglitz are studiously faithful to liberal social science orthodoxy. For example, despite shockingly obvious and intimate connections (of which it is literally impossible they are unaware), neither Marx's reserve army nor Kalecki's seminal work is even mentioned. Closely related contemporaneous work by technically sophisticated but "heterodox" economists like Stephen Marglin is also (and, it must be assumed, purposefully) ignored.[27] The model is, however, almost a bald-faced acknowledgement of "Kaleckian reactions" to politically empowering levels of employment, but it explains them as a "natural" product of employers' rational decisions, as opposed to the exercise of bosses' power or class conflict.[28] In other words, it presents a depoliticized account of destabilizing class politics—arguably a very Keynesian thing to do.

Indeed, one of the more interesting aspects of New Keynesian economics is that it depoliticizes Keynesianism in an effort to disavow its status as political economy. It is desperate to become merely "economics" in a strict sense, rejecting the renewal of political economy that earlier economists like Joan Robinson had celebrated. In that sense, it merely accepts Keynes's macro-empirics—markets do not clear, full employment is not inevitable, the nominal can affect the real, and things can very easily go from bad to worse—but justifies this acceptance with the same claims about human nature and collective well-being that found the classical and neoclassical schools. This is merely another way of performing the separation of politics and the economy, which is always based, as Keynes at least knew, on a kind of tacitly agreed-upon liberal mythology—because everyone

---

27   Stephen Marglin, *Growth, Distribution, and Prices*, Cambridge: Harvard University Press, 1984.

28   Wolfgang Streeck, "The Crises of Democratic Capitalism," *New Left Review* II: 71, 2011, 9.

knows, of course, there is no modern "economics" that is not always also political economy. Yet New Keynesian economics brings a distinctive twist to the Keynesian critique, because it often poses as merely a "disequilibrium" variation on a Walrasian theme. It assumes the posture of complete agnosticism concerning the liberal politics that founds it (a quality it shares with other neoclassical schools of thought), but it is nonetheless caught up entirely in the nervous legitimation of the social order. One would never describe orthodox royalty like Milton Friedman or Robert Lucas as involved in a nervous legitimation of the social order; they are caught up in an indignant denunciation of anyone who thinks the social order is not "natural," so its legitimacy never crosses their minds.

In this and several other dimensions, Shapiro–Stiglitz is an almost perfect example of the modern New Keynesian approach, deriving so-called "Keynesian" results from neoclassical "microfoundations." It is also suffused with the same attitude to the working class that saturates modern economic analysis: since political economy is by definition an elite knowledge and practice, workers are always "them." The workers Shapiro–Stiglitz have in mind—like Keynes and Kalecki—have, in modern economic terminology, "lower job-switching costs": they are employed "in lower paid, lower skilled, blue-collar occupations" in which they must always be cajoled or harried to perform work that is purely a disutility.[29] Presumably this is not the case for (political) economists themselves, who are exempt from the pressures associated with workers' "work"—they don't need to be supervised, and they do not need to be disciplined in the same way. Workers, on the other hand, are presumed to be motivated by simple utilitarian pain–pleasure stimuli. They "dislike putting forth effort but enjoy consuming goods"; they are all opportunistic, selfish, and lazy.[30] When they do not act according to this rational "psychology," they are said to have (at best) "predictably irrational" or even "mistaken" utility curves.[31]

---

29    Shapiro and Stiglitz, "Equilibrium Unemployment," 138–39.
30    Ibid., 126.
31    Dan Ariely, *Predictably Irrational: The Hidden Forces That Shape Our Decisions,*

We must remember that this is how Keynes and Kalecki talk about workers as well. Neither of them proposes a more robust or socially complex conception of workers' interests—in both cases rational selfish ends, as conceived by orthodox economics, drives the models and theories.[32] Like Shapiro–Stiglitz, for Keynes and Kalecki there is no utility in labor outside its pecuniary reward; it is categorically a "disutility." *The General Theory* rejects the second classical postulate (the equality of the utility of wages and the marginal disutility of employment) not because the kind of work workers do might be something other than a pure disutility, but because the equality it asserts does not in fact hold—labor is certainly always a disutility, just not necessarily to a degree that equals the utility of the wage. Kalecki, while certainly sensitive to the class dynamics of the struggle for full employment, and thus to the political causes of unemployment, was still more a Keynesian than a Marxist. Although operationalized in the "political" sphere, his theory of unemployment is just as mechanical an outcome of capitalist civil society as it is for Hegel, Keynes, and Shapiro–Stiglitz. Because the New Keynesians come to this conclusion in a different

---

New York: Harper Collins, 2008; Anthony Atkinson and Joseph Stiglitz, *Lectures on Public Economics*, Princeton: Princeton University Press, 2015, xiv.

32    As Samuel Bowles points out in an influential 1985 paper, published a year after Shapiro–Stiglitz, models like theirs "provide a microeconomic foundation consistent with Kalecki's suggestion that sustained full employment and the long-run survival of capitalist enterprise may be inconsistent"; see "The Production Process in a Competitive Economy: Walrasian, Neo-Hobbesian, and Marxian Models," *American Economic Review* 75: 1, 1985, 26. Bowles goes on to make the crucial point that a Marxian approach would require a radically different "labour extraction function" than the "Neo-Hobbesian" models with which he groups Shapiro–Stiglitz. For the Marxist, it is not labor per se that is a strict disutility, but labor in the social relations specific to capitalism. In other words, in any given labor process, the relative degree to which workers will commit to working and not shirking is not merely exogenously given by human nature, as Shapiro–Stiglitz and Kalecki and Keynes assume, but is endogenous to the production process and the social relations of production more broadly: "A more democratic structure of decision making and a more egalitarian distribution of the firm's net revenues, for example, might both reduce the incentive to pursue nonwork activities and heighten the cost of so doing by enlisting fellow workers as more effective enforcers of the pace of work, or more willing cooperators with the surveillance system" (p. 33). Kalecki is not a Marxian on these grounds, but rather marks one end of the Keynesian spectrum (see Chapter 12).

manner, then, it is worth looking at their analysis in a little detail, for there are some crucial dynamics that might be missed by a superficial scan.

### "Microfoundations" for Keynesian Macroeconomics: The Economics of Information

The Shapiro–Stiglitz argument is built on the conceptual infrastructure of the "economics of information," a subfield to which Stiglitz is a key contributor. An extension of a long tradition in institutional economics, the economics of information studies the effects of stocks and flows of information on market prices, institutional structures, regulatory design, and so forth.[33] It characterizes exchange as a contractual relation between "principals" and "agents" to exchange goods, services, information, or money. Principal-agent relations are commonly subject to so-called "information asymmetry," which engenders ubiquitous problems for principals, because in general they pay money—the quality and accepted value of which is virtually guaranteed—to agents for assets the quality and value or even delivery of which is much less certain. In other words, without direct supervision, the "agent" (the employee, for example) enjoys an information advantage over the "principal" (the employer, say). The work of Stiglitz (and others) argues that asymmetrical information virtually always impinges upon market relations: the employee, for example, has better information about the quality of production work than the employer; the borrower knows more about his or her capacity to repay than the lender; the firm knows more about its own behavior than the regulator.

If this is so (it does seem a reasonable description of capitalist markets), then in an economic theory in which agency is assumed

---

33  Stiglitz summarizes the "fundamental insight of information economics" as follows: it views "the neoclassical model as one that makes a particular assumption: that prices affect only quantities, and that prices carry no information which might affect incentives or sorting"; Joseph Stiglitz, "Post Walrasian and Post Marxian Economics," *Journal of Economic Perspectives* 7: 1, 1993, 109.

to be rational in the optimizing, *homo economicus* sense, actors can be expected to do their "boundedly-rational," budget-constrained best to overcome these information problems—or "information impactedness," as Oliver Williamson unfortunately labeled it—so as to be able to make informed decisions.[34] As economists understand it, information asymmetry explains a lot of otherwise inexplicably costly "irrational" and "inefficient" behavior on the part of principals and agents: it is the reason tenants are willing to pay damage deposits to their landlords, prospective employers ask job applicants for references, and regulators "stress-test" banks' capital cushions. It is the reason consumers do business with firms certified as "fair-trade" or "green" and potential investors examine a company's books. Contracts, especially those pertaining to complex exchange and regulatory relations, are of particular interest to information economists, because principals will attempt to structure contracts so as to overcome information asymmetry as much as possible: so-called "incomplete" contracting, the increasingly elaborate, conditional, and contingent character of the contracts that underwrite the global economy, has become a subspecialty all its own.[35]

Information economics suggests that information problems are a significant source of "Keynesian" rigidities and "stickiness" in the existing economy. For example, contracts fix wages and prices that "should" be flexible, or bind counterparties in ways that prevent them from seeking the lowest cost alternative for the duration of the contract. Alternatively, the long-term nature of many credit or supply relationships means that the expectation of future exchanges will lead to discriminatory (non-Walrasian) pricing. In other words, if the

---

34    Oliver Williamson, *Markets and Hierarchies: Analysis and Antitrust Implications*, New York: Free Press, 1975, 31.

35    The contract literature comes out of the seminal work on the theory of the firm, in particular Ronald Coase, "The Nature of the Firm," *Economica* 4: 16, 1937, 386–405, that eventually informed the so-called New Institutional Economics. For a rather technical introduction, see Bernard Salanié, *The Economics of Contracts: A Primer*, Cambridge: MIT Press, 1997. For a broad survey of recent work, see Philippe Aghion and Richard Holden, "Incomplete Contracts and the Theory of the Firm: What Have We Learned Over the Past 25 Years?" *Journal of Economic Perspectives* 25: 2, 2011, 181–97.

expected benefits derived from costs associated with reducing information problems outweigh the expected costs of ignorance, the principal will often be willing to pay what orthodox economists would consider above-market or inefficient prices. This will produce "Keynesian" outcomes by definition: sub-full resource employment in nonclearing markets.

There are three paradigmatic information problems for the discipline of economics: insurance, regulation, and the worker–employer relation.[36] The goal of Shapiro–Stiglitz's New Keynesian model is to inquire into the effects of the last on aggregate unemployment. Principal-agent problems are understood to be inherent to the wage relation and capitalist labor markets. If one assumes—like Keynes, Kalecki, and even radical political economy usually do—that workers' labor is a pure disutility for which the wage is compensation, then one will reasonably assume that if there is no penalty for "shirking," every worker will shirk as much and as often as he or she can.[37] By this reasoning, depending upon bosses' judgments of the costs of monitoring and ensuring worker effort relative to the costs of shirking, employers will undertake to "observe" or "monitor" the workforce. This has a dual benefit for the boss: first, it gives the firm better information regarding workers' individual and collective performance; second, if workers are aware of the monitoring system, they can be expected, like those

---

36 The respective literatures are usually traced to (in the case of regulation) Ronald Coase, "The Problem of Social Cost," *Journal of Law and Economics* 3, 1960, 1–43; (in the case of the employment contract) Armen Alchian and Harold Demsetz, "Production, Information Costs and Economic Organization," *American Economic Review* 62: 5, 1972, 777–95; and (in the case of insurance) Michael Rothschild and Joseph Stiglitz, "Equilibrium in Competitive Insurance Markets: An Essay on the Economics of Imperfect Information," *Quarterly Journal of Economics* 90, 1976, 629–49. For detailed overviews of this approach to political economy, see Jean-Jacques Laffont and Jean Tirole, *A Theory of Incentives in Procurement and Regulation*, Cambridge: MIT Press, 1993; Allan Drazen, *Political Economy and Macroeconomics*, Princeton: Princeton University Press, 2000; and Torsten Persson and Guido Tabellini, *Political Economics: Explaining Economic Policy*, Cambridge: MIT Press, 2000.

37 As noted earlier, although it is not always flagged explicitly, the premise of much radical political economy is that workers' labor *in a capitalist mode of production* is a pure disutility. It could be otherwise.

in Bentham's panopticon, to "behave" for fear of being identified as shirkers and paying the price. This, for example, would be an economist's explanation for the devices in fast-food restaurants that count off and record, in plain view, the seconds between customers' orders and service. The neo-Taylorist stopwatch is designed to ensure that employers have both disciplined employees and accurate data on work speeds.

These measures obviously assume there is a penalty to being caught shirking, which in political economy is always understood to involve a reduction in income: lower wages, fines, or—worst of all—"the sack." This was the basis of Kalecki's argument: if the labor market is sufficiently "tight," that is, near enough to full employment conditions, then workers are unlikely to fear being fired, since other jobs are readily available. According to Kalecki, capital's opposition to Keynesian full-employment policies is due, therefore, to the fact that they might actually work, and if they did, the hierarchy implicit in the wage relation would be entirely upended. For capital, job scarcity is absolutely essential to the institutional function of capitalist labor markets and production processes. They *require* some level of involuntary unemployment (even if the unemployed are then disingenuously blamed for their joblessness).

Shapiro–Stiglitz come at the problem from a different direction—from inside the labor market, as it were—to identify the ways in which classical and neoclassical behavior in "real" markets produces Keynesian outcomes. They claim to explain the "incentive role of unemployment."[38] Rather than positing a short-run politically determined structural equilibrium unemployment level, à la Kalecki, they argue that the problem lies in what might be called a microeconomic Kaleckian dynamic immanent to agents' rational behavior: in conditions of full employment, workers will always choose to shirk.[39] Consequently, "the inability of employers to costlessly observe workers' on-the-job effort" leads to a situation in which the "equilibrium

---

38   Shapiro and Stiglitz, "Equilibrium Unemployment," 126.
39   Kalecki too assumes that without fear of being fired, workers will become unruly, a form of shirking.

unemployment rate must be sufficiently large that it pays workers to work rather than to take the risk of being caught shirking."[40] This disciplinary "equilibrium" rate of unemployment is deemed "natural." In other words, it is endogenous to the labor market; state intervention in the form of unemployment benefits only exacerbates the problem, since it increases the wages with which employers must compete to overcome the incentive to shirk. They are forced, therefore, to pay "unnatural," higher-than-equilibrium wages. According to classical and neoclassical theories, the prevalence of these "efficiency wages" prevents the labor market from clearing, which is to say it prevents Say's Law from operating when it "ought" to come to the rescue by lowering wages until everyone who wants a job is employed.

Thus, on one level, Shapiro–Stiglitz merely reinforce liberal free-market common sense. It would seem that all would be well in a Walrasian world if only information asymmetry did not generate a "rational" choice to pay wage "premia" (nonequilibrium wages). Here we have a "market imperfection": microeconomically properly behaved classical and neoclassical actors producing improper macro outcomes. This is exactly what economists mean when they talk about providing "microfoundations": trying to find a way to show how rational self-interested optimizing behavior can produce inefficient markets. Shapiro–Stiglitz are, however, very careful to distance themselves from advocates of *laissez-faire* who would, presumably, insist that barring unwarranted distortions like workers' unreliability or moral turpitude, these problems would not arise. Instead, here unemployment is decidedly involuntary and "not of the standard search-theory type." In other words, in accordance with Keynes's definition of involuntary unemployment, Shapiro–Stiglitz assume there are no vacancies and that workers would be willing to work at less than market wages. If so, the market equilibrium produced by the model is not Pareto optimal, the standard gauge of free-market economic efficiency. There are "interventions in the market that would make everyone better off";

---

40   Shapiro and Stiglitz, "Equilibrium Unemployment," 123.

indeed, it is even possible that under certain circumstances wage subsidies are "desirable."[41]

Regardless of the route by which it is reached, this is a very Keynesian conclusion. Even when they have the capacity to enjoy full employment, modern communities must socially produce sufficient scarcity to make yield possible—in this case, to keep wages low enough, and productivity high enough, to generate profits.[42] If, relative to Kalecki's model, capital in this account does not play the bad-guy role and employers' self-interest expresses itself through more strictly "atomistic" rational behavior, the fundamental parallels between the two approaches to unemployment are not diminished. In both cases, classes and individuals are expected to behave in a manner consistent with their assumed self-interest, and in both cases the outcome is nontrivial: sustained or permanent involuntary unemployment, that is, suboptimal outcomes in the labor market caused by a scarcity ("job rationing") that is nothing if not immanent to the modern economy.


## Shirking Workers and the "Natural" Rate of Unemployment

To see how this works with Shapiro–Stiglitz, let's take a brief look at the model itself. Following Keynes by taking wages as a given—workers are "price-takers," unable to influence their wage—they assume the only choice a worker makes is effort level, selected to maximize his or her discounted utility stream. A "no-shirking condition" (NSC) exists at the wage level at which the "expected lifetime utility" of shirking is less than that for not shirking. Clearly, a

---

41   Ibid., 124. A Pareto optimal distributional arrangement is one in which any change will make at least one party worse off. At the risk of stating the obvious, neither social or collective value nor concern for the inequality of allocation is factored into this calculus. If there is $1 million to be distributed between two parties, a situation in which one has every one of those million dollars and the other has none is Pareto optimal. Any change will make one party less well-off. This is a small part of why Sen echoes Arrow in his article, "The Impossibility of a Paretian Liberal," *Journal of Political Economy* 78: 1, 1970, 152–57.

42   Nicholas Xenos, "Liberalism and the Postulate of Scarcity," *Political Theory* 15: 2, 1987, 225–43.

Kaleckian world in which workers have no fear of the sack is a world in which a no-shirking condition cannot hold.[43] But—and in this they put the emphasis on the *neoclassical* in the neoclassical synthesis—Stiglitz–Shapiro accept a variation on Milton Friedman's permanent income hypothesis in their focus on the long-run calculus implicit in the expected *lifetime* utility of shirking or not shirking. Workers in the model make decisions in the present in light of their expected income across their entire lives. Which is to say, just as many said of *IS-LM*, uncertainty is dismissed by fiat. Decisions in the present reflect a calculated, rational life plan regarding employment and "leisure," income and utility.[44]

Many will read this and have a justifiable urge to take this assumption as further proof of how "unrealistic" mainstream economics is. It is worth withholding that judgment, however, to step back from this or that assumption and look at the whole. If we accept this framing for a moment, then there will be a "critical wage," a threshold level of compensation at which workers will not shirk. The critical wage will be a positive function of required effort, the expected utility of unemployment, the rate of interest (because short-run gains from shirking are more heavily weighted), and the quit rate (because if you are quitting anyway, you will be more likely to shirk); it will be a negative function of the probability of being caught shirking. Obviously, taking the rest at face value, a high likelihood that shirking will be observed reduces the need to pay higher "efficiency" wages. Shirking is thus ultimately a negative function of the wage—other things can determine its level, but the higher the wage, the less the shirking.[45]

Similarly, the natural or equilibrium rate of unemployment is a positive function of the critical wage threshold. Wages will be relatively higher under the following conditions: there are high

---

43   Shapiro and Stiglitz, "Equilibrium Unemployment," 127–28.

44   Ibid., 127: "The key market variable that determines individual firm behavior is $V_u$, the expected lifetime utility of an unemployed worker."

45   Ibid., 130. The "critical wage" is defined by $\hat{w} \geq \bar{w} + e + \frac{e(a+b+r)}{q}$; where the critical wage $\hat{w}$ will be greater the higher the unemployment benefit, $\bar{w}$, the larger the required effort $e$, the higher the job acquisition rate $a$, the higher the quit rate $b$, the higher the interest rate $r$, and the smaller the detection probability $q$.

turnover rates (workers do not expect to be at the job for long);
workers have high discount rates (they value shirking now more
than they fear future penalties); there are more possibilities for
workers to opportunistically limit their effort (performance is
difficult to observe); or there are high costs to the employer associated with shirking (goods are perishable, say, or equipment is
very fragile or expensive to operate). The higher the critical wage,
say Shapiro–Stiglitz, the higher will be equilibrium
unemployment:

> If wages are very high, workers will value their jobs for two reasons:
> (a) the high wages themselves and (b) the correspondingly low
> level of employment (due to low demand for labour at high wages),
> which implies long spells of unemployment in the event of losing
> one's job. In such a situation employers will find they can reduce
> wages without tempting workers to shirk. Conversely, if the wage
> is quite low, workers will be tempted to shirk for two reasons: (a)
> low wages imply that working is only moderately preferred to
> unemployment, and (b) high employment levels (at low wages
> there is a large demand for labor) imply unemployment spells due
> to being fired will be brief. In such a situation, firms will raise their
> wages to satisfy the NSC.[46]

In conditions of Kaleckian full employment, no critical wage
could be set high enough to reach the threshold. Which means, *"no
shirking is inconsistent with full employment."*[47] If we assume that no
firm enjoys market power to set the wage, then all firms have to offer
the critical wage at a minimum, and labor market equilibrium will
be determined by the intersection of aggregate labor demand with
the aggregate no-shirking condition—not with the "natural" labor
supply curve.

Which is to say that the aggregate NSC is an "effective" labor
supply schedule, precisely the purpose of *The General Theory's*

---

46    Ibid., 129.
47    Ibid., 131.

"employment function."[48] The employment function describes the volume of employment corresponding to a given level of expected effective demand. The NSC is the level of the wage and employment at which firms can realize their labor demand with nonshirking workers. Aside from their technical-functional similarities in the economic theory of the labor market, there are therefore crucial over-laps in the politics that underwrite the labor supply claims of *The General Theory* and Shapiro–Stiglitz. To begin, both maintain the classical and neoclassical assumption of a passive workforce that reacts mechanically to capital's requirements; because workers drop in or out of the labor market in response to the wages on offer, the aggregate labor supply curve is a schedule determined, somewhat paradoxically, not by workers but by capital. The biggest difference is perhaps that for Shapiro–Stiglitz, as for Kalecki, its character is deter-mined by capital according to workers' characteristics *qua* factor of production. This is characteristic of New Keynesian analysis, which builds from mainstream "microfoundations," and, because it sees the world from the perspective of capital, understands labor solely as a cost, and not as a potential consumer. For Keynes, because he oper-ates without regard to firm-level (microeconomic) decisions, the NSC is determined in a more Weberian light, with regard to work-ers' (aggregate) characteristics *qua* consumers.[49]

The NSC also describes very Keynesian dynamics in that it imposes a wage level on the economy that workers cannot change, even if they wished to (see Chapter 10). So when demand for labor is reduced (because the critical wage is too high or rises), the NSC means "wages cannot fall enough to compensate for the decreased labor demand."[50] As Keynes says, labor can refuse to work for a wage less than the marginal disutility of labor, but it cannot demand to work for the wage that is associated with a particular level of employ-ment (in other words, it cannot demand a wage that is no greater

---

48   Keynes, *CW,* VII, 280–81; see the summary of Chapter 20 in the *Companion.*

49   Keynes claims that the employment function can "relate the amount of effective demand, measured in terms of the wage-unit, directly to a given firm," but it seems to me impossible to imagine how it might do so; *CW,* VII, 280.

50   Shapiro and Stiglitz, "Equilibrium Unemployment," 133.

than the marginal disutility of employment and thereby guarantee full employment in a classical world).[51] Real wages can only get reduced gradually—likely by inflation. This determines an "unemployment equilibrium," because from "the firm's point of view, there is no point in raising wages, since workers are providing effort and the firm can get all the labor it wants" at the going wage. "Lowering wages, on the other hand, would induce shirking and be a losing idea. From the worker's point of view, *unemployment is involuntary*"—and from Keynes's point of view too: the unemployed would gladly work at the going rate or lower "but cannot make a credible promise not to shirk at such wages."[52]

The Shapiro–Stiglitz framework thus effectively "naturalizes" or "rationalizes" unemployment, given the behavior of workers and the reactions of firms thereto. The very nature of work as pure disutility (in capitalism, we should add, even if Keynes and Shapiro–Stiglitz would not think to) "naturally" elicits behavior (shirking) that "rationally" generates unemployment. Keynes agrees (as does Hegel, hence the role of the *Korporation* in overcoming this emptiness and returning honor to the laborer). Indeed, nowhere does *The General Theory* suggest that workers are not a fundamental cause of unemployment—the proposition that high rates of employment require a slow, even hidden, ratcheting downward of real wages is all the proof we need of his tacit position. Instead, the difference between all these varieties of Keynesianism on one side, and liberal orthodoxy on the other, is that while both accept that workers are the *cause* of their own unemployment, Keynesians argue that they are not *responsible* for it.

This is because both the NSC and Keynes's employment function are intended as more "realistic" substitutes for the orthodox labor supply curve—and, to risk stating the obvious, "labor supply" is economics' catch-all description of workers' labor market behavior given the political and material conditions of life, cultural norms and constraints and expectations, and so forth. The Stiglitz–Shapiro

---

51    Keynes, *CW*, VII, 291.
52    Shapiro and Stiglitz, "Equilibrium Unemployment," 131 (emphasis added).

model reduces (however reluctantly) all of these factors to one—the disutility-income trade-off. But in the world in which we actually live, even this single "rational" trade-off (the tipping point of which is marked by the "critical wage") is a function of *Sittlichkeit*: life as it is lived in a real place and time, bound up in the interplay of stasis and change.[53] In other words, as Keynes, in his own way, makes as abundantly clear as Hegel, the necessarily abstracted activity of the individual worker-shirker in liberal capitalist civil society, shorn as it is of *Sitten*, leads inexorably to a positive aggregate level of involuntary unemployment. In this upside-down but very real world, the worker is a product of the model; the subject becomes predicate, the predicate becomes subject.

In contrast, for the mainstream market-clearing school, workers are both the *cause of* and *responsible for* their unemployment. They produce their own employment conditions, since in aggregate, unemployment results from individuals' decisions to remain unemployed because their so-called "reserve wage" is too high, insofar as the minimum compensation they will accept for the disutility of work is unreasonable. The constraints on the economy in both the Keynesian and mainstream analyses are worker imposed, but for Keynesians they are imposed involuntarily, even though it is workers' own fault. Consequently, even though it is "natural," the "*natural unemployment rate is too high.*"[54]

The corollary of this reasoning, it would seem, is that if firms could monitor costlessly and perfectly, we would overcome perhaps the principal force behind modern unemployment. This would also suggest (as Kalecki would lead us to believe) that the greater workers' autonomy in the workplace, the higher the rate of unemployment. Better monitoring would help workers (presumably as a class) by lowering the critical wage and improving labor market participation. By this logic, if all firms were McDonald's, there would be a lot more

---

53  The qualitative shift in a quantity like the wage is a function of what I have elsewhere called the "politics of measure"; see Geoff Mann, *Our Daily Bread: Wages, Workers and the Political Economy of the American West*, Chapel Hill: University of North Carolina Press, 26–28.

54  Shapiro and Stiglitz, "Equilibrium Unemployment," 134.

jobs. If there were no unemployment benefits, perfect and costless monitoring, significant penalties associated with job loss, and no discounting of the future on workers' part, then unemployment would fall as the critical wage diminished to the level (which Shapiro–Stiglitz designate $e$) at which the second classical postulate is satisfied, "the utility of the wages when a given volume of labor is employed is equal to the marginal disutility of that amount of employment."[55] Keynes, we know, rejected the second postulate because, he said, the social dynamics of modern liberal civil society prevent it from being realized. Shapiro–Stiglitz echo this judgment, if for different reasons.

It might seem that Shapiro–Stiglitz are proving Keynesians' libertarian trolls correct, in that Keynesian policies imply some degree of state authoritarianism, in this case the productivity and employment benefits of Big Brother-like surveillance. They are not. Instead, they consider the changes in the model's conclusions given different distributional regimes. They point out that if workers and owners were the same people, then Pareto optimality would demand the removal of all unemployment benefits, and the taxation of profits to subsidize wages; all income would take the wage form, and there would be a de facto tax on being unemployed.

But in contemporary capitalism workers and owners are almost never the same people. This means that the current distributional and property relations lead to the fundamental Keynesian conclusion: barring a fascist or authoritarian arrangement, capitalism must have unemployment. It must be (in Keynes's words) sufficiently and consistently impoverishing: "by reducing employment, workers are induced not to shirk. This enables society to save resources on monitoring (supervision)." In modern societies, "these gains more than offset the losses from the reduced employment."[56]

This is not to say that there are no important differences between this analysis and that of Keynes himself. The very fact that a "simplified general-equilibrium model" underwrites Shapiro–Stiglitz is

55   Keynes, *CW,* VII, 5.
56   Shapiro and Stiglitz, "Equilibrium Unemployment," 135.

reminder enough. Chief among these differences, perhaps, is the implicit acceptance of the microeconomic utilitarian or "welfare" foundations of orthodox economics, which posit "society" as a collective that benefits from aggregate income increases in a way that totally ignores internal inequalities. Even with the minor constraint provided by Pareto optimality, this assessment of social welfare is indefensible on Keynesian terms, and Keynes himself always railed against its "Benthamite calculus."[57] It celebrates unreservedly what Losurdo calls the "passive citizenship" of the masses that enables liberalism's privileged "community of the free": if their unemployment "enables society to save resources" that "more than offset [their] losses," then workers contribute to aggregate social welfare but are excluded from the "community" that enjoys it. So workers, figuratively incorporated into society for the purposes of justifying its generosity, individually and as a class pay the price of their de facto exclusion. These are the welfare implications of "the incentive role of unemployment," at least for everyone but the unemployed themselves.[58]

This would seem to be a perfect example of the "travesty" of which *IS-LM* stands accused by post-Keynesians: arriving at nominally "Keynesian" conclusions through a tautological mixture of classical means and assumed "rigidities," so that "the distinctive and revolutionary features of Keynesian theory vanish and dissolve into thin air."[59] The problem, as Shapiro–Stiglitz formulate it, does not begin as Keynes argued, that is, from the fact that Say's Law does not hold, and thus investment does not provide an economic context in which full employment is possible. The problem as they see it, rather, is in the microeconomics of the labor contract: "firms are assumed (quite reasonably, in our view) not to be able to monitor the activities of their employees costlessly and perfectly."[60] The logical conclusion

---

57   Ibid., 125; John Maynard Keynes, "The General Theory of Employment," *Quarterly Journal of Economics* 51: 2, 1937, 213; Keynes, *CW*, VII, 353.

58   Domenico Losurdo, *Liberalism: A Counter-History*, trans. G. Elliott, London: Verso, 2011, 184–88; Shapiro and Stiglitz, "Equilibrium Unemployment," 126.

59   Steindl, "J. M. Keynes," 291.

60   Shapiro and Stiglitz, "Equilibrium Unemployment," 131.

would seem to be that increasing what we might call the effective rate of exploitation would reduce unemployment. This sounds an awful lot like what a very strict "neoclassical" or orthodox economics would "discover."

And yet, let us think through this apparent irreconcilability for a moment. If we grant Shapiro–Stiglitz their argument, then the driver of unemployment is not a lack of coordinated capitalist investment and proper management of the "fetish of liquidity." The problem is the power relations of the workplace: despite themselves, workers are simultaneously *too* powerful and not powerful enough. The very fact that they always enjoy some capacity to shirk means that even if they *never would* shirk, they cannot organize their labor supply individually or as a class so as to clear the labor market and realize full employment. They are the *cause* of, but not *responsible* for, their unemployment. Consequently, while the state is nowhere invoked explicitly—as is true of much of New Keynesian economics—there is a spectral Arrovian collective "social choice" agent that underwrites the argument, an agent that has the capacity to do more than make things worse by legislating mandatory minimum unemployment benefits and raising the "critical wage." Because the (Pareto) "optimality" of the equilibrium "depends upon the distribution of wealth," the "standard separation between efficiency and income distribution does not carry over to this model."[61] It does not necessarily all work

---

61    Shapiro and Stiglitz, "Equilibrium Unemployment," 135. In the post–World War II Keynesian heydays, it was accepted that the state's efforts to optimize efficiency—through the provision of the (Pareto optimal) amount of public goods—will be unaffected by income redistribution, if it takes place through lump-sum taxes and transfers. Both allocation (efficiency) and distribution are assumed to proceed on Keynesian terms, that is, respective state institutions allocate "on the assumption of full employment of resources and that the proper distribution of income has been secured," and distribute assuming "a full-employment income is available for distribution and that the satisfaction of public wants is taken care of." The claim was famously formulated by Richard Musgrave, *The Theory of Public Finance: A Study in Public Economy*, New York: McGraw-Hill, 1959, Chapter 1. Musgrave understood that in practice, this separation was often unlikely to work, as later argued in Arthur Okun, *Equality and Efficiency: The Big Trade-Off*, Washington, DC: Brookings Institution, 1975; see Richard Musgrave, "U. S. Fiscal Policy, Keynes, and Keynesian Economics," *Journal of Post–Keynesian Economics* 10: 2, 1987–88, 171–72. Both Musgrave (who coined the term "macroeconomics") and Okun were influential Keynesian economists.

out in the end. The state—or something a lot like it, acting in the "social interest"—has a key role to play.

The main way in which it can play that role is through the "unemployment mechanism"—ensuring adequate unemployment, which is not necessarily a non-Keynesian conclusion.[62] As Shapiro–Stiglitz put it, if "it is costly to monitor individuals, competitive equilibrium will be characterized by unemployment," *but* the resulting "*'natural'* unemployment rate is too high*."[63] Which is to say—against the mainstream account—that the so-called "natural" rate of unemployment enjoys no legitimacy just because it is "natural." There is therefore a role for the agent of social welfare, the state, the sole agent that can coordinate the organization of legitimation ensuring a sustainable level of suffering and thus the sustainability of the social order. Moreover, the very idea that because liberal capitalism is *always* characterized by unemployment, political economy's main task is to determine whether the level of unemployment is unjustifiable ("too high"), exposes the politics-economy separation naturalized by liberalism as the social artifact it always is.

These are characteristics of the Keynesian critique of poverty and unemployment we can trace back two centuries. The "optimality" of the social arrangement and the standards by which it might be assessed are crucial here. We might legitimately question the Keynesian-ness of a diagnosis that suggests that the state's role is merely to achieve allocative Pareto efficiency under conditions in which nature does not produce it on its own. If Stiglitz–Shapiro take Pareto optimality as legitimate by definition, then the Keynesian critique of liberal common sense is arguably pretty trivial.

But they do not. Allocative efficiency is not self-justifying. Nor, I would argue, do they ultimately posit "optimality" as merely a problem of allocation alone. What is at issue here is in fact the concern at the core of Keynesianism and political economy as such: in any given "modern community," what is the appropriate organization of legitimation? Nature be damned; what liberal governmentality must

---

62   Shapiro and Stiglitz, "Equilibrium Unemployment," 138.
63   Ibid., 139.

determine is the acceptable level of unemployment, poverty, and inequality and how that level can be made acceptable. Or, alternatively, what state responses can justify an otherwise unjustifiable level of unemployment? How to ensure that the jobless live willingly with their joblessness?

These questions are merely muted twentieth-century variations of those the bourgeois members of the Convention were forced to ask themselves when confronted with Robespierre's demand for an honorable poverty: "Are we not witness," he asked, to conditions in which "those who have been provided with immense wealth are themselves a product of needs as great as their riches, in which their luxury and prodigality has created *poverty in the midst of plenty* [*rendu pauvres au sein de l'abondance*]?"[64] Shapiro and Stiglitz can only diagnose the problem and suggest some administrative medicine; they can neither answer these questions—political economy never can—nor can they avoid them, for ultimately, in Hegel's "modern society" or Keynes's "modern community," these questions are all that really matter.

---

64   Maximilien Robespierre, June 16, 1790, *Oeuvres Complètes,* vol. VI, Paris: Presses Universitaires de France, 1910, 410 (emphasis added).

# CHAPTER 14

# From Unemployment to Inequality in the Twenty-First Century

W̶hen Shapiro and Stiglitz's paper appeared in 1984, official unemployment hovered around 7.5 percent in the United States, 12 percent in the United Kingdom, just over 8.5 percent in France and Germany, and 11.5 percent in Canada. Three decades later, the situation was almost as bad: just over 7 percent in the United States and the United Kingdom, 10 percent in France, 7 percent in Germany, and 7 percent in Canada.[1] There had been a great deal of up-and-down in the meantime, but the problem of joblessness had clearly not diminished. And yet, while in 1984 unemployment was the main discursive category through which the experience of poverty was discussed in the affluent industrial nations of western Europe and North America, thirty years later things had changed. Unemployment certainly remains a key concern, but with the financial crisis following 2008, the mainstream object of political economic critique has shifted from unemployment to "inequality"—just as we can now see retrospectively that by Keynes's day unemployment had replaced poverty as the problem of the poor.

The reasons for this discursive transformation are not straightforward and merit their own detailed investigation. Surely it has several

---

1   Data from the Economic Research Division of the St. Louis Federal Reserve, available at research.stlouisfed.org.

related causes: the fallout of the crisis and the public exposure of finance capital's predations; the extraordinary acceleration of income and wealth inequality across liberal democracies; the awakened popular awareness of a global super-elite that live in unimagined luxury alongside the relative stagnation and even decline of real wages and incomes for most people.

But a cynic might suggest that many of these problems existed in almost as dire a state for many years prior, even as far back as 1984. The hegemony of "inequality," that cynic might say, is not due to a different understanding of the experience of poverty—especially absolute poverty—but is, rather, a product of the fact that these more recent developments have opened up a gap in the upper half of the income distribution. The poor, whether working or unemployed, remain poor in the sense that they do not have enough to live secure, dignified, healthy, joyful lives in a "modern community." But the top decile is now increasingly better off (at least in the material sense) than the second, third, and fourth, and the top percentile or one-tenth of a percentile is now absurdly rich compared to everyone else in the world. If this is in fact a driver of the categorical shift, then it is an ideological product of the very supercapitalist dynamics it condemns: "inequality" is the poverty of the bourgeoisie, the "deprivation and want" of the wealthy.

Without diminishing the actuality (in Hegel's sense) of the problem of inequality, I would suggest that the cynic is on to something, and an equally cynical assessment of the degree to which "inequality" has become a *cause célèbre*, especially among Keynesians, would confirm it. From popular films like *Inside Job* and Robert Reich's *Inequality for All* to bestsellers like *The Spirit Level* and Stiglitz's *The Price of Inequality*, inequality is the talk of the town among governing elites and the "universal class."[2] If

2  *Inside Job* (2011), dir. Charles Ferguson; *Inequality for All* (2013), dir. Jacob Kornbluth; Richard Wilkinson and Kate Pickett, *The Spirit Level: Why Greater Equality Makes Societies Stronger*, London: Bloomsbury, 2009; Joseph Stiglitz, *The Price of Inequality: How Today's Divided Society Endangers Our Future*, New York: W. W. Norton, 2012. We should also include in these developments the awarding of the 2015 Nobel Prize in economics to Angus Deaton—the author of *The Great Escape: Health, Wealth and the Origins of*

Hegel or Keynes were alive today, both would be paying a great deal of attention.[3]

This is the breach into which Thomas Piketty stepped in 2013 with *Capital in the Twenty-First Century* (translated into English in 2014). While widely read in the original in France, the English edition precipitated a sensation for which there is literally no comparison, at least not in post-World War II political economy. The book sent mainstream economists' superlative machine into overdrive: "Explosive." "Landmark." "Groundbreaking." "The book of the decade."[4] Lawrence Summers—like Stiglitz, a former Chief Economist of the World Bank—said it deserves a Nobel Prize.[5] All this for a massive (the French original is 950 pages), occasionally repetitive analysis of economic growth and inequality, chock-full of simple, virtually identically shaped, Excel charts. Yet it became nothing less than *un phénomène*, and the book and its author quickly became central to debates concerning the dynamics and trajectory of modern capitalism.

*Capital in the Twenty-First Century* was reviewed or discussed virtually everywhere, from newspapers, to the blogosphere, to *The New York Review of Books*. Often the comments came from influential public intellectuals—Dani Rodrik, Kenneth Rogoff, and others—and, as everyone from Slavoj Žižek to the Hoover Institution jumped in, part of the game was waiting to see what X had to say

---

*Inequality*, Princeton: Princeton University Press, 2015. Even Occupy Wall Street, the movement that coined the phrase "We are the 99 percent," is at least partly caught up in this. It was not organized by the poor, but by middle-class students (who else reads *Adbusters?*), not as an anti-poverty movement, but an anti-debt and anti-inequality movement. This is not to say that every movement is not similarly complex, nor is it to say that I do not support Occupy, but it seems to me essential to recognize the fraught nature of current oppositional politics reflected in the obsession with inequality.

3   And Hegel would note that just as Marx's *Capital* did in 2008 (*Wall Street Journal,* November 6, 2008), Jean-Jacques Rousseau's *Discourse on the Origin of Inequality* is "moving units" again!

4   Thomas Piketty, *Capital au XXIᵉ siècle*, Paris: Seuil, 2013; translated by Arthur Goldhammer as *Capital in the Twenty-First Century*, Cambridge MA: Harvard University Press, 2014. Citations refer to the French original (my translations).

5   Lawrence Summers, "The Inequality Puzzle," *Democracy: A Journal of Ideas* 33.

about Piketty.[6] On the political economy front, David Harvey, James Galbraith, and Paul Krugman all weighed in, as have other prominent figures in the world of mainstream economics (Brad de Long, Robert Solow, and more).[7] These engagements covered a wide political and ideological ground, and the debate was remarkably stimulating. Although some of them come from far right field, it must be said that virtually everyone had something useful to add, for there is indeed much to be said, and the book is so large, and its ambit so wide, that the conversation will likely continue.

Still, it seems to me that some crucial questions remain unasked. This is partly a function of the narrow approach taken by most responses to the book. The focus seemed stuck on largely empirical questions: whether and on what grounds the book was right or wrong; or whether the book is as right as other books; or whether Piketty's methodology, variable specification, or theoretical framework is adequate to his empirical claims or policy prescriptions. In radical and nonorthodox circles—David Harvey's and James Galbraith's reviews are exemplary—this strategy for the most part unfortunately involved holding Piketty's *Capital* up to the mirror of Marx's *Capital* and then cataloguing the ways in which, while an important read, the former misconstrues or simply falls (far) short of the latter.

I think this unfortunate, but not because these questions concerning methodological choices or theoretical framework are unimportant. On the terms with which they engage Piketty, I have little important to quibble with in Harvey's or Galbraith's

6   Dani Rodrik, "Piketty and the Zeitgeist," Project Syndicate, 2014, and Kenneth Rogoff, "Where is the Inequality Problem?" 2014, both available at: project-syndicate.org; Slavoj Žižek, "Slavoj Žižek comments on Thomas Piketty's 'Le Capital au XXIe siècle'," 2014, available at: criticatac.ro; Richard Epstein, "The Piketty Fallacy," 2014, available at:. hoover.org.

7   David Harvey, "Afterthoughts on Piketty's Capital," 2014, from his blog Reading Marx's Capital with David Harvey; James Galbraith, "*Kapital* for the Twenty-First Century?" *Dissent*, Spring 2014; Paul Krugman, "Why We're in a New Gilded Age," *New York Review of Books*, May 8, 2014; J. Bradford DeLong, "The Right's Piketty Problem," 2014, Project Syndicate; Robert Solow, "Thomas Piketty is Right," *New Republic*, April 22, 2014.

assessment and much to learn. It just seems to me, however, that such critiques miss the point, that the nature of the book as a "research program" cannot be the only way we read it. Despite his market-savvy title, Piketty is not trying to rewrite Marx, or, if he harbors that desire somewhere deep down, he almost certainly anticipated, and probably cares little, that some Marxists tell him he misunderstands the tendency of the rate of profit to fall or the nature of class struggle. That is not his audience, and that is not what the book is really about. No detailed critique of his engagement with Marx and communism or his account of the failures of militant radicalism will have a meaningful impact on the crucial question Piketty's *Capital* solicits.

In fact, I would go so far as to say that to make such questions central to an engagement with Piketty is to duck the responsibility that real critique entails, because it emphasizes what are essentially minor details in the book's architecture, however mistaken it is on any given point. The crucial "critical" question is not so much "Is Piketty right about this or that?" or "Is Piketty a contemporary substitute for Marx?" The question that must be asked of the book is, instead, "What does the Piketty phenomenon tell us about contemporary liberal capitalism?" What does the extraordinary reach and reaction the book has elicited tell us about the politics and political economy of the capitalist global North? In other words, the most significant lessons we can learn from *Capital in the Twenty-First Century* would be untroubled even if his argument turned out to be totally wrong-headed and all his data fabricated in a Paris basement. Any errors and shortcomings are not entirely irrelevant, but they are beside the point.

The point, rather, is that Piketty has offered, and many have desperately embraced, *The General Theory of Employment, Interest and Money* of our epoch. Piketty's affinities with Keynes and his "groundbreaking" "landmark" of 1936 are largely unreflexive. Keynes is mentioned twice, and Piketty briefly credits one of his fundamental laws (which ties the proportional burden of capital to the saving and growth rates) to the razor's edge of the Keynes-inspired Harrod-Domar growth models, essential building blocks in the economics of growth and development.[8] Nevertheless, the Keynesian critique as I have elaborated in the preceding chapters is the foundation of Piketty's account, and it manifests itself throughout *Capital in the Twenty-First Century*. The epistemology, the political stance, the methodological commitments, and the politics resonate with *The General Theory* in imperfect but remarkable harmony. All this is no accident, since the world in which Piketty's book appeared—the world that created the book's necessity—is haunted by Robespierre's ghost and thus trembling with the liberal capitalist form of anxiety Keynes, and Hegel before him, sought to diagnose and subdue.

## Keynes, Piketty and the Anxiety of Civil Society

At its most basic, Piketty's message is the same as Hegel's and Keynes's: if you are anxious about what the world is coming to right now, you are on to something. Whatever its merits, capitalism unchecked will always do two things that endanger the stability of the social order of modernity. First, it will increase inequality, a problem for which it has no "natural" or "immanent" solution. Second, it will leave a lot of people behind on both relative and absolute terms. Consequently— we do not know exactly when, but it is (always) probably soon—at some point those left behind or a significant fraction of them— Hegel's rabble—will refuse to accept their fate. *Notrecht* will assert itself, and the needs of many will cross some political economic threshold at which necessity means they have "nothing to lose" in unmaking the social order; others, dishonored, will act out of bitterness and perceived relative deprivation.

Hegel, Keynes, and Piketty in no way take this threat as presaging an incipient radical-democratic revolution, a cause for which all have some intellectual sympathy. Yet they are certain this will never happen; the masses are incapable of achieving anything so positive. The lesson history teaches them instead is that "the people" will choose destructive and demagogic means of rebuilding social order,

---

8  Piketty, *Capital*, 215, 348, 365.

and everyone will lose. As Piketty makes abundantly clear, he is no more worried about the promise of a socialist or communist horizon than Hegel or Keynes. The only "Marxian" dynamic on the horizon is the "Marxian apocalypse."[9] Civilization as a whole will likely go down with that ship.

In this context, attachment to abstract liberal principle (free trade, "pure" market-mediated distribution, individual meritocracy) is foolish, even apocalyptic. It does not matter a whit if according to some universal laws of Truth and Justice orthodox liberalism is formally "correct" or morally superior to other abstract principles of social organization. Maybe it is, maybe it is not; for Keynesians the question is moot if it renders the very foundations of society insecure. If liberal utopianism has any purpose at all, it is only in the long run, and "we"—those of us who feel we have something to look forward to tomorrow—know what happens in the long run. In the meantime, the only mechanisms that can secure a set of relations approximating liberalism are substantially illiberal, in and of themselves. To reject these relations on dogmatic principle is myopic, viciously destructive, and ultimately self-defeating. An unfettered liberal capitalism operating in the "freedom" of bourgeois civil society leads inexorably to its own destruction.

I should emphasize that my point is not that there is no difference between *Capital in the Twenty-First Century* and *The General Theory*, or that Piketty and Keynes propose identical theories of capitalism. They are writing for different worlds, just as Hegel and Keynes were. If only for these historical-geographical reasons, we should expect differences, and neither their theories nor their forecasts line up perfectly. For example, Piketty does not propose or anticipate anything so grandiose as "economic bliss," and, in stark contrast to Keynes, he self-consciously prioritizes empirical data analysis. (He even claims his work requires only a "minimal theoretical framework.")[10] However, there are remarkable similarities in their accounts, a product of a shared pragmatic intuitionism in

---

9   Ibid., 16, 28, 368.
10   Ibid., 65.

epistemology and, even more important, a common theory of capitalist civil society that neither of them invented but which both are convinced is so common sense as to be irrefutable. Which is to say that if one cannot find income subsidies, Philips curves, or a "sticky-price" model in Piketty, it does nothing to diminish the fact that he has written *The General Theory* for our times.

## The Keynesian Architecture of Piketty's General Theory

Keynes thought *The General Theory* identified the workings of the "delicate machine" that powered "modern communities." It solved the "paradox of poverty in the midst of plenty" through the "scarcity-theory" of capital: "capital has to be kept scarce enough" that return on its investment will be deemed acceptable by capitalists. Capital must be "kept scarce" to the point at which "we" become sufficiently impoverished so as to make profitable investment worthwhile.[11] Arguing precisely the same "stagnationist" point, Piketty puts it nicely: "Too much capital kills capital."[12]

Piketty's general line of argument has been covered elsewhere in such detail that I only offer a brief summary here, to isolate the ways in which its politics become more explicitly visible. At the outset, however, it is worth noting that the whole of his argument is couched in a pragmatic intuitionism much like Keynes's own epistemology. Piketty frequently emphasizes the applicability and accuracy of his assessments, relative to orthodox "neoclassical" conclusions, with phrases like "in practice," or "in reality."[13] He is also at pains to point out the significance of all-pervasive radical uncertainty. This uncertainty affects both our capacity to account for or anticipate the

---

11    Keynes, *CW*, VII, 30, 215, 217. In other words, scarce enough to produce a rabble; the rabble is a product of the fallacy of composition inherent in competitive ("individualistic") capitalism, and the condition in which it coalesces is the same condition necessary for profit. The rabble is the "unintended" consequence of the organization of life by the rule of value.

12    Piketty, *Capital*, 336.

13    See, for example, Ibid., 266, 288, 319, 568, 769.

future, but it also means that the quantities on which Piketty and other economists rely are general indicators that never capture all the forces that determine economic magnitudes: "we must distrust all economic determinism on these questions: the history of the distribution of wealth is always a deeply political history, and can never be reduced to purely economic mechanisms."[14] Consequently, and despite his reliance on a vast trove of numerical data, he is as suspicious as Keynes of economics' mathematical "fetish":

> The discipline of economics has never given up its infantile passion for mathematics and purely theoretical and often ideological speculation, to the detriment of historical research and a productive conversation with other social sciences. Too often, economists are obsessed with minor mathematical problems of interest to no one but themselves, and which grant them the appearance of scientificity and allow them to avoid answering other, more complicated questions posed by the world around them.[15]

This pragmatism is of course itself a product of our historical condition. The current situation seems to demand a willingness to "break the rules" to find a solution. "Dogma" and "doctrine," liberal or otherwise, is dismissed in the interests of getting things done. But in addition to suiting the crisis moment, it also provides the foundation for a Keynesian analysis that sets aside the minor details in favor of accurately capturing the general movements of capitalist market economies. Piketty's theory of that movement—the tendential laws of *laissez-faire*—is broadly the same as Keynes's, as it too recalls the Hegelian model of a civil society containing the seeds of its own destruction in the form of poverty and rabbledom, disorder, and even "apocalypse."

According to Piketty, the force behind this self-destructive tendency is the "fundamental inequality" $r > g$, that is, the return to capital $r$ tends to be meaningfully higher than the overall growth rate

---

14  Ibid., 47; see also 114, 145, 159, 272, 674, 772.
15  See, for example, Ibid., 63, 103, 156, 583, 769, 863.

g. If this inequality holds across most times and places—the *Trente Glorieuses* (the post-World War II Golden Age in the industrial-capitalist world) stand for Piketty as the exception that proves the rule—then clearly,

> wealth originating in the past is recapitalized faster than the progress of production and incomes. Those who inherit this capital thus need only save a limited part of the income from their capital for that capital to grow faster than the economy as a whole. In these conditions, it is almost inevitable that inherited wealth dominates wealth accumulated over the course of one's life, and that the concentration of capital reaches extreme levels, levels potentially incompatible with the ideals of meritocracy and principles of social justice that underpin our modern democratic societies.[16]

As we know, Keynes attributes the forces that threaten capitalist dynamism and accelerate inequality to insufficient inducement to productive (labor-utilizing) investment. The solution, he said, was to provide secure foundations for employment-producing investment by ensuring that the interest rate $r$ (for terms comparable to those for investment) was lower than the expected return on capital (or, more specifically the marginal efficiency of capital, $MEC$). In other words, the objective was to create conditions in which a money holder can earn higher yield funding entrepreneurship than buying debt. If this inequality is dependable, then entrepreneurs' "animal spirits" are activated, and money holders have an incentive to lend them capital.

This fundamental causal mechanism is a proto-Pikettian inequality. *The General Theory*'s explanation of capitalism's long-term crisis tendency—only very slightly simplified—is that, in general, the structural determinants of the rate of interest tend to prevent it from falling low enough, for long enough, to guarantee that the expected return to productive investment will dominate returns from debt purchase. In other words, $MEC$ is volatile enough, and $r$ resists

---

16   Ibid., 55.

approaching zero sufficiently strongly, that frequently, $r > MEC$.[17] Indeed, even during periods when $MEC > r$, the very fact that the relationship could so readily reverse increases uncertainty and liquidity preference, thus precipitating precisely that which was feared—a "flight to safety." Furthermore, this condition is more likely in the downturn, making bad times worse. Just as for Piketty "a global political community founded in justice and the common good" depends on a state-regulatory apparatus to ensure $g > r$, for Keynes, "economic bliss" lies in the long-term stability of $MEC > r$, that is, an animal spirits' playground[18]:

> If capitalist society rejects a more equal distribution of incomes and the forces of banking and finance succeed in maintaining the rate of interest somewhere near the figure which ruled on the average during the nineteenth century (which was, by the way, a little *lower* than the rate of interest which rules today), then a chronic tendency towards the underemployment of resources must in the end sap and destroy that form of society.[19]

Piketty's inequality is a reworking of the Keynesian inequality for the capitalist reason of the early twenty-first century. But before considering the ways in which these inequalities resonate with one another, we must address two key differences in the dynamics they specify. These differences are formally significant, but upon closer inspection they merely obscure deeper and more fundamental similarities.[20] The first concerns $r$. Although it is one side of both

---

17    Although Keynes does not state it so explicitly and formally as Piketty, this simple inequality is just as central to *The General Theory* as $r > g$ is to *Capital in the Twenty-First Century*. As he put it in late 1934: "So long as there is serious all-round unemployment I consider this proves that the equilibrium rate of interest is lower than the ruling rate"; *CW*, XXI, 345.

18    Piketty, *Capital*, 879.

19    Keynes, *CW*, XVI, 132.

20    Here I set aside the fact that in contrast to Keynes's explicitly expectational definition of *MEC*, Piketty does not define $g$ as a function of capital's expectations. His emphasis throughout on a radical Keynesian uncertainty implies it, however, and his belief that modern monetary policy can "anchor perceptions, expectations and hierarchies in monetary

inequalities, *r* clearly indicates something quite different in each case. Keynes's *r* is the interest rate (or more specifically, "the complex of rates of interest for debts of different terms and risks").[21] It "equalises the advantages of holding actual cash and a deferred claim on cash."[22]

Piketty defines *r* as "the rate of yield on capital (which is to say the annual return on average to capital in the form of profits, dividends, interest, rents and other sources as a percentage of its value)." This is a much more vaguely defined, catch-all variable. In fact, on *The General Theory*'s terms, Piketty's *r* is an awkward combination of both sides of Keynes's inequality, *r* and *MEC*, something like the (weighted?) average return available to capital through all yield-producing channels. (Piketty is not a lot of help on this front.) There is no distinction between, for example, buying sovereign debt (and earning Keynes's *r*) and investing in a new manufacturing concern (to enjoy Keynes's *MEC*). All yields from capital assets are collected in the homogeneous mass of "return [*rendement*] to capital."

The second difference is immediately evident in the light of the first. If *r* represents different phenomena in each inequality, then the two inequalities are not positing the same relation. Piketty's *g* is not a substitute for Keynes's *MEC*, and for Keynes, *g* and *MEC* are distinct. In fact, his economic bliss entails a constant fall in *MEC* toward zero but consistent per capita growth. The feasibility of this utopia aside, Keynes's fundamental inequality cannot be easily adapted to modern growth accounting because his understanding of economic development is not captured by rising GDP. In contrast, Piketty adopts this standard measure of progress. Despite some brief nods to the fact that certain forms of development might boost aggregate income while nevertheless hindering "real" progress (for

---

benchmarks," while today associated with "neoliberal" orthodoxy, is in fact a logical extension of Keynes's emphasis on the role of the state in maintaining the state of confidence. As Keynes said, money is "above all, a subtle device for linking the present to the future . . . we cannot even begin to discuss the effect of changing expectations on current activities except in monetary terms"; Piketty, *Capital*, 179; Keynes, *CW,* VII, 294.

21  Ibid., 207.
22  Keynes, *CW,* XIV, 206.

example, through increased carbon emissions or generating mass unemployment), his conception of growth is thoroughly orthodox.

Consequently, while Keynes posits that, concerning the self-destructive dynamics immanent to free-market civil society, the crucial distinction lies in what wealth holders do to extract yield (invest or buy debt), Piketty contends that this choice is not analytically important. This might seem a significant difference. Indeed it is, but it is largely a formal one, a product of changed political economic circumstances that mask a fundamental similarity in political content. To see this, we need to position Piketty's $r$ in its twenty-first century terrain. As noted above, his catch-all return to capital $r$ collapses the distinction between the interest rate (yield from holding debt) and capital gains (profits, dividends, rent from landed capital, and so on). This is to suggest that when it comes to the returns to owning wealth or capital in any form, in the end it is all the same thing: yield. Enjoying the yield from owning shares in a business that produces widgets, from rents extracted from tenants, or from coupon payments on sovereign debt: in the structure and effects of the fundamental inequality that threatens capitalist civilization, these differences are basically meaningless.

This is definitively not a category neoclassical economics would endorse, because it reflects a very unorthodox conception of capital. Piketty defines capital as "the set of nonhuman assets that can be owned and exchanged on the market," because "all forms of capital always play a double role, in part as factor of production and in part as store of value." Consequently—and this goes some way toward explaining the vague generality of $r$—"*capital is not a fixed category*: it reflects the state of development and the social relations that reign in a given society."[23] Piketty is no radical, but there is wisdom here. In explicitly rejecting the marginalist fetish of "productivity"—remember that in neoclassical theory, capital's share, like that of all other factors, is determined by its marginal productivity—Piketty not only dismisses mainstream orthodoxy's fundamentalist faith in the natural justice of market-based distribution. He also resurrects for our own time Keynes's critique of "productivity."

---

23 Piketty, *Capital*, 82, 85, 84 (emphasis added).

Recall that *The General Theory* emphasizes that capitalists are capitalists not because they want to possess capital for its own sake. They seek assets that yield, and yield is what drives them. But yield is *not* a return to productivity; lots of assets are productive but generate little or no yield, and some even produce a negative stream of profit. Yield, rather, is ultimately a function of *scarcity*. Keynes substitutes scarcity for productivity in the classical and new classical theories of growth and distribution, and in doing so he simultaneously identifies the "rent seeking" at the heart of all capitalist investment and puts the problem of poverty and necessity at the center of political economy. It is almost as if where mainstream liberal economics theorizes "positivity"—a dynamically reconfigured substantial "something"— Keynesian reason conceives "negation," a quasi-cyclical persistent undoing in the process of unfolding.[24] This negation is not (or not only) Schumpeter's "creative destruction," but, rather, the immanent creation of shortage, dearth, of not-enough-to-go-around-ness.

Returning to Piketty, we can see in his embrace of a fluid definition of capital (all exchangeable nonhuman assets) an elaboration of Keynes's insight that the ultimate purpose of capital is the extraction of yield. Increasing productivity—"growth"—is related to yield solely in a contingent manner. With capital, there is no necessary relationship between the two. Thus, Piketty's *r* is a vast catch-all because it is not the standard neoclassical measure of the return associated with capital's productivity (the justifiable earnings due to its contribution to the production process), but rather a measure of the yield that capital enjoys or extracts. (Compared to the common English phrase "return to capital," which carries with it all sorts of meritocratic ideological baggage, "yield to capital" or "capital's yield" is an awkward but probably more accurate translation of Piketty's "*rendement de capital*.")

All of which is to say that for both Keynes and Piketty, the fundamental purpose of *r* is to specify *rent* (perhaps this is why it is

---

24  Which would confirm Fredric Jameson's judgment of Deleuze as the unwitting creature of postmodern capitalism's eternal present in *A Singular Modernity: Essay on the Ontology of the Present*, London: Verso, 2002, 194–95.

"*r*"?)—in other words, income that "rewards the simple fact of ownership of capital, independent of any labour"—or, in Keynes's words, "what used to be called unearned income, and is now called investment income."[25] The purpose of Keynes's distinction between *MEC* and *r* is to distinguish between the entrepreneur—the hero of *The General Theory*—and the "rentier," the book's anti-hero, whose "euthanasia" is necessary to human progress.[26]

The distinction between the 1930s and today is that back in Keynes's day, the difference between "productive" and "unproductive" modes of capitalist being seemed relatively unproblematic, even common sense. Despite Hegel's most sincere hopes, the scent of aristocracy still hung in the air. But in the midst of the globalized and financialized capitalism of which Piketty writes, this difference is no longer meaningful. While he recognizes the nontrivial magnitude of income derived from "entrepreneurial labour," Piketty refuses to grant it anything more than the minor role it deserves. Capital, he says, "is always risky and entrepreneurial, especially in its early stages; and at the same time it tends always to transform itself into rent so as to accumulate without limit—this is its vocation, its logical destiny."[27] The "real economy" is increasingly financialized and securitized, the difference (if it ever existed) between "real" capital and "fictitious" capital has vanished, and the entrepreneur becomes rentier:

> The general lesson of my investigation is that the dynamic evolution of an economy based in markets and private property, left to itself, contains important internal forces that tend toward convergence, particularly those linked to the diffusion of knowledge and skills. But it also contains powerful forces that produce divergence, forces that pose potential threats to our democratic societies and the values of social justice on which they are founded. The

---

25  Piketty, *Capital*, 672; Keynes, *CW*, XIX, part 2, 846.

26  Keynes himself, along with most of his friends, was of course a rentier. Perhaps this is why he chose "euthanasia" over "elimination" or "assassination."

27  Piketty, *Capital*, 187.

principal destabilizing force has to do with the fact that the private rate of return on capital, $r$, can be significantly higher for long periods of time than the rate of growth of income and output, $g$. The inequality $r > g$ implies that wealth accumulated in the past grows more rapidly than output and wages. This inequality expresses a fundamental logical contradiction. The entrepreneur tends inevitably to transform him or herself into a rentier, and to dominate more and more completely those who possess nothing but their labour. Once established, capital reproduces itself, more rapidly than the growth of production. The past devours the future. The consequences for the long-term dynamics of wealth distribution are potentially terrifying . . . The problem does not admit of a simple solution.[28]

Hence the need for a revised $r$ to meet the needs of a renovated, but no less anxious, Keynesian political economy. The stakes are terrifyingly high.

### Regulation and the Rentier

I see, therefore, the rentier aspect of capitalism as a transitional phase that will disappear when it has done its work. And with the disappearance of its rentier aspect much else in it besides will suffer a sea change. It will be, moreover, a great advantage of the order of events which I am advocating, that the euthanasia of the rentier, of the functionless investor, will be nothing sudden, merely a gradual but prolonged continuance of what we have seen recently in Great Britain, and will need no revolution.[29]

One of Piketty's most powerful empirical claims is that Keynes's forecast of the deaths of rent and the rentier were only temporarily correct, and have, in the longer run, been totally and completely

---

28  Ibid., 942.
29  Keynes, *CW,* VII, 376.

mistaken.[30] But clearly, like Keynes, he understands the suppression of the rentier and of capital's tendency to rentification as the only "politically acceptable conclusion." Moreover, and in this he also follows Keynes, he takes the extant technical and institutional conditions of modern capitalism to be virtually fixed in the short term, or at least relatively immune to the effects of nonrevolutionary power and policy. There is little the state can do to alter $g$ or $MEC$. Regulations that suppress $r$ are the only feasible option.

> [W]hen Keynes wrote in 1936 of the "euthanasia of the rentier," he was just as deeply marked by what he observed going on around him: the world of the rentiers that preceded World War I was collapsing, and there was in fact no other politically acceptable solution to the ongoing budget and economic crises. In particular, Keynes knew very well that inflation, which the UK would only accept reluctantly, so strong was the attachment to the gold standard in the conservative climate before the war, was the simplest— if not necessarily the most just—way to reduce the burden of public debt and accumulated capital.[31]

Since his $r$ is the interest rate, Keynes proposes a primarily monetary strategy to this end. This might sound like a reassertion of the *Treatise*'s "magic formula": cheap money. But with *The General Theory*, Keynes identifies the reason that mechanically lowering interest rates by *fiat* only deals with the superficial aspects of the problem. As the depths of the Great Depression demonstrated, lowering interest rates cannot guarantee a response from entrepreneurs. The deeper issue is uncertainty. If uncertainty can be subdued, then not only will interest rates fall, but entrepreneurial "animal spirits"—the urge to invest and take risks—will rise, liquidity preference will fall, consumption will increase, and effective demand will rise. From a Keynesian perspective, this is a virtuous circle.

---

30   Piketty, *Capital*, 565, 675.
31   Ibid., 215.

The most expedient way to reduce uncertainty regarding the future is to introduce as much predictability as possible into capital, goods, and labor markets. If people feel like things are unlikely to oscillate, liquidity preference falls and they are more likely to put their money into market circulation. Indeed, the common medium (the "blood") of these markets is money, and for Keynes, money makes all the difference. It is the general equivalent, the store and expression of value across time and space. Money is "above all, a subtle device for linking the present to the future . . . we cannot even begin to discuss the effect of changing expectations on current activities except in monetary terms."[32] The highest policy priority in a monetary economy is thus to manage the link between the future and the present, so as to render it as stable as possible.

The means to this end are (a) skilled management of the rate of interest, which determines, for all intents and purposes, the terms upon which the present investment opportunities must compete with the future; (b) when necessary, state spending to maintain a stable or steadily increasing level of aggregate demand; and (c) as low inflation as is practically possible without too much disruption of the labor market, since it lowers the value of real wages, discourages investment, and can lead to vicious inflationary spirals.

Piketty's $r$ demands a different approach, for which interest rate-focused policies are inadequate, particularly in a historical context, so radically different to that of Keynes, of global flows and international deregulatory competition between states. His solution targets $r$ just as specifically but takes the form of a global tax on capital. It is perhaps unsurprising, if my argument holds, that although Keynes would have been unprepared for the scale of relations we now reference with the term "global," he also advocated a tax on capital at various points in his career and for the same reasons as Piketty.[33]

---

32 Keynes, *CW,* VII, 294.

33 When asked "Would you on general grounds be in favour of any kind of tax on capital?" Keynes responded: "The best way of doing that is by increasing the income tax on 'investment income' . . . I believe that, if you want to relieve current effort and to tax more heavily past accumulation, the way to do that is to increase the tax on what used to be called unearned income, and is now called investment income" (*CW,* XIX, part 2, 846; see also *CW,* XVII, 359, and *CW,* XVIII, 72).

Indeed, he too argued that if the technical or institutional challenges could be overcome (and they were "not unworkable"), it was sometimes "the best solution."[34] For both, however, the priority on regulating $r$ is due to its enormous influence on future economic potential, in particular because "the inequality $r > g$ means that the past tends to devour the future."[35]

Establishing confidence in the future, in the shadow of a menacing present and increasing political economic and ecological anxiety, is about as daunting a task as one can imagine. Piketty is adamant that capitalist civil society need not lead inexorably to the Hobbesian states of nature, reactionary fascisms, or totalitarian "communist" regimes that loom on the horizon; these are only some of our possible futures. (Those futures also include an "ideal society?" briefly referenced in Table 7.2 (Piketty's question mark)—is this Keynes's "economic bliss"?)[36] But, as he says, "if the tendencies observed in the period 1970–2010 were to continue until 2050 or 2100, we will approach social, political, and economic disequilibria of such magnitude, both within and between countries, that it is hard not to think of the Ricardian apocalypse."[37]

For Piketty and Keynes, the key is somehow to save liberal capitalist civilization from the Ricardian principle both know has historically been essential to it: scarcity, the rent scarcity generates for the rentier, and—always lurking beneath the surface—the "rabble mentality" inevitable to the dishonorable mass poverty scarcity produces. Scarcity is the origin of yield, the very basis of capital as a social relation, as an asset, and as a class. Radical thinkers have emphasized this feature of capitalism for centuries. But Keynes and Piketty distinguish themselves from their fellow economists because they suggest profound if immanent means by which to acknowledge and manage this dynamic. Each of them goes out of their way to point out that they are in no way "against" inequality, no more than

34   Keynes, *CW,* XIX part 2, 841; *CW,* XVIII, 72.
35   Piketty, *Capital,* 840, 600.
36   Ibid., 56, 391.
37   Ibid., 23.

Hegel thought it would be possible to be "against" poverty. "Inequality," Piketty writes, "is not necessarily inherently evil"; what is crucial is "to know if it is justified, if it has sufficient reasons." In other words, the problem is not poverty or inequality, but inequalities "being so great as at present," poverty without honor.[38] Nobody should understand themselves as having nothing to lose.

For Piketty, then, like all Keynesians, the challenge is to convincingly debunk the gospel Truth that capitalist civil society, in the operations of "the market," contains the solutions to its own problems, thereby reasserting the priority of the "social interest" in whose name "democratic" institutions act. The Fordist–Keynesian state built on the foundations of "the economics of Keynes"—less social safety net, and more low long-term interest rates, capital controls, and a relatively equalizing income distribution protected by long-term contracts—in many ways achieved this to a remarkable extent.

This ideological, political, and economic entangling, through what Negri calls the postwar "planner state," realized the political economic potential of what we might call "liberalistic" capitalism to a far greater extent than classical liberalism ever did or could.[39] It did so by producing a political condition in which the state and civil society (private markets involving firms and consumers) were understood as partners in a hegemonic "social interest"—one that paradoxically provided the essentially solidaristic common sense without which the neoliberal "counter-revolution" would have had no political legitimacy. The political viability of something like the Volcker shock of the late 1970s would have been unthinkable without Keynesian ideological foundations.[40] This—which was nothing less than the Thermidorian dream of a capitalist *Sittlichkeit*—was the

---

38   Keynes, *CW,* VII, 374; Piketty, *Capital,* 44.

39   Which is to say that neoliberalism was made possible by the (Hegelian) "passage" through Keynesianism.

40   The increase in interest rates was accompanied by Reagan's massive tax cut of 1981, which reduced government revenue by a third, and quintupled the US federal budget deficit by 1985. Richard Musgrave describes this as the moment the "most drastic Keynesian move (excepting only World War II) was undertaken under its most anti-Keynesian label"; Richard Musgrave, "U. S. Fiscal Policy, Keynes, and Keynesian Economics," *Journal of Post–Keynesian Economics* 10: 2, 1987–88, 180.

only political-economic common sense that could possibly legitimate a "collective" sacrifice to the war against inflation. Indeed, as a founding moment in neoliberal economic governance, we can see the Reagan era as a kind of snapshot of capitalist hegemony in "negative": working class pain is everyone's gain, even (they were told) the workers.[41]

The Keynes–Piketty proposition—that capital must "sacrifice" in the interests of the social order, in the interests of stable accumulation—is an unpalatable but pragmatic corollary of this reasoning. Keynes's and Piketty's emphasis on the "social interest" has no heritage in Rousseau: it is in fact almost a mirror image of the general will, since the collective interest is emphasized precisely because it serves individual interest. As Keynes said, "Marxists are ready to sacrifice the political liberties of individuals in order to change the existing economic order. So are Fascists and Nazis ... My own aim is economic reform by the methods of political liberalism."[42] I would suggest that if (like Hegel, Keynes, and Piketty) you understand the "rabble" as a constant immanent threat to social order, and thus necessarily to individual liberty, then this makes a lot of sense. I would also suggest that if you do, you are a "real" Keynesian, even if you are a quasi-neoclassical post-World War II New Keynesian like Krugman or Paul Samuelson:

> By proper use of monetary and fiscal policies, nations today can successfully fight off the plague of mass unemployment and the plague of inflation. With reasonably stable full employment a feasible goal, the modern economist can use a "neoclassical synthesis" based on a combination of the modern [i.e. Keynesian] principles of income determination and the classical truths. Paradoxically, successful application of the principles of income determination does result in a piercing of the monetary veil masking real conditions, does dissipate the topsy-turvy clashes between

---

41  Arguably, this ideological work is another way in which World War II made Keynesianism politically viable.

42  Keynes, *CW,* XXVIII, 28.

the whole and the part that gave rise to countless fallacies of composition, and does finally validate the important classical truths and vanquish the paradox of abortive thrift . . . Our mixed economy—wars aside—has a great future before it.[43]

Ultimately, the Keynesian problem Piketty has re-posed for liberals concerns that same essential problem that obsesses all Keynesians at all times: the political sustainability of modern ("bourgeois") privilege. The problem that Keynes struggled with, and Piketty confronts again today, is that rent and the rentier give wealth and privilege a bad name and tend constantly to produce levels of inequality for which popular "acceptance is hardly dependable or likely to last."[44] They expose the myths of meritocracy and the "bourgeois pillar." The rentier is thus nothing less than the "enemy of democracy," rent "the enemy of modern rationality."[45] This is why Keynesians are obsessed with the legitimacy of the social order, especially its inequalities. Keynes himself was particularly concerned with the persistence of levels of unemployment "so intolerably below [full employment] as to provoke revolutionary changes."[46] He attempted to address this legitimation crisis by isolating a clean, meritorious productive mode of capital from its parasitic sibling. The problem, he argued, was the residue of rentier capitalism in the modern economy, but with proper state-technocratic care, it would eradicate itself; good capital was sure to follow bad.

Piketty faces a much trickier "actually existing" capitalism, and he does so boldly, in a way that is hard not to admire at times. He recognizes that any proposed rentier/capitalist distinction is simultaneously untenable at a general level and evanescent in any given instance—profit tends to become rent, the entrepreneur becomes rentier. The categories themselves are unstable: "[a]ll wealth is partly justified and potentially excessive at the same time. Theft pure and

---

43    Paul Samuelson, *Foundations of Economic Analysis*, 3d ed., Cambridge: Harvard University Press, 1955, 590, 809.

44    Piketty, *Capital*, 566; see also p. 414.

45    Ibid., 671, 673.

46    Keynes, *CW*, VII, 308.

simple is rare, as is absolute merit."[47] Without recourse to the celebration of an untainted realm of accumulation, however, Piketty
faces a much more difficult task—one that, unacknowledged or
unwitting, has led him to resurrect a Keynes adapted to the 21st
century, in the form of a minimal tax on global capital.[48]

If Piketty cannot quite convince us that a progressive global tax on
capital is in fact the "ideal institution for avoiding an endless spiral
of inequality and retaking control of current dynamics," he does
show that it is "not nothing" either (*ce n'est pas rien*, a phrase Piketty
uses often). But the reason it would help is not, he says (correctly),
because it will improve the situation for low-income groups. The tax
is not intended to—and might have limited impact upon—the state's
social spending or on the distributional concerns of the poor. But the
point, again, is not to make the poor no longer poor. The "principal
function of the tax on capital is not to finance the welfare state [*l'État
social*], but to regulate capitalism" and to provide a veritable "global
financial cadaster" to improve our capacity to regulate banking and
finance through a vastly increased transparency.[49]

The conservative response to this proposal has been as stupid and
laughably predictable as the reactions to *The General Theory* in its
time: that it is "socialist," "Marxist," "double taxation," an attack on
property, and so forth. The proposed tax on capital is so far from any
of these it is almost funny. But neither is it a merely technical or
neutral addition to the state's arsenal, so pragmatic or obviously
necessary as to barely require deliberation among reasonable people,
as Piketty's champions sometimes suggest. Piketty himself is enjoya-
bly phlegmatic on the matter: "a tax is always more than just a tax: it
is always a means to clarify definitions and specify categories, to
produce norms, and to allow for the organization of economic activity in accord with the rule of law."[50] Such blithe reflections on the

---

47   Piketty, *Capital*, 709.
48   Ibid., 752.
49   Ibid., 842, 840. For an account of an attempt to impose such a tax at the local
scale, see Robin Harding, "Property: Land of Opportunity?," *Financial Times*, September
24, 2014.
50   Piketty, *Capital*, 843.

centrality of political economy to modern (bio)politics might sound like excerpts from Foucault's lectures, and indeed they expose the "liberalist" bases of Piketty's (and Keynes's) reluctantly logical critique of modern capitalism.

Echoing Keynes, Piketty is careful to endorse the abstract logic, even normative superiority, of liberalism while nonetheless exhorting us to recognize that in "the world in which we actually live" its principles cannot produce the world it anticipates. Just as Keynes suggested that with proper regulation we might produce a world in which eventually the "classical theory comes into its own again," Piketty notes, for example, that "ultimately"—in the long run, that is—"free trade and economic openness is in everyone's interest."[51] The problem is that "ultimately" we are all dead. In the meantime, we must be pragmatic, reasonable, realistic:

> It seems to me urgent that we approach this [tax] debate dispassionately, and give each argument and each fiscal policy tool the attention it is due. The capital tax is useful, even indispensable in the context of twenty-first century capital.

It is "simply" a better instrument than income tax to ensure payment of what individuals have the capacity to contribute, and it redistributes capital assets toward those who will put them to more dynamic purposes.[52]

And yet, despite these measured appeals to reason, the regulatory ambition of Piketty's proposals is in fact clearly about the "production of norms." The capital tax is "undoubtedly" (to use another of Piketty's favorite phrases, *sans doute*) an attempt to recreate a Keynesian "social interest" (however illusory it may or may not have been in reality) and to forge a Hegelian–Keynesian state-civil society "universality." "One might simply note," Piketty remarks, that "there is a massive chasm between the victorious declarations of responsible politicians and what they are really doing. This is extremely worrying

---

51   Keynes, *CW,* VII, 378; Piketty, *Capital,* 850.
52   Ibid., 857 n.1, 856.

for the equilibrium of our democratic societies."[53] The task is neither to rid society of inequality in wealth or income, nor to reinvigorate the socialist state, but to rebuild the legitimacy of liberal capitalism—its attendant and inevitable inequalities—in the twenty-first century.

If for some reason we did not realize this was not a reconstruction of Marx's *Capital* for the world after Lehman Brothers, we should now: "We must insist on this point: the central question concerns the justification of inequality, even more than its particular level."[54] This is a twisted, but eminently rational, realization of the revolutionary Declaration of the Rights of Man and Citizen of 1789, a document to which Piketty, like Robespierre, explicitly links his efforts.[55]

### Economics, Science, and a Revolution without Revolution

And yet I think it worth emphasizing that this link to revolutionary aspiration, through the Declaration, is neither superficial nor expedient nor accidental. Keynes and Piketty, like Hegel, are both caught up in a quasi-utopian effort to construct a state-civil society equivalence—even an indistinguishability or "universality"—that is also fundamental to, if differently inflected in, a wide range of Left thinking: from Marx and Engels's early ideas about communism, to Proudhon's mutualism, to Gramsci's integral state, and to Habermas's more social-democratic aspirations.[56] Consequently, contemporary knee-jerk Keynesianism on the center and Left—undoubtedly a major factor in the eager embrace of Piketty—is not a mere last resort defensive posture, as if the desperate attempts to fend off free market imperialism have simply made an otherwise unacceptable

---

53  Ibid., 848.
54  Ibid., 415.
55  Ibid., 63, 672.
56  Karl Marx, "Contribution to a Critique of Hegel's Philosophy of Law" [1843], *Marx-Engels Collected Works*, vol. III, New York: International Publishers, 1973, 29: "Democracy is the genus Constitution . . . Democracy is content and form."

Keynesianism comparatively attractive. It is also the case that at a vital and deeply historically embedded ideological level, the anxious political economy quaking beneath *The General Theory* and *Capital au XXIe siècle* resonates with many if not most "progressive" and social-democratic economic ideas currently in circulation in the global North.

The problem is that this thread in Keynesianism also resonates, often just as well, with other, much less emancipatory alternatives, like Schmitt's "total state" or the "market-based" noncapitalist system Giovanni Arrighi identifies with modern China in *Adam Smith in Beijing*.[57] Indeed, despite his hatred of fascism, Keynes was (notoriously) impressed by the Nazi state's economic achievements, which seemed to capture the way in which a radical shift in the popular understanding of the relation between state and civil society demonstrated that "there are no intrinsic reasons for the scarcity of capital" and exploded the idea that modern civil society requires us to "keep ourselves poor." But these pressing *political* complexities at the heart of Keynesianism are often suppressed by "progressives" in favor of attacks on the *analytical* merits of competing economic models.[58] This is the reason we still have to endure the endless heterodox and radical excoriation of orthodox or "neoclassical" economics—somehow the true source or legitimizing theory of neoliberalism—even when we are simultaneously convinced and bored out of our minds by the futility of preaching it to the converted over and over again.

Centrists, Marxists, and everyone in between constantly bemoan the ridiculous epistemological and pseudoscientific bases of modern economics: the assumptions about *homo economicus*, the perfect rationality and information requirements, the methodological individualism—all of which, we are told, are not only wrong but a deceitful disservice to the richness of human life, motivation, and potential. This is undeniably all absolutely true. Held up to measure against

---

57   Carl Schmitt, "The Way to the Total State" [1933], in *Four Articles, 1931–1938*, Corvallis, OR: Plutarch Press, 1999, 1–18; Giovanni Arrighi, *Adam Smith in Beijing: Lineages of the Twenty-First Century*, New York: Verso, 2007.

58   Moreover, while these models serve as tools of economic or policy "analysis," they are nonetheless always social theories.

the world in which we actually live, modern orthodox or mainstream economics, the self-proclaimed "queen of the social sciences" is indefensible. Wherever its "wisdom" is followed to the letter, the result is a disaster. It is, categorically, a defense of undeserved privilege and an apology for undeserved poverty. Only when those taking its advice are aware that it is ultimately fundamentally wrong has it proven even remotely beneficial to our collective welfare.

But these facts of the matter aside, progressive or left complaints are often disingenuous. For it is not clear that orthodox analysis would be the object of such scorn if its conclusions were not anathema to progressives' admittedly dynamic and diverse political goals. On essentially positivist grounds—the relative empirical accuracy of this or that economic account—the turn from orthodoxy to Keynes is "common sense." His economics, while still clearly flawed, is an infinitely better description of the *capitalist* order in which we "actually live."[59] Keynes really was objectively more correct, and many "progressives" hold him out as a logical basis for their opposition to the market order. But in the end, attacking the science of economics—berating its methods, debating its models, disproving its behavioral assumptions, and so forth—is a substitute, and not a very good one, for attacking its politics.[60]

The politics of what gets called "neoclassical" economics lies to a significant extent in its self-consciously apolitical posturing. It embraces a (false) scientific objectivity, thereby asserting not so much the "naturalness" of the status quo—for it is certainly recognized it could be otherwise—but some privileged insight into the "naturalness" of the human propensities that produce it. This privileged insight is of course something we might expect from scientists who actually talk to people and try to understand the "thickness" of their lives, but economists are virtually none of those scientists. And yet, on the basis of formalized, abstract, quasi-mathematical

---

59   Indeed, Piketty's praise adorns the cover of one of the latest revivals of Keynes, Peter Temin and David Vines, *Keynes: Useful Economics for the World Economy*, Cambridge: MIT Press, 2014.

60   Compare with Slavoj Žižek, *In Defense of Lost Causes*, London: Verso, 2008, 184.

theorizing—a Kantian science, you might say—they declare it "proven" that these human propensities are turned to greatest collective advantage, or given least destructive form, by "unfettered" markets. In other words, beneath the Smithian fundamentals, the liberal justification for the pursuit of individual self-interest is ultimately that it ensures *collective* well-being—what we might call socially responsible self-interest. So, we are assured, even though humans are naturally selfish, this is a collective evolutionary "adaptation": what recommends selfishness in the long run is not private interest but its social contribution.

Moreover—setting aside the almost otherworldly ridiculousness of these claims—if this is so then restricting the individual pursuit of self-interest is bad not only because it limits collective well-being, but also because it suppresses "human nature." This, economics is more than bold enough to suggest, is somehow going to result in people blowing some psychosocial valve and doing bad things. In other words, the neoclassical or orthodox position holds either that human "nature" is by definition a "good" to be nurtured (presumably because it is supposedly "natural")—and it is therefore wrong to suppress it—or human nature is immutable and, if unduly constrained, will lead to "perverse" outcomes we will deeply regret. All of which explains why, as Marx and Engels put it, "the bourgeois is a bourgeois—for the benefit of the working class."[61]

Keynes and Piketty make no less sweeping claims to apolitical scientific truth—remember that the title of *The General Theory* is meant to recall another "general theory" (Einstein's relativity), and *Capital au XXIe siècle* announces the revelation of the "fundamental laws" of capitalism.[62] Like all critics of (neo)liberalism, they also

---

61   Karl Marx and Friedrich Engels, "Manifesto of the Communist Party" [1847], *The Revolutions of 1848: Political Writings*, vol. 1, New York: Verso, 2010, 94. This is what Arendt calls the "communistic fiction" at the heart of "liberal economics"; Hannah Arendt, *The Human Condition*, Chicago: University of Chicago Press, 1958, 43–44, 44 n.36; compare with Gunnar Myrdal, *The Political Element in the Development of Economic Theory*, trans. Paul Streeten, Cambridge: Harvard University Press, 1954.

62   James Galbraith, "Keynes, Einstein, and the Scientific Revolution," *American Prospect*, Winter 1994; Roger Backhouse, "Samuelson, Keynes, and the Search for a General Theory of Economics," *Italian Economic Journal* 1: 1, 139–53.

make assertions about the social conditions in which humans best flourish or the ill that comes from suppressing "natural" human needs or desires, and both conclude we risk blowing the hydraulic social valve. But, despite the knee-jerk or intuitive appeal to some on the Left of arguments that condemn inequality or domination as destructive or unsustainable, on the basically scientific criteria we emphasize in our dismissal of (neo)classical economics' "unrealistic" theories, there is not a whole lot of evidence that progressive claims are more obviously universally and transhistorically "true." One could even argue that the part of Piketty's argument that has made him a progressive darling—the idea that inequality is bad for society—is founded on a theory of human motivation barely distinguishable from the self-interest the Left ridicules in the hands of mainstream economics. The expectation or demand that the poor or the working class or the subjugated should or will throw off the capitalist burden or embrace Occupy Wall Street is always based at least partly on the assumption that collective action is in the end self-interested. Inverting the classical sages' vision of self-interest as the means to collective welfare, the modern "progressive" holds that collective well-being is the path to self-interest—socially responsible self-interest versus effectively self-interested social responsibility. Recall the political paralysis of the Bush era, when the Left in Europe and North America struggled to understand, as Thomas Frank put it, "What's the matter with Kansas?" How could the poorest state in the United States vote for Republicans who would only further impoverish them? Why didn't the poor and disenfranchised act in their (presumably selfish) "interests"?[63]

One way to get out of this—which involves abandoning any claim to an economics devoid of politics and rejecting the sacred separation of politics and the economy (an act of disciplinary treason of which Piketty is constantly accused)—is to admit that "human nature," like capital, is a product of its time and place and to assert,

---

63  Thomas Frank, *What's the Matter with Kansas? How Conservatives Won the Heart of America*, New York: Metropolitan Books, 2004; Serge Halimi, "What's the Matter with West Virginia?" *Le Monde Diplomatique*, October 2004.

on political rather than scientific grounds, what a better "human nature" would be, and why. But any program to remake human nature has a nasty set of political predecessors. The compulsion to turn back at this frontier is ultimately where the appeal of Keynesianism lies. Keynesians tell us that, with proper stewardship and appropriate institutions, "human nature" is basically good enough and that, in conditions of reasonable social justice, it will do reasonably good things.[64] The question of political agency—outside the "universal class" of enlightened technocrats managing the state apparatus, at least—never arises and need not concern us.[65] We can safely denounce orthodox economics' celebration of the survival-of-the-fittest while remaining on the terrain of science and disavowing the realm of politics—the realm in which we might remake "human nature" and a realm that was the basis of many totalitarian projects.[66] We can indeed have a revolution without revolutionaries.

In other words, Keynes and Piketty tell us that the answers are ultimately not political but technical. The right science can manage the community so that we never have to turn to politics. There are very good reasons this message is so appealing, not just to worried liberals but also to many on the Left. For the rabble and disorder Hegel, Keynes, and Piketty fear is not revolutionary democratic transformation or egalitarian redistribution. They are not trying to suppress the emergence of the common, the multitude, or the "truth" of the working class in the political consciousness of collective freedom. Right or wrong, their fear is lynch mobs, *Kristallnacht*, neighbor informers, religious fundamentalists, the Tea Party, and Donald Trump. This is what many progressives in the capitalist global North fear too, because they have absorbed the same lessons as those they claim to oppose: it is unwise to trust the masses. The twentieth century taught them what the rabble can do. That is why Keynes is embraced so enthusiastically in every moment of capitalist crisis and

---

64    "[T]he important point is that one can hope that democratic deliberation in general leads in the direction of common sense [*bon sens*]"; Piketty, *Capital*, 878.

65    Hegel, *PhR*, §303.

66    For which the economy was to be not so much an object of governance as an instrument of transformation.

why Piketty has been given the mantle of knight in shining armor. He has come to subdue the rabble dragon without shedding any blood. But, just as with Keynes eighty years ago, and Hegel two centuries back, it is the existential anxiety at the heart of modern civil society that sent him on his quest.

# CHAPTER 15

# Revolution After Revolution?

In our own twenty-first century moment, the effusive embrace of Piketty indicates that anxious Keynesianism is alive and thriving. Modern political economy has always already been Keynesian in this sense: haunted by the memory of revolution and upheaval, and thus by a consciousness of the menace of popular rejection of the existing order, but convinced the right tax tweak or policy fix has the capacity to put off disaster so we can focus on economic bliss once more. If we think of political economy as identifying the conditions for the legitimation of a given distributional order (the latter being the problem of "who gets what and how much"), and economics as the problem of market function and price determination, then Keynesianism's reassembly in the wake of increasingly rapid-fire crisis shows how central political economy remains to liberal government, even when it claims it is only interested in economics.

Unsurprisingly, then, tension has filled the air since the collapse of Lehman Brothers in fall 2008, and almost a decade later, things hardly seem more promising. Joseph Stiglitz and Nouriel Roubini warn of austerity-driven fascism; Paul Krugman tells us that Greece's SYRIZA, even when it was still a party of the radical Left, did not go far enough; and Larry Summers is promoting "inclusive economies," rejecting his formerly doctrinaire defense of capitalism in a desperate bid to avoid point-of-no-return social unrest. Martin Wolf, one of liberal globalization's most articulate champions, titled his *Financial Times* commentary of May 27, 2014 "Disarm Our Doomsday Machine."[1] Angus Deaton, the 2015 Nobel laureate in economics, is warning of a middle class "epidemic of despair."[2] Political economy is how liberal government thinks, and Keynesianism's resurrection with 2008 is proof of how true this remains. This is a reengagement with Keynes's "paradox of poverty in the midst of plenty," with Hegel's struggle to understand why, "despite an *excess of wealth*, civil society is *not wealthy enough*" to prevent "an excess of poverty and the formation of a rabble." The anxiety triggered by the "rabble mentality" remains at the heart of liberal government. It is as crucial to the formation of Euro-American modernity as any other dynamic you care to name. These are the conditions Keynes warned us about: the poverty and inequality no one "of spirit" will accept for long.[3]

These fretting public intellectuals are all Keynesians, and Keynesianism is the political foundation for the house they are desperately trying to repair before it all falls to pieces. They all claim to speak in the name of the "average citizen," the working family and the "middle class." Indeed, a blurb on the jacket of the most recent edition of *The General Theory*—the one with an introduction by Paul Krugman—celebrates Keynes as "a workingman's revolutionary." One can only presume he merits the label (which he would have much appreciated) because the workingman and workingwoman need not stop working during the Keynesian revolution. Not that he or she would want to, of course:

---

1    "If Europe does not change its ways—if it does not reform the eurozone and repeal austerity—a popular backlash will become inevitable"; Joseph Stiglitz, "Europe's Lapse of Reason," Project Syndicate, January 8, 2014; Martin Wolf, "Disarm Our Doomsday Machine," *Financial Times*, May 27, 2014.

2    Anne Case and Angus Deaton, "Rising Morbidity and Mortality in Midlife Among White, Non-Hispanic North Americans," available at: princeton.edu/main/news/archive.

3    Hegel, *PhR*, §245 (emphasis in original); see also Jürgen Habermas, "Appendix I: Popular Sovereignty as Procedure," in *Between Facts and Norms: Contributions to a Discourse Theory of Law and Democracy*, trans. William Rehg, Cambridge: MIT Press, 1998, 474: "The welfare state was the innovation that democratized—and thereby stabilized—capitalism in the twentieth century"; Dani Rodrik, "Labor Saving Technology," Project Syndicate, 2015; Angus Deaton, "Rising deaths among white middle-aged Americans could exceed Aids toll in US," 2015, available at: theguardian.com.

for one reason or another, Time and the Joint Stock Company and the Civil Service have silently brought the salaried class into power. Not yet a proletariat. But a salariat, assuredly. And it makes a great difference . . . There is no massive resistance to a new direction. The risk is of a contrary kind—lest society plunge about in its perplexity and dissatisfaction into something worse. Revolution, as Wells says, is out of date.[4]

The "decaffeinated" *révolution sans révolution* Keynes proposed—like Hegel's before him—can unfold without the working man or woman worrying himself or herself too much: "If you leave it to me, I will take care of it."[5] In the hands of a bureaucratic universal class with the requisite expertise and breadth of vision, the technical problem of political economic transformation can proceed much more smoothly, and wisely, than if we all got involved. Ensuring the "necessaries" and honor that ground the modern social order, political economy can reconstruct an appropriate separation between Politics and the Economy, the former the superstructural realm in which popular participation is welcome, the latter the structural fundamentals not amenable to democracy.

The effort to properly define the realm of the economic in the interests of ring-fencing the political is not distinctively Keynesian. The assumption that it is not only possible but necessary is in fact "one of the deepest premises of liberalism: politics is necessary, but should not become too serious."[6] And the only way to ensure that it does not is to take "serious" questions off the political menu—questions like poverty, unemployment, inequality, and class struggle, all of which are bound to make the realm of the political a very fractious space.

Liberals have not discovered a consistent manner in which to effect this separation. More often than not, it has been introduced by

---

4   Keynes, *New Statesman & Nation*, November 10, 1934, in CW, XXVIII, 34.

5   Slavoj Žižek, *In Defense of Lost Causes*, London: Verso, 2008, 158: Žižek says "decaffeinated" means "1789 without 1793."

6   Tracy Strong, "Foreword," in Carl Schmitt, *The Concept of the Political*, trans. George Schwab, Chicago: University of Chicago Press, 2007, xxvi.

philosophical, ideological, statutory, or coercive fiat, the variation depending on the context. Sometimes, as in the Prussia of the Stein-Hardenberg reforms, in which Hegel first worked on his *Philosophy of Right*, it means administrative centralization to subdue internal discord among elites.[7] Other times, as in the "Keynesian" era following World War II, it means, as Keynes put it, entrusting "to science the direction of those matters which are properly the concern of science."[8] Today, among other things, it means proceduralizing international trade through undemocratic institutions like the World Trade Organization, abandoning economic sovereignty to organizations like the European Commission or the International Monetary Fund, and handing more and more of the domestic policy realm to the "neutral" technicians steering "independent" central banks.[9] The objective is to excise the "serious" questions by means of technical-scientific or jurisdictional surgery: to ensure that the "economic problem" is beyond "serious" public engagement.

## The Political Economy of Hope and Fear

In all cases this involves a paradoxical engagement with political economy: on one hand, the tools of political economy as science are the principal means by which liberal government implements and maintains this separation; on the other, the separation is produced so as to make the expression "political economy" appear oxymoronic, because the economic, which concerns the confrontation with necessity and the maintenance of the social order, is supposed to be (in the

---

7   Terry Pinkard, *Hegel: A Biography*, Cambridge: Cambridge University Press, 2000, 418–25.

8   John Maynard Keynes, "Economic Possibilities for Our Grandchildren," in *CW*, IX, 373. An internet search of this phrase will reveal how often this passage is cited and the remarkable extent to which it is mobilized by environmental science and its advocates in support of technocratic independence in the organization of everything from carbon mitigation to geoengineering.

9   On the way this undemocratic dynamic plays out in the monetary arena, for example, see Geoff Mann, "The Monetary Exception: Labour, Distribution, and Money in Capitalism," *Capital and Class* 37: 2, 2013, 196–215.

words of Hannah Arendt) "non-political" by definition. It is either a technical matter for the state, or a private affair for the household. What it is definitely not supposed to be is an object of struggle or negotiation.[10]

The capacity to construct and maintain this separation—which all Keynesians recognize as artifice, that is, as the social organization of legitimation—is the hinge in the dialectic of hope and fear at the heart of Keynesianism. Hope is only possible when the separation is acknowledged as legitimate, when the poor consent to their poverty. Without it, the economic seeps into politics, and all bets are off. This is the source of Keynesianism's fundamentally antidemocratic character. The separation is not "natural," and it can hardly be expected to hold if civil society self-regulates, since its very operation undermines its own stability, engendering the dishonored poverty that must be suppressed. The institutional and ideological buffer required by the "universal class" that operates the modern liberal state in intermittent concert with the elite capitalist leadership of civil society is thus a matter of life and death. Its legitimacy is, without exaggeration, an existential necessity for modern liberal capitalism, and Keynesian political economy is its principal knowledge and way of knowing. The universal class is the pharmacist of liberal capitalist civilization.

Keynesian explanations of history's moments of descent into "chaos" in "Western Civilization" almost always turn on the way an

---

10    Domenico Losurdo, *Hegel and the Freedom of Moderns*, Durham: Duke University Press, 2004, 237; Hannah Arendt, *The Human Condition*, Chicago: University of Chicago Press, 1958, 29. One of the more extreme variations on this excision of the economic from popular sovereignty is the libertarian argument for a "constitutional economics" by the likes of James Buchanan and Gordon Tullock of the "public choice school" (see Chapter 12). Although one might imagine that to suggest something is "constitutional" is to prioritize its political valence, "constitutional economics" would encode the mode of economic management—in this case, strict *laissez-faire* and neo-monetarism—into a nation-state's constitution, effectively removing it from debate because constitutions are very difficult to alter. Chicago School legend Robert Lucas has proposed something similar: for "efficient" monetary policy, "one must either permit an initial government to make decisions binding for all time . . . or restrict available strategies still further"; in other words, a policy rule that makes future policy changes impossible. James Buchanan, "The Domain of Constitutional Economics," *Constitutional Political Economy* 1: 1. 1990. 1–18; Robert Lucas, "Principles of Fiscal and Monetary Policy," *Journal of Monetary Economics* 17, 1986, 128.

attempt to construct "true" democracy leads to the contamination of the political by the economic. The inevitable impossibility of meaningful democracy is "proven" by what Keynesians consider to be the history of failure of what we might call *révolution avec révolution*. The moral to be taken from these stories is that the reassertion of order out of collapse always comes in populist-authoritarian form. Hence, the "Arrovian chaos" that followed the French Revolution led to the rise of Napoleon; the Bourbon restoration followed the brief liberal moment of Napoleonic Spain; the Second Republic collapsed with the victory of Louis Bonaparte on the backs of the alienated *lumpenproletariat*; vicious white "Redemption" followed Black Reconstruction in the US South; fascism emerged in barely consolidated Italy and Spain; and the Nazi disaster followed the chaotic end of the Weimar Republic.[11]

These are, sometimes, potted histories, even if they have some truth to them. But it is worth emphasizing that despite some superficial similarities, they are not Hobbesian—they are not about regress to a "state of nature" but instead about the outcome of dynamics particular, and endogenous, to modern liberal civil society. The disorder is not what modern communities protect us from, it is where they lead. These accounts describe capitalist civilization's tendential self-impoverishment, its *progressive* tendency to ruin. There are, then, some very interesting parallels one might draw with the radical historiography that has accumulated on any one of these developments. Radicals too argue that bourgeois-capitalist hegemony is fraught with self-destructive contradictions. They also often tell a similar story of the failure of revolutionary promise, but they usually attempt to show how, in many of these instances, it was not

---

11　Norman Schofield, "Social Orders," *Social Choice and Welfare* 34, 2010, 513–14; Norman Schofield, "Power, Prosperity and Social Choice: A Review," *Social Choice and Welfare* 20, 2003, 85–118. To take the history of Spain as a case study, see F. D. Klingender, *Goya in the Democratic Tradition*, London: Sidgwick and Jackson, 1948, 198–205; Robert Hughes, *Goya*, New York: Knopf, 2004, 274–328; Brendon Westler, "Between Tradition and Revolution: The Curious Case of Francisco Martínez Marina, the Cádiz Constitution, and Spanish Liberalism," *Journal of the History of Ideas* 76: 3, 2015, 393–416. It is no accident that Goya's despair is a common way for Keynesians to make sense of Spanish history. If Hegel had been a painter, he might have been Goya.

revolution but counterrevolution that precipitated authoritarian calamity. The failure of revolution, or the failure of revolution to arrive at all, is attributed to the constellation of forces that animated the moment and succeeded in preventing the realization of the revolution.

There is, however, a crucial Keynesian move in this retrospective assessment of revolution and "Western Civilization": Keynesianism does not engage in historiographical struggle. It places itself in the spectatorial position Arendt associated with Hegel, above the fray. From the Keynesian vista, the radical account of class forces and material and ideological struggle are accorded some truth-status. Keynesians empathize with revolutionaries. Unlike conservatives or classical liberals, they understand where revolution comes from—the dishonor engendered by poverty, unemployment, and inequality in liberal capitalism is real, and the masses are hardly to be expected to maintain an attachment to a modern community that neglects their welfare but cannot convincingly explain why. What Keynesians claim to "see" from their vista, but that radicals supposedly cannot, is that revolution is no more the "answer" than reaction. Neither revolution nor tradition is the solution. Bourgeois civilization—which all Keynesians understand to be the greatest achievement in history, however flawed—is always already on a tightrope. It contains the potential for bliss or disaster, but bliss is (as it were) only realizable at the end of the rope—a long and precarious walk—while disaster lies on both sides. We will never realize the long run without paying scrupulous attention to the fact that we could fall at any moment.

To Keynesians, therefore, revolution is as naïve a denunciation of modern liberalism's failures as *laissez-faire* is a celebration of its successes. Neither has the perspective or wisdom to look down and see the quivering rope beneath our feet. Hegel and Keynes, like all Keynesians, believe they are among the few that see the rope and get the balance right to make our way forward—which we must, because there is no standing still on a tightrope, and definitely no turning around. We cannot choose to stay where we are, and we cannot go back. Which is to say that often, "putting off disaster" is the only way to realize "economic bliss." That, obviously—or so it seems to Keynesians—is a job for the experts.

Keynes captured this sentiment in his Galton Lecture to the Eugenics Society, "Some Economic Consequences of a Declining Population," given a few months after the publication of *The General Theory*:

> If capitalist society rejects a more equal distribution of incomes and the forces of banking and finance succeed in maintaining the rate of interest somewhere near the figure which ruled on the average during the nineteenth century (which was, by the way, a little *lower* than the rate of interest which rules today), then a chronic tendency towards the underemployment of resources must in the end sap and destroy that form of society. But if, on the other hand, persuaded and guided by the spirit of the age and such enlightenment as there is, it permits—as I believe it may—a gradual evolution in our attitudes toward accumulation . . . we shall be able, perhaps, to get the best of both worlds—to maintain the liberties and independence of our present system, whilst its more signal faults gradually suffer euthanasia as the diminishing importance of capital accumulation and the rewards attaching to it fall into their proper position in the social scheme.[12]

This political path is a critique of both liberalism and radicalism at the same time, one that drops out of view when we speak of reaction and revolution and their mediation through "reform."

This is the crucial thread that Antonio Negri, in his deservedly famous 1967 essay on Keynes and Keynesianism, calls "bourgeois Utopianism." It invokes a "mystified notion" of the social interest "to represent an end-situation which could be attained 'without revolution'": "Capital becomes communist: this is precisely what Marx terms the communism of capital."[13] While Marx in fact never used

---

12  Keynes, "Some Economic Consequences of a Declining Population," *Eugenics Review* (April 1937), in *CW*, XIV, 132. Keynes's Malthusian interest in population—which he was certain was about to stabilize and then decline slightly, kept him interested in eugenics.

13  Antonio Negri, "Keynes and the Capitalist Theory of the State post-1929" [1968], in *Revolution Retrieved: Writings on Marx, Keynes, Capitalist Crisis and New Social Subjects*," London: Red Notes, 1988, 32–33.

the phrase "communism of capital" (nor "socialism of capital"), Negri touches on a crucial issue here.[14] His point is definitely not an endorsement of Peter Drucker's claim that we have reached an age of "pension-fund socialism." It is also very different than Žižek's critique of philanthro-capitalist "liberal communism"—Bill Gates or some other billionaire acting on Marx's dictum ("from each according to his abilities . . ."): fighting poverty or climate change, supplementing capitalism with "communism," putting a "humanitarian face" on exploitation.[15] Neither is it an anticipation of Paolo Virno's analysis of the post-Fordist (which is also, supposedly, post-Keynesian) neoliberal order as a "communism of capital." Virno argues that neoliberalism has operationalized a perverse capitalist variation on some of communism's central demands: wage labor is abolished, but only in favor of precarity for those fortunate enough to have any work at all; the state withers, but only in the interests of corporate power and market discipline; alienation is resisted, but by fetishizing difference, not building solidarity.[16]

Both Žižek and Virno identify crucial features of modern liberal capitalism. But Negri is pointing to something broader, an arguably more fundamental movement in its historical dialectic: "a secular phase of capitalist development in which the dialectic of exploitation was *socialised*, leading to its extension over the entire fabric of political and institutional relations of the modern state."[17] In this account, capital is "communist" in two basic senses: First, it is communist in that its "community of the free" is composed of the multitude of capitals; when households are left to their own private disasters and

---

14    Armin Beverungen, Anna-Maria Murtola and Gregory Schwartz, "The Communism of Capital?" *ephemera: theory and politics in organization* 13: 3, 2013, 484.

15    Peter Drucker, *Post-Capitalist Society*, New York: HarperBusiness, 1993; Slavoj Žižek, *Violence*, New York: Picador, 2008, 17–19. The flip side of the liberal communist coin is what Phillip Blond dubs a "Red Tory communitarianism," a liberal break with big business, a regulatory attack on monopoly, and support for worker-ownership, etc., in the interests of a "property-owning democracy"; "Rise of the Red Tories," *Prospect Magazine*, February 2009.

16    Paolo Virno, *A Grammar of the Multitude: For an Analysis of Contemporary Forms of Life*, trans. I. Bertoletti, J. Cascaito, and A. Casson, New York: Semiotext(e), 2004.

17    Negri, "Keynes and the Capitalist Theory of the State," 9.

banks are lavishly and uncritically bailed out, for example, the "community" to which the collective is dedicated "in common" is clear. To the extent that the worker participates in this communism, it is only as he or she is "massified," in other words, contributes to aggregate demand and is exploited in the interests of a "community of the free" to which he or she only "belongs" by virtue of that exploitation. Second, Keynesian capitalism is communist in the simple sense that it promises to attain, through an illiberal liberalism, a Utopia not entirely unlike (some visions of) communism: a world without rent, in which individual liberty and the social interest are both protected and the love of money and the scarcity value of capital are eliminated.

## The "Bourgeois Dialectic"?

And yet, Negri understandably does not trust the Keynesian promise. Indeed, it seems to him *impossible*. Remarking on Keynes's 1930 claim that the "problem of want and poverty and the economic struggle between classes and nations is nothing but a frightful muddle, a transitory and *unnecessary* muddle," Negri writes that there "is not even a sense of full and secure conviction: he is consciously disguising what is basically—and necessarily—an irrational obligation, an obscure substitute for any content of rationality."[18] Negri attributes this to Keynes's "clear-sighted conservatism," for which *The General Theory* is a "political manifesto": "a manifesto of conservative political thinking, in which a sense of present depression and anxiety for a doubtful future paradoxically combine to force a systematic revolutionising of the whole of capitalist economics." In other words, it is an attempt—by way of political economy, we might add—"to rule out a range of catastrophic possibilities and to cancel out the future by prolonging the present."[19] This is the core of what Negri calls Keynesianism's

18   Ibid., 21.
19   Ibid., 24–25.

"bourgeois dialectic," which "knows no sublation, it cannot over-throw its object."[20]

This is an incisive, stimulating, and welcome intervention. Yet there are ways in which its keenness exposes more than the ironic concept "bourgeois dialectic" is willing or able to handle. The phrase identifies an essential aspect of the Keynesian critique—its relation-ship to liberalism—but Negri does not pursue it very far. Instead, he uses it for rather un-dialectical purposes: to oversimplify (or deny entirely) Keynesianism's relation to modernity's revolutionary past and to exaggerate its correspondence with liberalism, at the expense of an understanding of some key aspects of the inner workings of both revolution and liberalism.

Negri evokes the "bourgeois dialectic" in the context of a critique of *The General Theory*'s celebrated dismantling of Say's law, which Negri holds to be a merely superficial attack on orthodoxy. To Keynes, the key to full employment was not classical liberalism's *lais-sez-faire* but reduced uncertainty—and yet, in *The General Theory*, he claimed that it was precisely by reducing uncertainty to encourage sufficient investment that classical *laissez-faire* would again become possible. Then Say's law would come back into force and orthodox analysis would be true to the world. Orthodoxy is only sustainable through unorthodox means. This is the culmination, without subla-tion, of the "bourgeois dialectic." As Negri puts it: Keynes's "destruc-tion" of classical economics

> served only for its reconstruction ... The bourgeois dialectic knows no sublation, it cannot overthrow its object. Whenever Keynes reaches the extreme limit of his critique, he is paralysed by a philosophy that stops him in his tracks.[21]

The question, though, is what obstacle sets the "limit" to the Keynesian critique? What is the philosophy that stops it in its tracks? Negri's answers are the revolutionary working class and communism.

---

20   Ibid., 21.
21   Ibid.

If only it were so. In fact, the answer to both questions is liberalism. For Keynesianism, liberalism is simultaneously capitalism's gravest problem and its only hope. This is what it actually means to say the "bourgeois dialectic knows no sublation, it cannot overthrow its object." Which is also to say that Negri unwittingly, but accurately, impugns the bourgeoisie with a double historical failure: not only is it an obstacle to the "emancipation" anticipated by so many communists, but it cannot get the movement of history right, even on its own limited terms. For a dialectic without sublation is no dialectic at all. It not only contradicts the inevitable radical emancipation upon which Negri's reading of Marxism depends entirely—and for this alone Negri condemns it out of hand—but it also goes so far as to deny what it cannot—the very force of history. It is, therefore, necessarily doomed by its own impossibility.

Because the first failure is merely a particular affront to Negri's own political theology, it is of little interest. If the problem with historical development is that it appears to contradict the answers he has formulated to questions that have not even been asked yet, that is not history's problem, but Negri's. The second failure is of far more interest and a far more important critical contribution. Neither the limits of Keynesian political economy, which Negri calls the "science of capital," nor the philosophy that "stops it in its tracks," is imposed externally upon the bourgeois dialectic. As Negri knows, the antagonistic nature of the working class and its politics—the "masses"—are a product of bourgeois capitalism's own contradictions. Although Negri develops a compelling and historically engaged account of the rise of the working class as the form "demand" takes in modern capitalism, it nonetheless fits quite readily into a rather standard Marxian mold, in which capitalism's crisis tendency emerges in part from its contradictory dependence on workers—they must simultaneously be producers paid as little as possible and consumers purchasing as many commodities as possible.

According to Negri, the particular but simultaneous problems *The General Theory* struggles to understand are economic (the Great Depression) and political (the "full independent expression" of working class politics in the Russian Revolution of 1917), but nonetheless two sides of the same process: the latter effectively triggered the former, he argues, because capital's terrified response to the Bolshevik victory led to the technological "repression" of the working class and hence to overaccumulation crises associated with unsustainable economywide organic compositions of capital. Negri identifies *The General Theory*'s distinctive merit in that it marks the point at which the real force of this dual crisis breaks the surface of capitalist thought. Keynes, he says, is the first to acknowledge—albeit without being fully aware of it—"the emergence of the working class and of the ineliminable antagonism it represented within the system as a *necessary feature of the system which state power would have to accommodate*."[22]

In Negri's analysis, then, Keynes represents the reluctant bourgeois recognition of the historical fact of working class autonomy.[23] In a postrevolutionary echo of Hegel's lordship and bondsman dialectic (the same dialectic discussed with regard to Haiti in Chapter 8)—the proletariat's fundamental independence forces itself into liberal consciousness: the proletariat does not need capital; capital needs the proletariat! Keynesian political economy is an attempt, in the face of the radical "philosophy that stops it in its tracks," to design a capitalism that can withstand the challenges posed by a working class autonomy Keynes could not help but admit when his critique reached its "extreme limit." It acknowledges

> the real problem facing capital: how to *recognise the political emergence of the working class*, while finding a new means (through a complete restructuration of the social mechanism for the extraction of relative surplus value) of *politically controlling this new class within the workings of the system*. The admission of working class autonomy had to be accompanied by the ability to control it politically.[24]

Negri developed this analysis in the 1960s, returning to it only intermittently and briefly in the years since, but it remains the best

22   Ibid., 10, 13.
23   Ibid., 28.
24   Ibid., 12.

critical account of the Keynesian contribution we have. His most crucial move is to read *The General Theory* as a "political manifesto"— not just because to do so offers new insights, but because that is, in fact, what it is. That it takes the form of political economy is an absolutely essential aspect of its politics (as I argued in Chapter 8 and as Hegel said two hundred years ago).

Nevertheless, Negri misconstrues his subject in fundamental ways. This is due in part to his selective engagement with Keynes and Keynesianism (perhaps a function of the material he could get his hands on), but to an even greater degree to his failure to embed the Keynesian critique in a liberal tradition that stretches back long before the Russian Revolution. This leads him to exaggerate *The General Theory*'s "decisive" breakthrough, as if it were an unprecedented capitalist response to the power of 1917, and thus, as many Marxists have done (and still do), he reads the Keynesian critique of modern capitalism as essentially a "mixed economy" *rapprochement* with the working class or the Left more broadly.[25] For Negri, Keynesianism ultimately represents the always contradictory effort to save capitalism from communism, the means to become a "planner state" (*stato plano*) that keeps the workers happy enough to prevent them from going red.[26]

Yet, because this is very clearly a part of what Keynes hoped to achieve, it leads Negri (and many others) to take the recognition of the need to "appease the masses" as evidence of a more fundamental motivation: the bourgeois fear of communism in the form of the revolutionary working class, embodied so powerfully in the Bolshevik Revolution. In other words—returning to the question of what Keynes came to save capitalism from and why he came to save it— Keynesianism here arrives to rescue capitalism from the proletarian liberation that marches inexorably toward it on all sides. Negri argues that Keynes offers a more effective solution to the *same problem* to

---

25  For example, see Charles Maier, *Recasting Bourgeois Europe: Stabilization in France, Germany, and Italy in the Decade After World War I*, Princeton: Princeton University Press, 1975.

26  Negri, "Keynes and the Capitalist Theory of the State," 13, 25.

which "immature ruling classes responded with fascist repression": the "inherent antagonism of the working class." "The British working class appears in these writings in all its revolutionary autonomy."[27]

This is not true. Or, if it is true, it is so partial and trivial that it is for all intents and purposes untrue. If it is not unreasonable to assume, first, that by "revolutionary" Negri means the kind of revolution he has spent his whole life working toward, and second, that his concept of "autonomy" suggests a capacity for the self-organization of such a revolutionary project, then his argument is based upon a crucially important misunderstanding.

Keynes-the-Edwardian-gentleman was of course concerned about the founding of the Soviet Union and class-conscious proletarian unrest. But anything more than a cursory engagement with his work will reveal his life-long commitment to the more complex Keynesianism traced in previous chapters, a Keynesianism that was a direct response to World War I and its aftermath, especially fascism. For him, the "inherent antagonism of the working class" is a poor and ultimately naïve description of the range of politics engendered by modern liberal capitalism. Insofar as capitalist civil society persistently produces poverty, and thus the immanent potential for the emergence of a rabble driven by necessity and unfreedom to undo the social order, then as far as Keynes was concerned, it was indeed a possibility that some collective that identified as "the working class" would be rendered "inherently" antagonistic to the social relations of liberal capitalism.

But this was only one possible form of "inherent antagonism," and all evidence suggests that for Keynes (and for Hegel also, if we can admit some anachronism), a class-conscious proletarian revolution in the struggle for communism in western Europe or North America was one of the more unlikely ways it would realize itself. Anything approaching what Negri means by "communism" would have appeared to Keynes and Hegel as the lesser of several evils. Keynes feared the radical Left, certainly, but no more (and arguably quite a bit less) than fascism, radical conservatism, authoritarianism,

---

27   Ibid., 10, 13, 19.

demagoguery, and anything else that smacked of dogmatic "funda-mentalism," because he understood all of them as undermining the stability of "civilization." Keynes feared the rise of an intransigent Right as much as a radical Left, since they both posed a serious threat to the precarious stability of modern communities by making them too inflexible. The Keynesianism of Hegel, Keynes, and Piketty is less a project to save capitalism from communism than to protect modern bourgeois civilization from disorder and the chaos and disastrous totalitarian fundamentalisms—Stalinist, National Socialist, or other-wise—to which they expect it inevitably leads. If that means saving some fundamental capitalist political economic architecture, well, then of course it must be done. *Révolution sans révolution* will always prioritize load-bearing features of the status quo.

And just as important, Keynesianism is not a project to save capi-talism from some threat because these forces menace "modern communities" from outside. On the contrary. The greatest threats to the social order to which Keynesians are committed are products of that very order. They take the "ethical" bases of liberal capitalism—the uncoordinated and unrestricted ("free") pursuit of individual self-interest in the inherently unequal context of a modern "mone-tary production economy"—to lead inevitably to poverty and thus to rabble mentality. If unaddressed through an adequately legitimat-ing ideological and institutional constellation, such conditions appear to render "the masses" all the more prone to the populist dogma to which they are susceptible even at the best of times. Since they do not understand how close to chaos we actually are, they are more willing than they should be to sacrifice measured practice to vengeful doctrine. The result will be a nightmare impossible to contain. The problem is not, then, the seeds that distributional radi-cals like Robespierre have always sown, but rather the soil in which they are sown, a soil that is cultivated by a liberalism afflicted with a sort of pathological far-sightedness: it is so convinced of its abstract, long run Truth and Reason that it is blind to the short run perils that threaten any such project.

But if the provision of necessaries and the promise of honor adequately buttress *Sittlichkeit* in a society, then these forces have no purchase. The Keynesian solution to this always-looming risk to civilization that lies at the heart of liberalism thus takes the form of a reluctantly radical, immanent critique of liberalism. Rather than freezing in its tracks when confronted with its extreme limit, the critique instead operationalizes the most sophisticated tools at liberalism's disposal—the tools provided by modern political economy—in the pharmaceutical, even surgical, management of the body of liberal capitalism itself. In the hands of the state, these instruments can (it is hoped) cure liberal civil society of its disorderly tendencies, thus literally saving its life—which is synonymous with saving civilization.

## I, Bourgeois

In the long run we are all dead, so let us not wait until then: this is the paradigmatic problem for bourgeois political economy. Indeed, it seems to me that whichever way we turn, we cannot avoid returning to the figure of the bourgeois at this conjuncture. The figure is fraught if only because to conjure it up is to expose oneself as anachronistic or to immediately identify oneself with a Marxian critique (at which point many stop listening) or both. Consequently, I bring up the figure of the bourgeois aware of its potential untimeliness but unable to shake the conviction that it captures something that is far from anachronistic. I do invoke a Marxian sensibility, but not only, and in any case Marx himself used the term "bourgeois" far more specifically than some Marxists, for whom it has become an insult, spat off-handedly at the habits of the professional and managerial classes. Despite all this, it seems to me that the bourgeois—as Hegel, Marx, and others since have analyzed him or her (mostly him)—is in fact crucial to Keynesianism, and alive and well, if not so coherent in his or her identity as perhaps was once the case.

On these grounds, the bourgeoisie is a key figure in a fractious and volatile modern age that really begins with the French Revolution. Since the end of the Terror, it has not only made up a significant part of the capitalist class, but of the professionals, managers, and well-paid workers, too. It is long associated with "culture" and "ideas" and "art"—"civilization," as it were. It is not reactionary but "conservative" in the bland sense of the word, interested in "disciplining change."[28] It has also long been dismissed as "rationalist and unheroic."[29] Hegel, the first to make the bourgeoisie the true protagonist of modernity, was also the first to diagnose in detail its essential political inadequacy: its members "find compensation" for their "political nullity" in

> the fruits of peace and of gainful employment, and in the perfect security, both as individuals and as a whole, in which they enjoy them. But the security of each individual is related to the whole, inasmuch as he is released from courage and from the necessity . . . of exposing himself to the danger of violent death, a danger which entails for the individual absolute insecurity in every enjoyment, possession, and right.[30]

We do not have to adopt the martial undertones of this denunciation, I think, to appreciate its capacity to capture an important quality of political life in modern liberal capitalism. This unheroic, anxious, absolute insecurity engenders in the bourgeois a "glorification of what exists" that is "always accompanied by the delusion that the individual—that which exists purely for itself, which is how the subject necessarily appears to himself in the existing order—is capable of the good." Adorno—whose sharp and prescient words these

---

28   Maier, *Recasting Bourgeois Europe*, 1.

29   Joseph Schumpeter, *Capitalism, Socialism and Democracy*, New York: Harper & Row, 1942, 138. Carl Schmitt celebrates Hegel for capturing the nature of the bourgeois as "essentially apolitical and in need of security"; Carl Schmitt, "Hegel and Marx," *Historical Materialism* 22: 3-4, 2014, 390.

30   G. W. F. Hegel, *Political Writings*, Cambridge: Cambridge University Press, 1999, 150. This was written between 1798 and 1802, a few years before the *Phenomenology of Spirit*, whose famous lordship-bondsman dialectic is clearly foreshadowed here. Reading the dialectic with this in mind lends some support for Alexandre Kojève's influential lectures on Hegel in the 1930s, in which lordship and bondage stand in for the bourgeoisie and the proletariat; Alexandre Kojève, *Introduction to the Reading of Hegel: Lectures on the Phenomenology of Spirit*, trans. James Nichols, Ithaca, NY: Cornell University Press, 1980.

are—claims that "Hegel destroyed this illusion."[31] That seems to me patently untrue. If anything, Hegel, and Keynes even more so, have made it possible for the illusion—if indeed it is an illusion—to persist long past the end it would have suffered without them. Keynesianism rescues the bourgeois in the modern sense—the sense in which it is epitomized by Hegel the wine connoisseur, by Keynes and his Bloomsbury colleagues, by contemporary "progressive" (and even some "radical") cosmopolitan academics and professionals.

This is certainly due in part to "the bourgeois spirit [that] has spread well beyond the bourgeoisie," and the bourgeois "illusion" is arguably far more generalized today, in Piketty's moment, than when Hegel or even Keynes was writing.[32] And if the bourgeois spirit has spread, it is almost certainly among the self-identified middle class. In the affluent global North, that is not a small fraction of the populace. As of 2015, while the number is declining due to the fallout of the "Great Recession" and (probably even more because of) accelerating inequality, between 50 and 60 percent of US households still self-identified as middle class.[33] A 2008 survey found that almost half of respondents with annual incomes below $20,000, and a third of those with incomes above $150,000, considered themselves middle class. There is of course no reason to identify the bourgeoisie as coextensive with the "middle class," and it is important not to generalize the US experience across other liberal capitalist nation-states, but they are certainly overlapping categories, especially since the dawn of the "Keynesian" era following World War II.

Consider the following, from a 2010 US Department of Commerce report to the Vice President:

> Income levels alone do not define the middle class. Many very high and very low-income persons report themselves as middle

---

31    Theodor Adorno, *Hegel: Three Studies*, trans. Sherry Weber Nicholsen, Cambridge: MIT Press, 1993, 48.

32    Maurice Merleau-Ponty, "An Epilogue to *Adventures of the Dialectic*," in Ted Toadvine and Leonard Lawlor (eds.), *The Merleau-Ponty Reader*, Evanston, IL: Northwestern University Press, 2007, 304.

33    Gallup, "Fewer Americans Identify as Middle Class in Recent Years." 2015.

class. Social scientists have explained this by defining "middle class" as a combination of values, expectations, and aspirations, as well as income levels. Middle class families and those aspiring to be part of the middle class want economic stability, a home and a secure retirement. They want to protect their children's health and send them to college. They also want to own cars and take family vacations. However, aspirations alone are not enough; middle class families know that to achieve these goals they must work hard and save.[34]

These aspirations are obviously the historical product of the Keynesian Golden Age, but some combination of them would seem to me to accurately characterize at least a substantial portion of any twenty-first century incarnation of Hegel's unheroic and insecure bourgeois as well as the "bourgeois and intelligentsia" whom Keynes celebrated as "the quality in life and surely carry the seeds of all human advancement."[35] There are moments when many, myself included, can find themselves in the thrall of these aspirations. Which is to say that, if it is possible to live this identity, which should be (and is) riven with contradictions, it is because of two bourgeois delusions: first, that the individual (though not only the individual) is capable of the good; second, as Habermas said typifies the bourgeois, to be bourgeois today is to be a member of a class that has convinced itself it no longer rules.[36]

*This* is the "bourgeois dialectic" that "cannot overthrow its object." According to Negri it "knows no sublation" since its first and last moments appear to him identical. Liberalism begets liberalism. But it is not really so simple. The bourgeois or Keynesian dialectic is not a sorry attempt to stall the force of history. It is structurally akin not to Marx's account of the emergence of capitalist social relations from their precapitalist predecessors, but to his account of the specificity

---

34  US Department of Commerce, Economics and Statistics Division, *Middle Class America* (Executive Summary), Washington, DC: US Department of Commerce, 2010.

35  Keynes, *CW,* IX, 258.

36  Jürgen Habermas, *Legitimation Crisis,* trans. Thomas McCarthy, Boston: Beacon Press, 1975, 22.

of capital as a sociohistorical relation. Just as in the operation of capital the commodity stands for Marx as a middle term in the expansion of value—$M$-$C$-$M'$—the Keynesian dialectic captures a dynamic at the core of two centuries of actually existing, illiberal liberalism, in which the state is the middle term: $L$-$S$-$L'$. At least since Thermidor, liberalism has been renewed and reconstituted through the state and its political economy, a process that continues. If $M$, $C$, and $M'$ constitute the moments in the movement of value, for Hegel and Keynes $L$, $S$, and $L'$ are the moments in the historical development of freedom, in which the gradual evolution of $L'$ to $L''$ represents the consolidation of a conception of freedom that embraces the necessity toward which the state constantly and pragmatically turns it. Freedom develops in the recognition of necessity's necessity.

Keynesianism's decisive contribution to liberalism is to have legitimized its hegemony by continually, pragmatically, and scientifically generalizing a worldview in which the welfare of the state and the prosperity of civil society are conceptually inseparable: this is in fact the *definition* of "civilization." Its inescapably illiberal liberalism has proven essential to the survival of even the most dogmatically classical liberalism, providing it with an anxious political logic without which it would never have survived without the constant use of brute force. The bourgeois and the middle class are thus both effect and cause of Keynesian "civilization." "Civilization" provides the ground upon and against which many—especially but not only those enjoying any degree of privilege—have come to build a life. If there is a bourgeois dialectic whose engine consistently stalls on the on-ramp to the highway of History, it is because the bourgeois dialectic has been carefully constructed, politically, ideologically, and materially, so as to avoid at all costs overcoming its object. Surely no "civilization" in history has been so persistently and increasingly tweaked, groomed, massaged, sutured, studied, and monitored as modern liberal democratic capitalism. Surely no modern "civilization" has been so introspectively and pragmatically attentive not just to the order of government or the state, but to the "arrangement of society as whole."[37]

---

37  Habermas, "Popular Sovereignty," 478.

None of which is to defend that "civilization," with or without scare quotes. But it is to say that its very object—to (paradoxically) *not* "overcome its object"—is premised on deferral. The interplay between hope and fear at the heart of Keynesianism, between the promise of "economic bliss" and the threat of disaster, erases something crucial to deep social transformation or revolutionary politics. It is not so much that the future is collapsed into the present (a variation on Fredric Jameson's description of postmodern temporality) but rather that for many, it no longer seems reasonable to imagine we could construct a future of our own choosing. Too much could happen between now and then. That is a long-run project, and in the long run we are all dead.

Moreover, although Joan Robinson tells us that Keynes tended to go through moods when capitalism enraged him, and others when he sang its praises, the self-arresting bourgeois dialectic of hope and fear at the heart of Keynesianism and modern bourgeois (Keynesian) "civilization" is less and less a trampolinelike experience in which we confront the world in successive stages: a lift of optimism, followed by a fall of pessimism, then bouncing optimism again. Today, I would argue that our political "animal spirits" are not moved by a rhythm of hope, then fear, then hope once more. Instead, it is both hope and fear, all at once, all the time. At times it becomes difficult to know one from the other. My hopes for my children, for example, are not that they will "do better" than I have, or achieve more than I have or will (as we are told was the case for the previous generation). My greatest hope for my children is that their future will not turn out to be as disastrous as I fear it will be. From this perspective, a revolutionary Leap of Faith seems simultaneously absolutely necessary and a very bad idea.

This is not liberalism, but bourgeois-dom, and it is the force that never lets Keynesianism go. Revolution will always frighten Keynesianism, because revolution claims to guarantee what Keynesians think they know is *impossible*. Everything they have ever thought tells them so, all the history they know tells them so, even when they know that the *status quo* is untenable. Maybe, just maybe, there is something up the road; you never know: "If we are at peace in the short run, that is something. The best we can do is put off disaster, if only in the hope, which is not necessarily a remote one, that something will turn up."[38]

In the post-Golden Age conjuncture of accelerating capitalist political-economic volatility, ecological degradation, and the threat or likelihood of catastrophic climate change, all this makes perfect sense. This is where the increasingly widespread urge to embrace the promises of "Green" Keynesianism comes from: a combination of technocracy and technology, state and private enterprise, that will—somehow—not only get us out of our ecological bind, but will stimulate growth and jobs, counteract inequality, promote international cooperation, and produce a world which can only be a better, more environmentally friendly version of "civilization's" status quo.[39] All without significant interruption, too: it will be a "workingman's revolution." The new and improved modernity will of course struggle with the same tragic tendencies to the production of poverty, unemployment, and inequality, but they will be less pressing, and, because our attention to the constant political-ecological and political-economic panic will no longer be so urgent, we will have greater resources to dedicate to making modernity even better still. Who would not want to participate in this collective act of wish fulfillment? If nothing else, it is better than the apparent alternative (awaiting the arrival of "Arrovian chaos" and the demagoguery to which it is sure to lead).

## Doctor Marx and Mister Keynes

Some readers of an early version of the first chapter of this book—committed, engaged, effective young activists I feel fortunate to even

---

38 Keynes, *CW,* XXVIII, 61.

39 Like all Keynesianisms, in an age of crisis Green Keynesianism appeals to a wide range of otherwise seemingly incompatible political positions. See, for example, Edward Barbier, *A Global Green New Deal: Rethinking the Economic Recovery,* Cambridge: Cambridge University Press, 2010; Susan George and Walden Bello, "A New, Green, Democratic Deal," *New Internationalist,* no. 419, 2009; Martin Sandbu, "This Shouldn't Be Difficult," *Financial Times,* November 30, 2015.

know, let alone to have read my writing—suggested that even if this analysis of the current moment does not justify this conservatism, it nonetheless conveys the message that hope for radical change is lost, that their admirable work to change things is a waste of time. I tried, and failed, to convince them that to acknowledge this Keynesian common sense "out loud" is neither to defend nor to accept it, nor even to admit its (capital T) Truth. Nor is it to claim that it is futile or foolish to resist this promise—which, I might seem to be saying, they should welcome because it is the "best we can hope for" or for some other pragmatic reason. It is neither. If nothing else, I am as certain as I can be that something like "Green Keynesianism" is no solution to the ecologically and politically destructive trajectory we are on. The question of what politics and political economy, bourgeois or not, will look like in the future will largely, I think, be a product of how that failure unfolds and on whose watch, if anyone's.[40]

Instead, the importance of acknowledging the ideological power of Keynesianism lies in the fact that it is one of the toughest obstacles any project of more-than-trivial social transformation will face. Currently, I would venture to suggest, it hegemonically defines the horizon of the peacefully possible for both those who understand themselves as in fundamental political opposition to much of the current liberal capitalist order and those whose dogmatic and unwavering faith in austerity is always tacitly back-stopped by a Keynesianism-of-last-resort. Insofar as nonviolent transformation is the goal, Keynesianism is the politics and political economy to which many people "nearest" to the Left feel most attached, because on the terms of that politics, letting go is to abandon reason and relinquish control by throwing one's fortunes in with the masses. From that perspective, a lot has gone wrong, and a lot more could yet. If a nonviolent constraint is not binding, then the political project is all the more daunting, since a constituency that might rally around

---

40   For more on this assessment of the political implications of climate change, see Joel Wainwright and Geoff Mann, "Climate Leviathan," *Antipode* 45: 1, 2013, 1–22; and Wainwright and Mann, "Climate Change and the Adaptation of the Political," *Annals of the Association of American Geographers* 105: 2, 2015, 313–21.

Žižek's call—however qualified and mystified—to embrace and renew a revolutionary Terror has yet to realize itself.[41] Outside the lunatic fringe of neo-Nazis like Golden Dawn and US militias, there is not yet virtue in terror again; in the age of the Islamic State of Iraq and Syria and imperialist drone attacks, the idea seems, if nothing else, entirely and justifiably discredited.

Indeed, there are many who might not be willing to grant revolution and revolutionaries much credit any longer. Keynesianism is premised, among other things, on the recognition that there is no best or permanent "solution" to the problem of sustaining "civilization" and a legitimate and stable social order. There being no "right" answer to the challenges of this or any other conjuncture, and especially no *single* "right" long-run destination, the arrogance on the part of the stereotypical revolutionary to claim there is a right answer, and the assumption of the omniscience to name it, might be difficult to put up with anymore. At the very least, when, for good or ill, revolution or radical transformation commonly conjure up Stalin, Mao, or Castro (and, perhaps, Ho Chi Minh, Franco, or Ben Bella), the historical support for the Leap seems weak. None of these stories ended well for the very "people" who supposedly thought they were finally taking the reins of their own history. The fact that in actuality, all of these histories are more complicated, that in many cases the revolutions were crushed or betrayed by domestic reactionaries or

---

41    Žižek, *In Defense of Lost Causes*,157–210; Žižek, *Violence*, 178–217; Žižek, *Living in the End Times*, Afterword, and elsewhere. Žižek's defense of what he once glibly named *Linksfascismus*, "left fascism," is a strange and mostly, as far as I can tell, merely provocative sensationalism. His insistence on the simultaneously macho and monastic issue of Terror— of the demand to cull the "traitor" to the revolution, to commit to the logic of minoritarian Truth, to never fear death—is always qualified, parenthesized, and complicated by un-explained references to Lacanian terminology, as if everyone has just re-read the Seminars last week. I have no idea where the embrace of "divine violence" is supposed to go, what is supposed to happen, or who we might expect to still be standing, if anyone, once we have made the "Leap of Faith" (only the Just? the Mighty?). In this same *salto mortale* vein, Žižek is fond of quoting Alain Badiou's "*mieux vaut un désastre qu'un désêtre*" (better a disaster than the "dis-being" of "eventless utilitarian-hedonist survival" in which the rest of us live), but again, it hardly seems to matter, which is probably good for those upon whom *désastre* might actually descend (it is unlikely to be Žižek or Badiou). See also Alan Johnson, "The Power of Nonsense," *Jacobin* 3–4, 2012.

imperial forces, that however bad it turned out, it might still be better than what would have been—none of this, unfortunately, is all that important unless we can tell those histories differently, in ways and places that can be widely heard and embraced. Until then, at least in the part of the planet with "something to lose," Keynesianism always appears the more "realistic" proposition.

These failures are not lost on the young activists who read my draft chapter. Their persistently hopeful resistance in thought and action is not naïve; they are not "radical" merely because they are youthful, starry-eyed, or full of rebellious contempt for their elders. On the contrary, they seem much older than they are, more jaded than they "should" be, but unwilling to give up. Habermas, whose late politics epitomize much of Keynesianism, nonetheless accurately captures some of this.

> The Revolution itself has slipped into tradition: 1815, 1830, 1848, 1871, and 1917 represent the caesurae of a history of revolution-ary struggles, but also a history of disappointments . . . Melancholy is inscribed in the revolutionary consciousness—a mourning over the failure of a project that *nonetheless cannot be relinquished.*[42]

At a political level, a consciousness caught up in a fusion of these positions is no doubt appropriate to its material conditions, Doctor Marx might say. The quotidian concerns of Mister Keynes constantly break in on and destabilize an intellectual–political life informed by the good Doctor.

When I began this project many years ago, I planned to write a Marxian–Gramscian critique of Keynes's resurrection in the wake of the financial meltdown of 2008. What I found in the writing, however, was the reluctant, even repressed, Keynesian in myself. And yet I would argue that in the end, I have in fact written a Marxian–Gramscian critique of Keynesianism through political-intellectual history. It is not the radical destruction of Keynes I planned it to be—far from it. But it is, or is intended to be, an attempt to make

---

42  Habermas, "Popular Sovereignty," 467, 471.

Keynes our Hegel, and through Keynesianism to understand the operation of a remarkably robust, immanent critique of modern liberal capitalist "civilization."

The question this contradictory condition poses for anyone who experiences it will of course be what to do. The Marxist in him or her will suggest he or she must "choose," and, in Lenin's words, only the "shame-faced" coward will choose Keynes. That, however, is not true—or we had certainly better hope it is not true—not least because ideology and the sediment of *Sittlichkeit* are not that easily sloughed off. If one imagines that the necessary revolution involves the more-or-less rapid and voluntary renunciation, by millions, of ideology that most of us cannot even recognize as ideology (that is how ideology works), then I think it is fair to say we are doomed.

This poses particular challenges for the Left in the capitalist global North, a diverse mix whose one shared quality is perhaps a special sensitivity to the precarious meaning of the past. The idea that popular revolution was once a useful tool of historical progress but is no more—properly "social revolution," as opposed to mere regime-changing "political revolution"—may be completely wrong-headed. Revolution might very well be the way in which we turn modernity around and orient it in the direction of a just and planet-worthy future. But the idea that revolution has had its day and is no longer a viable option is not incompatible with some aspects of contemporary "progressive" and "radical" politics. And if some have concluded that many of the struggles of the past and their political methodology have exhausted themselves or have ultimately failed, it would be foolish to say that conclusion is entirely unjustifiable. The problem is not just that it is hard to blame someone who is not convinced that one more protest march will matter all that much, or that a traditional class party is no longer an appropriate means to emancipatory ends. It is also that many revolutions have turned out very badly for the very people they were supposed to redeem. Not that there is nothing to learn or admire in the revolutionary politics of the past, but it takes a particularly sanguine—one might even say revisionist—historical perspective to defend the trajectory of the Soviet or Maoist experiments, for example.

Yet the idea that revolution is a thing of the past is complete anathema to others on the Left, and for equally good reasons. For them, the shadow of currently looming disasters (endless war, climate change and environmental degradation, accelerating concentrations of wealth and de-democratization, and so on), the disavowal of the resources of the past before a future that seems to have no history leads to two political errors, both tempting but untenable. The first is the belief that the past has no resources from which to draw at this daunting moment. If it sometimes appears that history is of no use, its movements ultimately no more than a rearranging of the deck chairs on a planetary Titanic, part of my goal is to show that this is not true or at least need not be true. The second mis-step is that in rejecting its own history—which depends only tendentially on chronology—the Left is too easily tempted to excuse itself from political complicity in the fact that the available options are so unsatisfactory. While those of us in "opposition" to the current order—whatever that may mean, and it can clearly mean a lot of different things— seem increasingly willing to accept partial responsibility for the "state we are in," we rarely understand our complicity is perhaps partly bound up in, if not entirely reducible to, a renunciation of the Left's revolutionary heritage.[43] It may be that what has "gone wrong" is due not only to revolutionary failures, but to our own inability or unwillingness to follow through on the revolutionary promise.

Wendy Brown once wrote of the need to overcome what she called (after Walter Benjamin) "Left melancholy," the "sorrow, rage, and anxiety about broken promises and lost compasses that sustain our attachments to left analyses and left projects." That effort, she says,

---

43   This is, I would suggest, a more productive direction in which to elaborate a Left self-critique than that proposed by Slavoj Žižek in his *In Defense of Lost Causes*, 175–76: "What this means is that, even if—or, rather, especially if—one submits the Marxian past to ruthless critique, one has first to acknowledge it as 'one's own,' taking full responsibility for it, not to comfortably reject the 'bad' side of things by attributing it to a foreign element (the 'bad' Engels who was too stupid to understand Marx's dialectics, the 'bad' Lenin who did not grasp the core of Marx's theory, the 'bad' Stalin who spoilt the noble plans of the 'good' Lenin, and so on)."

demands a spirit that embraces the notion of a deep and indeed unsettling transformation of society rather than one that recoils at this prospect, even as we must be wise to the fact that neither total revolution nor the automatic progress of history will carry us toward whatever reformulated vision we might develop. What political hope can we nurture that does not falsely ground itself in the notion that "history is on our side" or that there is some inevitability of popular attachment to whatever values we might develop as those of a new left vision? What kind of political and economic order can we imagine that is neither state-run nor utopian, neither repressive nor libertarian, neither economically impoverished nor culturally gray? How might we draw creative sustenance from socialist ideals of dignity, equality, and freedom, while recognizing that these ideals were conjured from historical conditions and prospects that are not those of the present?[44]

I would contend that while Keynesianism usually falls far short of this critical spirit, it is nevertheless the thread that ties the Left to its often knee-jerk Keynesian sensibility that allows us to identify it. If the task of the Left is to maintain the struggle for a transformed "political and economic order," that project must be Keynesian insofar as it embraces impossibility, hope, and fear as inescapable elements of both politics and the future toward which we hurtle. There is no denying the fact that we will never get it finally and perfectly right, that there is no "solution" and no historically ordained agent, like the proletariat, that will necessarily light or lead the way. Consequently, we will much of the time be terrified of what might be just around the corner. To deny this seems the purest folly. Necessity and freedom are not, except in an ultimately meaningless one-sided abstraction, separable, just as Hegel attests. The only realizable practice of freedom must involve a recognition of necessity, and the only realizable practice of collective freedom—the lived experience of freedom in a social world, which is surely what freedom always must be—depends upon recognizing and providing the necessaries that ensure

44   Wendy Brown, "Resisting Left Melancholy" *boundary 2* 26: 3, 1999, 26–27.

a dignified, secure, and joyful life for all, regardless of their individual "contribution." The fact that scarcity in the straightforward hunger-and-shelter sense will, in the ecologically nonsensical world capitalism has wrought, increasingly impinge upon that practice of freedom is undeniable. Green capitalism or any other promissory cure-all will not open a hidden escape-hatch through which we can exit the labyrinth. No revolutionary doctrine, Marxist or otherwise, can guarantee us deliverance, either. That is not a reason not to pursue revolutionary thought and action—indeed, it *"cannot be relinquished"* because the injustice that solicits it remains—but it is a reason to remain critically skeptical of guarantees.[45]

This Keynesian sensibility is, however, Marxian insofar as radical politics in the rich world, partly in and through the refusal of Keynesianism's Eurocentrism, will have no choice but to focus increasingly on necessity. It must, because it will be impelled to, build a foundation upon which radicalism (in its truest, from-the-roots sense) can grow. This will be, as Gramsci recognized all efforts must be, a stuttering scramble up the scree slope of history, accelerated no doubt by environmental pressures. If not, then however frantic the conditions, radicalism will pose as it so often seems to: as a shrill lesson from the "universal class" of revolutionaries, who can see the Truth and know the Way.[46] That is a political dead-end, a true disaster, and we need the room, the courage, and the wisdom to say it without thereby affirming the calamitous and unjust present or some technocratic mitigation of its terribleness. If that takes us to revolution, then fair enough. We will have hacked a clearing in which to gather for what comes next.

The radical kernel at the heart of Keynesianism, which Keynes and even Hegel could never see, lies here, in the refusal either to throw out or to cling desperately to what we have, but to admit those things "we simply do not know." Keynesianism's bourgeois dialectic stutters

---

45  Domenico Losurdo, *War and Revolution: Rethinking the 20th Century*, trans. Gregory Elliott, London: Verso, 2015.

46  Maurice Merleau-Ponty, *Humanism and Terror*, trans. John O'Neill, Boston: Beacon Press, 1969 [1947], 9: "Revolutionary honor is itself only a species of bourgeois dignity."

on its dependence upon the experts or elites to find a safe haven, however temporary: "something will turn up." A radical Keynesianism refuses this also, but it does not pretend or have the temerity to claim we need a bit of divine violence to knock us out of the rut we are in. No one "needs" violence, and surely not (à la Sorel or Žižek) "on principle." We need a new world, certainly. But we also must think about what we want to rescue, if anything, from the world we have; I cannot imagine there is nothing at all.

# Index

## A

absolute freedom, 127, 128, 129, 130, 131, 132, 141
absolutely necessity, rule of, 51
*abzuhelfen* (to remedy), 172
actual is rational, 137, 138–9, 149
actually-existing capitalism, 233–9, 356
actually-existing economy/price mechanism, 240, 241, 276
*Adam Smith in Beijing* (Arrighi), 360
Adorno, Theodor, 43, 121, 383
aggregate demand, 194, 244, 245, 248, 251n12, 255, 263, 276, 309, 352, 375
aggregate supply, 244, 245, 248, 249n9, 251n12, 309
ahistorical and aspatial linear developmentalism, 66–67n25
allocation, 169, 192, 241, 249, 324n41, 332n61, 333
Althusser, Louis, 224n14
American Civil War, slavery and, 189n13
American War of Independence/American Revolution, 85, 133, 136, 185, 186
animal spirits, 9–10n15, 294, 295n35, 344, 345, 351, 387
antifascism, 67
anti-Keynesians, 3, 64, 186n8, 285, 289, 313, 354n40

antipopulism, 21, 22
anti-Ricardian, 198
anxiety
    of civil society, 340–2, 365
    as generated by tragedy in continued force of Keynesian ideas, 63
    at heart of Keynesianism, 278
    Keynesian reason as scientific form of political anxiety, 258
apocalypse, 343. *See also* Marxian apocalypse; Ricardian apocalypse
Apostles, 40
Arendt, Hannah, 38, 49, 55, 86, 102n41, 122, 144–5, 146, 148, 149, 164–165n5, 185, 186, 259n6, 278, 302, 370, 372
Arrighi, Giovanni, 360
Arrovian chaos, 290, 371, 388
Arrovian collective social choice agent, 332
Arrow, Kenneth, 61n9, 285–6, 287, 288, 289, 290
*AS-AD*, 309
atomicity, principle of, 11, 173–174n18, 176
Audier, Serge, 39n8
*Aufklärung* (enlightenment), 123, 128
austerity, 202, 297, 297n39, 314, 367n1, 389
automatic stabilizers, 227
Avineri, Shlomo, 177n28

**B**

Badiou, Alain, 75, 85, 112, 113, 117, 390n41
Bailey, Samuel, 243
bank intermediation, 252n13
Baran, Paul, 36–7, 38
bastard Keynesianism, 60, 311, 313
Bees, Fable of the, 139, 180
Benjamin, Walter, 393
Bentham, Jeremy, 322
Benthamite, 199, 260n9, 289, 331
Beveridge, William, 282, 283, 299n42, 300
Beveridge Report (*Social Insurance and Allied Services*), 281
Blackburn, Robin, 24
Blair, Tony, 49
Blinder, Alan, 313n23
Blond, Phillip, 373n15
blueback scheme, 17n32
Bodin, Jean, 49, 150
Bolivarian revolution, 214
Book 1ers/Part 1ers, 61, 62, 309. *See also* New Keynesians
bourgeois, 77, 154n30, 382–8
bourgeois dialectic, 375–82, 385, 386, 387, 395
bourgeois liberalism, 90, 132, 172
bourgeois order, 68, 90, 116, 175n22, 197, 202, 204
bourgeois political economy, 382
bourgeois public sphere, 55, 278
bourgeois revolution, 85, 108, 109, 185, 186
bourgeois socialism, 75–76n40
Bowles, Samuel, 318n32
Bradley, A. C., 72
Bretton Woods Agreements, 47, 48
Brontë, Charlotte, 282
Brown, Wendy, 393
Buchanan, James, 289, 289n20, 370n10
Buck-Morss, Susan, 207, 208, 209
bureaucratization, 55
*bürgerliche Gesellschaft* (civil society or modern community), 38, 45, 150, 153
Burke, Edmund, 183, 190

**C**

Cambridge controversy, 312–313n20
Cambridge savings equation, 312
capital
    according to Piketty, 347
    as communist, 373–4
    marginal efficiency of capital (*MEC*). *See* marginal efficiency of capital (*MEC*)
    scarcity theory of, 238, 239, 268–73, 342
    tax on, 352n33, 357, 358
    as tending toward fascism, 301
    ultimate purpose of, 348
*Capital* (Marx), 337n3, 338, 359
*Capital in the Twenty-First Century* (*Capital au XXe siècle*) (Piketty), 10, 17, 337, 338, 339, 340, 341, 360, 362
capitalism
    capitalist abundance as self-destructive proposition, 12
    capitalist scarcity as produced by, 12
    consolidation of in post-1789 Europe, 271
    crisis tendency of, 344
    as endangering stability of social order, 340
    individualistic capitalism, 238n40, 259, 265, 342n11
    Keynes as attempting to save, 64, 65, 66
    Keynes as committed to rewriting, 65
    Keynes as most influential theorist of in twentieth century, 36
    Keynes's theory of, 229
    liberal capitalism. *See* liberal capitalism
    managerial capitalism, 55
    as monetary production economy, 234
    theory of actually-existing capitalism, 233–9
    unemployment as a must, 330
capitalist modernity, x, 11, 35, 291, 314

Carlyle, Thomas, 183
causal priority, 233–234n30
centrality of centrality, 53
Césaire, Aimé, 205, 208, 209
Chapter 12ers, 61, 62, 309. *See also*
    post-Keynesians
civil dissension, 15, 83
civilization
    defined, 9–10n15, 386
    Keynes as seeing self riding to rescue
        of, 274
    Keynes's theory of, 23
    as in need of saving, 66
    precariousness of, 18
    problem of maintaining, 85, 204
    theory of, 63–72
    thin crust of, 205, 228, 273–9
*Civilization and Its Discontents* (Freud),
    9–10n15
civil society
    according to Hegel, 150–7, 270
    analysis of, 52
    anxiety of, 340–2, 365
    defined, 271
    disorganization of as Hegel
        proposal, 173, 177
    failures of, 52
    as historical force, 53
    *Notrecht* and, 146–50
    principle of, 283
    as source of difficulties, 55–6
    theory of, 52–3
classical economics, 14n24, 58, 217,
    227, 228n21, 230, 233, 240, 241,
    242, 245, 249, 251, 252, 253,
    254, 256, 260, 305, 307n6, 311,
    314, 363, 376
classical liberalism, 68, 71, 181, 250,
    354, 376, 386
climate change, x, 18, 19, 374, 388,
    389n40, 393
climate Leviathan, 19, 389n40
Clinton, Bill, 313n23
coefficient (of Kalecki), 294n34
Cold War, Keynesian heights of, 22
Colletti, Lucio, 37, 190
colonialism, relationship of political
    economy to, 205–14
colossal muddle, 49, 180, 237

commerce, freedom of, 94, 95, 97, 99,
    100. *See also* trade, freedom of
Committee of Public Safety, 27, 86,
    102, 111, 189
common element, 127, 177
communism, 11, 16, 22, 66, 67, 77,
    93, 302, 339, 359, 371, 373, 374,
    375, 376, 379, 380
community of the free, 109, 110, 112,
    114, 141, 187, 271, 331, 374, 375
complete markets, 230n27
concrete freedom, 128, 140–3, 150,
    165
conservatism, 22, 23, 50, 73, 76, 87,
    106, 115, 134, 134n49, 135,
    137, 183, 184, 187, 211, 222,
    297, 351, 357, 372, 375, 380,
    383, 389
constitutional economics, 370n10
consume, propensity to, 237n39, 246,
    247, 248, 260, 263, 270
consumption, 15, 196, 237, 245, 246,
    247, 248, 263, 266, 276, 283,
    293, 298, 351
contracting, 320, 320n35
"Contribution to a Critique of Hegel's
    Philosophy of Law" (Marx), 223,
    224
Convention of 1792, 50
crisis
    capitalism's most significant legiti-
        mation crisis, 17
    crisis tendency of capitalism, 344
    financial crisis (2007–2008). *See*
        financial crisis (2007–2008)
    political and economic conditions
        identified as crises, 83
    political economy as science of, 84
    twenty-first century triple crisis, 7–8
    use of term, 84
crisis-oriented fiscal policy, 226–7
critical wage, 325, 325n45, 326, 327,
    329, 330, 332
curse of Midas, 157, 294. *See also* fate
    of Midas

**D**
*Daily Telegraph*, 64, 182
David, Jacques-Louis, 182

De Angelis, Massimo, 218
*The Death of Marat* (painting), 182
Deaton, Angus, 336–337n2, 367
Debreu, Gérard, 61n9
Declaration of the Rights of Man and Citizen (1789), 359
deficit spending, 227
defunct economists, 132
Deleuze, Gilles, 348n24
delicate machine, 237, 238, 240, 342
DeLong, J. Bradford, 313n23, 338
demand
    aggregate demand, 194, 244, 245, 263, 276, 309
    effective demand. *See* effective demand
    priority of, 249n9
    supply and demand. *See* supply and demand
de Mandeville, 139, 154, 258
*denrées* (foodstuffs), 97, 168, 198
de Tocqueville, Alexis, 85
Dewey, John, 42
*direzione*, 68. *See also* Gramsci, Antonio
"Disarm Our Doomsday Machine" (Wolf), 367
*Discourse on Colonialism* (Césaire), 205–6
*Discourse on Inequality* (Rousseau), 156, 337n3
disembedded liberalism, 48
disequilibria, 61, 243, 246, 266, 312, 312n19, 317, 353
disorder
    abolition of, 170
    fear of, 51, 54, 364
    inevitable transformation as needing to be accomplished without, 53
    keeping of at bay, 23
distribution
    challenge of as one side of problem of poverty, 168
    as classical focus of political economy, 192
    concerns of/problems of, 67–68n25, 92, 168, 357
    distributional radicals, 381
    distributional regimes, 330

economic distribution, 192
    legitimation of, 366
    market-mediated/market-based distribution, 341, 347
    and narrative of revolution, 209
    Pareto optimal distributional arrangement, 324n41
    and standard summary of economics, 265
    of wealth and incomes, 37, 115–16, 117, 292, 332, 332n61, 336, 343, 345, 350, 354, 373
doctrine of separation, 11
Douglas, Paul, 228
Drucker, Peter, 373
Durkheim, Émile, 271

E
ecological disintegration, 19. *See also* climate change
economic, separating of from political, 10–11, 55. *See also* political-economic separation
economic bliss, 14, 15, 58, 201, 236, 239, 303, 341, 345, 346, 353, 366, 372, 387
*Economic Consequences of the Peace* (Keynes), 3n2
economic liberalism, 68
economic pessimism, 13–14, 54n33
"Economic Possibilities for Our Grandchildren" (Keynes), 13, 369n8
economic problem
    as beyond serious public engagement, 369
    liberalism as incapable of containing, 73
    poverty as, 279
    reining in of, 56
    solving of, 12, 13, 15n28, 54, 70, 204, 236
    as supposedly disappeared, 72
    use of term, 16, 278
economics. *See also* macroeconomics; microeconomics
    classical economics. *See* classical economics
    constitutional economics, 370n10

of information, 319, 320
neoclassical economics. *See* neoclassical economics
neoclassical microeconomics, 240, 241
new classical economics, 240
Ricardian economics, 199, 230n27
economic thought, mathematization of, 61n9
*Economist*, 64, 206
economists. *See also specific economists*
defunct economists, 132
freshwater economists, 242, 242n2, 258
saltwater economists, 242n2
effective demand, x, 29, 30, 61, 155, 194, 197, 198, 237, 239, 243–5, 246, 247, 248, 249, 263, 264, 265n20, 266, 274, 276, 277, 292, 309, 309n9, 327, 351
efficiency wages, 323, 325
elite managerialism, 20
elites, 12, 17, 18, 19, 21, 22, 27, 29, 65, 69, 74, 75, 79, 83, 92, 110, 111, 118, 134n49, 180, 183, 193, 198, 201, 207, 212, 282, 336, 369, 370, 396
embedded liberalism, 47, 48, 48n22
employment, 196, 243, 245, 246–7, 248, 249, 250, 251, 253, 254, 256, 263, 267, 268, 269, 283, 297, 303, 305, 316, 318, 325, 326, 328, 329, 330, 383. *See also* full employment; unemployment
employment function, x, 327, 327n49, 328
Engels, Friedrich, 75, 79, 223, 359, 362
enlightenment, 122, 123, 124
entrepreneuriat, 235, 235n34, 244, 245, 246, 247, 294, 299, 344, 349, 351
equality. *See also* inequality
formal equality, 73, 90–1, 103, 104, 156
liberty and, 99–106
equilibria, 233, 243, 250, 253, 255, 266, 274, 286, 287, 289, 305,

307, 311, 312n19. *See also* disequilibria; full employment equilibrium; macroeconomic equilibrium; unemployment equilibrium
equilibrium unemployment, 304–34. *See also* unemployment equilibrium
"Equilibrium Unemployment as a Worker-Discipline Device" (Shapiro and Stiglitz), 315
estate (*Ständ*), 174, 175, 175n22
ethical non-naturalism, 40
ethical state, structure of, 173–81
Euro-American, use of term, 46
European colonialism, 158n42
European Commission, 369
extremism, 86, 93, 188

**F**
Fable of the Bees, 139, 180. *See also* de Mandeville
Fama, Eugene, 241
fascism, ix, 13, 42, 53, 67, 84, 274, 285, 301, 302, 302n52, 353, 360, 366, 371, 380, 390n41
fatal purity argument, 102
fate of Midas, 237, 269. *See also* curst
Ferguson, Charles, 193
feudalism, 115, 135, 140, 207
Feuerbach, Ludwig, 224, 225
Fichte, Johann Gottlieb, 149
financial crisis (2007–2008)
dynamics that helped trigger, 266
inequality as mainstream object of political economic critique since, 335–6
responses to, 24, 314
return of Keynesianism following, x, 3–5, 4–5n6, 16–17, 25–6, 36, 44, 59–60, 222
*Financial Times*, 206
fiscal conservatism, 297
Fordist–Keynesian state/Keynesian–Fordist Golden Age, 324, 354
formal equality, 73, 90–1, 103, 104, 156
formal freedom, 128, 154, 156
formal universality, 152

Foucault, Michel, 84, 145, 154, 163, 191, 193, 209, 210, 211

Frank, Thomas, 21, 363

free, community of the. *See* community of the free

freedom
 absolute freedom, 127, 128, 129, 130, 131, 132, 141
 abstract and concrete, 140–3
 concrete freedom, 128, 140–3, 150, 165
 formal freedom, 128, 154, 156
 identity of as heart of modern life, 123
 post-French Revolution, 119–43
 poverty as opposite of, 12, 73, 129
 practice of, 96
 principle of, 96
 universal freedom, 131, 140, 160

freedom of commerce/freedom of trade, 94, 95, 97, 99, 116, 166, 167, 169, 170

free markets, 29, 62–63n14, 79, 95, 186n8, 199, 235, 238, 255, 273, 276, 323, 347, 360

free trade, 48, 99, 199, 212n60, 341, 358

French Revolution. *See also* Robespierre, Maximilien; Terror
 as contemporary event, 190
 failures of, 126–7, 134
 as founding moment of Keynesianism, 214
 fractious and volatile modern age as beginning with, 382
 Hegel and, 121–5
 Hegel as struggling to make sense of, 39, 43, 119
 Hegel's critique of liberalism as based on, 132–3
 as heralding revolutionary birth of modern political liberalism, 85
 influence of on birth of liberalism, 44
 legacy of, 182, 183–4, 191, 207
 as lens through which to assess progress of modernity, 87
 and liberal ambivalence, 184–91
 liberal reaction to, 71

origins of Keynesianism in, 5–6

origins of social choice theory as traced to, 289

Thermidorian reaction as most powerful inheritance of, 106. *See also* Thermidor/Thermidorian Convention

as universal earthquake, 85

freshwater economists, 242, 242n2, 258

Freud, Sigmund, 9–10n15

Friedman, Milton, 52, 241, 284n7, 285, 289, 317, 325

full employment, 29, 155, 230, 239, 243, 246, 248, 249, 250, 252, 253, 255, 266, 268, 277, 285–96, 298–9, 301, 304, 318, 322, 324, 326

full employment equilibrium, 30, 233, 242, 243, 246, 253, 255

*Full Employment in a Free Society* (Beveridge), 282

full unemployment, 281–303

fundamental inequality $r > g$, 343–4, 350, 353

fundamentalism, 381

fundamental psychological law, 246, 260–1, 294

Furet, François, 93

**G**

$g$ (rate of economic growth), 343–6, 351

Galbraith, James K., 68, 313, 338

Galbraith, John, 68, 313

Gates, Bill, 373

general good, 167, 168, 170, 171, 172

general possibility theorem, 285–286n11

*The General Theory of Employment, Interest, and Money* (Keynes), ix–x, 3, 8, 11, 12, 16, 34, 37, 39, 47, 50, 57, 58–9, 60, 61, 62, 63, 65, 70, 71, 79, 80, 132, 193, 199, 200, 201, 203, 205, 217, 218, 219, 226, 227, 228, 229–30, 232, 233, 235, 236, 238, 242, 243, 244, 246, 249, 253, 258, 259, 265, 268, 270, 274, 278, 282,

283, 291, 293, 294, 304, 305, 311, 312, 315, 318, 326, 327, 328, 339, 340, 341, 342, 344, 349, 351, 357, 360, 362, 367, 374, 375, 376, 377, 378
general will, 48, 87, 89, 127, 130, 131, 355
Geoghegan, Thomas, 4
Gesell, Silvio, 17, 17n32
Giddens, Anthony, 49
Gilroy, Paul, 208
Girondins, 94, 95, 99, 109, 189
Godwin, William, 196
gold standard, 228, 237n37, 351
government
  as province of universal class, 180n40
  state. *See* state
governmentality, 121, 154, 163, 210, 212
government debt, 247, 297
government intervention, 300, 301n48, 302, 303. *See also* state intervention
Goya, Francisco, 371n11
Gramsci, Antonio, 68, 139, 190, 359, 395
Great Depression, 43, 54, 59, 251, 254, 266, 269, 270, 282, 283, 285, 300, 314, 351, 376
*The Great Escape: Health, Wealth and the Origins of Inequality* (Deaton), 336–337n2
Great Recession, 384. *See also* financial crisis (2007–2008)
Green, T. H., 39
Green Keynesianism, 388, 388n39, 389
guild system, 173–174n18, 176

**H**

Habermas, Jürgen, 16n30, 55, 164, 185, 278, 302, 359, 385, 391
Haiti, Hegel and, 123n15, 208
Haitian Revolution, 21, 47, 85, 121, 136, 139n69, 207, 208, 214, 377
Hansen, Alvin, 305
Hardenberg, Karl August von, 137n58
Harrod, Roy, 60

Harrod-Domar growth models, 339
Harvey, David, 158n42, 338
Hayek, Friedrich, 185, 289
Hayekians, 185, 289n20, 290n25
Haym, Rudolph, 135
Hegel, G. W. F., v, 7, 10, 35, 36, 37, 38, 39–44, 46, 47, 49, 50, 51, 56, 73, 77, 78, 79, 80, 95, 115, 119–43, 144, 146, 147, 148, 149–62, 163, 164, 165–6, 184, 185, 187, 190, 191, 193, 200, 201, 204, 207, 209, 210, 212, 220, 220n7, 221, 222–6, 259, 271, 272, 273, 274, 275, 277, 278, 289, 290, 300, 328, 329, 383
"Hegel and Haiti" (Buck-Morss), 207
Hegelian-Keynesian critique, 45
Heine, Heinrich, 103
Hicks, John, 305, 306, 307, 309
Hicks-Hansen framework, 305
Hirsch, Fred, 202n37
Hirschman, Albert O., 45, 64, 213
Hitler, Adolph, x, 87
Hobbes, Thomas, 23, 32, 51, 54, 71, 123, 146–7, 148, 151, 154, 178–9, 179n36, 259, 259n6, 270, 273
Hobbesian/Hobbesianism, 46, 51, 52, 54, 259, 260, 353
Hobhouse, Leonard, 42
Hobsbawm, Eric, 8
Hobson, John, 42
*homo economicus*, 258, 288, 320, 360
*Homo sacer*, 72n37, 148n10
honourable poverty/honorable poverty, 73, 78, 90, 91–9, 103, 104, 111, 112, 113, 116, 117, 118, 172, 203, 204, 334
Hoover Institution, 64, 337
human nature, 52–53n30, 123, 258, 316, 362, 364
Hume, David, 270

**I**

idealism/idealist, 37, 41, 87, 122, 124, 129, 149, 190, 191, 201, 205, 221, 221n9, 225, 258
ideal society, 353

IMF (International Monetary Fund), 114, 213, 369
imperfections, 201, 242, 250, 276
impossibility theorem, 285–6, 285–286n11, 287n16, 288, 290. *See also* Arrow, Kenneth
*In Defence of the Terror* (Wahnich), 184
individualistic capitalism, 238n40, 259, 265, 342n11
individual liberty, 48, 49, 52, 53, 171, 180, 355, 375
inducement to invest, 237, 237n39, 247, 248, 260, 309
inequality, x, 7, 12, 20, 30, 79, 89, 90, 103, 115, 156, 172, 196, 197n30, 202, 203, 243, 312, 314, 324n41, 334, 335–7, 336–337n2, 340, 344, 345, 345n17, 346, 347, 350, 353, 354, 356, 357, 359, 363, 367, 368, 372, 384, 388. *See also* fundamental inequality *r > g*
*Inequality for All* (film), 336
information, economics of, 319, 320
information asymmetry, 319, 320, 323
*Inside Job* (film), 336
interest, rates of, 17, 117, 232, 234, 235, 238, 239, 247, 263, 267, 268, 277, 295n35, 307, 351. *See also* negative interest rates
International Monetary Fund (IMF), 114, 213, 369
*International Socialist Review*, 64
interventionist state, 276
investment, 17n32, 61, 169, 218, 229, 231, 232, 235, 238, 247–8, 249, 252, 261, 263, 264, 265, 267n25, 269, 270, 276, 294, 307, 331, 344. *See also* inducement to invest; private investment; public investment; saving
involuntary unemployment, 251, 255, 256, 257, 258, 277, 295, 296, 322, 323, 324, 329
Ireland, struggles, 84, 211
Islam, political 76
*IS-LM*, 305, 306–15, 325, 331
*Ius necessitatis*, 88, 95, 97, 99, 144, 146, 147

**J**
Jacobin Club, 86, 92, 110
Jacobins, 87n7, 92, 93, 94, 99, 106, 109, 111, 119, 127, 146, 147, 173n16
James, C. L. R., 208
Jameson, Fredric, 348n24, 387
Japan, experiments of with Keynesian policy, 47
Jefferson, Thomas, 52
Jevons, William, 243, 304
joblessness, 282, 322, 334, 335. *See also* unemployment

**K**
Kalecki, Michal, 284, 290–6, 297, 298, 299, 300, 302–3, 304, 313, 314, 315, 316, 317, 318, 322, 324, 325, 326, 327, 329
Kant, Immanuel, 23, 40, 54, 87, 88, 91, 103–4, 123, 124, 126, 131, 144, 146, 147, 150, 164, 190, 270, 272
Karlsbad Decrees of August 1819, 137
Keynes, John Maynard
   analysis of modern political economy as tragic, 11–12
   antifascism of, 66
   as attempting to save capitalism, 64, 65, 66, 218, 378
   belief of in capacities of scientific management, 15
   belief of in masses as only capable of destruction, 16
   characterization of by critics on Left, 217–18, 219
   as committed to rewriting capitalism, 65
   as compared to Hegel, 36–8, 39, 39n7
   defense of *laissez-faire*, 62–63n14
   detractors of, 64
   difference between Keynes and Kalecki, 292
   economics of, 226–39
   as enemy of cult of tradition/nostalgia, 134
   as fearing rise of intransigent Right as much as radical Left, 381

foundation of work of, 56
as having inspired left- and right-traditions, 39
as helping to save capitalism and liberalism, 24
as known for witticisms, 227, 229, 234
legacy of, 134
letter of New Year's Day 1935, 58
on Malthus, 196–9
merger of with Keynesianism, 34
mismatch between readership of and influence of, 3n2
most famous remark by ("in the long run ..."), 51, 227, 228, 298
as most influential theorist of capitalism of twentieth century, 36
as no radical, 8
as not a democrat, 70
as not a left thinker, 68
as not committed to capitalism at all costs, 66
as not first Keynesian nor last, x, 5
as opposed to mathematization of economics, 304
as our Hegel, 222–6
political economy of as rooted in theory of civilization not theory of capitalism, 63
as pragmatist, 220, 284
putting of in proper historical place, 45
quote from, v
radical kernel at heart of, 12
radical potential in work of, 291
reputation of as sowing confusion or creating a stir, 59
as secret Hegelian, 43
visit to Soviet Union (1925), 69n30
as workingman's revolutionary, 367
writings of. *See The General Theory of Employment, Interest, and Money* (Keynes), 3n2, 13, 56–7, 203, 229, 273, 369n8, 372
Keynesian critique, 5, 26, 45–57, 132, 218, 296–303
Keynesian–Fordist Golden Age/ Fordist–Keynesian state, 314, 354
Keynesianism

as about production of credible stability in face of crisis, 15
antidemocratic character of, 370
anxiety as at the heart of, 278
appeal of, 24, 25, 55, 364
approach of to relation between individual liberty and social collective, 48
bastard Keynesianism, 60, 311, 313
as better science, 257
bourgeois as crucial to, 382
as conflated with economics of Keynes, 227
core of, 7, 262, 333
counterrevolution against, 7
decisive contribution to liberalism by, 386
defined, 32–57
as defined by relation between liberalism and revolution, 87
dialectic of hope and fear as heart of, 14, 16, 18, 284, 370, 387
as distinctively postrevolutionary politics and political economy, 118
early and later distinctions in, 14
as effort to shorten temporal units of history and deny effective force of long run, 116
Eurocentrism of, 214
function of rabble in, 160
Green Keynesianism, 388, 388n39, 389
heart of, 14, 16, 18, 21, 284, 370, 387, 395
hold on liberal capitalism of, 226
ideological power of, 389
as immanent critique of revolutionary radicalism and classical liberalism, 71
lack of reach outside western Europe and North America, 47
Left as bound to, 19
as liberalism's most significant theoretical and political development in face of revolutionary menace, 85, 206
logic at heart of, 21
as managing postrevolutionary transition in bourgeois order, 204

meaning of for progressives, 8
and necessity of political economy
  to modernity, 192
as not equivalent to political economy in Hegelian sense, 191
as obsessed with containing problems to their proper sphere, 55
origins of, 5
as part of effort to carve out space
  for honorable poverty, 117
premise of, 8
quasi-paralyzing conclusions as
  partly defining, 20
radical kernel at heart of, 395
raison d'être, 19
reassembly of, 366
return of/affirmation of with financial crisis (2007–2008), x, 3–5,
  4–5n6, 16–17, 25–6, 36, 44,
  59–60, 222
several lives of, 36
shared origin of with political economy, 145
supposed death of, 314, 315
as taking market- and state-
  mandated capitalist production
  and exchange relations for granted,
  202
as trying to stave off calamity caused
  by capitalism in hope something
  better will come along, xi
unrepentant lack of precision of, 193
use of term, 6, 33
vista of, 115, 119
as weaving immanent critique of
  revolution and liberalism, 44
Keynesian propositions, 50–3
Keynesian reason
  as alive and well, 44
  as conceiving negation, 348
  as demanding find-tuning, 53
  as demanding fundamental skepti-
    cism regarding all popular/populist
    modes of politics, 52
  fear of disorder as fundamental
    driver of, 51
  goal of, 49
  as having hold on progressive
    thought, 8

Hegel as first to fully elaborate, 39
as neither property nor product of
  Keynes alone, 36
as recognizing bourgeois public
  sphere, 278
as scientific form of political anxiety,
  258
use of term, 35
Keynesians. See also anti-Keynesians;
  New Keynesians; post-Keynesians
  as empathetic with revolutionaries,
    372
  examples of, 4
  origins of, 59
Keynesian state, defined, 54
Keynes–Piketty proposition, 355
Kindleberger, Charles, 6n9
King, Martin Luther, 139
kingdom of ends, 87n7, 88
Klasse (class), 174
Klein, Lawrence, 301, 310
Knight, Frank, 228
Koch brothers, 22
Kojève, Alexandre, 383n30
Korporation, 173–7, 178, 328
Kouvelakis, Stathis, 127
Krugman, Paul, 4, 34, 54, 60–1, 62,
  64, 206, 240, 242, 257, 258, 276,
  309, 338, 355, 366, 367

L
labor, as disutility, 251, 253, 317, 318,
  321, 321n37, 327, 328, 329, 330
labor supply, 250–1, 254, 295, 326,
  327, 328, 332
labor theory of value, 264n18
laissez-faire, 43, 59, 62–63n14, 64, 66,
  74, 170, 171, 181, 195, 196n28,
  219, 227, 230, 233, 240, 243,
  250, 257, 268, 269, 283n5, 286,
  298, 323, 343, 370n10, 372, 376
La Montagne, 189n12
Latin America, Keynesian policy as
  part of limited conversation in, 47
laws
  fundamental psychological law, 246,
    260–1, 294
  Say's Law. See Say's Law
Leap of Faith, 387, 390n41

Left
  as bound to Keynesianism, 19–20
  ghost of Robespierre as haunting, 79
  reaction to working class votes for conservatives, 76
  self-critique of, 393n43
  signal claim of, 75
  task of, 394
  as wanting democracy without populism, 21
left fascism, 390n41
left-Keynesian, 60, 69, 301
legitimation, 17, 28, 192, 202–3, 228, 314, 317, 333, 356, 366, 370
Lehman Brothers, x, 16, 228, 359, 366
Leijonhufvud, Axel, 33
Lenin, Vladimir, 54, 74, 139, 190, 392
*les Enragés*, 92n16
*Leviathan* (Hobbes), 146
liberal ambivalence, revolution and, 184–91
liberal capitalism
  as always characterized by unemployment, 333
  anxiety of, 84
  as calamity, xi
  civilization as under threat because of, 260
  critique of, 74
  current trajectory of, 19
  development of, ix–x
  emergence of, 140
  failures of, 278
  as form civilization took, 274
  as having distrust of the masses, 20
  as involving/producing poverty and disorder, 210
  Keynesian critique/Keynes's critique as running throughout history of, 44, 219
  Keynesianism as resting on, 7
  Keynesianism description of, 262
  Keynes's understanding of, 78
  as not holding self responsible for poverty, 72
  persistence of, x
  as potentially dead in the long run, Keynesian in short run, 25
  theory of, 7, 8
  as unsustainable if left to self-regulate, 79
liberal civil society, 45, 56, 233, 330, 371, 382
liberal elite, 21
liberalism
  according to Hegel, 142–3
  attractions Keynes found in, 67
  bourgeois liberalism, 90, 132, 172
  as capitalism's gravest problem and only hope, 376
  classical liberalism, 68, 71, 181, 250, 354, 376, 386
  coining of term, 187, 187n9
  core premise of, 23
  critique of, 49
  current efforts/varieties of, 22, 26
  defined, 135n51
  disembedded liberalism, 48
  economic liberalism, 68
  as effectively rewriting its own history, 93
  embedded liberalism, 47, 48, 48n22
  founding of, 42
  Hegel on, 43, 132–9, 169
  history of in nineteenth century, 42
  ideological hegemony of, 66
  immanent critique of, 11
  immanent critique/reform of, 7, 66, 85
  *laissez-faire* liberalism, 59, 74
  modern liberalism, 10, 22, 27, 111, 185, 270, 372
  necessity as greatest obstacle to, 144
  new liberalism, 42
  radical critique of, 7
  relation of to revolution according to Robespierre, 87
  as renewed and reconstituted through the state and its political economy, 386
  role of political economy in, 209
liberal realism, 229–33
liberal syllogism, 23, 38
liberty
  and equality, 99–106

individual liberty. *See individual liberty*
  problem of, 188
  simultaneously volatile possibilities of, 142
Lippman, Walter, 39n8, 86
liquidity, fetish of, 261–8
liquidity preference, 232, 233, 234, 235, 247, 261, 263, 267, 305, 307, 307n6, 308, 309, 311, 311n16, 345, 351, 352
loanable funds, 231, 294, 307n6, 311n16
Locke, John, 23, 49, 52, 54, 186
long-run monetary neutrality, 253n14
Losurdo, Domenico, 109, 114, 138, 331
Lucas, Robert, 7, 186n8, 317, 370n10
*lumpenproletariat*, 77–8, 295, 371
Luxemburg, Rosa, 139, 213, 265n20

**M**

Machiavelli, Niccolò, 11, 32, 221
MacPherson, C. B., 270
macroeconomic equilibrium, 306–15
macroeconomics, 199, 240n1, 241, 253n14, 261, 282, 288n18, 310n13, 311, 319, 332n61
macromorality, 202n37
Magri, Lucio, 6, 7
Malthus, Thomas, 165, 193–4, 194–195n23, 195, 196, 197, 198, 199, 200, 210, 211, 212, 222, 270, 272
Malthusian, 96, 193
managerial capitalism, 55
Mandevillean, 46, 260
Manichean, 89, 170
*Manifesto* (Marx), 77, 79, 139
Mankiw, Gregory, 313n23
Marat, Jean-Paul, 182
marginal efficiency of capital (*MEC*), 232, 238, 247, 248, 263, 264, 267, 268, 269, 294, 344–5, 349, 351
marginal productivity theory, 312
marginal product of labor, 250, 255
Marglin, Stephen, 316
market failures, 242, 277

market imperfection, 284n7, 323
marketing, 265
markets, 168, 176, 230, 230n27, 231, 250, 271. *See also* free markets
market society, 167
Marshall, Alfred, 40, 199, 200, 200n35, 243, 264n18
Marx, Karl, 3, 24–5, 32, 35, 36, 37, 39, 43, 45, 52, 75, 76, 77, 78, 79, 80, 86, 103, 122, 136, 139, 149, 165, 190, 209, 210, 220, 221, 222–6, 243, 264n18, 284, 292, 293, 295, 339, 359, 362, 372–3, 382, 385
Marxian apocalypse, 22, 341
Marxism, 20, 22, 32, 43, 224, 292n27, 377
mass consumption, 298
masses, state and, 163–81
mass politics, 18, 20, 74, 111, 201
mass psychology, 235
materialism, 79, 149n13, 190, 224
Mattick, Paul, 218
Mazzetti, Giovanni, 63
*MEC* (marginal efficiency of capital). *See* marginal efficiency of capital (*MEC*)
Menke, Christoph, 73n38
microeconomics, 288, 288n18, 331. *See also* neoclassical microeconomics
microfoundations, 288n18, 317, 319–24, 327
Midas, curse of/fate of, 157, 237, 269, 294
middle class, 26, 367, 384–5, 386
Mill, John Stuart, 42, 199, 243, 270
minimum wage policies, 241
Minsky, Hyman, 311, 313
mixed economy, 49, 49n23, 54, 227, 227n18, 356, 379
modern communities, 8, 16, 38, 45, 46, 51, 56, 115, 143, 169, 202, 212, 230, 236, 239, 260, 268, 272, 275, 277, 278, 279, 283, 294, 302, 324, 333, 334, 336, 342, 371, 372, 381
modernity, signature problem of, 46
modern liberalism, 10, 22, 27, 111, 185, 270, 372

modern society (of Hegel), 334
monetarism, 240
monetary production economy, 231, 234, 264n18, 381
monopoly, 94, 173–174n18, 220, 292–3
*Monthly Review*, 20, 37
Mont Pèlerin Society, 289
Moore, G. E., 40, 41, 42
moral autonomy, 124, 125, 129
*Moralität*, 129
morality, custom and freedom, 125–32
"Mr Keynes and the Classics" (Hicks), 305
muddled confusion, 50
multilateralism, 48, 48n22
Musgrave, Richard, 332n61, 354
Mussolini, Benito, 86

**N**

Napoleon Bonaparte, 75, 106, 119, 135, 136, 137, 183, 290, 371
*Nation*, 20
Nazi system, 301, 301n48, 360, 371
*necessitas non habet legem*, 88, 97, 99, 100
necessity/necessities
    as civilization's thin crust, 205, 228
    problem of, 168, 348
    provision/regulation of, 171, 172, 180
    and the rabble, 144–62
    right of, 88, 94, 100, 148
negative interest rates, 17, 267
Negri, Antonio, 15–16, 107, 108, 109, 110, 113, 218, 310, 354, 372, 373, 374–5, 376, 377, 378, 379, 380, 385
Neithammer, Immanuel, 135
neoclassical economics, 36, 251, 310, 347, 360, 361, 363
neoclassical microeconomics, 240, 241
neoclassical synthesis, 30, 60n7, 61, 284, 287, 309, 310, 312n19, 313, 325, 355
new classical economics, 240
New Classicals, 241
New Keynesians, 33, 35, 60, 60n7, 61, 64, 240, 241, 242, 249, 250, 276,

284, 309, 313, 315, 316, 317, 319, 327, 332, 355. *See also* equilibrium unemployment
new liberalism, 42
*New York Review of Books*, 20, 337
9 Thermidor, 87. *See also* Thermidor/Thermidorian Convention
99 percent, 22, 23
Nisbett, Nick, 207, 208
nonrevolutionary revolution, 56
non-Walrasian, 30, 61, 321
no-shirking condition (NSC), 324, 325, 326, 327, 328
*Notrecht*, 95, 146–50, 158, 161, 162, 165, 168, 171, 178, 198, 340

**O**

Obama, Barack, 33, 313n23
Occupy movement, 18, 336–337n2, 363
Okun, Arthur, 332n61
"On the Jewish Question" (Marx), 223
open economy dynamics, 47
organicism, 40–41n11, 40–2, 122
Ortega y Gasset, José, 71
Owl of Minerva, 149n15

**P**

Paine, Thomas, 196
Pareto efficiency, 333
Pareto optimality, 323, 324n41, 330, 331, 332, 333
Paris Commune (1871), 75
particularity, right of, 156
Pasinetti inequality, 312
passive citizenship, 331
perfect foresight, 241
*Phenomenology of Spirit* (Hegel), 41, 47, 137, 207
Phillips curve, 253n14, 312
*Philosophy of Right* (Hegel), 37, 47, 119, 135, 137, 138, 140, 149, 150, 157, 165, 173, 187, 207, 222, 224, 225, 369
Physiocrats, 209, 210, 230
Pigou, Cecil, 243, 245, 264n18
Piketty, Thomas, 7, 10, 11, 17, 22, 206, 238, 266, 269n30, 299, 337, 338, 339–40, 341, 342–50,

350–9, 360, 362, 363, 364, 366,
  384
Pilling, Geoff, 218
planner state (*stato plano*), 354, 379
Plato, 40
"Political Aspects of Full Employment"
  (Kalecki), 315
political business cycle, 302, 314
political-economic separation, 10–11,
  55, 201, 259, 317, 333, 368,
  369–70
political economy
  according to Hegel, 164, 165–70
  analytical core of, 194
  bourgeois political economy and
    Western civilization, 205–14
  centrality of to governmentality, 163
  as central to liberal government,
    366
  concern at core of, 333
  dedication to politics-economy
    separation as built into, 201
  defining lesson of, 210
  distribution as classical focus of, 192
  emergence of, 150
  Eurocentrism as plaguing, 183
  final shape of according to Marx,
    165, 210
  future as focal point of, 193
  of hope and fear, 369–73
  as how modern state thinks, 164
  Kant as excluding of from practical
    philosophy, 164
  main task of, 333
  as one of sciences that arose out of
    conditions of modern world, 163
  as postrevolutionary, 165
  postrevolutionary origins of,
    191–205
  principal function of according to
    Keynes, 210–11
  problem of poverty and necessity at
    center of, 348
  as product of Western civilization
    and colonialism, 212
  relationship of to colonialism,
    205–14
  role of liberalism in, 209
  as *savoir* and *connaissance*, 168

  as science of liberal capitalist
    government, 84
  as science of liberal government,
    191
  as science of modern government,
    181
  as science of relations of present to
    future, diagnosis to prescription,
    162, 172
  shared origin of with Keynesianism,
    145
  state as protagonist of, 167
  theory of, 182–214
political Islam, 76
political realm, as inadequately isolated
  from economic problems, 56
political transformation, problem of
  according to Keynes, 78
politics, as continuously distorted by
  fact of poverty, 56
politics of measure, 329n53
*Polizei*, 170, 173
Pol Pot, 92
population, principle of, 197, 212
populism, 18, 21, 285
Posner, Richard, 4
posteconomic world, 236
post-Keynesians, 33, 34, 60, 60n7, 61,
  62, 249, 276, 309, 331, 373
Poulantzas, Nicos, 258
poverty
  as agonizing/haunting, 172
  consent to remain poor, 201–5, 278
  as defining problem of modern soci-
    eties especially, 273
  distributional challenge as one side
    of problem of, 168
  as economic problem/social ques-
    tion, 279
  as endemic to modern communities,
    275
  as having no proper sphere, 72
  and honor, 170–81
  honourable poverty/honorable
    poverty. *See* honourable poverty/
    honorable poverty
  inability to eradicate or contain, 72
  as inevitable, 196
  as not amenable to cure, 172

as opposite of freedom, 12, 73, 129
as of our making, 72, 73, 171
paradox of in richest societies, 63
paradox of in the midst of plenty, 238, 249, 272, 275, 293, 342, 367
politics as continuously distorted by, 56
problem of as center of political economy, 348
as serving no purpose, having no place, not justifiable, 12
as side by side with excessive wealth, 300
tragedy of, 58–80
as transhistorical, 172
practical reason, 179n36
pragmatism, 51, 102, 104, 220, 221, 284, 343
Prebisch, Raúl, 283n5
price controls, 94, 171
*The Price of Inequality* (Stiglitz), 336
prices, 61n9, 96, 192, 230, 233, 235, 240–2, 250, 252–3, 254, 255, 276, 298, 305, 311, 319, 319n33, 320, 321
primary social goods, 288n17
*Principia Ethica* (Moore), 40
principle
of atomicity, 11, 173–174n18, 176
of civil society, 283
of freedom, 96
of population, 197, 212
real principle, 95, 96, 116
Ricardian principle, 353
*Principles of Political Economy* (Mill), 196, 199
private investment, 302
private property, 92, 95, 96, 271
privilege, political sustainability of modern (bourgeois) privilege, 356
production, 15, 45, 46, 65, 76, 157, 158n42, 164, 165, 192, 195, 202, 230, 231, 232, 233, 233–234n30, 237, 244–5, 250, 252, 255, 257, 264n18, 266, 267, 268, 276, 284n7, 293, 294, 318n32, 321n37, 322, 327, 344, 347, 348, 350. *See also* monetary production economy

productivity, 157, 158, 254, 264, 283, 324, 330, 347, 348
progressives, 5, 8, 19–20, 21, 22, 65, 189n13, 360, 361, 364
propensity to consume, 237n39, 246, 247, 248, 260, 263, 270
propositional framework (of Keynesianism), 50–3
proto-Pikettian inequality, 344
Proudhon, Pierre-Joseph, 359
public choice school, 289, 370n10
public expenditure, theory of, 287
public goods, 170, 276–277n50, 287, 288, 332n61
public investment, 298, 302, 303
public works, 196, 198, 227
pushing on a string, 295n35

Q
Quesnay, François, 209, 210

R
*r* (rate of interest/return on capital), 343–6, 347, 348, 349, 350, 351, 352
*r* > *g* (Piketty inequality), 343–6, 350, 353
rabble, 77, 112, 157–62, 163, 171, 175, 176, 228, 238n40, 260, 271, 272–3, 283n6, 295, 298, 300, 301, 340, 342n11, 355, 364, 365, 367, 380
rabble mentality, 162, 171, 172, 272, 283, 353, 367, 381
rabble problem, 76
radical, use of term, 187
radicalism, 18, 43, 71, 75, 86, 92, 93, 106, 115, 116, 197, 223, 339, 373, 395
radical moral autonomy, 124, 129
radical uncertainty, 15, 61, 179, 181, 200, 342
Rancière, Jacques, 76, 77
Rawls, John, 91, 270, 278, 287, 287n16, 288n17
Reagan, Ronald, 313, 315
real business cycle theory, 240
realism, 55, 65, 221, 229–33
real principle, 95, 96, 116

real wages, 250, 251, 253, 254, 255,
    328, 336, 352
reason
    of Hegel, 126
    historical unfolding of, 138
    identity of as heart of modern life,
        123
    Keynesian reason. *See* Keynesian
        reason
    practical reason, 179n36
Reason (capital-R Reason), 6, 38, 117,
    122, 123, 124, 126, 127, 128,
    139, 141, 178n32, 179, 179n36,
    207, 208, 296, 381
*Recht*, 164, 165
redistribution, 22, 63, 92, 116, 364
redistributive taxation, 46
Red Tory communitarianism, 374n15
reformism, 114–15
regulation, 166, 169–70, 180, 192,
    321, 350, 351, 358. *See also*
    self-regulation
Reich, Robert, 336
Reinhart, Carmen, 297n39
relative wages, 254
rent/rentier, 78, 227, 278, 298, 349,
    349n26, 350–8, 356
reserve army of labor, 284, 284n7,
    292, 295
reserve army of unemployed, 295
reserve wage, 329
revolution
    after revolution, 366–96
    bourgeois revolution, 85, 108, 109,
        185, 186
    as category of social dynamics, 83
    centrality of in Hegel's thought, 121
    failures of, 73, 75
    Hegelian analysis of, 80
    as an idea, 84
    inevitable transformation as needing
        to be accomplished without, 53
    Keynesianism as immanent critique
        of, 85
    and liberal ambivalence, 184–91
    modern liberal capitalism as shaped
        by anxious memory of, 84
    as necessary tragedy/tragic necessity,
        73

    nonrevolutionary revolution, 56
    as now unnecessary, 50
    as out of date, 70
    relation of to liberalism according to
        Robespierre, 87
    with revolution as not inevitable,
        277
    without revolution, 50, 53–7, 80,
        85, 101, 173, 277, 359–65, 368,
        371, 373, 381
    without revolutionaries, x, 21, 53,
        79, 134, 364
Revolution (capital-R Revolution)
    as absent presence, 84
    American War of Independence/
        American Revolution, 85, 133,
        136, 185, 186
    French Revolution. *See* French
        Revolution
    Haitian Revolution. *See* Haitian
        Revolution
    Russian Revolution, 274, 376, 377,
        378
revolutionary ideology/Revolutionary
    ideology, 90, 111, 112–13
Ricardian apocalypse, 11, 11n18, 353
Ricardian economics, 199, 230n27
Ricardian faith, 193
Ricardian formalization and abstrac-
    tion, 199–200
Ricardian heritage, 211
Ricardian principle, 353
Ricardian school, 200
Ricardian victory, 194, 217, 230n27
Ricardo, David, 61n9, 117, 154, 165,
    193, 194, 194–195n23, 195, 197,
    199, 211, 212, 243, 258, 272
right of necessity, 88, 94, 100, 148
right of particularity, 156
rigidities, 33, 242, 250, 257, 276, 320,
    331
Ritter, Joachim, 121
"Rival Views of Market Society"
    (Hirschman), 45
Roberts, Michael, 218
Robertson, Dennis, 243
Robespierre, Maximilien, x, 8, 50, 73,
    74, 79, 80, 86–106, 107, 108,
    110, 112, 113, 114, 116, 117,

118, 130, 131, 142, 144, 146, 157, 158, 160, 168, 171, 172, 173, 184, 188, 191, 198, 202, 203, 204, 290, 300, 334, 340, 359, 381

Robinson, Joan, 60, 200, 219–20, 275, 283n6, 285, 288, 316, 387

Rodrik, Dani, 337

Rogoff, Kenneth, 297n39, 337

Roubini, Nouriel, 366

Rousseau, Jean-Jacques, 54, 86, 87, 88, 89, 123, 124, 127, 131, 140, 142, 151, 156, 190, 337n3, 355

Ruda, Frank, 161

rule of absolutely necessity, 51

Russian Revolution, 274, 376, 377, 378

Ryan, Alan, 129n34

**S**

*salto mortale*, 25, 258, 390n41

saltwater economists, 242n2

Samuelson, Paul, 287, 288, 310, 355

Savigny, Friedrich Carl von, 134n49

saving, 231, 232, 235, 247, 252, 252n13, 267, 267n25, 269, 294, 306, 307, 307n6, 312, 339. *See also* investment

*savoir et connaissance*, 168, 193

Say, Jean-Baptiste, 154, 193, 197, 209, 230

Say's Law, 61, 61n9, 230, 231, 232, 233, 242, 243, 245, 248, 249, 252, 263, 276, 309, 311, 321, 323, 331, 375

scarcity
  as inevitable, 196
  as necessary social condition of capitalist political economy, 265
  as origin of yield, 353
  principle of, 116, 117
  problem of, 270
  production of, 265–6
  scarcity theory of capital, 268–73
  theory of, 342
  yield as function of, 348

Schelling, Friedrich Wilhelm Joseph, 149

Schmitt, Carl, 360

Schumpeter, Joseph, 12, 348

*Science of Logic* (Hegel), 138

Scott, David, 208

secular stagnation theory, 269

*Sein*, 126, 178, 194, 230, 241

self-adjustment, 230n27

self-destructive forces/tendencies, 43, 49–50, 58, 65, 150, 293, 343, 347, 371

self-interest, 45, 95, 96, 154, 170, 173, 173–174n18, 261, 271, 278, 296, 323, 324, 362, 363, 381

self-regulated markets, 248, 256

self-regulation, 156, 157

Sen, Amartya, 288

separation, doctrine of, 11

Shapiro, Carl, 313n23, 315–17, 335

Shaw, George Bernard, 58

shirking, 318n32, 321, 322, 322n39, 323, 324–34. *See also* no-shirking condition (NSC)

*Sitten*, 125, 126, 128, 298, 329

*Sittlichkeit*, 125–6, 128, 129, 134, 143, 151, 152, 169, 178, 202, 287, 329, 354, 381, 392

Skidelsky, Robert, ix, 226

Smith, Adam, 139, 154, 165, 170, 180, 186, 193, 195, 209, 270, 273, 362

social choice theory, 288, 289, 290, 332

social collective, 48, 49

social contract, 51, 204

social democracy, 69, 218

*Social Insurance and Allied Services* (Beveridge Report), 281

social interest, 55, 179, 239, 262, 270, 273, 275, 276, 277, 289, 333, 354, 355, 358, 373, 375

socialism, 23, 32, 66, 223, 264n18, 302, 374. *See also* bourgeois socialism

socialistic bourgeois, 77

social order
  as important cause of human unhappiness, 46n19
  Keynesianism as taking up burden of ensuring sustainable social order, 79

threats to, 381
social question, 12, 56, 278
social welfare, 282, 286, 286n12, 287, 289, 331, 333
*societas civilis*, 150
*Sollen*, 126, 178, 194, 230, 241, 287
Solow, Robert, 310, 338
"Some Economic Consequences of a Declining Population" (Keynes), 372
Sorel, Georges, 26, 396
sound finance, 297
Spanish republicanism, 75
Spinoza, Baruch, 40
*The Spirit Level* (Pickett), 336
Sraffa, Piero, 291
stagnation, 37, 195, 238, 269–70, 336, 342
Stalin, Josef, 92, 115
Stalinism, 21, 75
state
  interventionist state, 277
  as neither natural nor arbitrary according to Rousseau, 127
  as political economy's protagonist, 167
  role of, 54, 64, 67, 74, 162, 163–81, 275, 276, 277, 283
  welfare state. *See* welfare state
state authoritarianism, 330
state intervention, 170, 227, 323. *See also* government intervention
state of confidence, 246, 297, 345–346n20
state of government, transition to, 163–164n1
state of justice, transition from, 163–164n1
state of nature, 51, 123, 179n36, 260, 371
state subsidies, 241
state surveillance, 46
Stein, Karl von, 137n58
Stein-Hardenberg reforms, 137n58, 173–174n18, 369
Steuart, James, 154, 167, 193
stickiness, 242, 320
Stiglitz, Joseph, 4, 206, 240, 249, 284, 313n23, 315–17, 319, 335, 337, 366

Stiglitz–Shapiro/Shapiro–Stiglitz model, 315–17, 321, 322, 323, 324, 325, 326, 327, 328–9, 330, 331, 332, 333, 334
Summers, Lawrence, 240, 337, 366
super-elite, 336
supply and demand, 211, 232, 243, 246, 249, 250, 251, 307, 321
supply-demand mismatch, 293
supply-demand scissors, 199, 251
Sweezy, Paul, 230n27

**T**
*Tableau Économique* (Quesnay), 210
*tabula rasa* politics, 67–68n25, 89, 119
*The Tailor of Ulm* (Magri), 6
taxation
  on capital, 352n33, 357, 358
  double taxation, 357
  of profits to subsidize wages, 330
  to provide services to meet basic human needs, 276–277n50
  redistributive taxation, 46
Taylor, Charles, 121, 124, 179n36
Taylor, John, 313n23
Taylor, Lance, 213
Tea Party (United States), 20, 21, 23, 64, 76, 364
techno-bureaucratic solutions/expertise, 10, 55, 67, 180
technocratic managerialism, 278
Terror, 21, 75, 86, 93, 102, 106, 109, 111, 114, 127, 128, 131, 132, 133, 140, 177, 183, 184, 188, 189, 191, 209, 382
Thatcher, Margaret, 76, 197, 289n20, 313, 315
theorems
  general possibility theorem, 285–286n11
  impossibility theorem, 285–6, 285–286n11, 287n16, 288, 290
theories
  labor theory of value, 264n18
  marginal productivity theory, 312
  real business cycle theory, 240
  scarcity theory of capital, 268–73
  secular stagnation theory, 269

social choice theory, 288, 289, 290, 332
theory of capitalism, 229
theory of civilization, 23, 63–72
theory of civil society, 52–3
theory of liberal capitalism, 7, 8
theory of political economy, 182–214
theory of public expenditures, 287
theory of scarcity, 342
*Theory of Economic Dynamics: An Essay on Cyclical and Long-Run Changes in Capitalist Economy* (Kalecki), 292
Thermidor/Thermidorian Convention, 106, 107–12, 114, 118, 184, 290, 310, 354, 386
third way, 10, 49, 219
tight money, 297
Tily, Geoff, 309n10
Tobin, James, 310
*Tract on Monetary Reform* (Keynes), 56–7, 203, 273
trade
    freedom of, 95, 116, 166, 167, 170
    free trade, 48, 99, 199, 212n60, 341, 358
trade-off, 46, 99, 253n14, 312, 329
Treasury School, 64
*Treatise on Money* (Keynes), 229
*Trente Glorieuses*, 344
Trump, Donald, 20, 364
trust in the people, 112–18
Truth, ix, 80, 102, 115, 124, 129, 258, 284, 301, 341, 354, 381, 389, 395
Tugan-Baranovsky, Mikhail, 265n20
Tullock, Gordon, 289, 289n20, 370n10

**U**
uncertainty
    economic effect of, 234
    radical uncertainty, 15, 61, 179, 181, 200, 342
unemployment, 235–6, 251, 253n15, 255, 256, 263, 269, 270, 282, 283, 284, 285, 302, 315, 318, 324, 324–34, 329, 330, 331, 332,

335. *See also* equilibrium unemployment; involuntary unemployment; joblessness
unemployment equilibrium, 328
Unger, Roberto, 5
universal class, 10, 180, 180n40, 181, 275, 290, 310, 336, 364, 368, 370, 395
universal freedom, 131, 140, 160
universality, 99, 130, 131, 149, 152, 154, 155, 168, 170, 173n16, 179, 181, 296, 359
universal will, 130, 131
utopianism, 11, 14, 55, 64, 68, 75, 79, 117, 140, 233, 274, 286, 341, 346, 359, 373, 375, 394

**V**
Viner, Jacob, 228
Virno, Paolo, 373
Volcker, Paul, 314
Volcker shock, 314, 314–315n25, 354
von Haller, Albrecht, 134

**W**
Wade, Robert, 24
wage goods, 171, 254
wages
    critical wage, 325, 325n45, 326, 327, 329, 330, 332
    efficiency wages, 323, 325
    real wages, 250, 251, 253, 254, 255, 328, 336, 352
    relative wages, 254
    reserve wage, 329
Wahnich, Sophie, 184
Wainwright, Joel, 19
Waldron, Jeremy, 72–73n37
Walras, Léon, 61n9, 249, 286, 304
Walrasian, 61n9, 284n7, 286, 317, 323
*The Wealth of Nations* (Smith), 170
Weber, Max, 152, 178n32, 271, 327
welfare benefits, 241
welfare state, 34, 35, 59, 202n37, 218, 226, 244, 281, 314, 357, 367n3
Western civilization, bourgeois political economy and, 205–14

will
  general will, 48, 87, 89, 127, 130,
    131, 355
  universal will, 130, 131
Williamson, Oliver, 320
witticisms (of Keynes), 227, 229, 234
Wolf, Martin, 4, 366
World Trade Organization, 369

**X**
Xenos, Nicholas, 270

**Y**
Yellen, Janet, 240, 249
yield, 229, 238, 247, 263, 264, 265,
    266, 267, 288, 294, 299, 324,
    344, 346, 347, 348, 353

**Z**
Žižek, Slavoj, 75, 93, 102, 112–13,
    117, 161, 337, 373, 390, 393n43,
    396